SUSTAINABLE FACADES

SUSTAINABLE FACADES

DESIGN METHODS FOR HIGH-PERFORMANCE BUILDING ENVELOPES

AJLA AKSAMIJA, Ph.D.
PERKINS+WILL

WILEY

Cover image: © Benjamin Benschneider/OTTO

Cover design: Michael Rutkowski

This book is printed on acid-free paper.

Copyright © 2013 by Ajla Aksamija and Perkins+Will

All rights reserved.

Published by John Wiley & Sons, Inc., Hoboken, New Jersey

Published simultaneously in Canada

No part of this publication may be reproduced, stored in a retrieval system, or transmitted in any form or by any means, electronic, mechanical, photocopying, recording, scanning, or otherwise, except as permitted under Section 107 or 108 of the 1976 United States Copyright Act, without either the prior written permission of the Publisher, or authorization through payment of the appropriate per-copy fee to the Copyright Clearance Center, 222 Rosewood Drive, Danvers, MA 01923, (978) 750-8400, fax (978) 646-8600, or on the web at www.copyright.com. Requests to the Publisher for permission should be addressed to the Permissions Department, John Wiley & Sons, Inc., 111 River Street, Hoboken, NJ 07030, (201) 748-6011, fax (201) 748-6008, or online at www.wiley.com/go/permissions.

Limit of Liability/Disclaimer of Warranty: While the publisher and author have used their best efforts in preparing this book, they make no representations or warranties with the respect to the accuracy or completeness of the contents of this book and specifically disclaim any implied warranties of merchantability or fitness for a particular purpose. No warranty may be created or extended by sales representatives or written sales materials. The advice and strategies contained herein may not be suitable for your situation. Neither the publisher nor the author shall be liable for damages arising herefrom.

For general information about our other products and services, please contact our Customer Care Department within the United States at (800) 762-2974, outside the United States at (317) 572-3993 or fax (317) 572-4002.

Wiley publishes in a variety of print and electronic formats and by print-on-demand. Some material included with standard print versions of this book may not be included in e-books or in print-on-demand. If this book refers to media such as a CD or DVD that is not included in the version you purchased, you may download this material at http://booksupport.wiley.com. For more information about Wiley products, visit www.wiley.com.

Library of Congress Cataloging-in-Publication Data:

Aksamija, Ajla.
 Sustainable facades : design methods for high-performance building envelopes / Ajla Aksamija, Ph.D., Perkins+Will.
    pages cm
 Includes bibliographical references and index.
 ISBN 978-1-118-45860-0 (cloth); ISBN 978-1-118-54964-3 (ebk); ISBN 978-1-118-54971-1 (ebk); ISBN 978-1-118-54975-9 (ebk)
 1. Facades--Design and construction. 2. Exterior walls--Design and construction. 3. Sustainable design. I. Title.
 TH2235.A426 2013
 729'.1--dc23

2012037882

Printed in the United States of America

10 9 8 7 6 5 4 3 2

CONTENTS

Figure Credits	ix
Acknowledgments	xi
Introduction	xiii

CHAPTER 1   CLIMATE-BASED DESIGN APPROACH FOR FACADES   1

Climate Classifications and Types	3
Climate-Specific Design Guidelines for Facades	8
Environmental Considerations and Design Criteria	8
Design Strategies and Climate	9
Chapter Summary	14

CHAPTER 2   CHARACTERISTICS OF SUSTAINABLE FACADES   17

Energy Efficiency	18
Orientation	19
Fenestration	24
Facade Types and Materials	40
Opaque Building Facades	40
Glazed Building Facades	48
Materials and Properties	54
Properties of Facade Materials and Components	54
Embodied Energy of Materials	62
Thermal Behavior and Moisture Resistance	66
Control of Heat Transfer, and Air and Moisture Movement	66
Steady-State Heat and Moisture Transfer Analysis for Opaque Building Facades	69
Hygrothermal Analysis for Opaque Building Facades	74
Heat Transfer Analysis for Glazed Building Facades	79
Chapter Summary	83

CHAPTER 3   DESIGNING FOR COMFORT   85

Thermal Comfort   86
    Methods of Measurement   87
    Facade Design and Thermal Comfort   91
Daylight and Glare   95
    Daylighting Strategies   95
    Glare   109
Acoustic Comfort and Air Quality   115
    Acoustics   115
    Air Quality   118
Chapter Summary   119

CHAPTER 4   EMERGING TECHNOLOGIES IN FACADE DESIGNS   121

Emerging Materials and Technologies   122
    Advanced Facade Materials   122
    Smart Materials   126
Double-Skin Facades   135
    Double-Skin Facades in Hot and Arid Climates   141
    Double-Skin Facades in Cold Climates   143
Facades as Energy Generators   149
Control Systems for Facades   153
Chapter Summary   155

CHAPTER 5   CASE STUDIES   157

Building Orientation and Facade Design   159
    Arizona State University Interdisciplinary Science & Technology Building   159
    Center for Urban Waters   167
Tectonic Sun Exposure Control   178
    Kuwait University College of Education   178
    King Abdullah Financial District Parcel 4.01 Building   186
    King Abdullah Financial District Parcel 4.10 Building   200
External Shading Elements   211
    University of Texas Dallas Student Services Building   211
Facade Materials and Wall Assemblies   218
    Bigelow Laboratory for Ocean Sciences   218

APPENDIX   **CASE STUDIES INDEX**   227

    Chapter 2   228

        Case Study 2.1: Vincent Triggs Elementary School, Clark County Elementary Prototype (Las Vegas, Nevada)   228

        Case Study 2.2: Hector Garcia Middle School (Dallas, Texas)   228

        Case Study 2.3: Kendal Academic Support Center, Miami Dade College (Miami, Florida)   229

    Chapter 3   229

        Case Study 3.1: Centers for Disease Control and Prevention, National Center for Environmental Health (Atlanta, Georgia)   229

    Chapter 4   230

        Case Study 4.1: Princess Nora Bint Abdulrahman University for Women Academic Colleges (Riyadh, Saudi Arabia)   230

        Case Study 4.2: Tinkham Veale University Center, Case Western Reserve University (Cleveland, Ohio)   230

    Chapter 5   231

        Interdisciplinary Science & Technology Building, Arizona State University (Tempe, Arizona)   231

        Center for Urban Waters (Tacoma, Washington)   232

        Kuwait University College of Education (Shadadiyah, Kuwait)   232

        King Abdullah Financial District Parcel 4.01 Building (Riyadh, Saudi Arabia)   233

        King Abdullah Financial District Parcel 4.10 Building (Riyadh, Saudi Arabia)   233

        University of Texas Dallas Student Services Building (Dallas, Texas)   234

        Bigelow Laboratory for Ocean Sciences (East Boothbay, Maine)   234

Index   235

FIGURE CREDITS

Figure 2-6a: Jeff Green

Figure 2-6b: Jeff Green

Figure 2-20: Steinkamp Photography

Figure 2-21: Steinkamp Photography

Figure 3-19: Nick Merick © Hedrich Blessing

Figure 3-21: Nick Merick © Hedrich Blessing

Figure 5-4: Steinkamp Photography

Figure 5-5: Steinkamp Photography

Figure 5-6a: Steinkamp Photography

Figure 5-6b: Steinkamp Photography

Figure 5-9: Steinkamp Photography

Figure 5-10: Steinkamp Photography

Figure 5-11: Steinkamp Photography

Figure 5-15: Benjamin Benschneider

Figure 5-17: Benjamin Benschneider

Figure 5-20: Benjamin Benschneider

Figure 5-21: Benjamin Benschneider

Figure 5-22: Benjamin Benschneider

Figure 5-23: Benjamin Benschneider

Figure 5-24: Benjamin Benschneider

Figure 5-25: Benjamin Benschneider

Figure 5-67: Charles Smith

Figure 5-68: Charles Smith

Figure 5-69: Charles Smith

Figure 5-72: Charles Smith

Figure 5-73: Charles Smith

Figure 5-76: Charles Smith

Figure 5-77: Charles Smith

Figure 5-80: Christopher Barnes © ChristopherBarnes.com

Figure 5-82: Christopher Barnes © ChristopherBarnes.com

Figure 5-83: Christopher Barnes © ChristopherBarnes.com

Figure 5-84: Christopher Barnes © ChristopherBarnes.com

Figure 5-87: Christopher Barnes © ChristopherBarnes.com

ACKNOWLEDGMENTS

I would like to acknowledge Bill Schmalz, RK Stewart, and Bruce Toman for their input, comments, and tremendous support during the writing of this book. Also, project team members of the featured case studies were crucial in providing the necessary documentation and comments, and I am deeply grateful for their involvement: Curt Behnke, Pat Bosch, Ryan Bragg, Alejandro Bragner, Eric Brossy de Dios, Jane Cameron, Matthew Crummey, Patrick Cunningham, Anthony Fieldman, James Giebelhausen, Patrick Glenn, Andrew Goetze, David Hansen, Scott Kirkham, Devin Kleiner, Aki Knezevic, Richard Miller, Tom Mozina, Michael Palmer, Camila Querasian, Deborah Rivers, Bryan Schabel, Dan Seng, Gary Shaw, Calvin Smith, Ron Stelmarski, Angel Suarez, Jolly Thulaseedas, Deepa Tolat, Ashwin Toney, and Mark Walsh. I would also like to thank Wajdi Abou-Izzeddine (The Dar Group) for his valued input. My research assistants, Negin Beyhaghi and Abul Abdullah, deserve special recognition for their assistance: Negin for collecting information about some of the case studies in the book, and Abul for preparation of some of the diagrams. Kathryn Bourgoine, Donna Conte, Danielle Giordano, and the Wiley production team deserve special recognition for their input during the production of this book.

Lastly, I would like to acknowledge Zlatan and Nur Aksamija for their undivided love and support.

INTRODUCTION

Buildings, as the largest users of energy in our society, are also our greatest opportunity for energy conservation and protection of the environment. The rapidly growing world energy use has raised global concerns over continued depletion of energy resources and their negative environmental impacts. Current predictions show that this growing trend will continue.

The facade is one of the most significant contributors to the energy budget and the comfort parameters of any building. As energy and other natural resources continue to be depleted, it has become clear that technologies and strategies that allow us to maintain our satisfaction with the interior environment while consuming fewer of these resources are major objectives for contemporary facade designs.

This book focuses on the strategies and approaches for designing sustainable, high-performance building facades, and provides technical guidance for architects and designers. Building facades act as barriers between the interior and exterior environment. To provide building occupants with a comfortable and safe environment, a facade must fulfill many functions, such as:

- Provision of views to the outside
- Resistance of forces from wind loads
- Bearing its own weight
- Implementation of daylighting strategies to minimize use of artificial lighting
- Protection from solar heat gain
- Protection from noise
- Resistance to rainwater and moisture penetration

Control of physical environmental factors (heat, light, sounds) must be considered during the design process, as must design strategies that improve occupant comfort (thermal, visual, acoustic, and air quality). Therefore, sustainable facades must block adverse external environmental effects and maintain internal comfort conditions with minimum energy consumption. The location and climate thus are crucial factors in selecting appropriate design strategies for sustainable facades.

Strategies and technical guidelines for designing environmentally sensitive, energy-efficient facades based on scientific principles are the basis of this book (such as climate-specific approaches for minimizing energy consumption, thermal behavior of different facade systems, and materials and their properties), which illustrates with case studies how these approaches have been implemented on real-life architectural projects. It also discusses emerging facade technologies, materials, and systems.

CHAPTER 1 discusses different climate classification systems, climate-based design strategies, and energy code recommendations for building envelopes. Different design strategies are required for different climatic regions. Heating-dominated climates benefit from solar collection and passive heating, heat storage, and conservation through improved insulation and use of daylight to reduce lighting demand. For cooling-dominated climates, opposite strategies should be applied; in these climates, protection from sun and direct solar radiation is advantageous, as well as reduction of internal and external heat gains. In mixed climates, combined strategies must be implemented to balance solar exposure and access to daylight.

CHAPTER 2 presents characteristics of sustainable facades, as well as guidelines for minimizing energy consumption associated with facade design. It examines appropriate strategies based on building orientation, different facade types and materials, and material properties. Opaque facades, usually constructed of masonry materials, precast-concrete panels, metal cladding, and other solid materials, respond differently to environmental conditions than do curtain walls or other types of transparent envelopes. The components, material selection, and construction methods for each are different, as is thermal behavior. This chapter also discusses control of heat, air, and moisture movement; and different analysis methods that can be used for design decision-making.

CHAPTER 3 presents design methods for improving occupants' comfort, which is a key component of sustainable, high-performance facades. Thermal, visual, and acoustic comfort and indoor air quality affect the satisfaction and productivity of building occupants. This chapter covers methods for measuring thermal comfort conditions, design strategies for improving daylight levels and elimination of glare in interior spaces, acoustic comfort metrics and material properties influencing acoustic behavior, and methods for minimizing air infiltration and leakage through facades.

CHAPTER 4 discusses emerging facade technologies and innovative design approaches that affect their functions and aesthetics. It focuses on advanced and smart materials, and describes their properties and applications for building facades. It also discusses double-skin facades, covering their components, design strategies for different climates, and their effects on energy consumption. Building-integrated photovoltaic systems and their applications in building facades are covered too, as are control systems.

CHAPTER 5 presents in-depth case studies and illustrates how the various design strategies discussed in previous chapters have been implemented on various building types located in different climates. Different ways of approaching sustainable facade design are detailed, including proper design and passive strategies based on building orientation; control of solar exposure and self-shading mechanics through tectonic building form; design of external shading elements; selection of facade materials; and design of exterior wall assemblies.

SUSTAINABLE FACADES

CHAPTER 1

CLIMATE-BASED DESIGN APPROACH FOR FACADES

Building facades perform two functions: first, they are the barriers that separate a building's interior from the external environment; and second, more than any other component, they create the image of the building. *High-performance sustainable facades* can be defined as exterior enclosures that use the least possible amount of energy to maintain a comfortable interior environment, which promotes the health and productivity of the building's occupants. This means that sustainable facades are not simply barriers between interior and exterior; rather, they are building systems that create comfortable spaces by actively responding to the building's external environment, and significantly reduce buildings' energy consumption.

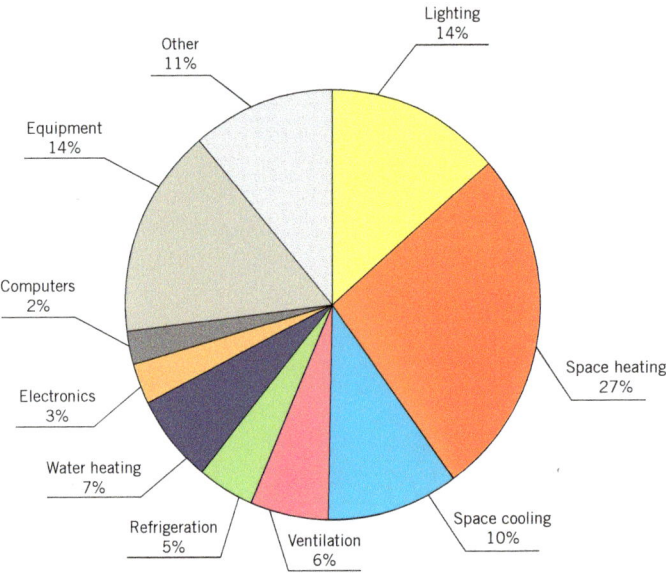

Figure 1-1 Energy use breakdown for commercial buildings (Adapted from DOE, 2012).

Average energy use for commercial buildings is shown in Figure 1-1. Heating, cooling, lighting, and ventilating interior spaces account for more than half of the energy use. The performance of the building facade can significantly affect the energy consumed by these building systems.

Designers of sustainable facades should use the specific characteristics of a building's location and climate, as well as its program requirements and site constraints, to create high-performance building envelopes that reduce the building's energy needs. Climate-specific guidelines must be considered during the design process. Strategies that work best in hot and arid climates are different from those that work in temperate or hot and humid regions.

In this chapter, we look at the different ways of classifying climates, and the characteristics of each climate zone. We also discuss some of the factors that must be considered when designing high-performance sustainable facades, based on climatic environmental characteristics.

CLIMATE CLASSIFICATIONS AND TYPES

Climate encompasses the sum of temperature, humidity, atmospheric pressure, wind, rainfall, atmospheric particles, and other meteorological characteristics over extended periods of time. Climate is affected, in varying degrees, by latitude, terrain, and altitude, as well as by nearby mountain ranges or bodies of water. In the United States, for example, the coastal regions of the Pacific Northwest are at the same latitudes as the northern Great Plains. However, due to the tempering effects of ocean currents, its coastal winters are mild compared to the harsh winters on the northern plains. The effects of the Gulf Stream, an ocean current in the northern hemisphere, are responsible for moderating the climate of western Europe. Therefore, countries such as the United Kingdom and France have relatively warm winters, although they are positioned along the same latitude as Canada.

The Koppen Climate Classification System was one of the first methods to categorize different climates. It consists of five major climate groups, each of which is further divided into one or more subgroups. The five primary groups are labeled by the letters A through E, and the subgroups by two- and three-letter codes to designate relative temperature, average precipitation, and (where relevant) native vegetation. The entire world can be classified using this system, as shown in Figure 1-2. Table 1-1 summarizes the basic characteristics of all Koppen climate groups and subgroups, and indicates representative locations.

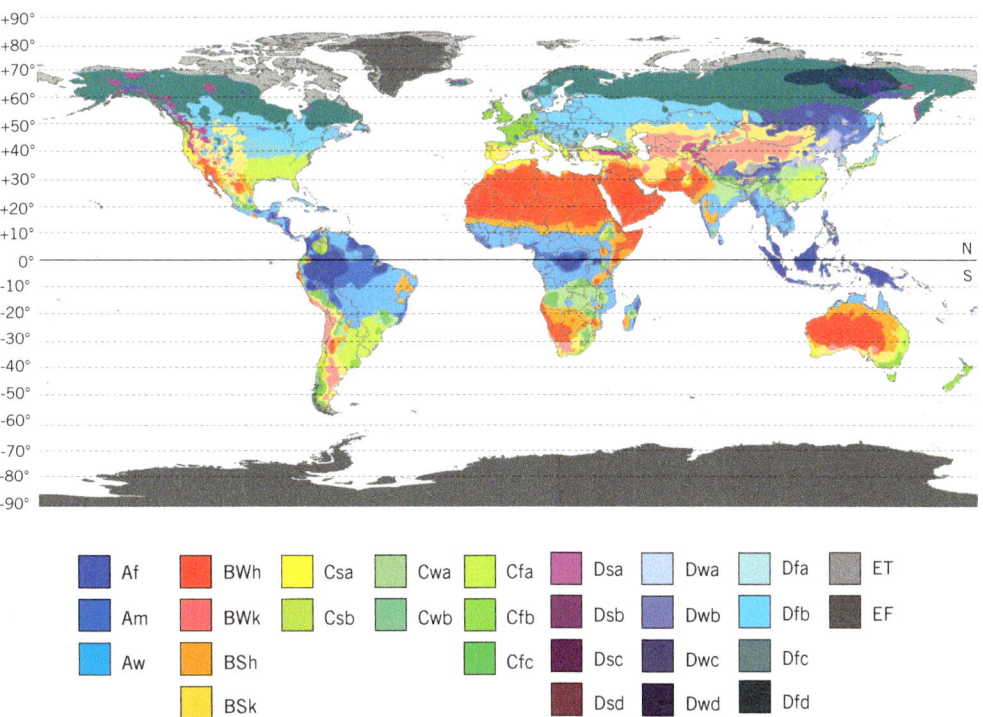

Figure 1-2 Koppen Climate Classification System (Adapted from Peel et al., 2007).

Table 1-1 Koppen Climate Classification System.

Group	Subgroups	Characteristics	Regions
A: Tropical climate Nonarid climate throughout the entire year Mean temperature of 64°F (18°C) Warm to hot, and moist, during the entire year Af: Tropical rainforest Am: Tropical monsoon Aw: Tropical wet and dry or savannah climate	Af: Tropical rainforest	No dry season, average annual rainfall at least 2.4 in. (60 mm)	Typically within 5°–10° latitude from the equator
	Am: Tropical monsoon	Short wet season and long dry season, annual precipitation less than 2.4 in. (60 mm)	Most common in southern Asia and West Africa
	Aw: Tropical wet and dry or savannah climate	Distinct dry season, annual rainfall less than 2.4 in. (60 mm)	Most common in central Africa
B: Dry climate (arid and semi-arid) Severe lack of precipitation Annual evaporation exceeds annual precipitation BS: Steppe climate BW: Desert climate	BSh: Hot steppe climate	Subtropical desert with average temperature greater than 64°F (18°C) Hot semi-arid climate with extremely hot summers and mild to warm winters	Low latitudes (0°–10°) of central Africa, north and east parts of Australia
	BSk: Cold semi-arid climate	Cool dry climate	Temperate zones and continental interiors in middle latitudes (10°–30°), away from large bodies of water
	BWh: Hot desert climate	Precipitation too low to sustain much vegetation; precipitation less than 10 in. (250 mm) per year Very high diurnal shifts in temperature	Central and northern Africa, parts of southwestern United States, central Australia
	BWk: Cold desert climate	Found in temperate zones, typically in the rain shadow of high mountains; hot summers and very cold and dry winters	Close to high mountain ranges, typically at high altitudes, such as southern parts of South America

Group	Subgroups	Characteristics	Regions
C: Temperate climate Cw: Temperate climate with dry winters Cs: Temperate climate with dry summers Cf: Temperate climate with significant precipitation	Csa/Csb: Dry summer subtropical climates	Warmest month average temperature above 72°F (22°C), with at least four months averaging above 50°F (10°C)	Western sides of continents between latitudes of 30° and 45° (such as southern California coastal regions in North America, Mediterranean regions)
	Cfa/Cwa: Humid subtropical climates	Humid summers, precipitation present during all seasons	Interiors or east coasts of continents, mainly between 30° and 45° latitudes (such as Florida in the United States)
	Cfb: Marine temperate climate	Changeable weather, cool summers and mild winters	Western sides of continents between 45° and 55° latitudes (such as the Pacific Northwest of North America)
	Cwb: Temperate climate with dry winters	Noticeably dry winters and rainy summers	Typically associated with highlands in the tropics
	Cfc: Maritime subarctic climate	Cold winters and very mild summers	Narrow coastal strips (such as southern Alaska coastal regions of North America)
D: Continental climate Dw: Continental climate with dry winters Ds: Continental climate with dry summer Df: Continental climate with significant precipitation during all seasons	Dfa/Dwa/Dsa: Hot summer continental climates	Warmest month temperatures greater than 71.6°F (22°C)	Interiors of continents and on eastern coasts, such as northeastern part of South America
	Dfb/Dwb/Dsb: Warm summer continental climates	Warmest month temperatures averaging below 71.6°F (22°C), but with at least four months averaging above 50°F (10°C)	Immediately north of hot summer continental climates (northern part of North America, northern Europe, parts of South America)
E: Polar climate ET: Tundra climate EF: Ice cap climate	ET: Tundra climate	Warmest temperatures below 50°F (10°C) during all seasons	Polar regions and high elevations
	EF: Ice cap climate	Temperature almost never exceeds 32°F (0°C); covered by permanent layer of ice	Antarctica and Greenland

Although the Koppen Classification System can be used to classify climate and environmental conditions for any location in the world, its complexity makes it difficult for designers to use when relating local climate to energy-reduction design strategies. The International Energy Conservation Code (IECC), in conjunction with the American Society of Heating, Refrigerating and Air-Conditioning Engineers (ASHRAE), has developed a climate classification system for the United States that is easier for designers to use. The IECC climate map provides a simplified, consistent approach based on widely accepted descriptions of world climates, as well as the number of cooling and heating degree days for each location. This classification system divides the United States into eight temperature-based climate zones (labeled by numbers 1 to 8), and three subzones based on humidity levels (labeled by letters A, B, and C).

The eight climate zones are:

- Zone 1: very hot
- Zone 2: hot
- Zone 3: warm
- Zone 4: mixed
- Zone 5: cool
- Zone 6: cold
- Zone 7: very cold
- Zone 8: subarctic

The three subcategories based on the location's humidity are:

- A: humid
- B: dry
- C: marine

Every location in the United States has an associated IECC climate zone and humidity subcategory, as seen in Figure 1-3. The IECC and ASHRAE standards, and the energy codes that are based on them, use this classification system.

Although the IECC climate classification system is useful for designers, and is referred to frequently throughout this book, it has some limitations. The IECC system does not recognize local microclimates. For example, the entire Chicago metropolitan region falls within climate zone 5A. However, the microclimate within a mile of Lake Michigan is different from an inland location such as O'Hare International Airport (one of the weather stations where Chicago weather data are collected). Another example is the city of Los Angeles, which is located in climate zone 3B. However, the microclimate near the Pacific Ocean shore is significantly different from the microclimate of the San Fernando Valley, which is 600 or more feet above sea level and entirely surrounded by hills. For buildings in urban areas, designers should research local microclimate conditions, which may vary from the IECC climate zone description.

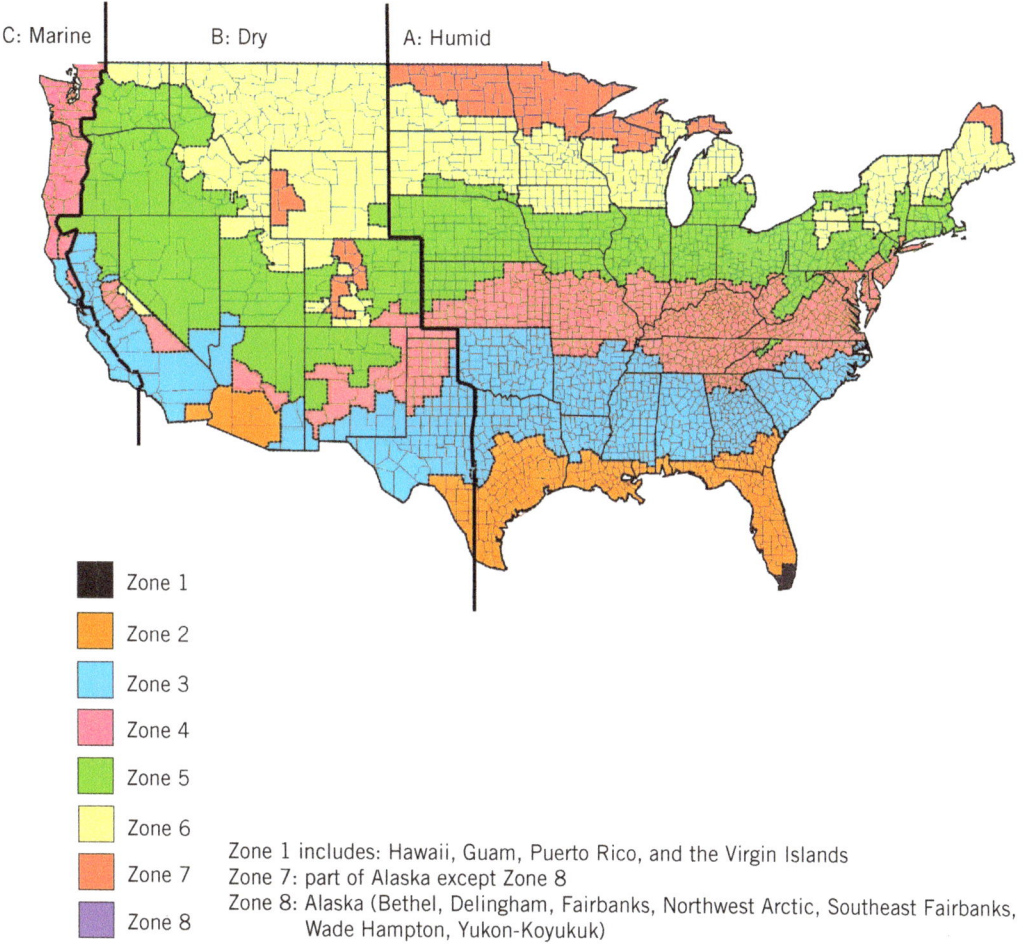

Figure 1-3 Climate classification for the United States.

Energy performance modeling for buildings is typically based on historical weather data, which are collected over a specific time period, such as thirty years. Temperature, relative humidity, wind speeds, precipitation, and solar radiation data are collected and statistically analyzed to identify typical weather patterns that can be used to predict heating and cooling loads when used in performance modeling. In addition to historic weather data, predictive climate models are currently being developed, which can be used to predict future conditions for a specific location (Lawrence and Chase, 2010). Predictive climate models account for climate changes, impacts of existing and projected greenhouse gas emissions, and slight increases in temperatures. Predicted weather data can be used instead of historical data for modeling a building's energy consumption, thus taking into account these future changes in climate and their effects on energy consumption.

CLIMATE-SPECIFIC DESIGN GUIDELINES FOR FACADES

Environmental Considerations and Design Criteria

For most buildings, the facade affects the building's energy budget and the comfort of its occupants more than any other system. To provide occupants with a comfortable and safe environment, a facade must fulfill many functions, such as providing views to the outside, resisting wind loads, supporting its own dead-load weight, allowing daylight to interior spaces, blocking unwanted solar heat gain, protecting occupants from outside noise and temperature extremes, and resisting air and water penetration (Aksamija, 2009).

Designers need to consider the external environment, building orientation, space dimensions, and occupants' comfort expectations. Table 1-2 shows how air temperature, solar radiation, humidity, wind velocity, noise, ground reflectivity, and dimension and location of external obstacles (e.g., buildings, topography, or plantings) can affect thermal, visual, and acoustic comfort. The relative importance of these criteria will affect design decisions, such as the properties of opaque materials (thickness, density, conduction, reflectivity) and transparent (glazing) materials (thickness, number of layers, heat transmission, light absorption, reflection).

Table 1-2 Environmental conditions and properties of facade elements that affect thermal, visual, and acoustic comfort.

Environmental conditions	Thermal comfort	Visual comfort	Acoustic comfort
Outdoor design criteria	Sun and wind obstructions	View and daylight obstructions	Noise obstructions
	Building dimensions	Building dimensions	Building dimensions
	Air temperature range	Latitude and location	Exterior noise level
	Relative humidity range	Time of day	Exterior noise source
	Wind velocity	External horizontal illuminance	
	Solar radiation	Ground reflectivity	

Environmental conditions	Thermal comfort	Visual comfort	Acoustic comfort
Indoor design criteria	Space dimensions User's activity level User's clothing insulation	Space dimensions Colors of surfaces Working plane location	Space dimensions Absorption coefficients of interior surfaces
Indoor comfort criteria	Air temperature Relative humidity Air velocity Mean radiant temperature	Illuminance level and distribution Glare index	Acceptable interior noise levels
Opaque facades	Material properties of cladding Amount of insulation Effective heat resistance properties (R-value)	Window-to-wall ratio	Material selection and properties
Glazing	Orientation Number of glass layers Layer thicknesses Heat transfer coefficient (U-value) Visual transmittance Solar heat gain coefficient (SHGC)	Orientation Window properties, size, location, and shape Glass thickness and color Visual transmittance Reflectance	Number of layers Layer thicknesses Layer density
Frames and supporting structure for glazed facades	Thermal properties of the frames		Material types

Design Strategies and Climate

Different design strategies are required for different climatic zones. Basic methods for designing high-performance building facades include:

- Orienting and developing geometry and massing of the building to respond to solar position
- Providing solar shading to control cooling loads and improve thermal comfort
- Using natural ventilation to reduce cooling loads and enhance air quality
- Minimizing energy used for artificial lighting and mechanical cooling and heating by optimizing exterior wall insulation and the use of daylighting

In choosing design strategies, we need to consider the conditions of the climate zone to minimize their impacts and reduce energy consumption. In Table 1-3, we see how design strategies are affected by climate types (Aksamija, 2010). Heating-dominated climates (zones 5 through 8) benefit from collection of solar radiation, passive heating, heat storage, improved insulation to reduce heating demand, and the use of daylighting to reduce lighting demand. In cooling-dominated climates (zones 1 through 3), protection from sun and direct solar radiation becomes more important. In mixed climates (zone 4), combined strategies that balance solar exposure and access to daylight should be implemented. In some cases, localized climate conditions, or microclimates, may be different from the generalized conditions of that climate zone. Designers need to respond to the specific characteristics of a building site.

Table 1-3 Facade design strategies for different climate zones.

Climate type	Design strategies for sustainable facades
Heating-dominated climates Zones 5, 6, 7, 8	*Solar collection and passive heating:* collection of solar heat through the building envelope
	Heat storage: storage of heat in the mass of the walls
	Heat conservation: preservation of heat within the building through improved insulation
	Daylight: use of natural light sources and increased glazed areas of the facade, use of high-performance glass, and use of light shelves to redirect light into interior spaces
Cooling-dominated climates Zones 1, 2, 3	*Solar control:* protection of the facade from direct solar radiation through self-shading methods (building form) or shading devices
	Reduction of external heat gains: protection from solar heat gain by infiltration (by using well-insulated opaque facade elements) or conduction (by using shading devices)
	Cooling: use of natural ventilation where environmental characteristics and building function permit
	Daylight: use of natural light sources while minimizing solar heat gain through use of shading devices and light shelves
Mixed climates Zone 4	*Solar control:* protection of facade from direct solar radiation (shading) during warm seasons
	Solar collection and passive heating: solar collection during cold seasons
	Daylight: use of natural light sources and increased glazed areas of the facade with shading devices

Many energy codes reference ASHRAE 90.1, *Energy Standard for Buildings except Low-Rise Residential Buildings*, which provides recommendations for building envelopes (ASHRAE, 2007). ASHRAE 90.1 is periodically updated based on increasing expectations of building performance. These recommendations are based on building location and climate zone, using the IECC climate classification system of eight zones and three subzones (Figure 1-3). If ASHRAE 90.1 has been adopted as part of the state energy or building code, then the ASHRAE recommendations become the required metrics of building performance. ASHRAE's requirements are categorized based on the basic building function and occupancy, including: (1) nonresidential conditioned space (daytime use, higher internal loads), (2) residential conditioned space (24-hour occupancy, building envelope-dominated due to lower internal loads), and (3) nonresidential and residential semiheated space.

ASHRAE identifies four types of exterior walls:

- Mass walls, generally constructed of masonry or concrete materials
- Metal building walls, consisting of metal members spanning between steel structural members (not including spandrel glass or metal panels in curtain walls)
- Steel-framed walls, with cavities whose exterior surfaces are separated by steel framing members (including typical steel stud walls and curtain walls)
- Wood-framed and other walls

ASHRAE requirements are prescribed in three ways for all climate zones:

- Minimum allowable thermal resistance (R-value) for the different exterior walls
- Maximum allowable heat transfer coefficients (U-value) for the facade assembly (including the thermal bridging effects of framing members)
- Maximum allowable solar heat gain coefficient (SHGC) for the glazed portions of a facade assembly

Thermal resistance (R-value) is an assembly's or a material's resistance to heat transfer, and is expressed in h-ft^2-°F/Btu or m^2-°K/W. Individual materials have specific R-values, usually listed as R-value per inch (see Chapter 2). The overall R-value of a facade assembly is calculated by adding the R-values of individual material layers. R-values are typically used to define the thermal performance of opaque areas of facades built up from multiple layers of materials.

Heat transfer coefficient (U-value) is the inverse of R-value. It measures the heat transmission through a material or a facade assembly. U-values are expressed in Btu/hr-ft^2-°F or W/m^2-°K, and are usually used to define thermal performance of glazed parts of facade assemblies.

The *solar heat gain coefficient (SHGC)* quantifies the amount of solar radiation admitted into a building's interior through glass, and is expressed as a number between 0 and 1, with 0 meaning that no radiation is admitted and 1 meaning that no radiation is blocked.

Figure 1-4 shows ASHRAE recommendations for minimum R-values for nonresidential conditioned spaces, for each climate zone and four types of wall construction. R-values for mass walls are highly dependent on the climate, and increase from warmer to colder climates. Recommended minimum R-values for metal building walls are virtually identical for all climate types. The exception is for very cold and arctic climates, which demand significantly higher insulation. Recommended minimum R-values for steel-framed walls are the same for mixed and colder climates. Recommended minimum R-values for wood-framed walls vary depending on climate zone. In general, steel-framed and wood-framed walls require higher levels of insulation than the other wall types.

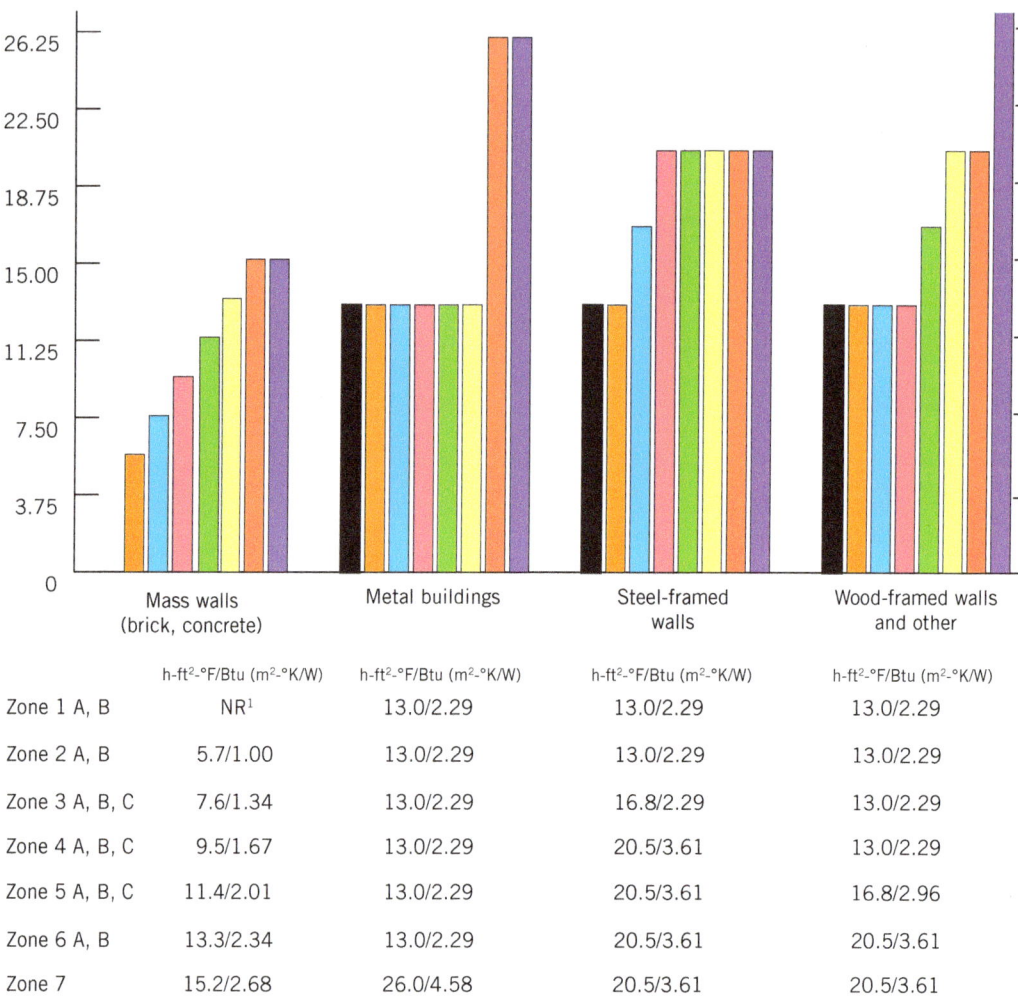

	Mass walls (brick, concrete)	Metal buildings	Steel-framed walls	Wood-framed walls and other
	h-ft²-°F/Btu (m²-°K/W)	h-ft²-°F/Btu (m²-°K/W)	h-ft²-°F/Btu (m²-°K/W)	h-ft²-°F/Btu (m²-°K/W)
Zone 1 A, B	NR[1]	13.0/2.29	13.0/2.29	13.0/2.29
Zone 2 A, B	5.7/1.00	13.0/2.29	13.0/2.29	13.0/2.29
Zone 3 A, B, C	7.6/1.34	13.0/2.29	16.8/2.29	13.0/2.29
Zone 4 A, B, C	9.5/1.67	13.0/2.29	20.5/3.61	13.0/2.29
Zone 5 A, B, C	11.4/2.01	13.0/2.29	20.5/3.61	16.8/2.96
Zone 6 A, B	13.3/2.34	13.0/2.29	20.5/3.61	20.5/3.61
Zone 7	15.2/2.68	26.0/4.58	20.5/3.61	20.5/3.61

Figure 1-4 Minimum R-value recommended by ASHRAE 90.1-2007 based on wall construction type for all climate zones.

Figure 1-5 identifies maximum U-values recommended by ASHRAE for different facade assemblies (for nonresidential conditioned buildings); like Figure 1-4, it is based on four wall types and all climate zones. The recommendations are for entire wall assemblies, including glazed and opaque areas. All wall types in colder climates require lower overall U-values. Requirements for masonry, steel-framed, and wood-framed facades tend to decrease as climates get colder. In contrast, required U-values for metal building walls fall into two clusters: very cold climates and all the others. Steel-framed walls require lower U-values than mass walls for all climate types, due to thermal bridging effects. Wood-framed walls require the lowest U-values for most climate types.

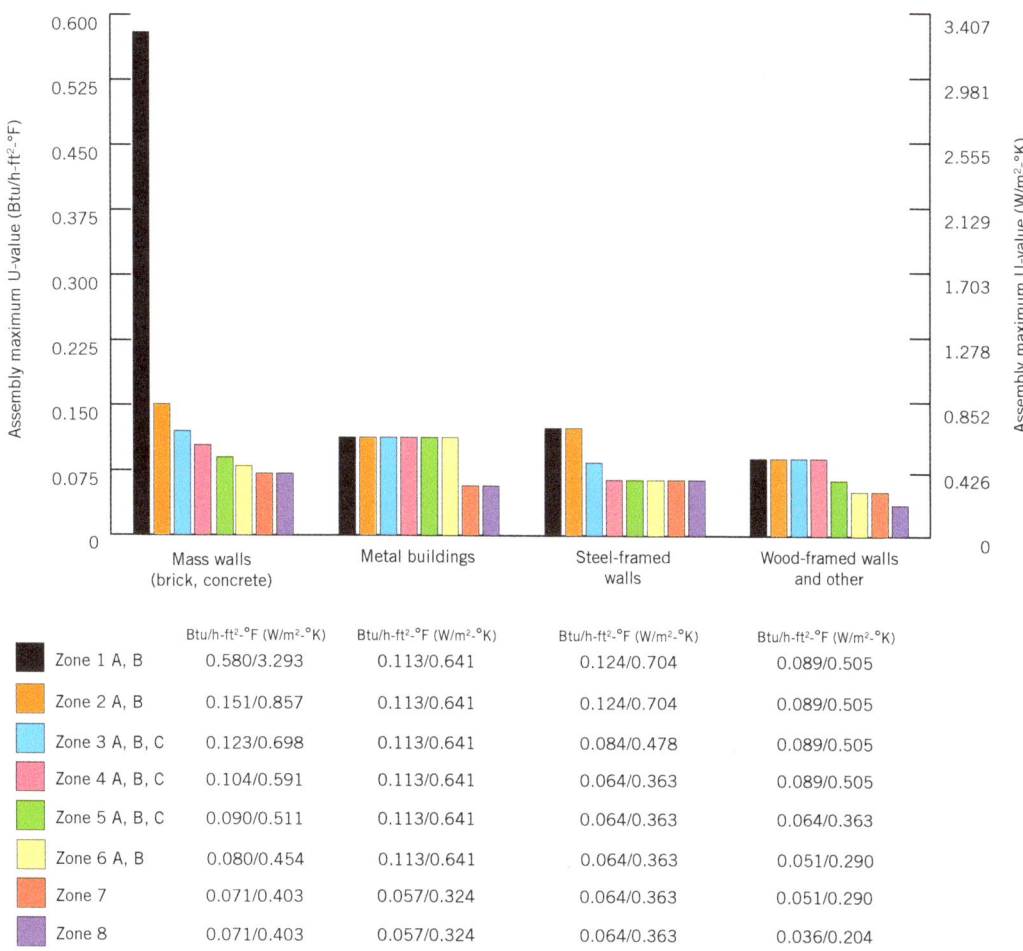

Figure 1-5 Maximum assembly U-values for exterior walls recommended by ASHRAE 90.1-2007 based on wall construction type for all climate zones.

Figure 1-6 shows ASHRAE recommendations for maximum SHGC for glazed areas of the facades. For warmer climates, lower SHGC, not exceeding 25%, is desirable, as excess solar radiation should be blocked. For colder climates, higher SHGCs can support passive solar heating, but should not exceed 45%.

14   CLIMATE-BASED DESIGN APPROACH FOR FACADES

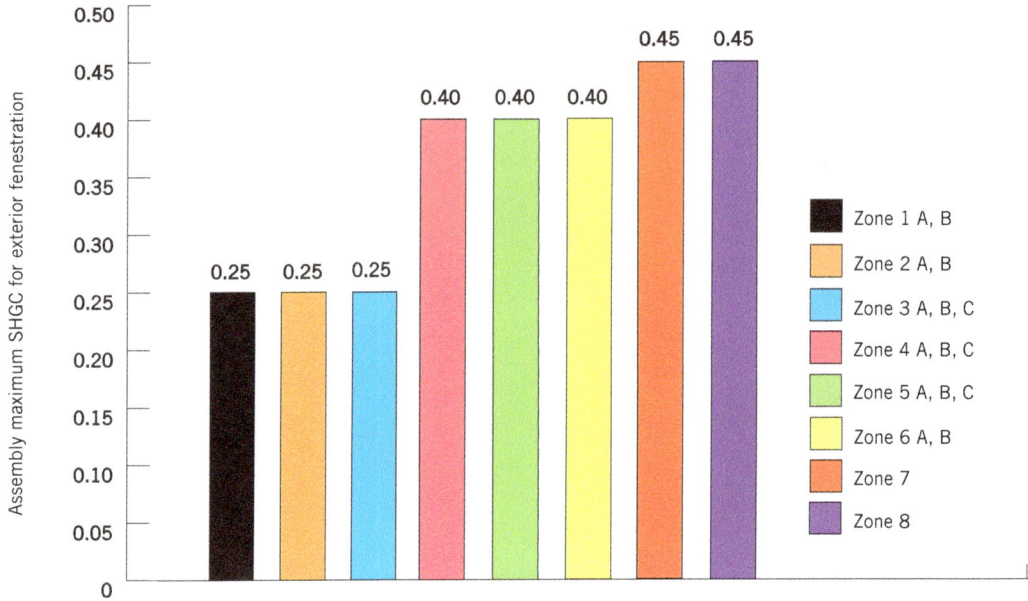

Figure 1-6 Maximum SHGCs for fenestration recommended by ASHRAE 90.1-2007 for all facade types and climate zones.

CHAPTER SUMMARY

This chapter discussed climate classification systems; climate-based design strategies for sustainable, high-performance facades; and energy code requirements for building envelopes. Standards prescribed by the energy codes, such as ASHRAE 90.1, only establish minimum requirements for improving energy efficiency of buildings. Sustainable facades, which use high-performance materials and glazing, and daylight harvesting strategies, shading devices, and control systems to monitor and adjust their performance, typically aim for better performance than those the energy codes prescribe. They also improve overall building envelope operation, thermal behavior, and occupants' thermal and visual comfort.

REFERENCES

Aksamija, A. (2009). "Context Based Design of Double Skin Facades: Climatic Consideration During the Design Process." *Perkins+Will Research Journal,* Vol. 1, No. 1, pp. 54–69.

Aksamija, A. (2010). "Analysis and Computation: Sustainable Design in Practice." *Design Principles and Practices: An International Journal,* Vol. 4, No. 4, pp. 291–314.

ASHRAE. (2007). *BSR/ASHRAE/IESNA 90.1-2007, Energy Standard for Buildings except Low-Rise Residential Buildings.* Atlanta, GA: American Society of Heating, Refrigerating and Air-Conditioning Engineers, Inc.

DOE. (2012). *Buildings Energy Data Book 2011.* Washington, DC: Department of Energy. Retrieved from http://buildingsdatabook.eren.doe.gov/default.aspx.

Lawrence, P., and Chase, T. (2010). "Investigating the Climate Impacts of Global Land Cover Change in the Community Climate System Model." *International Journal of Climatology,* Vol. 30, No. 13, pp. 2066–2087.

Peel, M., Finlayson, B., and McMahon, T. (2007). "Updated World Map of the Koppen-Geiger Climate Classification." *Hydrology and Earth System Sciences,* Vol. 11, No. 5, pp. 1633–1644.

CHAPTER 2

CHARACTERISTICS OF SUSTAINABLE FACADES

Highly glazed facades have been with us since the Crystal Palace was built in 1851. However, it was not until the early 1950s that building technology and postwar economic prosperity allowed the extensive use of curtain walls worldwide. For decades after that, designers placed much greater priority on aesthetics and views than on how facades can improve the energy performance of an entire building. Starting with the oil shortages of the 1970s, architects became increasingly concerned about worldwide energy resources, global climate change, and the importance of designing energy-efficient buildings and high-performance facades.

Four basic mechanisms—thermal heat transfer, solar heat gain, air leakage, and lighting loads—determine how facades affect overall building energy use. There are numerous strategies and tools designers can use to improve the performance of facades. Improved wall insulation will reduce conductive heat losses. Solar shading and high-performance glazing will control solar heat gain. Continuous air barriers and well-designed window systems will prevent air leakage. Increased daylighting of interior spaces will reduce the need for and reliance on electric lighting. In this chapter, we discuss the properties of high-performance facades and factors that influence their design.

ENERGY EFFICIENCY

What are the properties of energy-efficient building facades? They include allowing daylight into a building; preventing unwanted solar heat from entering the building; storing heat within the mass of the wall; preventing heat transfer through improved insulation; preventing air or moisture from passing through the facade; and allowing natural ventilation to cool the building's interior. As we saw in Chapter 1, these properties are highly dependent on climate, as well as a building's function, occupancy patterns, orientation, and equipment loads.

There are essentially two types of facades:

- *Opaque facades,* which are primarily constructed of layers of solid materials, such as masonry, stone, precast concrete panels, metal cladding, insulation, and cold-formed steel framing. Opaque facades may also include punched opening or windows.
- *Glazed facades,* such as curtain walls or storefront facades, which primarily consist of transparent or translucent glazing materials and metal framing components.

Physical behaviors of these two facade types differ because their components, materials, and construction methods are different. Opaque facades typically have more mass, greater insulation levels, and better heat retention than glazed facades. In contrast, glazed facades usually allow more daylight into the interiors, provide better views for occupants, and impose less dead load on the building structure than opaque facades.

This section reviews two basic elements in the design of any type of energy-efficient facade: orientation and fenestration.

Orientation

The orientation of a building determines its exposure to sunlight. Because the angle of the earth relative to the sun varies throughout the year and the sun moves across the sky during the day, solar exposure on a facade is continually changing. To simplify the issue, four days of the year—the solstices, December 21 (when the sun is at its lowest) and June 21 (when it is at its highest); and the equinoxes, March 21 and September 21—can be used to analyze solar exposure, as seen in Figure 2-1.

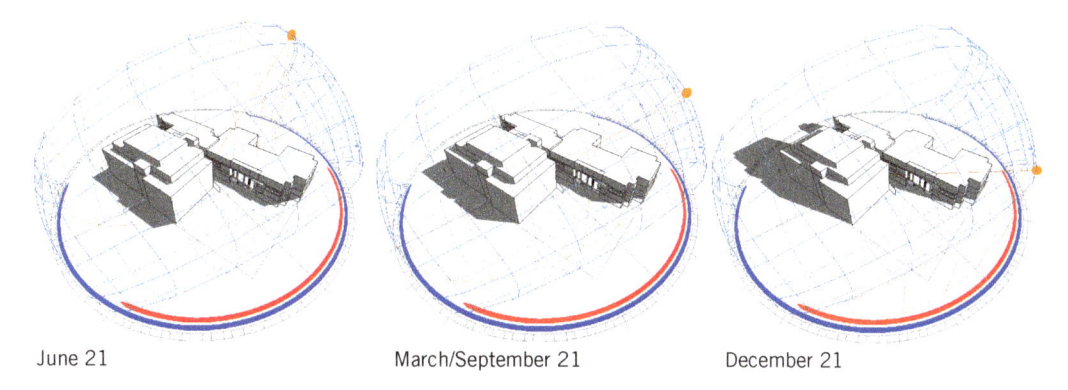

June 21   March/September 21   December 21

Figure 2-1 Building orientation and solar position during the different times of the year.

Strategies for controlling solar heat gain depend on the building's orientation. As we saw in Chapter 1, solar heat gain can benefit buildings in colder climates during winter months. In warmer climates, interior spaces have to be shaded from direct sunlight for much of the year. The optimal orientation of the building, from the perspective of solar heat gain, balances desirable solar heat gain during winter months with solar shading during summer months.

Figures 2.2 and 2.3 show solar diagrams for very hot and cool climates, using typical latitudes for those climatic zones. Both diagrams show the optimal building orientation in relation to solar heat gain. For example, Figure 2-2 shows that in very hot climates (zone 1), solar heat gain must be kept as low as possible during the entire year, but especially during summer months. In cool climates (zone 5), more balance is needed across the seasons. In winter months, solar exposure should be used to passively heat the building.

20 CHARACTERISTICS OF SUSTAINABLE FACADES

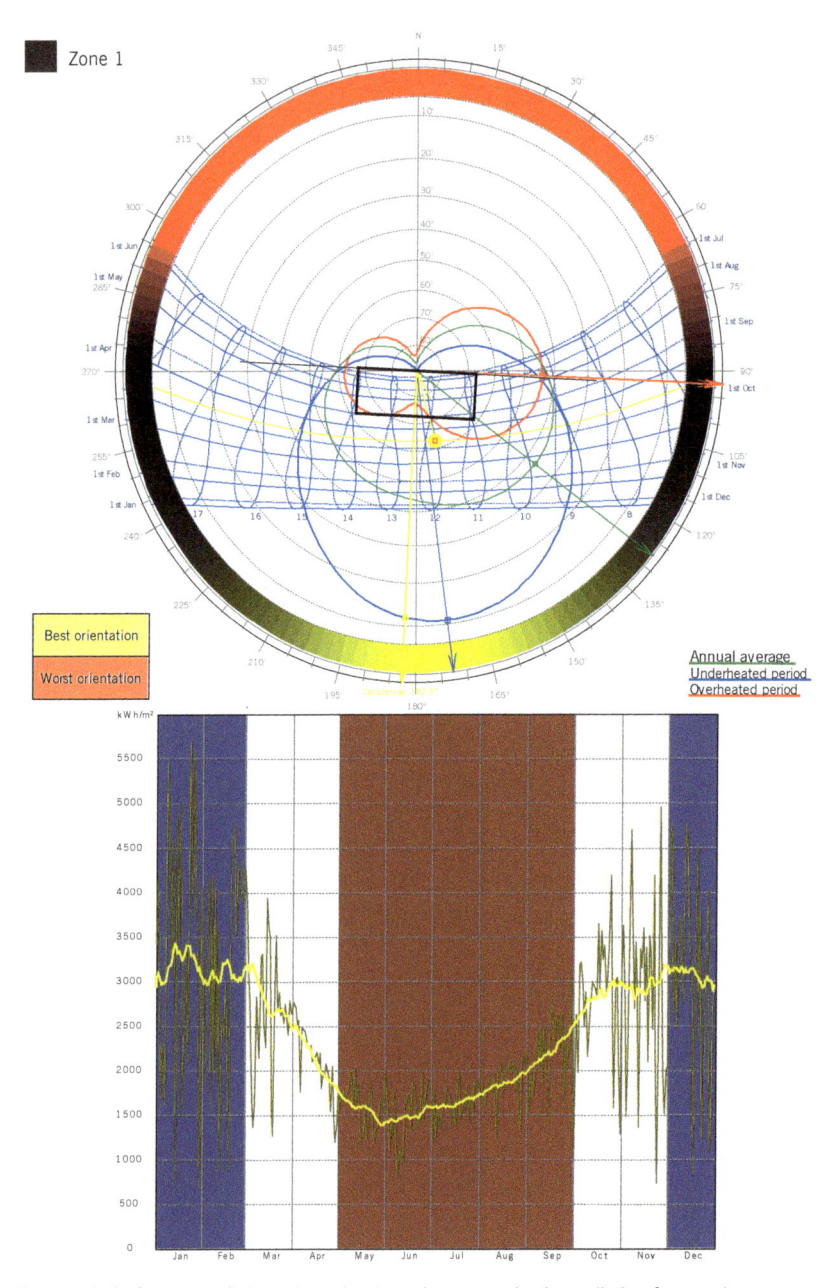

Figure 2-2 Optimal building orientation based on annual solar radiation for very hot climate (zone 1).

ENERGY EFFICIENCY 21

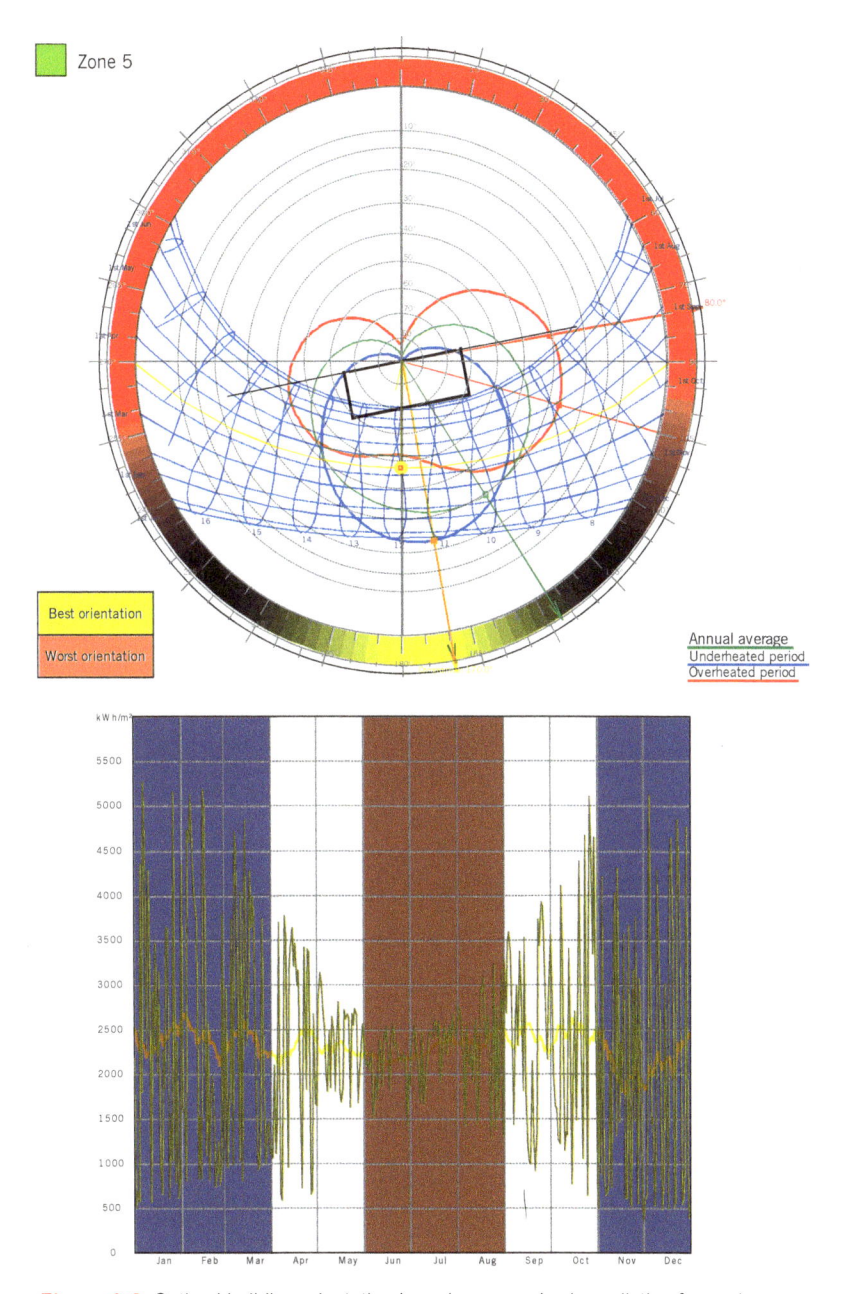

Figure 2-3 Optimal building orientation based on annual solar radiation for cool climate (zone 5).

Building orientation is not always under the designer's control. The configuration and orientation of the site, zoning or planning code requirements, or other similar considerations may determine it. Because the passive effects of solar orientation are so significant, the orientation of the facades should be considered early in the design process. The environmental conditions and solar radiation are different and require differing responses for facades facing north, south, east, and west. For example, northern and southern exposures are beneficial for daylighting, on the north because the light is indirect and on the south because the sun is high enough in the summer to allow shading of the direct sunlight. There is usually a daylighting advantage in maximizing these exposures. In contrast, because the sun is usually low in the east and west, as little of the facade as possible should face these exposures, to prevent unwanted solar radiation. If, because of site constraints, designers have no choice but to orient the building east and west, deep vertical fins on those facades can usually block most of the low morning and afternoon sunlight. When a building is designed to take advantage of its orientation, comfortable living and working conditions inside the building will be achieved at a relatively low consumption of energy.

CASE STUDY 2.1 VINCENT TRIGGS ELEMENTARY SCHOOL

When the Clark County Elementary School District in Las Vegas, Nevada, began its building program, it set a simple but daunting challenge to designers: each new school building was to use two-thirds the energy of the district's existing benchmark buildings, but with 5–10% more program area and for no more than 80% of the construction cost. A design competition resulted in four school designs, and a prototype of each was built. Vincent Triggs Elementary School is the first of the built prototypes (Figures 2-4 to 2-7). Located in the mixed, arid climate of southern Nevada (zone 4B), the building relies on passive design strategies, including optimized building orientation, climate-appropriate massing, and a thermally improved building envelope to reduce energy use.

Figure 2-4 Rendering of the Clark County Elementary School prototype.

ENERGY EFFICIENCY   23

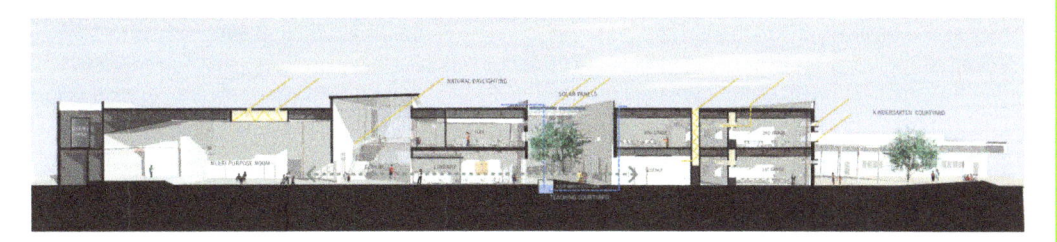

Figure 2-5 Diagrammatic section.

Figure 2-6 (a) Entry along the south facade.

Figure 2-6 (b) Deep overhang over the entry.

The building's east-west orientation minimizes solar exposure for the east and west facades, and maximizes north and south exposures. A central courtyard, a common feature in indigenous architecture in these climates, helps ventilate the surrounding interior spaces. The two-story courtyard provides shading for the building and uses reflected daylight to reduce the need for artificial lighting and to soften the glare of the bright desert sky. Light tubes efficiently direct daylight from skylights to the classrooms.

CHARACTERISTICS OF SUSTAINABLE FACADES

Most of the building's facade consists of opaque panels containing punched windows, with shading devices on the south and west sides. The north and south ends of the main entry lobby are enclosed with a full-height curtain wall. Deep overhangs are used to shade these facades and reduce solar heat gain.

Insulated tilt-up concrete panels were selected as the opaque facade material. These panels, often used for industrial, warehouse, or big-box retail buildings, were a low-cost way to provide high thermal performance. Each panel is composed of three layers, with the insulation sandwiched between precast concrete skins. This panel construction minimizes the direct transfer of outside heat to the inside. The concrete mass of the panels also provides thermal storage, which is beneficial in this type of climate due to the large daily temperature shifts. All glazing assemblies are composed of high-performance, low-e insulated units set in thermally broken frames.

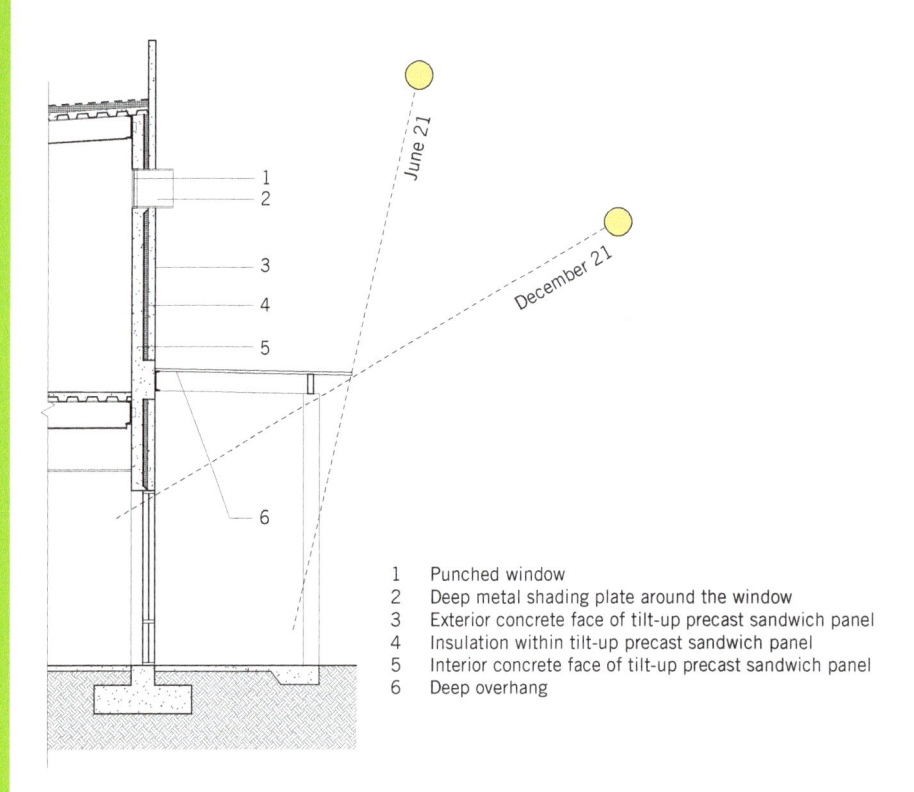

1 Punched window
2 Deep metal shading plate around the window
3 Exterior concrete face of tilt-up precast sandwich panel
4 Insulation within tilt-up precast sandwich panel
5 Interior concrete face of tilt-up precast sandwich panel
6 Deep overhang

Figure 2-7 Exterior wall section (south facade).

Fenestration

Fenestration components (windows, curtain walls, clerestories, skylights) are significant elements of envelope design, from both aesthetic and performance perspectives. They allow natural light to enter interior space, but also allow heat transfer between the outside and inside. Fenestration elements affect a building's overall energy consumption, as well as its occupants' well-being, health, comfort, and productivity. When choosing fenestration materials, the designer must consider properties of glass, such as U-values, SHGC, and visual transmittance. The design of the fenestration framing system is also important. Poor fenestration system design and construction may result in drafts, glare, noise, condensation, and excessive heat loss or gain, ultimately causing discomfort for the building's occupants and excessive use of energy.

Recently developed fenestration products use new advances in building technology to allow transparent yet energy-efficient facades. Glazing units can be insulated using two, three, or more layers of glass. The spaces between the glass layers can be filled with inert gases or aerogel insulation to lower the U-value of the unit. Low-e, reflective, or ceramic frit coatings can be applied to the glass to reduce transmission of solar heat gain. The glass itself can be tinted with a color. Interlayer films within laminated glass can also provide shading. Aluminum frames can be thermally broken or thermally improved to raise the unit's U-value. New glass types are continually being introduced into the market to satisfy a variety of functional, security, and aesthetic requirements.

An important metric of a facade's characteristics is the window-to-wall ratio (WWR), that is, the proportion of glazed to opaque facade area. This ratio is a significant contributor to a facade's solar heat gain and energy consumption. In most cases, higher WWRs result in greater energy consumption, as the thermal resistance of even a well-insulated glazed facade is typically lower than that of an opaque facade.

To show the relationship between WWR and energy consumption, Figures 2-8 to 2-19 present the effects on energy consumption for north-oriented office space located in twelve U.S. cities. Each figure represents a different climate zone and subzone, with WWRs of 20%, 40%, 60%, and 80%. For all these examples, the characteristics of the interior space (dimensions, occupancy patterns, equipment and lighting loads) are identical, as are the properties of the opaque and glazed areas of the facade. The opaque elements of the facade in each case are designed according to the minimum recommendations for insulation prescribed by ASHRAE 90.1-2007. The glazed area in each case consists of air-filled glazing units, using clear glass with a low-e coating on the second surface. The latitude for each city is also shown, since solar radiation on a site is dependent on the latitude (as well as other environmental conditions, such as number of cloudy days).

For hot and warm climates (Figures 2-8 to 2-12), increased WWRs cause cooling loads to increase due to increased solar heat gain. However, note in Figure 2-8 that while the WWR increases 300% (from 20% to 80%), the annual cooling loads increase only 33% (from approximately 36 to 48 kBtu/ft^2). This is the result of at least three factors. First, the facade is not the only component of a building determining its energy efficiency. Other components, including roof construction, the number of doors and the frequency of their use, and the heat load produced by the building's occupants, influence cooling loads. Second, the opaque portions of these facades are insulated to only the minimum ASHRAE level; if the walls were more heavily insulated, the effect of increasing the WWR would be less pronounced. Third, these diagrams do not assume a reduction of energy loads for electrical lighting resulting from the increased WWRs. For mixed and colder climates (Figures 2-13 to 2-19), higher WWRs also affect heating loads, especially for buildings located in cold and very cold climates. In all these examples, reducing the WWR (by increasing the amount of opaque facade relative to glazed facade) improves the energy efficiency.

26 CHARACTERISTICS OF SUSTAINABLE FACADES

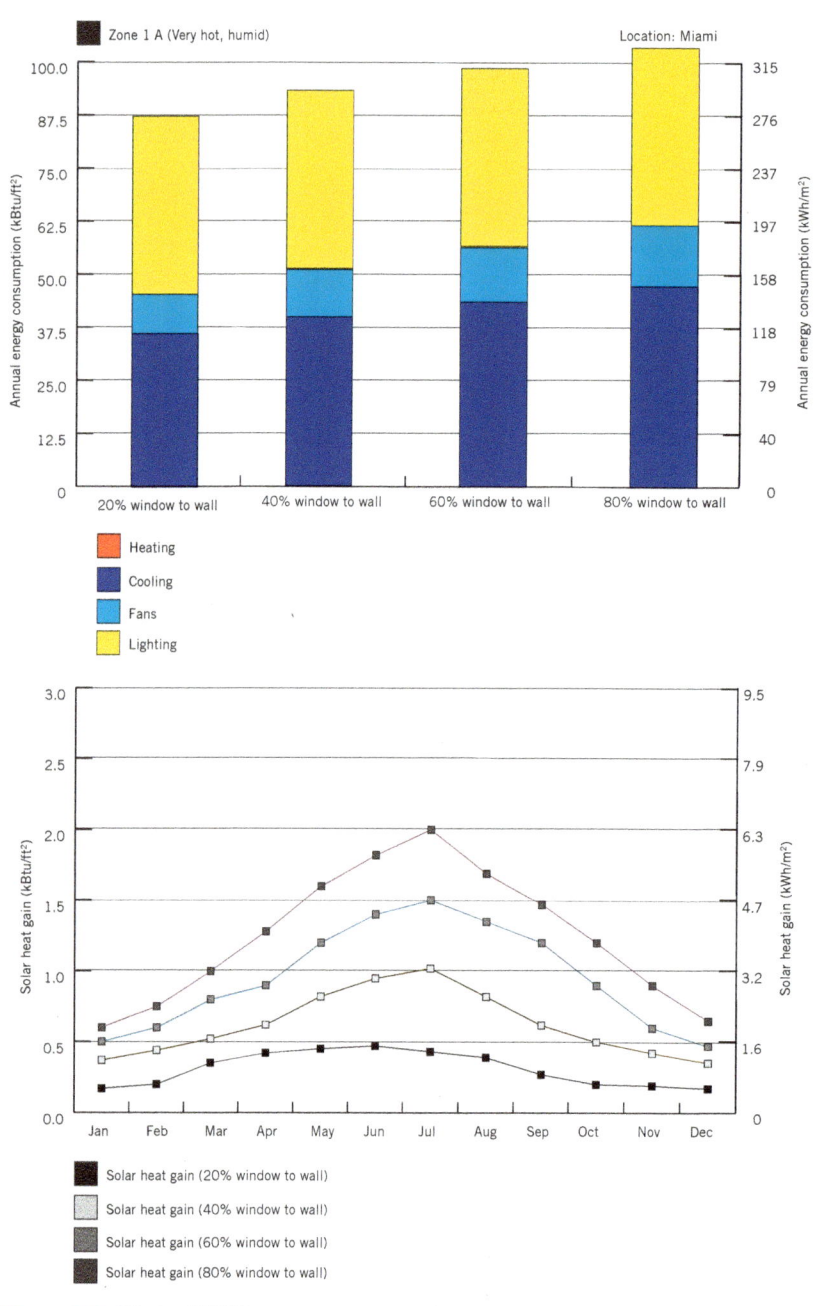

Figure 2-8 Effects of WWR on energy consumption and solar heat gain for zone 1A climate.

ENERGY EFFICIENCY 27

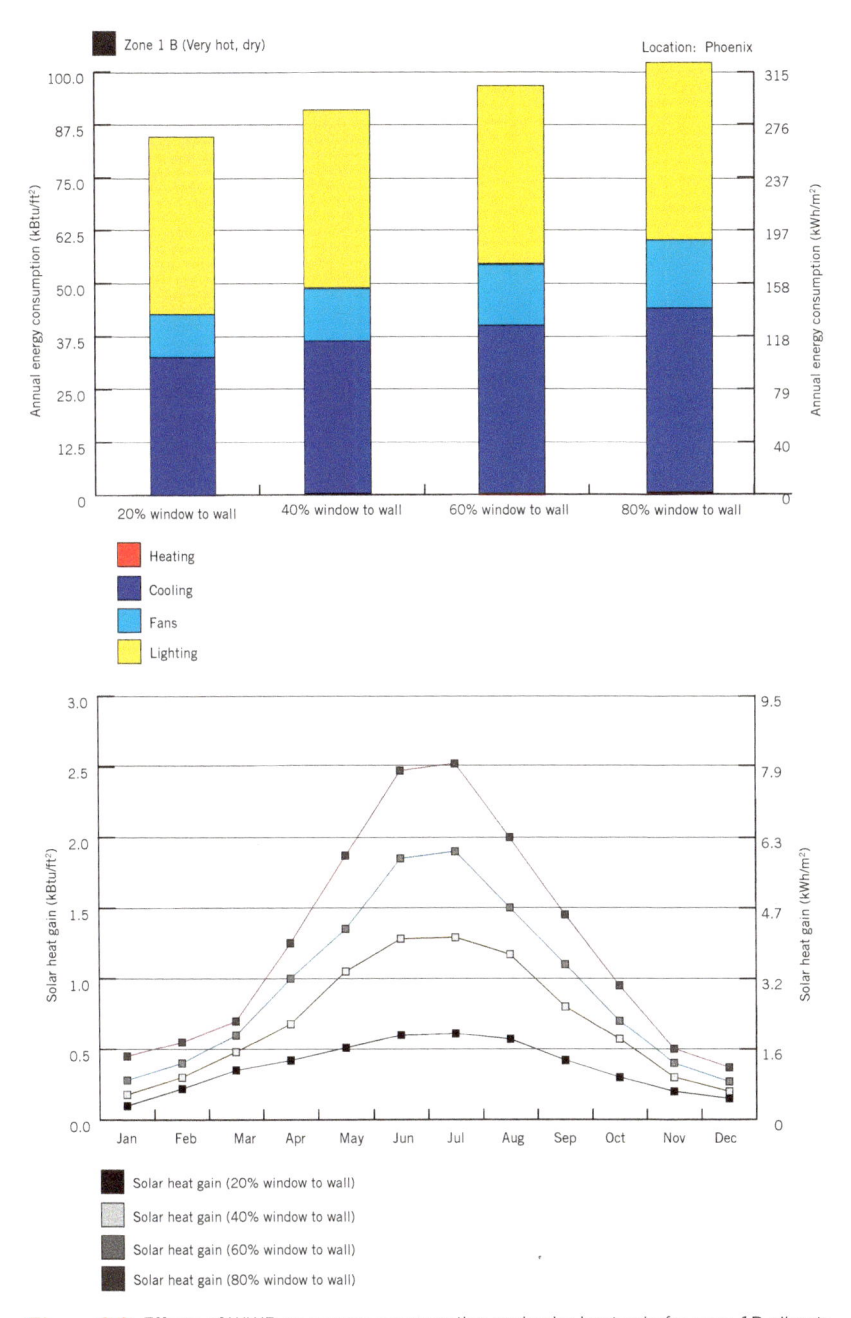

Figure 2-9 Effects of WWR on energy consumption and solar heat gain for zone 1B climate.

28 CHARACTERISTICS OF SUSTAINABLE FACADES

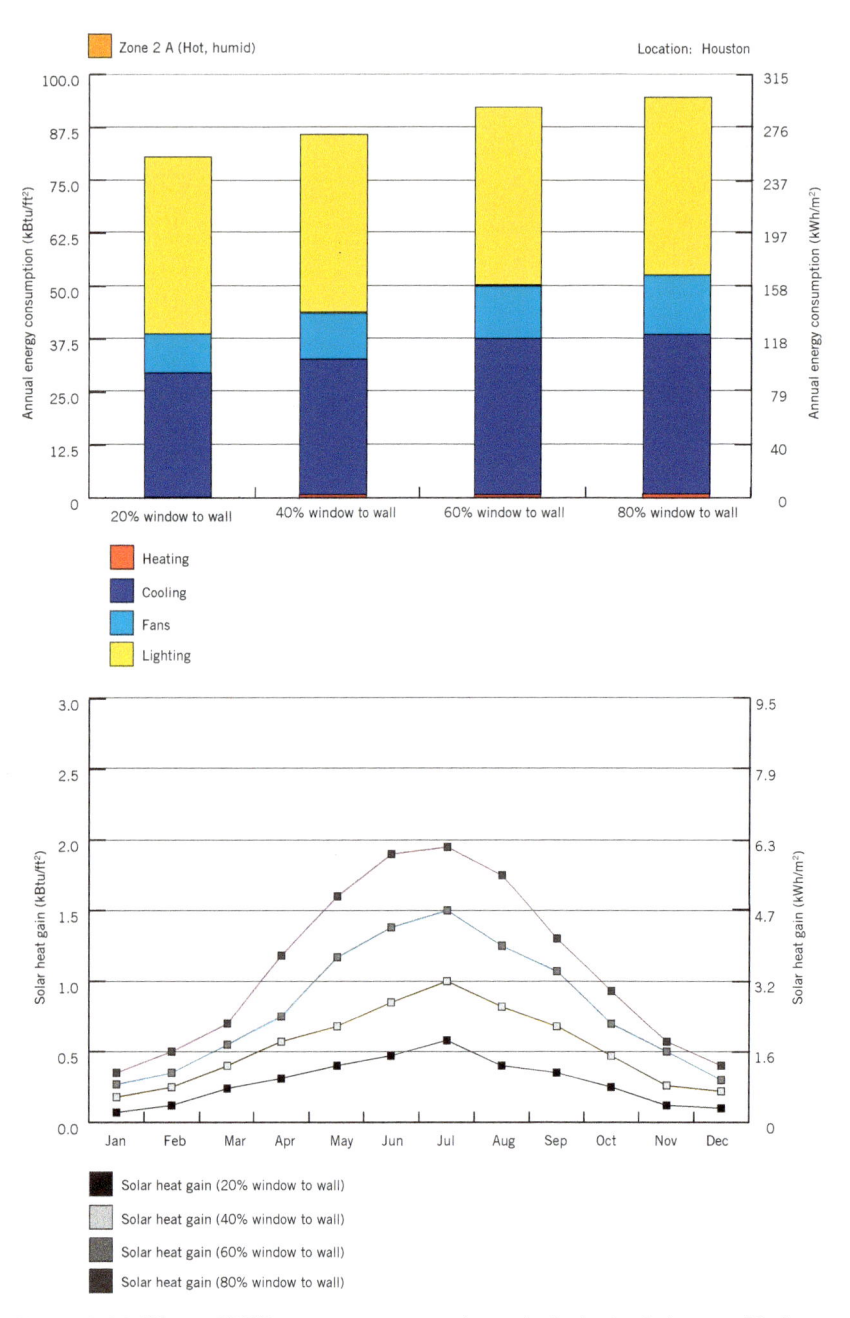

Figure 2-10 Effects of WWR on energy consumption and solar heat gain for zone 2A climate.

ENERGY EFFICIENCY   29

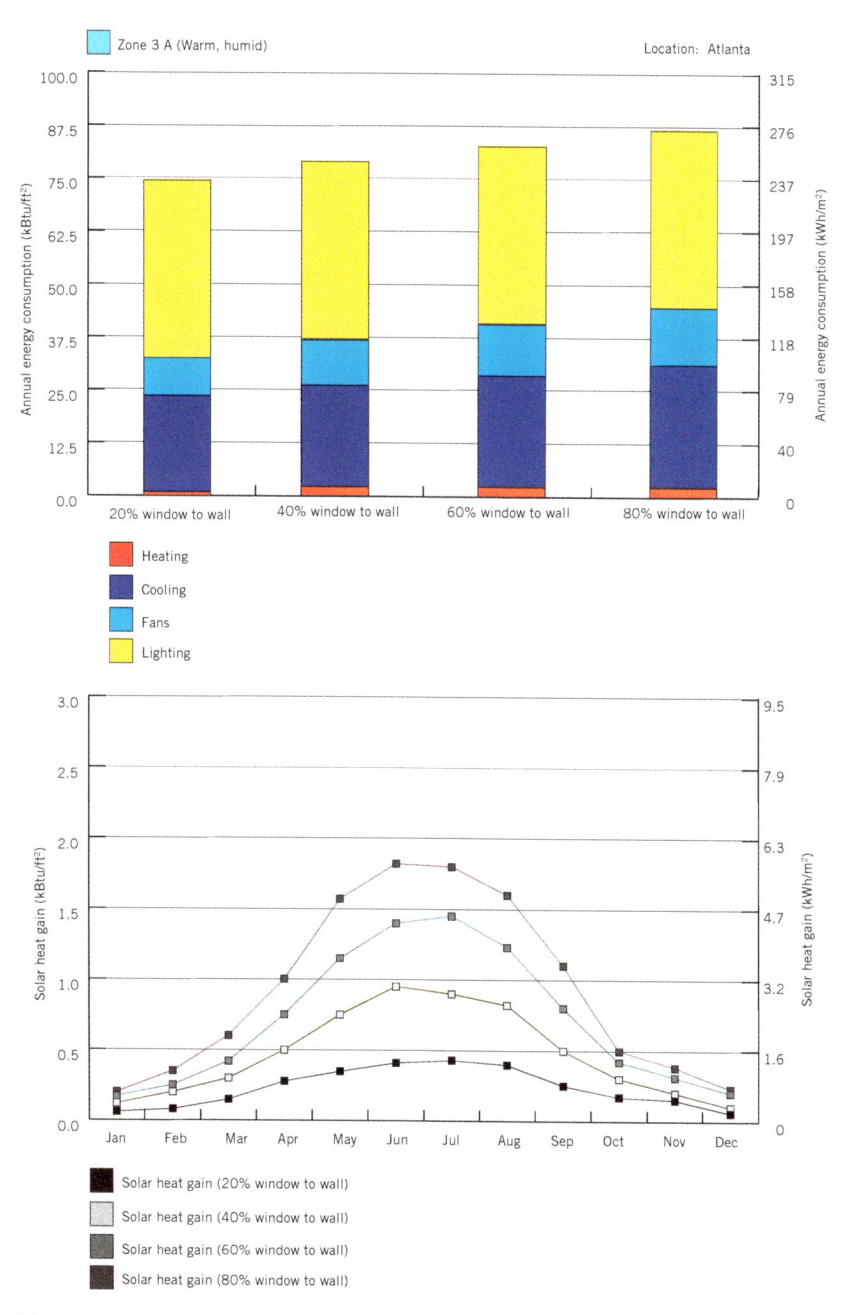

Figure 2-11 Effects of WWR on energy consumption and solar heat gain for zone 3A climate.

30 CHARACTERISTICS OF SUSTAINABLE FACADES

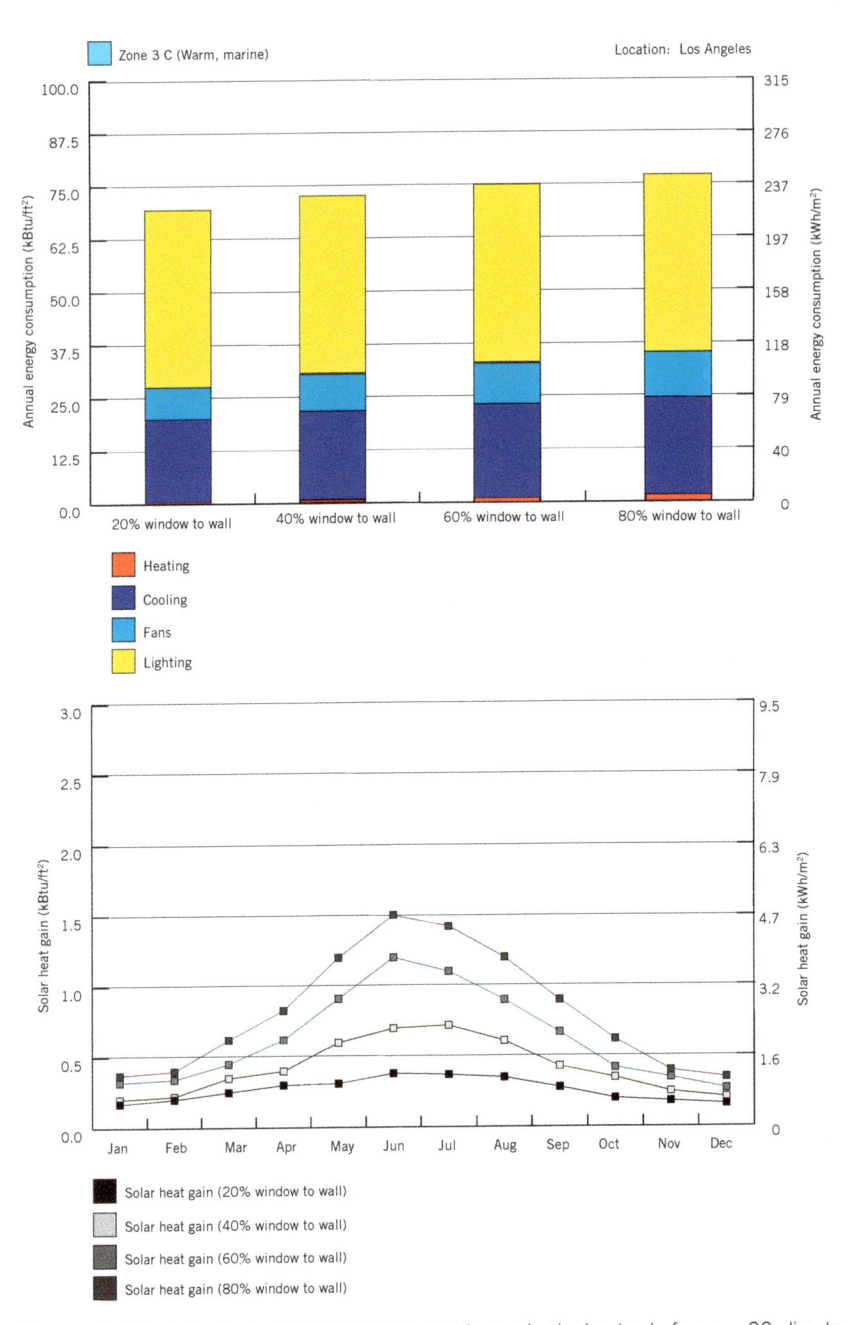

Figure 2-12 Effects of WWR on energy consumption and solar heat gain for zone 3C climate.

ENERGY EFFICIENCY 31

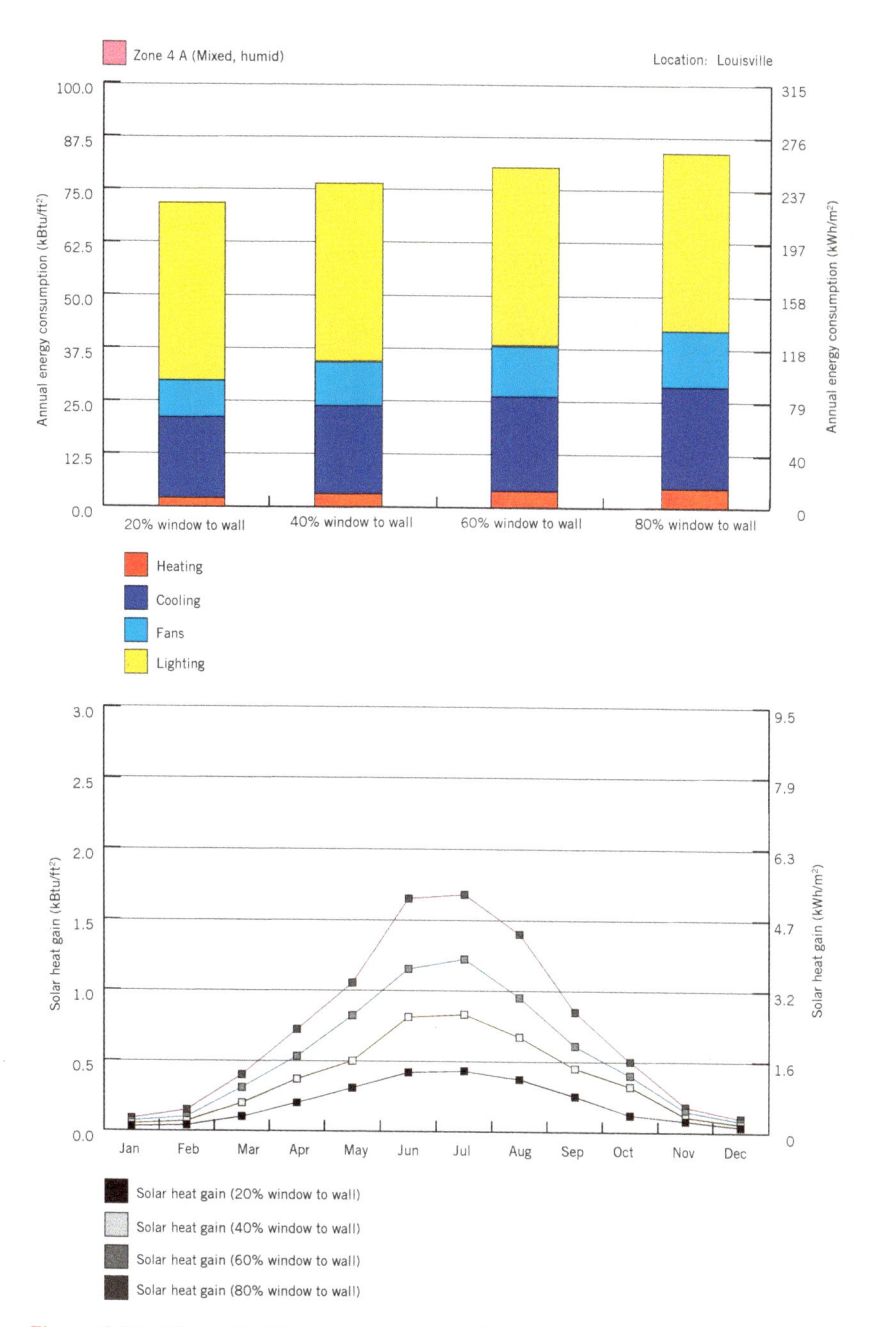

Figure 2-13 Effects of WWR on energy consumption and solar heat gain for zone 4A climate.

32 CHARACTERISTICS OF SUSTAINABLE FACADES

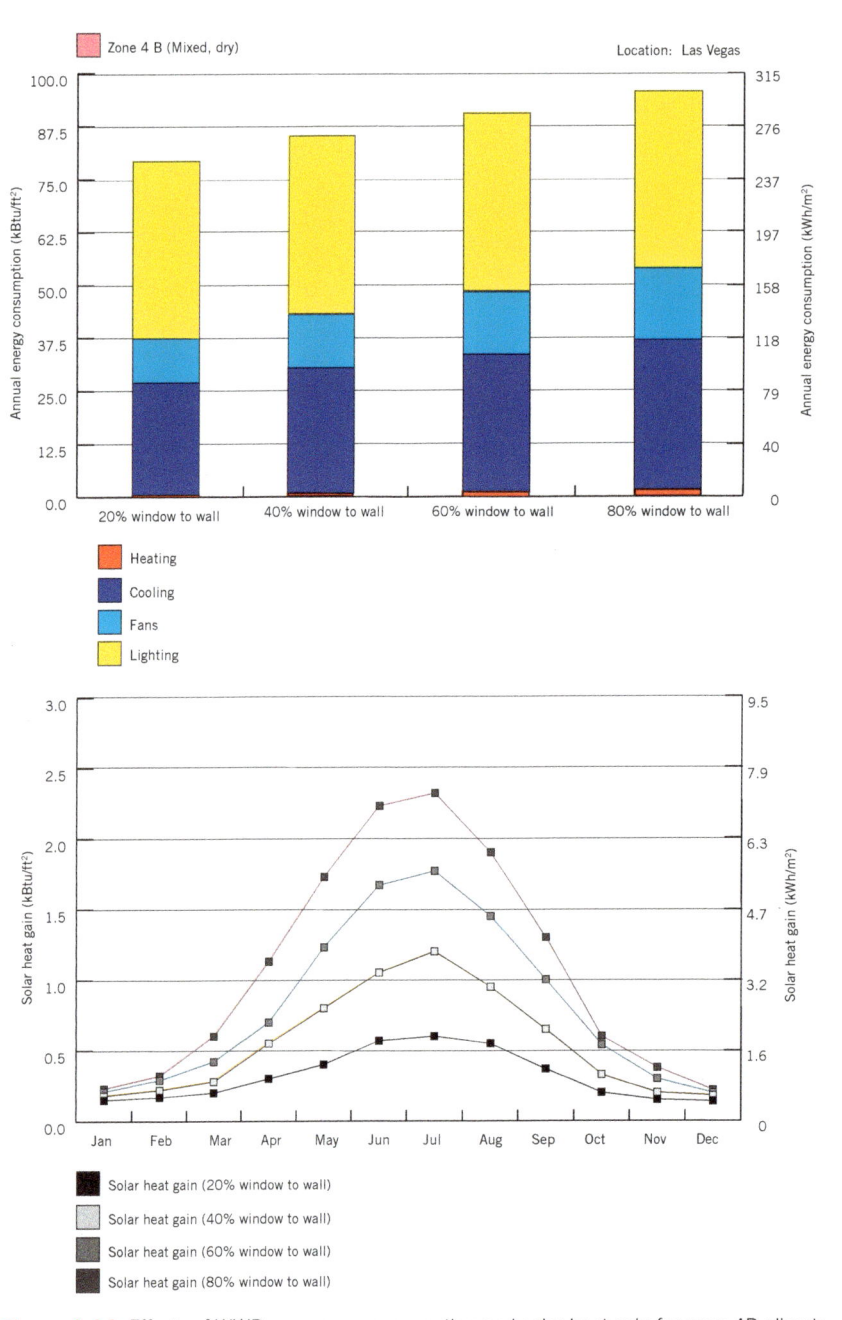

Figure 2-14 Effects of WWR on energy consumption and solar heat gain for zone 4B climate.

ENERGY EFFICIENCY 33

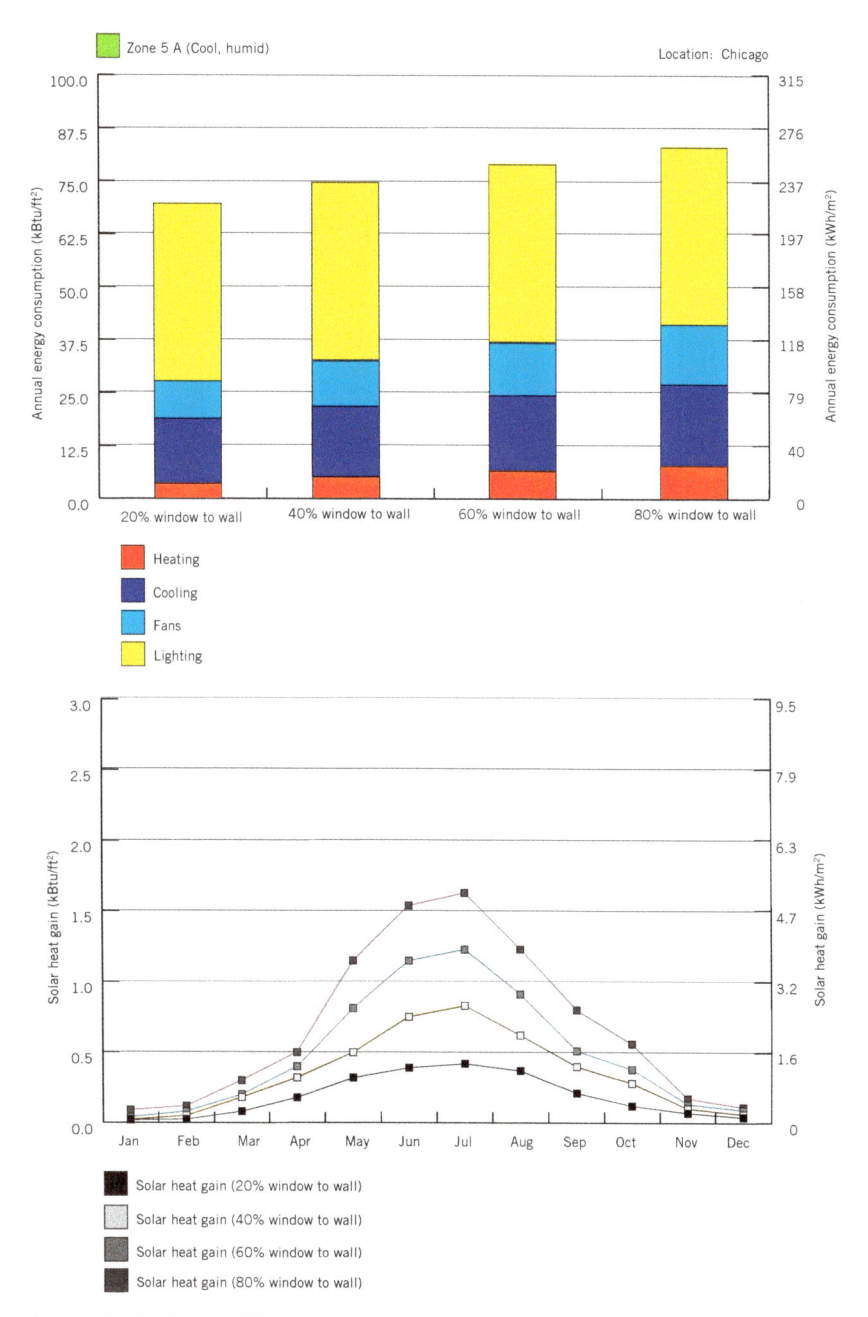

Figure 2-15 Effects of WWR on energy consumption and solar heat gain for zone 5A climate.

34 CHARACTERISTICS OF SUSTAINABLE FACADES

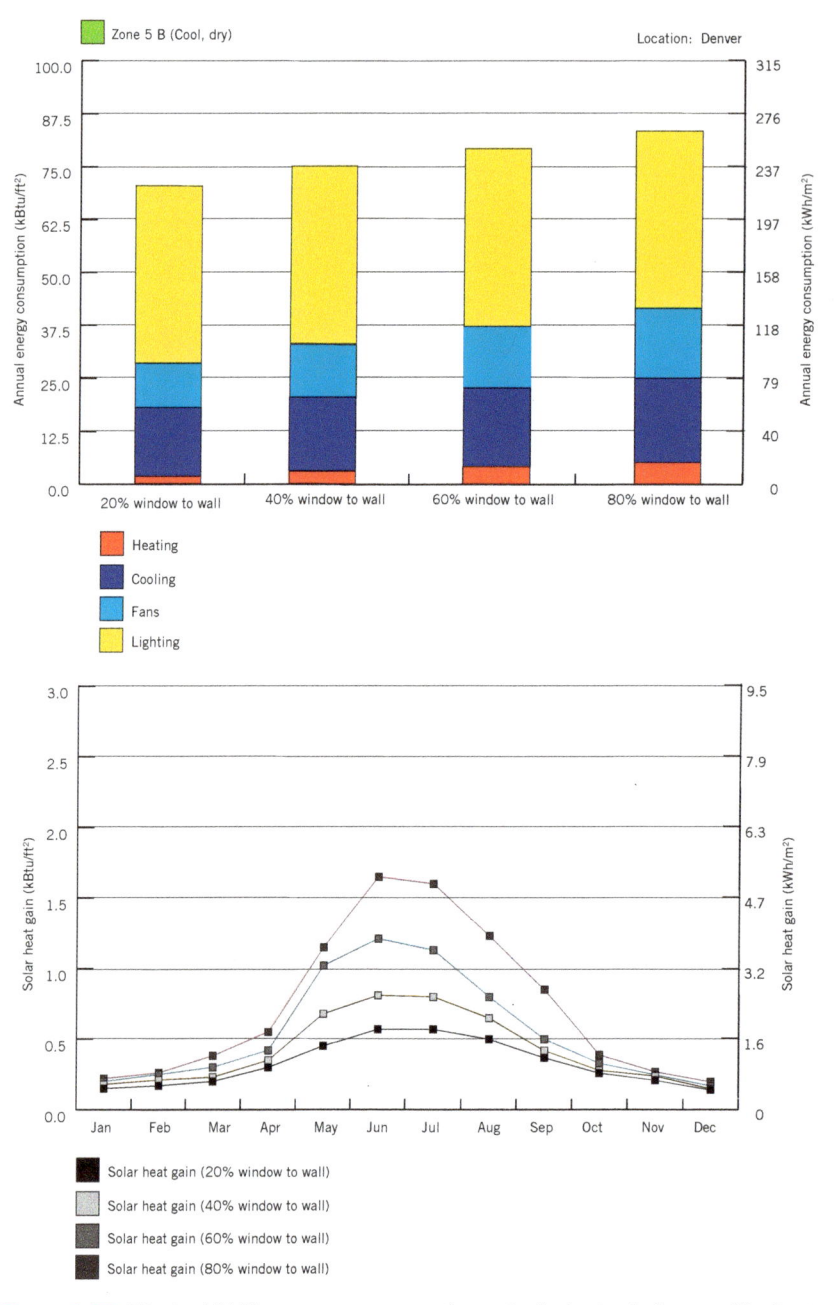

Figure 2-16 Effects of WWR on energy consumption and solar heat gain for zone 5B climate.

ENERGY EFFICIENCY   35

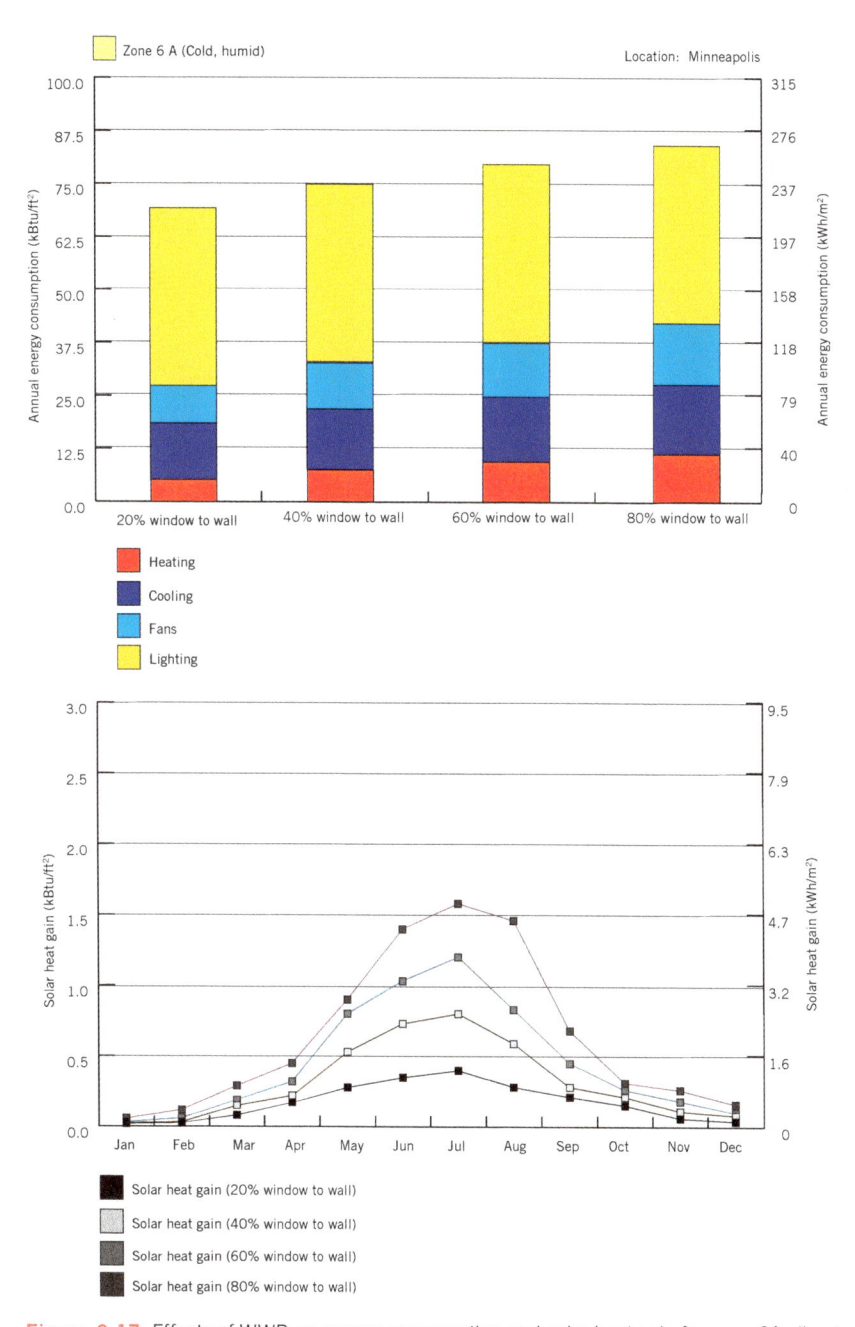

Figure 2-17 Effects of WWR on energy consumption and solar heat gain for zone 6A climate.

36 CHARACTERISTICS OF SUSTAINABLE FACADES

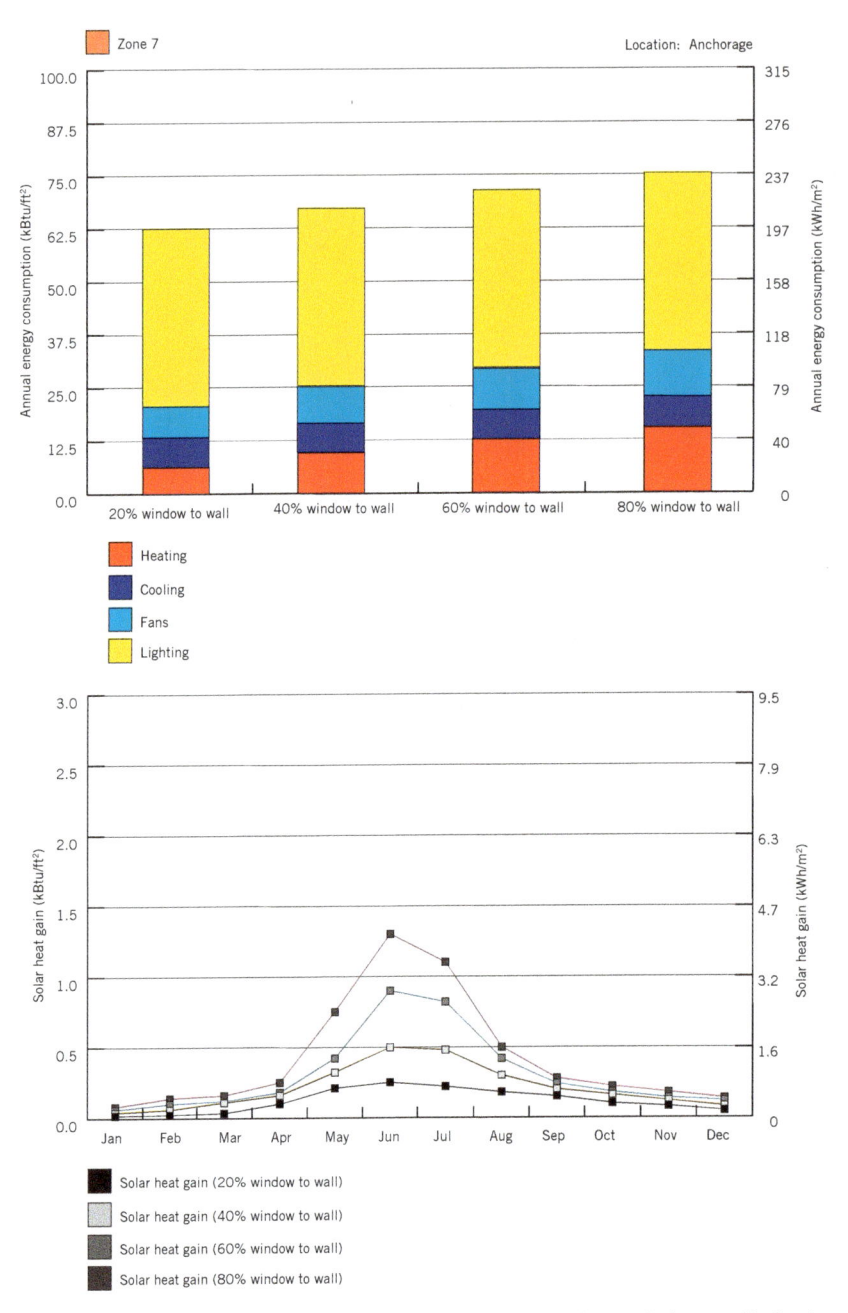

Figure 2-18 Effects of WWR on energy consumption and solar heat gain for zone 7 climate.

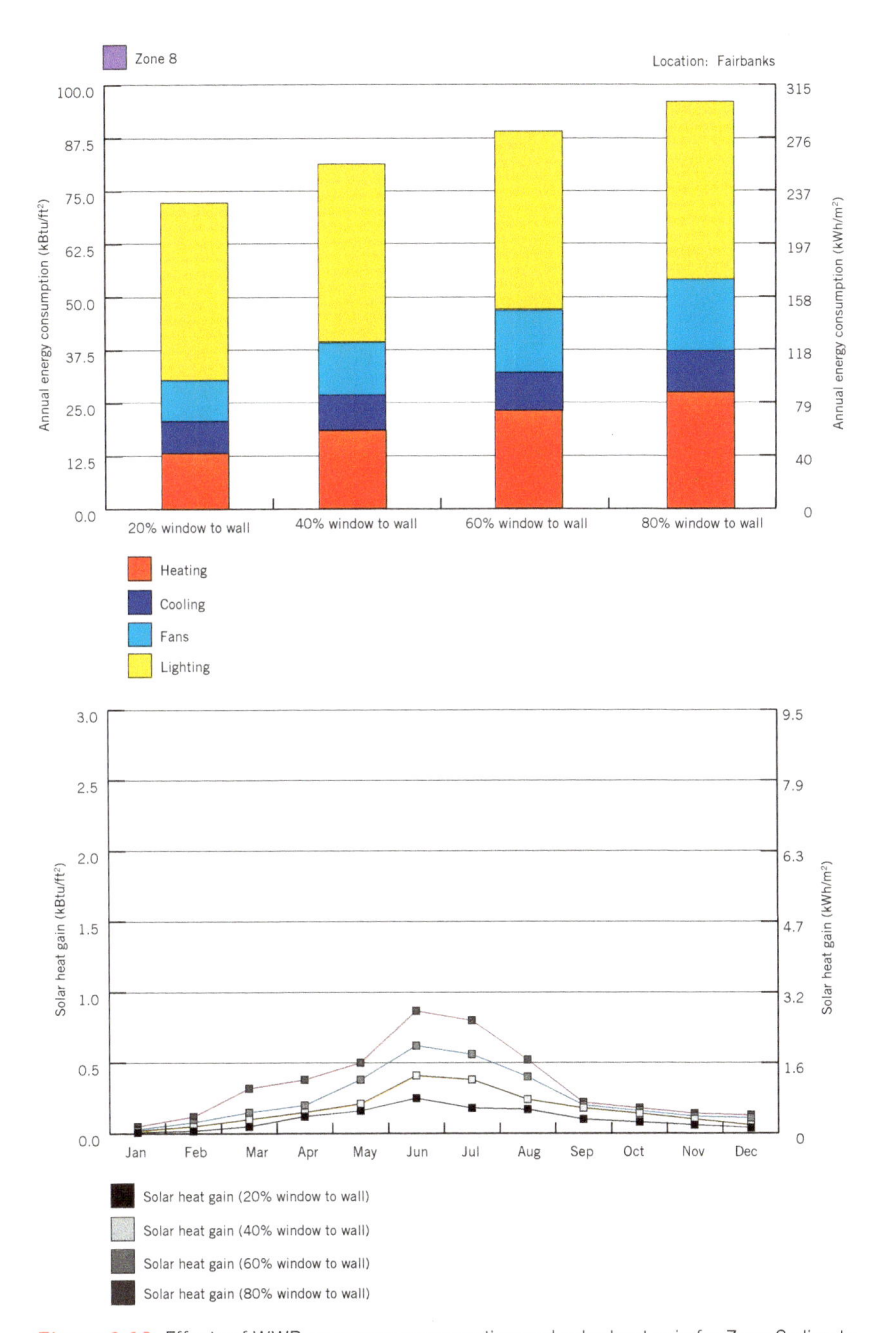

Figure 2-19 Effects of WWR on energy consumption and solar heat gain for Zone 8 climate.

CASE STUDY 2.2 HECTOR GARCIA MIDDLE SCHOOL

Hector Garcia Middle School is located in Dallas, Texas (zone 3A). It is oriented in the east-west direction to limit its east and west exposures (Figures 2-20 to 2-22). Because the classrooms are grouped along the north orientation, they have a consistent energy demand. This orientation also minimizes cooling loads by protecting the classrooms from the harsh south, east, and west sun exposures. The north facade's WWR of 70% takes advantage of the available daylight and provides views to the outside. The facade at the second and third levels is a two-story curtain wall with clear and colored glazing. At the ground level is a brick cavity wall with metal framing, punctuated by a series of long strip windows.

Figure 2-20 North facade.

Large-volume instructional spaces and other program spaces that require minimal natural light are located along the south facade. The WWR for this facade is 30%. Several exterior wall systems are used: brick cavity wall with metal framing, metal panels, aluminum curtain wall, storefront facade, and punched windows. A deep roof overhang shades the curtain wall from the south sun.

Figure 2-21 South facade.

ENERGY EFFICIENCY 39

The east and west facades consist primarily of brick cavity wall. The openings in these facades are kept to a minimum, with a 0% WWR on the east facade and a 10% WWR on the west facade.

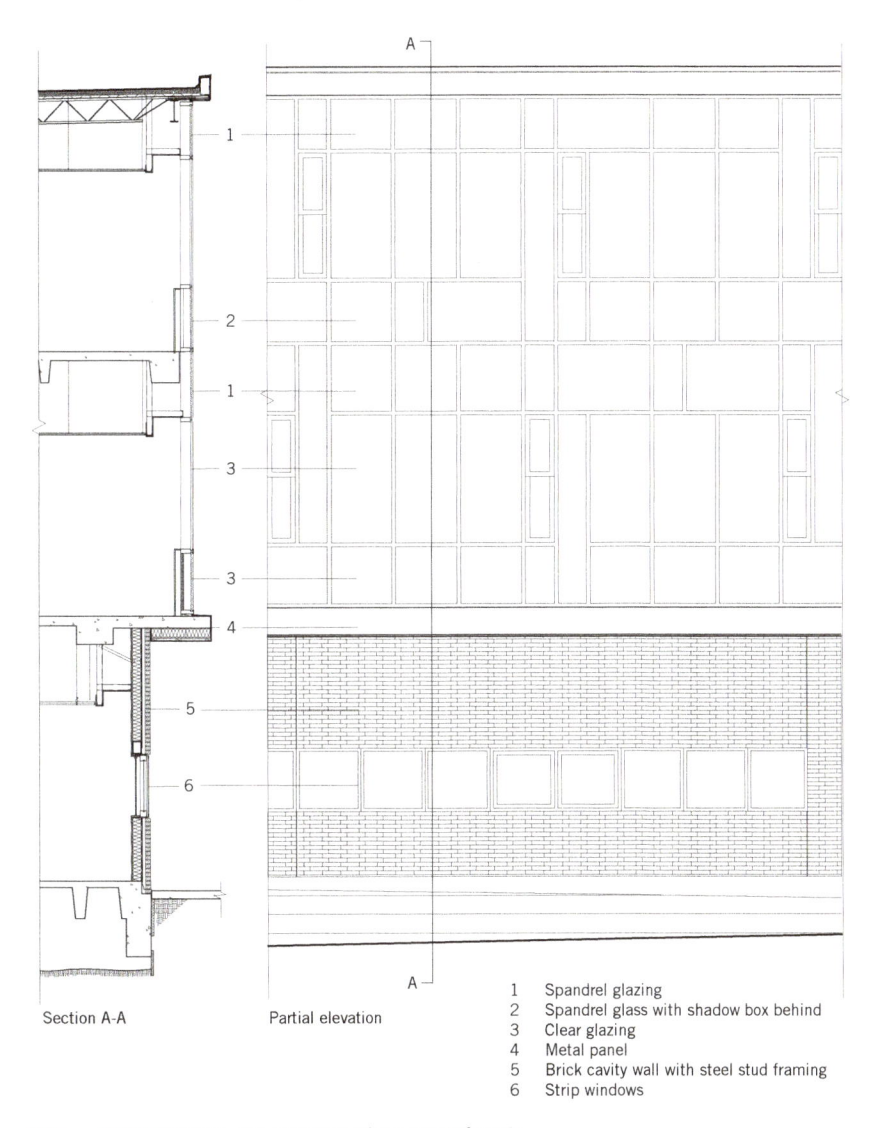

Section A-A   Partial elevation

1 Spandrel glazing
2 Spandrel glass with shadow box behind
3 Clear glazing
4 Metal panel
5 Brick cavity wall with steel stud framing
6 Strip windows

Figure 2-22 Section and elevation of the north facade.

FACADE TYPES AND MATERIALS

Opaque Building Facades

Brick veneer facades consist of single exterior wythes of nonstructural brick masonry, supported by cold-formed steel framing (Figure 2-23) or by a concrete masonry unit (CMU) wall (Figure 2-24). An air space, or cavity, between the outer layer of brick and the inner support system functions as a drainage zone, allowing any water that penetrates the exterior brick layer to drain at the bottom of the cavity. Rigid insulation within the air space, or batt insulation between the steel framing members, will improve the thermal performance of the wall. When the brick veneer is supported by CMU, insulation is adhered to the exterior side of the CMU (Figure 2-24).

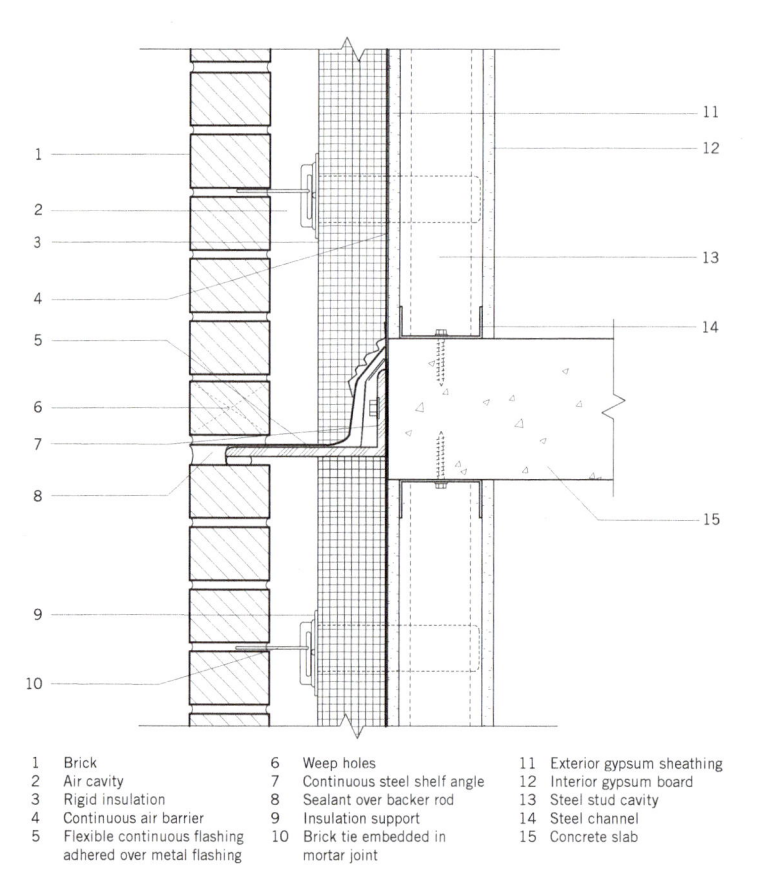

1 Brick
2 Air cavity
3 Rigid insulation
4 Continuous air barrier
5 Flexible continuous flashing adhered over metal flashing
6 Weep holes
7 Continuous steel shelf angle
8 Sealant over backer rod
9 Insulation support
10 Brick tie embedded in mortar joint
11 Exterior gypsum sheathing
12 Interior gypsum board
13 Steel stud cavity
14 Steel channel
15 Concrete slab

Figure 2-23 Brick cavity wall with steel stud framing.

FACADE TYPES AND MATERIALS   41

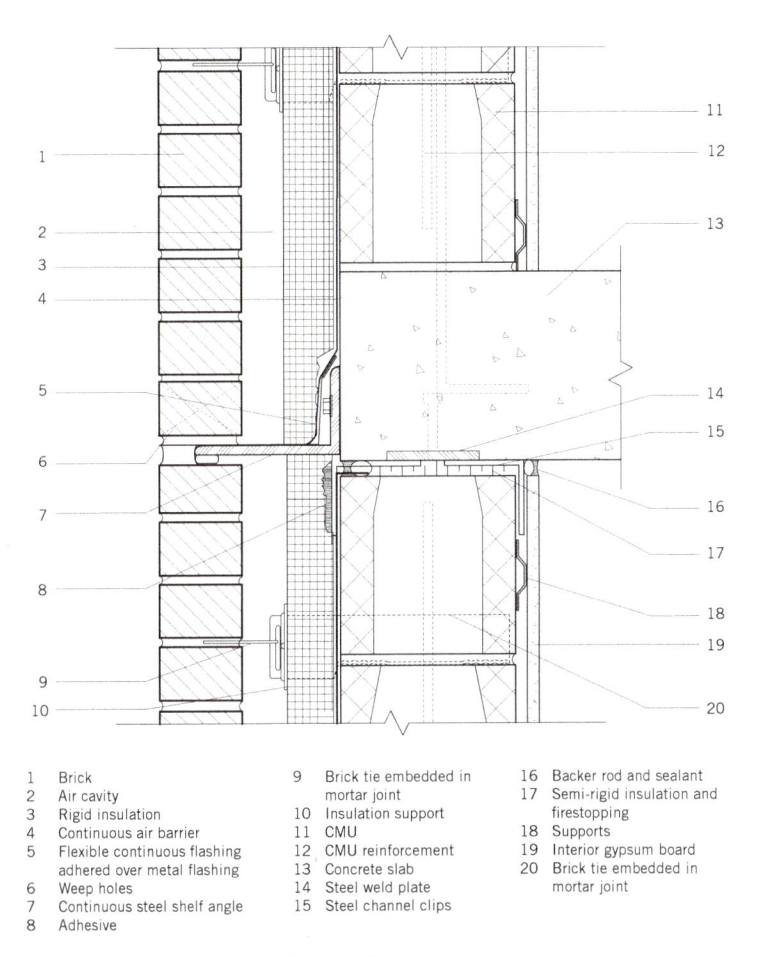

1	Brick	9	Brick tie embedded in mortar joint	16	Backer rod and sealant
2	Air cavity	10	Insulation support	17	Semi-rigid insulation and firestopping
3	Rigid insulation	11	CMU	18	Supports
4	Continuous air barrier	12	CMU reinforcement	19	Interior gypsum board
5	Flexible continuous flashing adhered over metal flashing	13	Concrete slab	20	Brick tie embedded in mortar joint
6	Weep holes	14	Steel weld plate		
7	Continuous steel shelf angle	15	Steel channel clips		
8	Adhesive				

Figure 2-24 Brick cavity wall with CMU backing.

There are several types of *concrete facades*: precast concrete panels used as cladding material with secondary structure (Figure 2-25), cast-in-place concrete walls, and insulated tilt-up concrete panels.

Other types of concrete facades include insulating concrete forms (ICFs) and insulating concrete block (ICB). ICFs consist of extruded or expanded polystyrene panels acting as the formwork for cast-in-place concrete; a finish coating covers the polystyrene panels inside and outside. These types of facades are typically used for residential or small-scale commercial buildings. ICBs are concrete masonry units that have expanded polystyrene sandwiched between the two faces of each block.

42 CHARACTERISTICS OF SUSTAINABLE FACADES

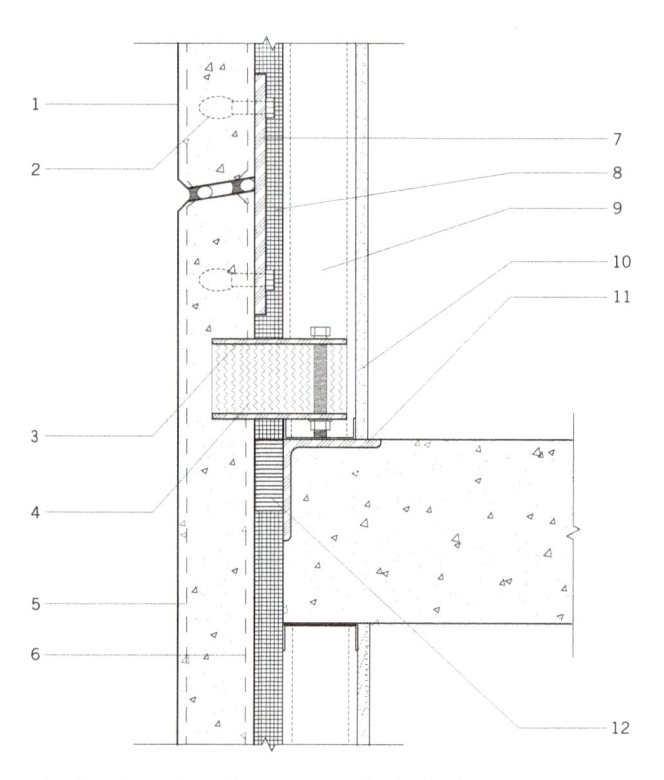

1 Precast concrete panel
2 Precast concrete panel anchor
3 Shear connection cast into panel
4 Spray insulation fill
5 Line of weather seal at panel joints
6 Line of air seal at panel joints
7 Anchor plate
8 Rigid insulation
9 Stud cavity
10 Interior gypsum board
11 Cast-in-place anchor
12 Firesafing and smoke seal

Figure 2-25 Precast concrete panel with steel stud framing.

CASE STUDY 2.3 KENDAL ACADEMIC SUPPORT CENTER, MIAMI DADE COLLEGE

The Kendall Academic Support Center (Figures 2-26 to 2-30) is located on the Miami Dade College campus. The building's program includes classrooms, student support, and administrative spaces. An atrium connects the administrative areas to the learning spaces.

The south facade is composed of thin-shell precast concrete panels. The sizes and positions of windows were determined by daylighting studies (Figure 2-27).

FACADE TYPES AND MATERIALS   43

Figure 2-26 Rendering of the south facade.

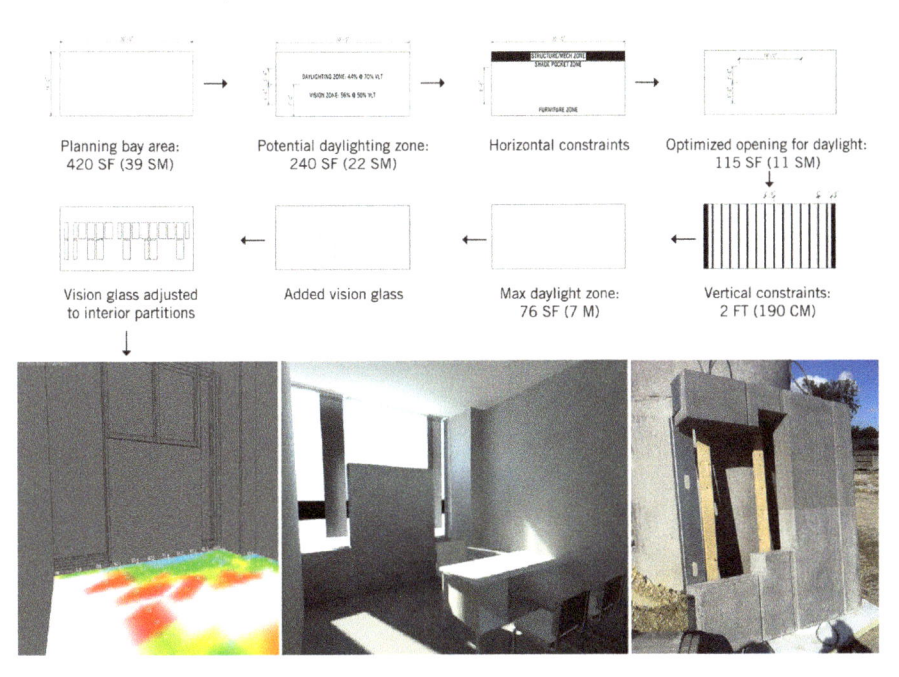

Planning bay area: 420 SF (39 SM) → Potential daylighting zone: 240 SF (22 SM) → Horizontal constraints → Optimized opening for daylight: 115 SF (11 SM)

Vision glass adjusted to interior partitions ← Added vision glass ← Max daylight zone: 76 SF (7 M) ← Vertical constraints: 2 FT (190 CM)

Figure 2-27 Daylight study used to determine the window pattern in the precast concrete panels.

44 CHARACTERISTICS OF SUSTAINABLE FACADES

Thin-shell precast concrete panels consist of roughly 2 in. (50 mm) of concrete cast onto light-gauge, cold-formed steel framing. The concrete provides durability and the desired finished look of the facade. The steel studs provide the structural support for the thin-shell precast concrete panels. The resulting panels are low in weight compared to standard precast panels, thus reducing structural frame, transportation, and installation costs. Two finishes are used for the panels: smooth finish to match the structural columns and board-formed texture on the ground-level facade.

To improve the thermal performance of the facade, foam insulation is embedded within the thin-shell concrete precast panels.

Figure 2-28 Section perspective through the south facade.

FACADE TYPES AND MATERIALS   45

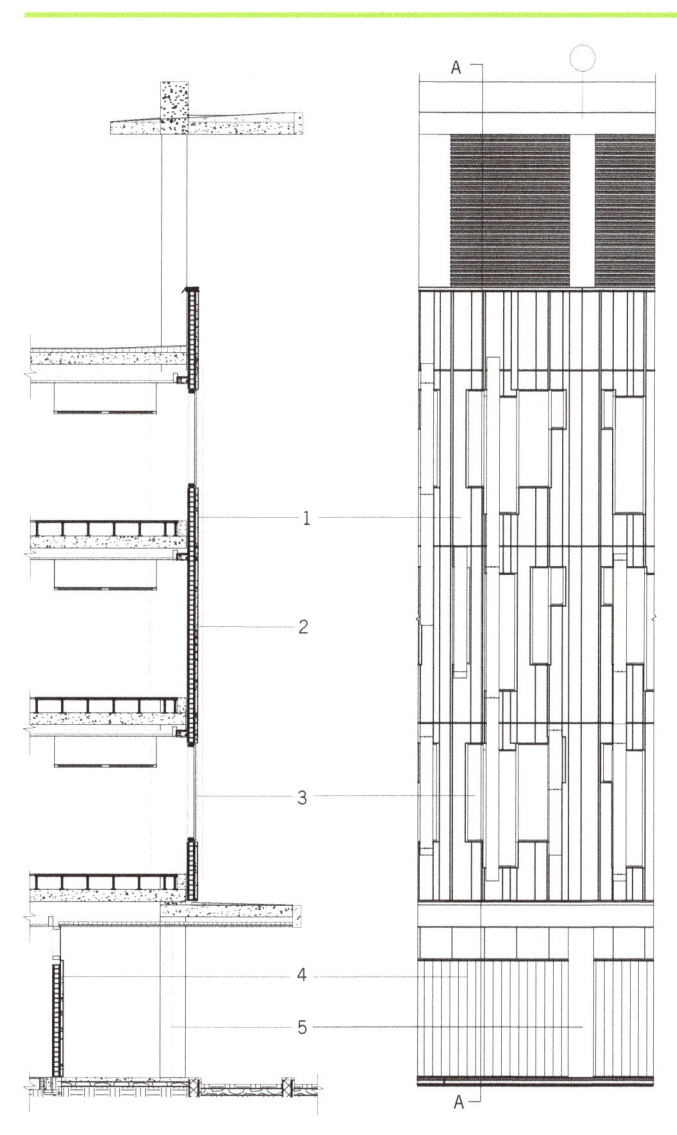

1 Thin-shell precast concrete panel (smooth finish)
2 Foam insulation
3 Glazing
4 Thin-shell precast concrete panel (board-formed finish)
5 Concrete column

Figure 2-29 Exterior wall section and partial elevation of the south facade.

46 CHARACTERISTICS OF SUSTAINABLE FACADES

Figure 2-30 Installation of the precast concrete panels.

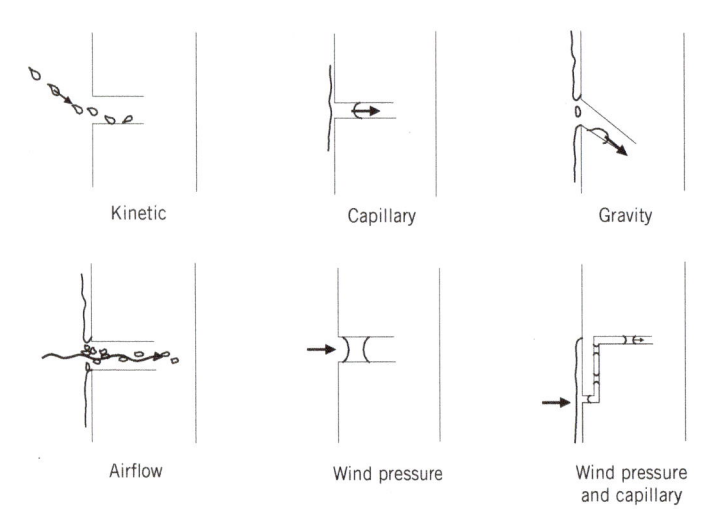

Figure 2-31 Rain penetration forces.

Rainscreen facades reverse the traditional approach for protecting the building's interior from air and moisture infiltration. Most non-rainscreen facade systems rely on two lines of defense. The first line of defense—the outermost surface of the facade—is the primary barrier against air and moisture, designed to stop all of the air and water. The second line of defense is intended to stop small amounts of air and water vapor that may penetrate the first line.

The rainscreen concept utilizes an outermost facade layer differently, as it is not designed to be impervious to air and water. Instead, it acts as a barrier against rain, but relies on a weatherproof inner layer to block air and moisture penetration. Figure 2-31 shows forces that produce rain penetration. Water entry resulting from an air-pressure difference can be controlled by the introduction of an air space in the wall. Between the outer and inner layers is a ventilated air cavity that drains water to the outside. The cavity (including the inner surface of the cavity) acts as the primary line of defense against air and water penetration.

Cladding material is selected primarily for its appearance. The cladding is usually panelized and can be made of a variety of materials, such as stone, precast concrete, terra cotta, cement composite, crystallized glass, or metal. Because the inner layer is not visible in the completed construction, it is not designed for its visual qualities. Instead, it must be designed to withstand wind and seismic loads, to thermally and acoustically insulate the building, and to prevent air or water from entering the building. Figure 2-32 shows a back-ventilated rainscreen facade with metal cladding.

1	Metal cladding	6	Flashing
2	Vertical channel	7	Exterior gypsum sheathing
3	Air cavity	8	Steel stud cavity
4	Rigid insulation	9	Interior gypsum board
5	Waterproofing membrane	10	Steel channel

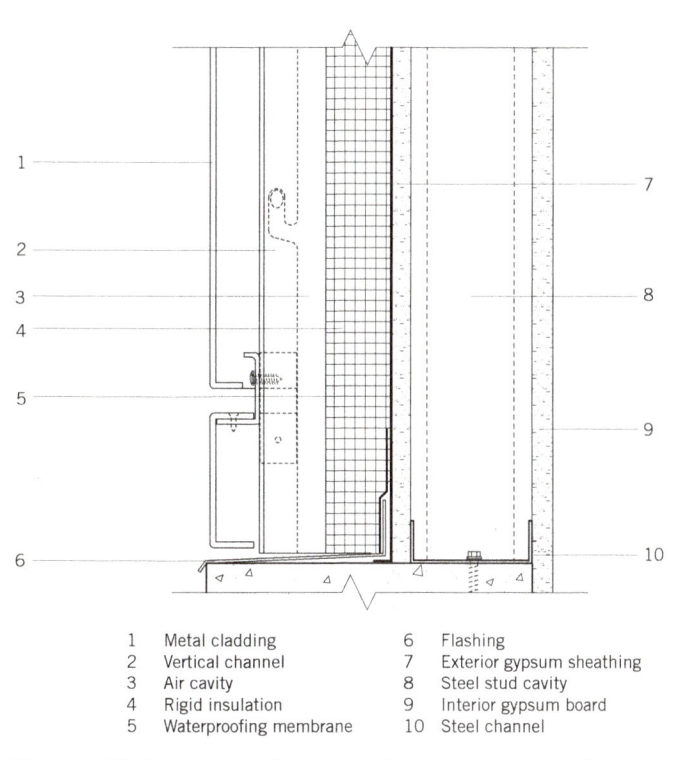

Figure 2-32 Back-ventilated rainscreen facade with metal cladding.

A variation of the rainscreen concept is the *pressure-equalized rainscreen (PER)*. In a PER, the air pressure within the inner air cavity is made equal, or close to equal, to the air pressure at the exterior face of the facade, as seen in Figure 2-33. This prevents air and water from being pulled into the cavity. To achieve pressure equalization, openings acting as vents must be designed into the outer facade surface. The larger the openings, the more equal the inner and outer pressures will be. If the PER is designed well, the combination of equalized pressures and gravity will force rainwater to drain to the exterior. Figure 2-34 shows components of a pressure-equalized rainscreen facade with metal cladding and steel framing.

48 CHARACTERISTICS OF SUSTAINABLE FACADES

1 Plane of air barrier system
2 Air cavity
3 Compartment separator
4 Cladding

Pe Exterior pressure
Pc Compartment pressure
Pi Interior pressure

$Pe \sim Pc > Pi$

Assembly designed to address pressure equalization

$Pe > Pc > Pi$

Assembly not designed to address pressure equalization

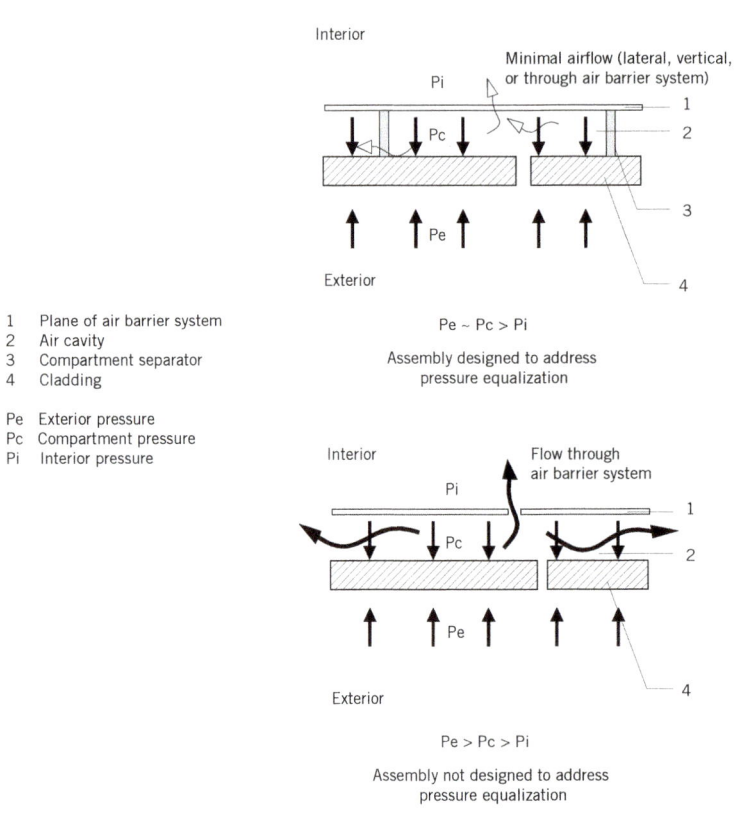

Figure 2-33 Pressure equalization concept diagram.

Glazed Building Facades

Curtain walls are lightweight facade systems, usually framed with aluminum extrusions attached to the building's primary structure. Curtain walls do not carry structural loads, other than wind loads and their own dead load. Figures 2-35 and 2-36 show the three major components of curtain walls: mullions, vision glass, and spandrel areas. The methods of fabrication and installation of curtain walls classify them as either stick or unitized systems.

Figure 2-34 Pressure-equalized rainscreen with metal cladding and steel framing.

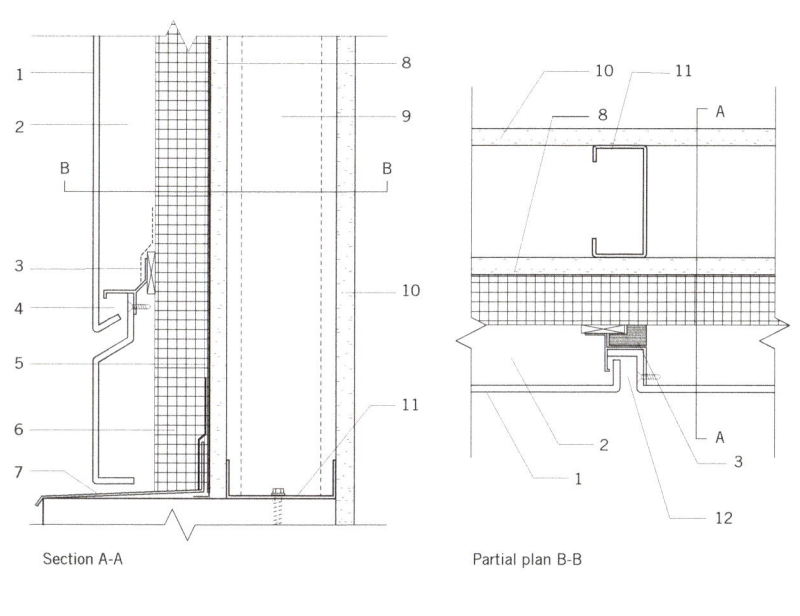

1 Metal cladding
2 Air cavity
3 Horizontal air block for compartmentalization
4 Path for pressure equalization and drainage
5 Waterproofing membrane
6 Insulation
7 Flashing
8 Exterior sheathing
9 Steel stud cavity
10 Interior gypsum board
11 Steel stud
12 Vertical drainage channel

Stick systems consist of components (mullions, glass, and spandrel panels) that are installed on the building structure piece by piece to form the building skin, as shown in Figure 2-37. Stick-system curtain walls can be further differentiated by the method of glazing. Interior-glazed systems allow vision glass to be installed into the curtain wall openings from the interior of the building. Exterior-glazed systems, in contrast, can be glazed only from the exterior. Exterior glazing is typically used for low-rise construction with easy access to the building's exterior.

Unitized systems are assembled and glazed as modular units in a factory. The modular units are typically one vision pane wide and one or two stories high. Figure 2-38 shows typical components of a unitized system. Installation of unitized systems is usually quicker than that of stick systems, requiring less field labor, because the components are preassembled. Because the assembly of the system occurs primarily in controlled factory conditions, the quality control and performance of unitized systems are better than with stick systems.

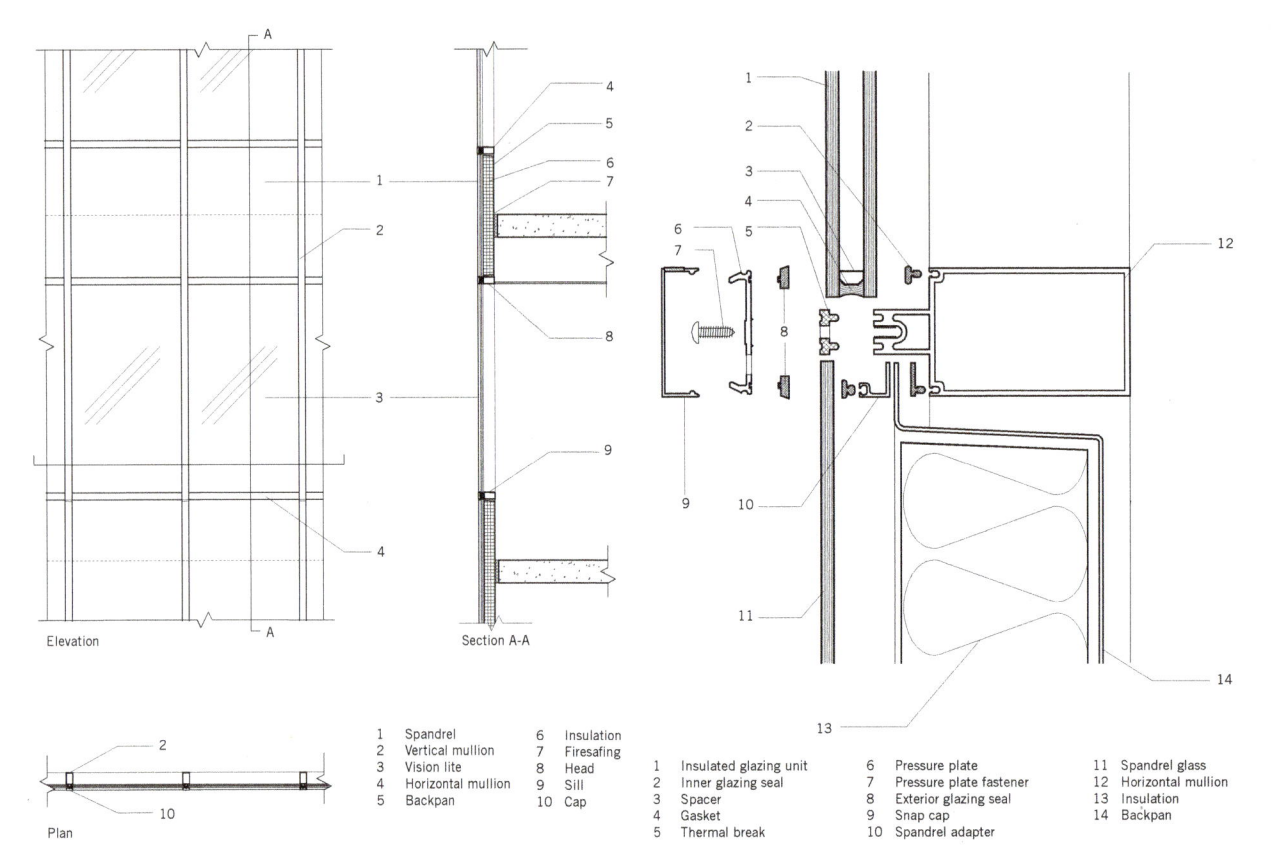

Figure 2-35 Basic components of a curtain wall.

1	Spandrel	6	Insulation
2	Vertical mullion	7	Firesafing
3	Vision lite	8	Head
4	Horizontal mullion	9	Sill
5	Backpan	10	Cap

Figure 2-36 Materials and components of a curtain wall.

1	Insulated glazing unit	6	Pressure plate	11	Spandrel glass
2	Inner glazing seal	7	Pressure plate fastener	12	Horizontal mullion
3	Spacer	8	Exterior glazing seal	13	Insulation
4	Gasket	9	Snap cap	14	Backpan
5	Thermal break	10	Spandrel adapter		

Thermal performance of curtain wall assemblies depends on the design and interaction of individual components: mullions, glazing units, spandrel units, anchor/attachment components, and the perimeter closures. Because aluminum has very high thermal conductivity, aluminum mullions are typically prone to transfer heat or cold through the assembly. To enhance the thermal performance of aluminum mullions, thermal breaks can be incorporated into their design. *Thermal breaks* consist of low-conductivity materials, such as urethane, neoprene rubber, or polyester-reinforced nylon, which separate the mullion's outer and inner metal parts, including the fasteners. With thermally broken mullions, exterior metal surfaces are not in contact with the inside metal. A less costly, and less effective, variation is "thermally improved" mullions, which also have thermal-break material separating exterior and interior extrusion parts, but have fasteners or other elements that span the thermal break. Because of the metal-to-metal contact at the fasteners, cold or hot temperatures can move through thermally improved mullions.

FACADE TYPES AND MATERIALS   51

Stick-system curtain wall components

1 Horizontal mullion
2 Vertical mullion
3 Corner block
4 Shear mullion
5 Expansion joint
6 Snap cap
7 Pressure plate
8 Thermal break
9 Anchor
10 Spandrel
11 Vision glazing

Unitized system curtain wall components

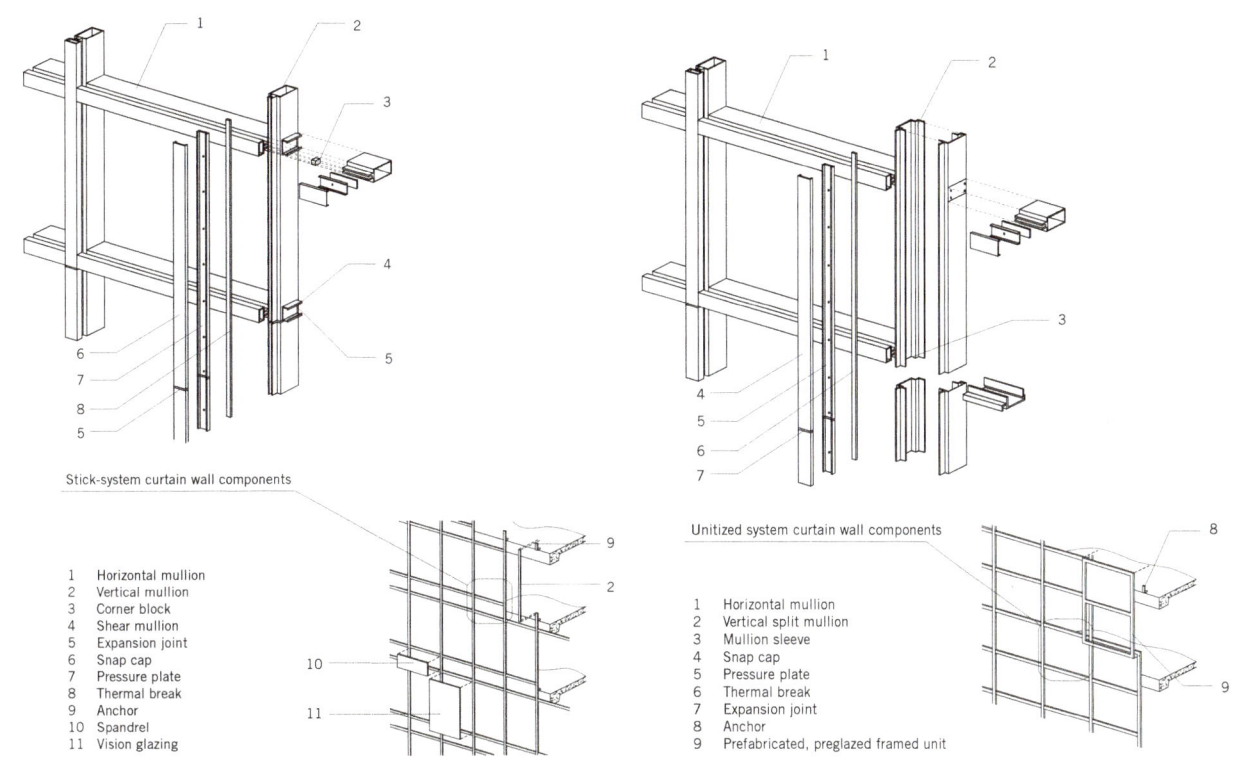

1 Horizontal mullion
2 Vertical split mullion
3 Mullion sleeve
4 Snap cap
5 Pressure plate
6 Thermal break
7 Expansion joint
8 Anchor
9 Prefabricated, preglazed framed unit

Figure 2-37 Components of a stick curtain wall system.

Figure 2-38 Components of a unitized curtain wall.

The type of *glazing* can significantly affect a curtain wall's performance. Although clear vision glass may be desirable for daylighting, views, and building appearance, it performs poorly with regard to insulation or shading. However, there are a number of ways to improve the performance of the vision-glass areas of a wall system. First, the glass itself can be integrally tinted. Heavily tinted glass can block a substantial amount of direct sunlight. Unfortunately, tinted glass also blocks daylight and may restrict views. A single lite of glass—any kind of glass—provides almost no insulation. Therefore, tinted glass is usually the lowest-cost but least effective way of improving glass performance.

Insulating glass units using two lites of glass separated by a desiccated air space can significantly improve glazing performance. Because air is a poor conductor of heat, double-glazed insulating units perform significantly better than a single lite of glass. Further performance improvements can be achieved by adding another lite of glass (and another air space). Triple-glazed units perform better than double-glazed ones; however, the incremental improvement is less than when going from single glazing to double-glazed units.

A cost-to-benefit analysis is needed to determine if the additional cost for triple glazing is justified by the increased performance. Other materials, such as argon gas or transparent silica aerogel, can be used in lieu of the desiccated air between the lites of glass to improve the insulating qualities of the glazing unit.

Coatings can be applied to glass to improve its thermal and light-transmission performance. Low-emissivity (low-e) coatings applied to the glass surface can block and reflect some daylight (thus making the glass look darker and more reflective). Through improvements in the formulation of the coating materials and their application processes, manufacturers are continually introducing better-performing, yet clearer, low-e glass. Because low-e coatings are susceptible to damage and require protection, they can only be applied to the inner surfaces of an insulating glass unit. Glass surfaces of double-glazed insulating units are usually designated by a number, with the #1 surface on the outside of the unit and the #4 surface on the building interior. Therefore, low-e coatings are applied to either the #2 or #3 surfaces.

Another type of commonly used coating is ceramic frit. Ceramic frits can have varying levels of opacity, and can be applied in patterns with varying levels of glass coverage. Glass that is coated with a 50% pattern of opaque frit will block twice the direct sunlight as unfritted glass. Because frit is baked onto the surface of glass, it is durable and does not require the same level of protection as low-e coatings. Frit can be applied to any glass surface; however, designers need to remember that all glass, even the most transparent, has some amount of inherent tinting. If a frit is applied to the #4 surface, then light that is reflected off the frit must pass through four lites of glass.

The three most common glazing methods are exterior batten, applied stops, and structural silicone (Figure 2-39). With the exterior batten method, a pressure plate holds the glass lite in place. The pressure plate is fixed to the mullion with screws that apply pressure to gaskets or glazing tapes between the glass and the mullion. The exterior gasket prevents most water from entering the system, while the interior seal provides the real air and water barrier. The applied stops method consists of an exterior or interior removable glazing stop that holds the glass lite in place. An interior applied stop method allows glass replacement from the interior of the building, which could be beneficial for building maintenance. The structural silicone method uses specially formulated silicone sealant to hold the glass lite in place. Structural silicone can be either two-sided or four-sided. In the first case, either the vertical or the horizontal edges of the glass are adhered to mullions with structural silicone sealant, and the other two edges are mechanically fixed, usually with pressure plates. With four-sided structural silicone, all four edges of the glass are adhered to mullions with structural silicone sealant.

Opaque areas of a curtain wall include spandrels. A *spandrel* is a horizontal band of opaque curtain wall between continuous strips of vision glass. Spandrels are generally the best-insulated parts of a curtain wall, so increasing their area can significantly improve the overall performance of the facade. There are four types of spandrels: solid materials, back-coated glass, glazed shadow boxes, and louvers.

A variety of solid materials can be used for spandrel areas, the most common being metal panels. The panels can have integral insulation, or insulation can be a separate layer behind them.

Exterior batten glazing method

1. Exterior cap
2. Pressure plate
3. Glazing cavity
4. Exterior gasket
5. Glazing unit
6. Interior gasket
7. Frame
8. Pressure plate screw
9. Thermal break
10. Frame cavity

Applied stop glazing method

1. Exterior fixed stop
2. Glazing tape
3. Glazing unit
4. Rubber gasket
5. Interior removable stop
6. Thermal break
7. Gasket air seal

Structural silicone glazing method

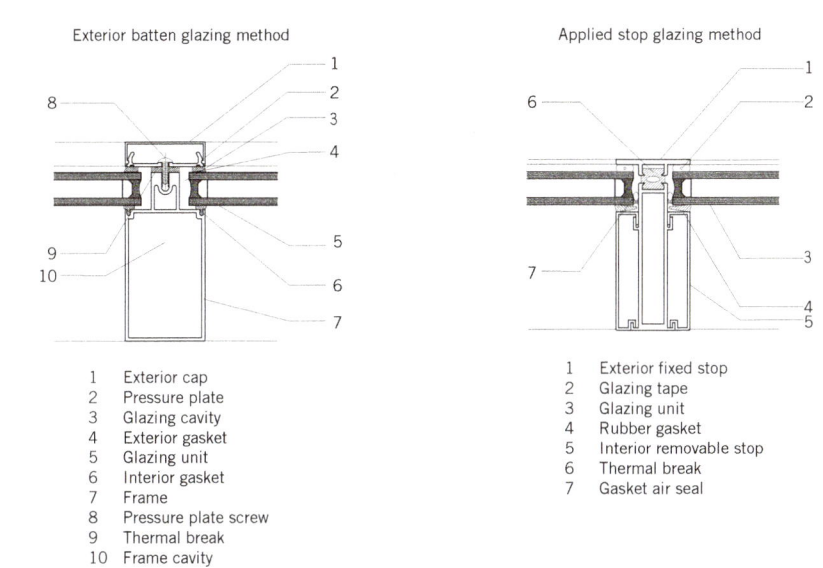

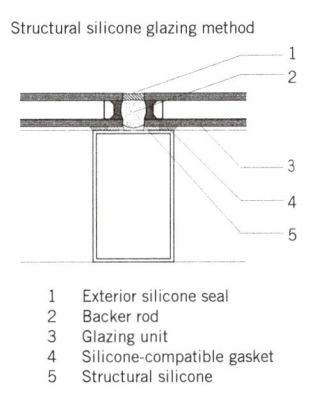

1. Exterior silicone seal
2. Backer rod
3. Glazing unit
4. Silicone-compatible gasket
5. Structural silicone

Figure 2-39 Different glazing methods and mullion types.

Back-coated glass can be either a single lite of glass or an insulating unit. In either case, the inner surface of the glass is completely coated with ceramic frit to make an opaque spandrel. Whether the glass spandrel is single- or double-glazed, an additional insulation layer is recommended to improve its thermal performance.

Shadow boxes are created by placing painted metal boxes behind vision glass. The purpose of shadow boxes is to give spandrels the appearance of occupied space. A deep shadow box, with a carefully selected paint color, can come close to creating this illusion. A layer of insulation should be added behind the shadow box.

Louvers in spandrels can be functional, to allow air to enter or be exhausted from the building; or decorative, with some form of solid material behind them. Functional spandrel louvers are usually used adjacent to mechanical rooms, so they are tied to fully insulated internal building systems. Decorative louvers require insulation behind them.

Storefront facades are primarily used at the ground or second floor of a building. Like curtain walls, they consist of aluminum frames and glass components, and do not carry significant structural loads. However, the assembly and frame components are different than in curtain wall applications and the performance criteria are less stringent. For example, frames may have smaller dimensions, or gaskets may be made of different material (vinyl for storefront applications and silicone for curtain walls).

MATERIALS AND PROPERTIES

Properties of Facade Materials and Components

Material selection is an important factor in designing sustainable facades. All materials have specific physical properties, such as density, thermal conductivity, thermal resistance, and permeability. Insulating materials are selected for their thermal resistance, and vapor barriers for their permeability. Table 2-1 lists the thermal resistance (R-values) of typical building materials used for opaque building envelopes. The nominal thermal resistance of an opaque building facade can be calculated by adding the R-values of each material layer, including air spaces.

Table 2-1 Thermal resistance properties of typical components for opaque building envelopes.

Material	R-value (h-ft^2-°F/Btu)	R-value (m^2-°K/W)
Brick	0.10–0.40 per inch	0.68–2.77
CMU, 8 in. (200 mm)	1.11–2.0	0.20–0.35
CMU, 12 in. (300 mm)	1.23–3.7	0.22–0.65
Concrete (sand and gravel aggregate)	0.05–0.14 per inch	0.35–0.99
Concrete (limestone aggregate)	0.09–0.18 per inch	0.62–1.26
Concrete with lightweight aggregate	0.11–0.78 per inch	0.76–5.40
Stone (quartzitic and sandstone)	0.01–0.08 per inch	0.10–0.53
Stone (limestone, marble, granite)	0.03–0.13 per inch	0.23–0.90
Mineral batt insulation, 6 in. (150 mm)	22	3.67

Material	R-value (h-ft²-°F/Btu)	R-value (m²-°K/W)
Expanded polystyrene insulation	5 per inch	34.7
Spray-applied foam	6.25 per inch	43.3
Gypsum board, 0.500 in. (12.7 mm)	0.45	0.08
Gypsum board, 0.625 in. (15.9 mm)	0.56	0.10

Source: © 2005, ASHRAE (www.ashrae.org). Used with permission from *ASHRAE Handbook of Fundamentals* Chapter 25 (2005).

Table 2-2 calculates the overall R-values for five brick veneer wall assemblies. For each assembly, the overall R-value is calculated by adding the thermal resistance of individual material layers (determined by multiplying its R-values per unit thickness by the material's overall thickness). Table 2-2 compares various combinations of back-up wall systems: CMU wall, and cold-formed steel framing spaced 16 inches (406 mm) and 24 inches (610 mm) apart. Insulation materials for the five assemblies are rigid mineral batt insulation, polystyrene spray foam insulation, or mineral wool insulation. The five wall assemblies have the following components:

- Assembly 1: Brick veneer with rigid batt insulation and CMU back-up wall
- Assembly 2: Brick veneer with polystyrene insulation and CMU back-up wall
- Assembly 3: Brick veneer with cold-formed steel framing (16 in. or 406 mm o.c.) and rigid mineral wool insulation in the stud cavity
- Assembly 4: Brick veneer with cold-formed steel framing (16 in. or 406 mm o.c.) and spray foam insulation in the stud cavity
- Assembly 5: Brick veneer with cold-formed steel framing (24 in. or 610 mm o.c.) and rigid mineral wool insulation in the stud cavity

Table 2-2 Calculated R-values for five brick veneer exterior wall assemblies.

Wall assembly materials	R-value (h-ft²-°F/Btu)	R-value (m²-°K/W)
Assembly 1: Brick veneer with rigid batt insulation and CMU back-up wall		
4 in. (100 mm) brick veneer	4 in. x 0.20/in. = 0.80	0.14
2 in. (50 mm) air space	2 in. x 0.56/in. = 1.13	0.20
3 in. (75 mm) of rigid mineral batt insulation	11.00	1.95
Air and vapor barrier	0	0
8 in. (200 mm) CMU	1.11	0.20
0.625 in. (15.9 mm) interior gypsum board	0.56	0.10
Overall R-value	**14.60**	**2.59**

Wall assembly materials	R-value (h-ft²-°F/Btu)	R-value (m²-°K/W)
Assembly 2: Brick veneer with polystyrene insulation and CMU back-up wall		
4 in. (100 mm) brick veneer	4 in. x 0.20/in. = 0.80	0.14
2 in. (50 mm) air space	2 in. x 0.56/in. = 1.13	0.20
3 in. (75 mm) of expanded polystyrene	3 in. x 5/in. = 15.00	2.66
Air and vapor barrier	0	0
8 in. (200 mm) CMU	1.11	0.20
0.625 in. (15.9 mm) interior gypsum board	0.56	0.10
Overall R-value	18.60	3.30
Assembly 3: Brick veneer with insulated steel stud framing (16 in. or 406 mm o.c.) and rigid mineral wool insulation		
4 in. (100 mm) brick veneer	4 in. x 0.20/in. = 0.80	0.14
2 in. (50 mm) air space	2 in. x 0.56/in. = 1.13	0.20
3 in. (75 mm) of rigid mineral wool insulation	3 in. x 4/in. = 12.00	2.12
Air and vapor barrier	0	0
0.5 in. (12.7 mm) exterior gypsum sheathing	0.45	0.08
6 in. (150 mm) stud cavity with batt insulation	7.10*	1.26
0.625 in. (15.9 mm) interior gypsum board	0.56	0.10
Overall R-value	22.04	3.90
Assembly 4: Brick veneer with insulated steel stud framing (16 in. or 406 mm o.c.) and spray foam insulation		
4 in. (100 mm) brick veneer	4 in. x 0.20/in. = 0.80	0.14
2 in. (50 mm) air space	2 in. x 0.56/in. = 1.13	0.20
0.5 in. (12.7 mm) exterior gypsum sheathing	0.45	0.08
3 in. (75 mm) of spray foam insulation in 6 in. (150 mm) steel stud cavity	19.80*	3.50
0.625 in. (15.9 mm) interior gypsum board	0.56	0.10
Overall R-value	22.29	3.94
Assembly 5: Brick veneer with insulated steel stud framing (24 in. or 610 mm o.c.) and rigid mineral wool insulation		
4 in. (100 mm) brick veneer	4 in. x 0.20/in. = 0.80	0.14
2 in. (50 mm) air space	2 in. x 0.56/in. = 1.13	0.20
3 in. (75 mm) of rigid mineral wool insulation	3 in. x 4/in. = 12.00	2.12
Air and vapor barrier	0	0
0.5 in. (12.7 mm) exterior gypsum sheathing	0.45	0.08
6 in. (150 mm) stud cavity with batt insulation	8.60*	1.52
0.625 in. (15.9 mm) interior gypsum board	0.56	0.10
Overall R-value	23.54	4.16

*Note: Values for insulated stud cavities are from ASHRAE Standard 90.1-2007 (Insulation correction factor for determining thermal resistance of wall assemblies containing metal framing).

MATERIALS AND PROPERTIES 57

The simple additive method does not work well for facades supported by cold-formed steel framing. In these facades, the low thermal resistance of the highly conductive steel members will be quite different from that of the insulation between the members. The zone method has been developed for calculating the R-values in these cases. For example, a brick veneer wall that uses steel framing can be divided into two zones: a zone containing steel framing, and a zone between the framing. The thermal resistance of each zone can be calculated using the additive approach. By calculating the R-values of each zone and factoring in the relative areas of each zone, the overall thermal resistance of the facade can be determined.

Thermal bridging within a wall occurs where a highly conductive material, such as a metal veneer support, penetrates the facade's insulation layer. This can affect the thermal performance of the wall. Thermal bridging can occur in all types of facades. Thermally unbroken aluminum mullions in curtain walls are highly conductive and transfer heat from the exterior to the interior, reducing the overall thermal performance of the facade. When an opaque facade has a significant amount of thermal bridging, the effective R-value of the wall assembly will be less than its nominal R-value. Figure 2-40 shows the differences between nominal and effective R-values of brick veneer facades with three types of supports: vertical Z-girts, horizontal Z-girts, and wire ties. For all three conditions, there is a layer of insulation within the air space, and no insulation between the cold-formed steel framing. The thermal bridging occurs where the Z-girts or wire ties penetrate the insulation layer. The difference between nominal and effective overall thermal resistance can be significant (Lawton et al., 2010). For example, for a brick veneer wall with vertical Z-girts and a nominal R-value of 33 h-ft^2-°F/Btu (5.8 m^2-°K/W), thermal bridging results in an effective R-value of 10.6 h-ft^2-°F/Btu (1.9 m^2-°K/W).

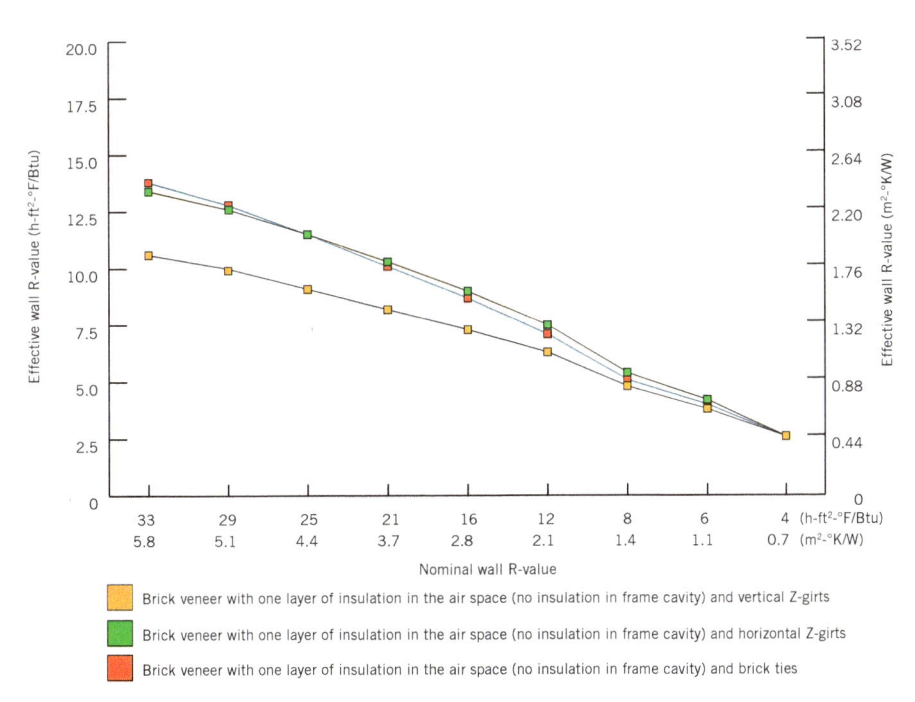

Figure 2-40 Effects of thermal bridging on thermal resistance of brick veneer walls with one layer of insulation (Adapted from Lawton et al., 2010).

Brick veneer walls with either wire ties or horizontal Z-girts perform better than walls with vertical Z-girts, although there is still a significant reduction of effective R-value.

Figure 2-41 shows the nominal and effective thermal resistance of brick veneer walls with two layers of insulation—one layer of rigid insulation within the air space and one layer of batt insulation between the steel framing.

■ Brick veneer with two layers of insulation (in the air space and frame cavity) and vertical Z-girts
■ Brick veneer with two layers of insulation (in the air space and frame cavity) and horizontal Z-girts
■ Brick veneer with two layers of insulation (in the air space and frame cavity) and brick ties

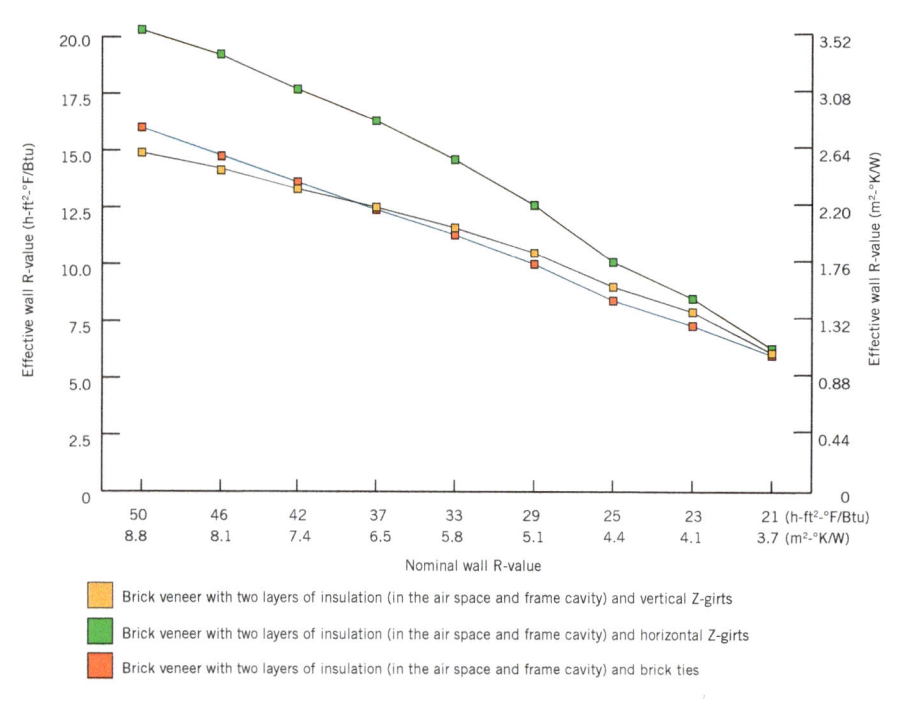

Figure 2-41 Effects of thermal bridging on thermal resistance of brick veneer walls with two layers of insulation (Adapted from Lawton et al., 2010).

For glazed facades, thermal and optical properties of the glazing units must be considered. These properties include the solar heat gain coefficient (SHGC), the shading coefficient (SC), the visual transmittance (Tv), and the light-to-solar-gain (LSG) ratio.

The solar heat gain coefficient (SHGC) quantifies the amount of solar radiation transmitted through the glass. It is expressed as a number between 0 and 1, with 0 meaning that no radiation is admitted and 1 meaning that no radiation is blocked. Low-e coatings significantly reduce admitted solar radiation and can reduce SHGC for all types of insulated glazing units.

Thermal bridging negatively affects the overall thermal resistance in all cases. For example, a brick veneer wall with two layers of insulation and a nominal R-value of 50 h-ft^2-°F/Btu (8.8 m^2-°K/W) has an effective R-value of 14.9 h-ft^2-°F/Btu (2.6 m^2-°K/W) with the vertical Z-girts. The wall assembly with horizontal Z-girts performs better than the other two assemblies, but still shows a significant reduction of R-values.

R-values are most appropriate for determining the thermal performance of wall systems that consist of multiple layers of materials, each with its own R-value. For glazed facades, the coefficient of heat transfer, or U-value, is used to represent thermal properties. Because U-values are the inverse of R-values, they decrease as the thermal performance of a glazed wall area increases. The U-value of a glazed assembly is calculated using an area-weighted approach that considers three separate U-values: at the frames, at the center of the glass, and at the perimeter of the glass, 2.5 inches (64 mm) from the frame. U-values are typically lowest at the center of the glass and highest at highly conductive metal frames. The methods for determining the overall U-value are defined by the National Fenestration Rating Council (NFRC, 2010).

Lower overall U-values can be achieved by selecting high-performance glass or by designing framing systems that limit heat transfer. Insulating values of glazing units are improved by increasing the number of glass lites and by filling the spaces between the lites with inert gases, such as argon or krypton, instead of air. Thermally broken aluminum frames, or structural glazing that puts a layer of silicone between the outside glass and the metal framing, reduce thermal transmittance through glazed facades. Table 2-3 presents typical U-values for different types of curtain walls and different types of glazing. Center of glass, edge of glass, and overall U-values are shown for insulated glazing units with different types of gases (air, argon, and krypton), different thicknesses of the insulating space, and different types of framing systems.

Table 2-3 Heat transfer coefficients for different types of curtain walls.

Glazing type	Center of glass	Edge of glass	Aluminum without thermal break	Aluminum with thermal break	Structural glazing
Double glazing					
1/4 in. (6 mm) air space	0.55 (3.12)	0.64 (3.63)	0.79 (4.47)	0.68 (3.84)	0.63 (3.59)
1/2 in. (12 mm) air space	0.48 (2.73)	0.59 (3.36)	0.73 (4.14)	0.62 (3.51)	0.57 (3.26)
1/4 in. (6 mm) argon fill	0.51 (2.90)	0.61 (3.48)	0.75 (4.28)	0.64 (3.65)	0.60 (3.26)
1/2 in. (12 mm) argon fill	0.45 (2.56)	0.57 (3.24)	0.70 (3.99)	0.59 (3.36)	0.55 (3.11)
Double low-e glazing (coating on glass surface 2 or 3)					
1/4 in. (6 mm) air space	0.45 (2.56)	0.57 (3.24)	0.70 (3.99)	0.59 (3.36)	0.55 (3.11)
1/2 in. (12 mm) air space	0.35 (1.99)	0.50 (2.83)	0.62 (3.50)	0.51 (2.87)	0.46 (2.63)
1/4 in. (6 mm) argon fill	0.38 (2.16)	0.52 (2.96)	0.64 (3.65)	0.53 (3.02)	0.49 (2.77)
1/2 in. (12 mm) argon fill	0.30 (1.70)	0.46 (2.62)	0.57 (3.26)	0.46 (2.63)	0.42 (2.38)

U-value for glass only (Btu/h-ft^2-°F) and (W/m^2-°K); Overall U-value for curtain walls based on frame type (Btu/h-ft^2-°F) and (W/m^2-°K)

Glazing type	U-value for glass only (Btu/h-ft²-°F) and (W/m²-°K)		Overall U-value for curtain walls based on frame type (Btu/h-ft²-°F) and (W/m²-°K)		
	Center of glass	Edge of glass	Aluminum without thermal break	Aluminum with thermal break	Structural glazing
Triple low-e glazing (coating on surface 2, 3, 4, or 5)					
1/4 in. (6 mm) air space	0.33 (1.87)	0.48 (2.75)	0.59 (3.34)	0.48 (2.73)	0.42 (2.41)
1/2 in. (12 mm) air space	0.25 (1.42)	0.42 (2.41)	0.52 (2.95)	0.41 (2.33)	0.35 (2.02)
1/4 in. (6 mm) argon fill	0.28 (1.59)	0.45 (2.54)	0.54 (3.09)	0.44 (2.48)	0.38 (2.16)
1/2 in. (12 mm) argon fill	0.22 (1.25)	0.40 (2.28)	0.49 (2.80)	0.38 (2.19)	0.33 (1.87)
Quadruple low-e glazing (coating on surface 2 or 3 and 4 or 5)					
1/4 in. (6 mm) air space	0.22 (1.25)	0.40 (2.28)	0.49 (2.80)	0.38 (2.19)	0.33 (1.87)
1/2 in. (12 mm) air space	0.15 (0.85)	0.35 (1.96)	0.43 (2.45)	0.32 (1.84)	0.27 (1.52)
1/4 in. (6 mm) argon fill	0.17 (0.97)	0.36 (2.05)	0.45 (2.55)	0.34 (1.94)	0.29 (1.62)
1/2 in. (12 mm) argon fill	0.12 (0.68)	0.32 (1.83)	0.41 (2.31)	0.30 (1.69)	0.24 (1.38)
1/4 in. (6 mm) krypton fill	0.12 (0.68)	0.32 (1.83)	0.41 (2.31)	0.30 (1.69)	0.24 (1.38)

Source: © 2005, ASHRAE (www.ashrae.org). Used with permission from *ASHRAE Handbook of Fundamentals* Chapter 31 (2005).

The shading coefficient (SC) is the ratio between the SHGC of a glazing system and that of a reference pane of clear glass. It measures only the direct solar radiation. It does not measure the radiant temperature effects that result when the sun's rays heat the glass.

Visual transmittance (Tv) is the amount of visible light energy that enters through the glass, expressed as a percent from 0% to 100%. The higher the Tv of a glazing unit, the more visible light is admitted into the interior spaces. A high Tv is not always suitable. A high visual transmittance usually means a higher SHGC, so the designer must find a balance between allowing light into the building while blocking solar radiation. Figure 2-42 shows relationships between these two properties for low-e coated glass produced by five glass manufacturers.

The light-to-solar-gain (LSG) ratio is the ratio between the amount of light transmitted by the glass and the amount of absorbed solar heat gain. The LSG ratio is calculated by dividing Tv by SHGC for a specific glass product. Facades located in colder climates benefit from lower LSG ratios, as some solar heat gain is beneficial for passive heating. Higher LSG ratios are appropriate for facades located in warmer climates, to keep solar heat gain as low as possible. In those climates, spectrally selective glazing, with LSG ratios of 1.25 or more, should be used for sustainable facades.

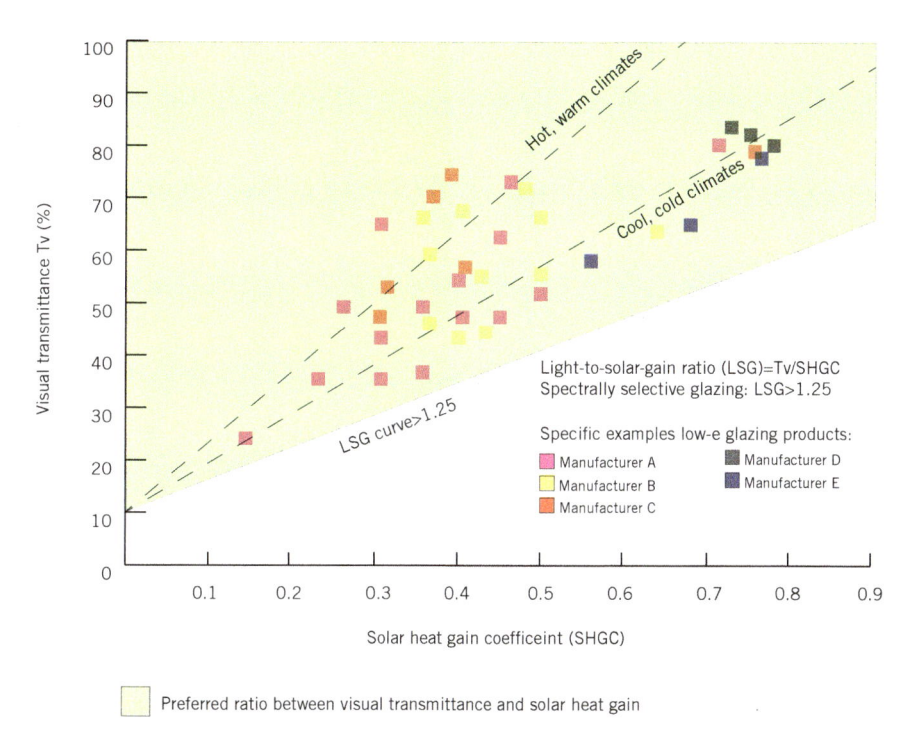

Figure 2-42 Light-to-solar-gain ratio as balance indicator between visual transmittance and solar heat gain for glass.

Shading elements integral with the curtain wall and ceramic frit coatings on glass can further reduce solar heat gain and energy consumption. Well-designed shading devices can be highly effective in reducing building peak heat gain and cooling requirements, while improving the quality of natural daylighting for interior spaces. They should be selected or designed based on the orientation of the facade. Vertical shading devices, such as vertical louvers or fins, are useful primarily for east and west exposures. Horizontal shading devices, such as overhangs, are most appropriate for south facades. For intermediate orientations, horizontal and vertical shading devices can be combined. Operable shading devices are more effective than static systems, as they can track position of the sun and respond appropriately; however, unlike fixed shading devices, they require ongoing maintenance to assure their effectiveness in solar control.

Though not as effective as shading devices, ceramic frit coatings can be a lower-cost way of reducing solar heat gain. Unlike shading devices, which keep direct sunlight from hitting the glass, frit reflects most of the direct sunlight that hits it but allows some solar energy to be absorbed into the glass and transferred to the building interior.

Figure 2-43 shows energy consumption for a southeast-oriented office with a curtain wall located in a mixed humid climate. This type of climate is problematic for designing energy-conserving facades. Direct sunlight during cold seasons can be beneficial in heating the building, but has to be blocked during warm seasons to prevent unwanted heat gain. The graph compares four curtain wall designs for a southeast-facing office space. Option 4—a combination of fritted glass, horizontal overhangs, mullion extensions used as vertical fins, and daylighting controls—would result in nearly 50% less energy consumption than Option 1, which has none of these features.

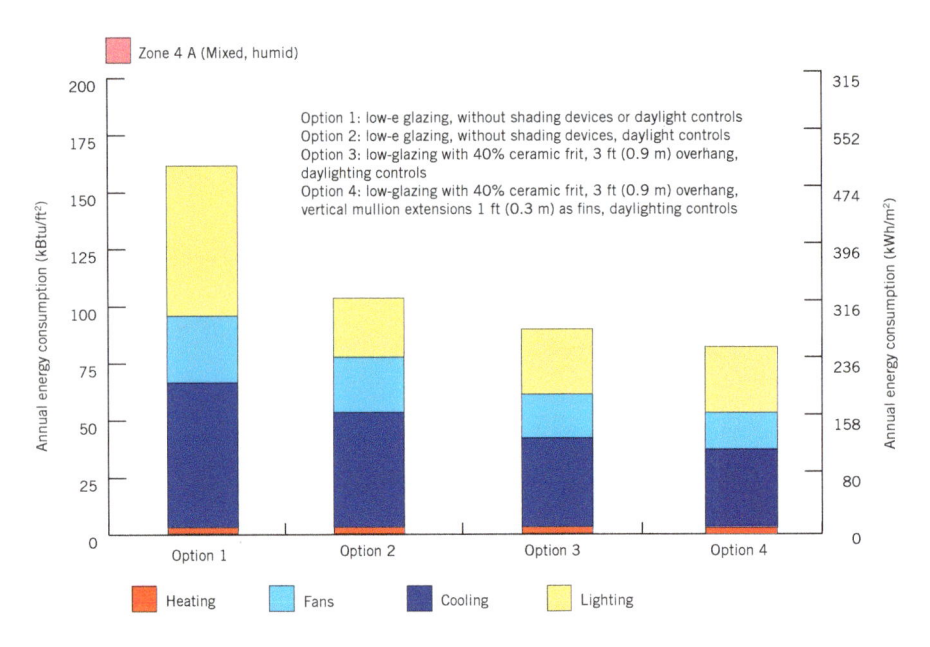

Figure 2-43 Effects of shading strategies (fritted glass, combination of appropriate shading devices) and daylight controls on energy consumption in mixed humid climate.

Embodied Energy of Materials

The preceding section discussed physical properties of facade materials that relate to thermal performance. Material selection also has an environmental impact. It is becoming increasingly important to select materials that have the least negative effect on the environment. The life-cycle assessment approach can be used to determine environmental impacts of material selection, where material contents, production methods, energy requirements, and waste are analyzed to identify the real cost of a material, reflecting the total amount of its environmental impact. The International Standards Organization specifies methods to be followed for the life-cycle analysis (ISO, 2006).

Another property designers should consider when choosing sustainable facade materials is embodied energy. This is the amount of energy required to extract, process, transport, install, and recycle or dispose of a material. The embodied energy is commonly measured in megajoules (MJ) per units of mass (lbs or kg) or volume (ft^3 or m^3) of the material.

Table 2-4 compares the embodied energy, by mass, for selected materials. There are numerous factors to consider when determining a material's embodied energy. For example, the table includes energy required for mining or harvesting the raw materials, shipping and transporting them to the manufacturing facility, processing the raw materials into the building products, and shipping the building products to the construction site. Disposal and recycling when the building is demolished must also be taken into account. The calculation is difficult and complex, and involves many project-specific variables: How close to the project site are the points of extraction and manufacture? What will be the means of shipping? How long is the building expected to last? These and other questions may not be answerable by the project team. Therefore, Table 2-4 shows values that can be used for comparative analysis of the general types of materials, but not for precise calculations for a specific project.

Table 2-4 Embodied energy of general facade materials.

Material	Embodied energy (MJ/lbs)	Embodied energy (MJ/kg)
Aluminum		
Cast virgin	497	226
Cast recycled (33%)	55	25
Extruded virgin	471	214
Extruded recycled (33%)	75	34
Rolled virgin	477	217
Rolled recycled (33%)	62	28
Brick	6.6	3.0
Cement		
Portland	2.09	0.95
Fly ash (6–20%)	1.96 to 1.67	0.89 to 0.76
Fly ash (21–35%)	1.65 to 1.36	0.75 to 0.62
Mortar	0.49	0.22
Concrete		
General	2.2	1.0
Fly ash (15%)	2.13	0.97
Fly ash (30%)	1.96	0.89
Precast	3.3	1.5

Material	Embodied energy (MJ/lbs)	Embodied energy (MJ/kg)
Glass		
Primary	33	15
Toughened	52	24
Insulation		
Fiberglass	62	28
Mineral wool	37	17
Polystyrene	195	87
Polyurethane	224	102
Fiber board	44	20
Glass fiber reinforced polymer	220	100
Polycarbonate	249	113
Paint	154	70
Steel		
Virgin	78	35
Recycled	21	9
Stainless	125	57
Stone		
Granite	24	11
Limestone	3.3	1.5
Marble	4.4	2.0
Sandstone	2.2	1.0
Slate	0.2 to 2.2	0.1 to 1.0
Wood		
General	22	10
Glue laminated	26	12
MDF	24	11
OSB	33	15
Plywood	33	15
PV panels		
Monocrystalline	10,450	4,750
Polycrystalline	8,954	4,070
Thin film	2,871	1,305

Source: Inventory of Carbon & Energy (ICE), V.2 (Hammond and Jones, 2011).

When comparing the embodied energy of facade systems, the measurements are based on area (ft^2 or m^2) instead of mass or volume. The embodied energy of individual components and materials of the facade must be considered. Table 2-5 compares the average embodied energy of general types of exterior walls.

Table 2-5 Comparison of embodied energy of different facade systems.

System and components	Embodied energy (MJ/ft^2)	Embodied energy (MJ/m^2)
CMU		
Brick cladding, continuous insulation and polyethylene membrane	247	23.0
Steel cladding, continuous insulation and polyethylene membrane	370	34.4
Precast concrete cladding, continuous insulation and polyethylene membrane	291	27.0
Cast-in-place concrete		
Brick cladding, continuous insulation and paint	113	10.5
Steel cladding, continuous insulation and paint	236	21.9
Stucco cladding, continuous insulation and paint	99	9.2
Steel framed (16 in. or 406 mm o.c.)		
Brick cladding, continuous insulation, cold-formed steel framing, cavity insulation and polyethylene membrane, gypsum board and paint	96	8.9
Steel cladding, continuous insulation, cold-formed steel framing, cavity insulation and polyethylene membrane, gypsum board and paint	219	20.4
Wood cladding, continuous insulation, cold-formed steel framing, cavity insulation and polyethylene membrane, gypsum board and paint	61	5.7
Precast concrete cladding, continuous insulation, cold-formed steel framing, cavity insulation and polyethylene membrane, gypsum board and paint	141	13.1
Steel framed (24 in. or 610 mm o.c.)		
Brick cladding, continuous insulation, cold-formed steel framing, cavity insulation and polyethylene membrane, gypsum board and paint	91	8.5
Steel cladding, continuous insulation, cold-formed steel framing, cavity insulation and polyethylene membrane, gypsum board and paint	213	19.8

System and components	Embodied energy (MJ/ft^2)	Embodied energy (MJ/m^2)
Wood cladding, continuous insulation, cold-formed steel framing, cavity insulation and polyethylene membrane, gypsum board and paint	55	5.1
Precast concrete cladding, continuous insulation, cold-formed steel framing, cavity insulation and polyethylene membrane, gypsum board and paint	135	12.5
Curtain wall		
Vision glazing and frames	148	13.8
Opaque glazing	159	14.8
Metal spandrel panel	138	12.8

Source: Athena Sustainable Materials Institute, EcoCalculator for Commercial Assemblies.

THERMAL BEHAVIOR AND MOISTURE RESISTANCE

Control of Heat Transfer, and Air and Moisture Movement

Heat transfer through facades follows a basic principle of physics: heat flows from higher to lower temperatures. This takes place through one or more of the following processes:

- Conduction (heat flows between two facade materials in contact with each other)
- Convection (heat is conveyed by air currents within the facade)
- Radiation (heat flows as electromagnetic energy through materials and air spaces within the facade)
- Air leakage (heat is conveyed by air passing through the facade)

The rate of heat transfer through the building skin depends on the difference between the interior and exterior temperatures and the capacity of the facade to control heat flow. Factors that influence heat flow within the facade include the overall thermal resistance, material properties, and air-leakage control. Design strategies for controlling heat flow include using a continuous thermal barrier (i.e., insulation layer), filling air gaps between material layers to prevent conduction, providing a continuous air barrier to prevent heat loss through air leakage, and avoiding thermal bridging. "Controlling" heat transfer does not always mean preventing it. In some cases, a sustainable design strategy may be to use heat transfer to help heat a building's interior.

Air leakage can affect a building's overall energy consumption, as it permits unwanted warm air to enter the building (increasing cooling loads) or warm inside air to escape to the colder outside (increasing heating loads). Exterior air can also carry moisture (as vapor) into the building envelope and the building itself, causing condensation and, potentially, mold and damage to building materials. Air leakage is never desirable, but it can never be completely prevented. Even the standard performance criteria for air leakage established by ASTM allow for a small amount of air to penetrate the wall (ASTM, 2005).

An *air barrier* is any element, or combination of elements, that reduces the movement of air through a building enclosure. Air barriers control airflow between unconditioned and conditioned spaces. Air barriers are intended to resist differences in air pressure between interior and exterior. They can be located anywhere in the building enclosure (the exterior surface, the interior surface, or somewhere in between). Air barriers must be continuous over the entire building enclosure, and be impermeable to airflow. Air barrier standards are established in ASTM E 2178, which requires that air leakage not exceed 0.004 cfm/ft^2 at 1.57 psf (0.02 L/s/m^2 at 75 Pa) (ASTM, 2003). Table 2-6 compares three types of air barrier from one manufacturer.

Table 2-6 Examples of specific air barrier products and their properties.

Type/Property	Elastomeric emulsion 1	Elastomeric emulsion 2	Microporous laminate
Air barrier	Yes	Yes	Yes
Vapor barrier	No	No	No
Air leakage (per ASTM E 2178)	0.0002 cfm/ft^2	0.0016 cfm/ft^2	0.002 cfm/ft^2
Vapor permeance (per ASTM E 96)	12.3 perms	11.6 perms	37 perms
Application method	Trowel, spray, brush	Trowel or spray	Self-adhesive

Source: Henry Air Barrier Systems. © 2012 Henry Company, LLC.

Similar to air leakage is *vapor infiltration*. *Vapor* is water in its gaseous state. It is a normal component of air, making up around 1% to 4% of the atmosphere in most habitable regions. The amount of vapor that air can "hold" depends on the air temperature, with warmer air being able to hold more vapor than colder air. Relative humidity measures the amount of vapor in the air as a percentage of the maximum amount of vapor that the air, at a certain temperature, can hold.

An important point about vapor is how it moves through an exterior wall. Vapor is carried in the air, but it moves from higher density to lower density air through a process called *diffusion*.

Why is understanding vapor important to facade design? Because vapor is carried by air—and we have already seen that air infiltration cannot be completely eliminated—then it follows that some vapor is inevitably entering the exterior wall. The problem occurs when the vapor-bearing air encounters a material that is colder than the air. When the air cools, its capacity for carrying vapor is reduced. If the air cools off enough, the vapor condenses into water. This is called the *dew-point temperature*, or *dew point*. If the vapor condenses within the wall, the resulting water can saturate materials. That water may create an environment that promotes the growth of mold, which can have a serious effect on the building's occupants and their health. Sustainable facades are designed so that vapor condensation will happen in a location in the wall where the water can drain to the outside.

Vapor barriers reduce the movement of moisture and vapor diffusion through the building enclosure. The amount of water vapor passing through materials, or *permeance*, is measured in *perms*, with one perm equal to 1 grain of water vapor per hour, per square foot, per inch of mercury. Vapor barriers are categorized based on permeance values, when tested according to ASTM E 96 Test Method A (ASTM, 2010). They are grouped into three classes:

- Class I (vapor impermeable): materials with permeance of 0.1 perm or less (such as sheet polyethylene or nonperforated aluminum foil)
- Class II (vapor semi-impermeable): materials with permeance between 0.1 and 1.0 perm (such as kraft-faced fiberglass batt insulation)
- Class III (vapor semi-permeable): materials with permeance between 1.0 and 10 perms (such as latex or enamel paint)

Air barriers limit the infiltration of air through walls, while vapor barriers limit the movement of moisture. Some air barriers may also resist vapor diffusion, in which case they act as both air and vapor barriers. Impermeable vapor barriers can also function as air barriers. Their placement within the wall assembly depends on the climate type. For example, in colder climates (zones 5, 6, 7, and 8), the vapor barrier is usually placed on the inside (warm) surface of the insulation. In hot or warm climates (zones 1, 2, and 3), especially in the humid subzones, the vapor barrier is usually on the exterior side of the insulation layer. In mixed climates (zone 4), there is no ready answer for placement of vapor barriers. Prevailing temperature and humidity conditions, both inside and outside the building, should be considered. There should never be two vapor barriers within a wall assembly, as this could trap moisture and not allow it to drain or evaporate. Table 2-7 shows permeance and other properties of five vapor barrier products by one manufacturer.

Table 2-7 Examples of specific vapor barrier products and their properties.

Type/Property	Elastomeric bitumen	Synthetic rubber adhesive	Elastomeric emulsion	Rubberized asphalt 1	Rubberized asphalt 2
Air barrier	Yes	Yes	Yes	Yes	Yes
Vapor barrier	Yes	Yes	Yes	Yes	Yes
Air leakage (per ASTM E 2178)	0.000023 cfm/ft²	0.0026 cfm/ft²	0.00012 cfm/ft²	0.0001 cfm/ft²	0.0001 cfm/ft²
Vapor permeance (per ASTM E 96)	0.02 perms (Class I)	0.03 perms (Class I)	0.08 perms (Class I)	0.03 perms (Class I)	0.05 perms (Class I)
Application method	Trowel or spray	Trowel, spray, brush	Trowel or spray	Self-adhesive	Self-adhesive

Source: Henry Air Barrier Systems. © 2012 Henry Company, LLC.

Steady-State Heat and Moisture Transfer Analysis for Opaque Building Facades

Although the previous section provides general guidelines for determining vapor barrier requirements, it is recommended that a specific dew-point analysis be performed for each building. By analyzing specific conditions (such as relative humidity and exterior and interior temperatures) and the properties of individual material layers, designers can identify the thermal and moisture performance of the opaque parts of a building envelope. To perform this analysis, designers can choose either the steady-state method or the transient-analysis method.

The *steady-state method* is used to determine the dew point within the exterior wall. As discussed earlier, the *dew point* is the temperature at which airborne water vapor condenses to liquid water. The two factors that determine the dew point are the temperature of the air (or of the surface that is in contact with the air) and the relative humidity of the air. The dew-point temperature equals the air temperature when the relative humidity is 100%. In other words, the lower the relative humidity, the cooler the air must be to condense water saturated in that air.

Dew-point analysis assumes that *steady-state conduction* governs heat flow and *steady-state diffusion* governs water vapor flow (ASHRAE, 2005). By steady-state conduction, we mean that the temperature differences between exterior enclosure materials remain the same. Steady-state diffusion means that the concentration of water molecules within the components (including air spaces) of the exterior enclosure is constant. In other words, both the heat flow and the vapor diffusion within the enclosure assembly have reached a point of equilibrium. Other factors affecting moisture transfer, such as initial moisture content of materials, solar radiation, and effects of rain, are not addressed by this analysis method.

Dew-point analysis is one-dimensional, as it considers heat flow and vapor diffusion along a straight line passing through the exterior wall. It compares the saturated vapor pressures, which represent the calculated dew point at each material surface, with the actual vapor pressures within the envelope, calculated by steady-state vapor diffusion. Saturated vapor pressures are based on temperature and relative humidity, and indicate the point where water vapor condenses (the dew point). The results are approximations, and their validity and usefulness depend on the accuracy of the data used, including interior and exterior temperature and relative humidity, and the thermal resistance and permeance of the materials. The method, which estimates seasonal average conditions, involves the following steps:

- Determination of inside and outside air temperature and humidity levels for different seasons (summer and winter)
- Determination of thickness, thermal resistance (R-value), and permeance of each material within the portion of the exterior wall assembly being analyzed
- Calculation of thermal gradient, which graphs the temperature at the face of each component of the wall assembly, for summer and winter conditions; this calculation is based on the R-values of individual material layers
- Calculation of saturated vapor pressure (dew point) across the assembly based on temperature gradient
- Calculation of actual vapor pressures across the wall based on the permeance of individual material layers
- Comparison of actual and saturated vapor pressure; condensation occurs if the actual vapor pressure is above the saturation (dew) point

To see how this method is applied, an example for a cool and humid climate (Chicago, climate zone 5A) is described in this section. The location has very cold winters, but also hot and humid summers. The brick veneer facade consists of these material layers:

- Brick
- Air space (bridged by wire brick ties)
- Insulation (expanded polystyrene)
- Vapor barrier (Class II, vapor semi-impermeable)
- Exterior gypsum sheathing

- Cold-formed steel framing
- Interior gypsum board

Table 2-8 shows the exterior and interior summer and winter temperatures and humidity levels. Selected exterior temperatures and humidity levels represent upper limits (for summer conditions) and lower limits (for winter conditions). Interior conditions are based on the normal levels for thermal comfort. Table 2-9 shows properties of each of the material layers. Thermal resistance and permeability values of materials are used to calculate the thermal gradient, as well as vapor pressures, across the assembly.

Table 2-8 Interior and exterior conditions used in the dew-point analysis example.

Conditions	Exterior temperature °F (°C)	Exterior relative humidity	Interior temperature °F (°C)	Interior relative humidity
Winter	10 (−12)	60%	71 (22)	40%
Summer	90 (32)	80%	73 (23)	50%

Table 2-9 Material properties for each layer of the brick veneer facade with cold-formed steel framing used in the dew-point analysis example.

Material	Interior gypsum board	Steel framing cavity	Exterior gypsum sheathing	Vapor barrier	Insulation	Air space	Brick
Thickness (in.)	0.625	6	0.625	0.004	2	1.25	4
R-value (h-ft²-°F/Btu)	0.56	0.79	0.56	0.06	10	1.12	0.8
Permeability (perm-in.)	18.75	120	20	0.5	0.76	120	8
Vapor resistance (perm/in.)	0.053	0.008	0.050	2.000	1.325	0.008	0.125
Vapor resistance	0.033	0.050	0.031	0.008	2.649	0.010	0.500

Figure 2-44 shows thermal gradients and vapor pressure graphs for winter conditions for this exterior wall assembly. The left side of the graph shows interior conditions and the right side shows exterior conditions. The upper part of the graph shows the thermal gradient across the wall, which is calculated by taking into account respective R-values of the individual material layers, and temperature change from the outside to the inside. From this, we can see that the insulation layer provides most of the resistance to the heat flow in the assembly.

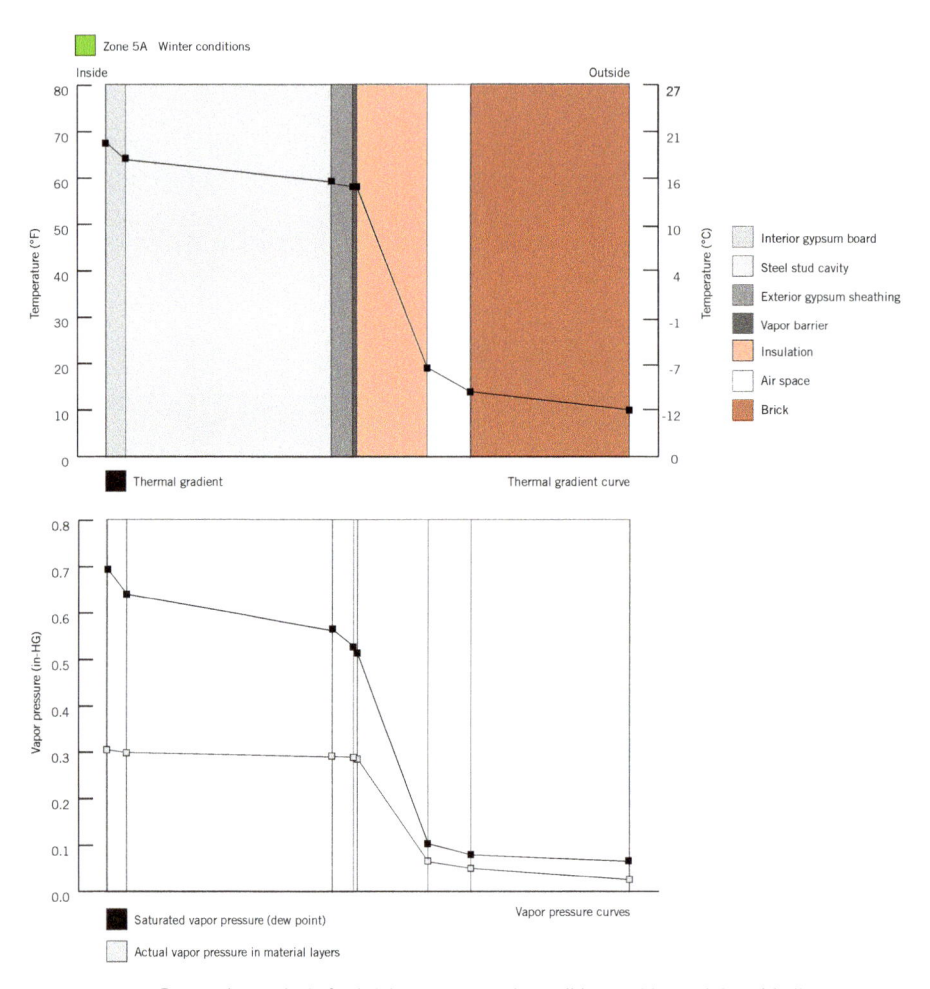

Figure 2-44 Dew-point analysis for brick veneer exterior wall located in cool, humid climate (winter conditions).

The lower portion of the graph shows saturated and actual vapor pressure curves. The saturation curve is calculated based on the thermal gradient, and indicates the dew point for each material surface within the assembly. Actual vapor pressure is calculated based on the thickness and vapor resistance of individual material layers. The graph shows that actual vapor pressure in all material layers is well below the dew point. Figure 2-45 shows comparable results for summer conditions.

THERMAL BEHAVIOR AND MOISTURE RESISTANCE   73

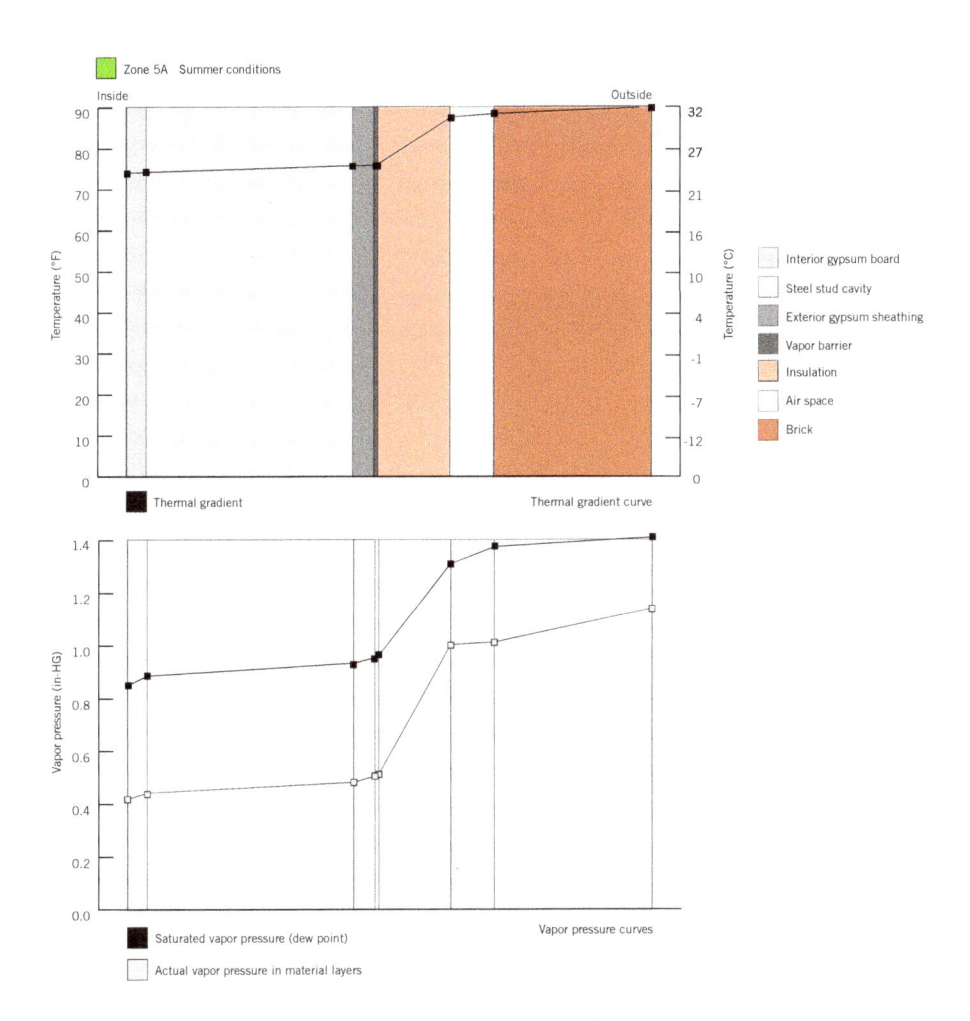

Figure 2-45 Dew-point analysis for brick veneer exterior wall located in cool, humid climate (summer conditions).

Steady-state analysis is based on the assumption that daily temperatures during a season are generally constant. In climates where daily temperatures can vary significantly during a season, the *transient-analysis method*, which can address either a fixed point in time or a period of time, is more appropriate for analyzing heat, moisture, and air movement. One form of transient analysis is hygrothermal analysis.

Hygrothermal Analysis for Opaque Building Facades

We have seen how steady-state dew-point calculations can be used for analyzing heat and moisture movement through a wall, and for determining the potential for vapor condensation within the wall. This is a simple and effective method for approximating dew points. A drawback to this approach is that the calculations represent a specific point in time. In addition, many variables, such as water content of individual material layers (that is, their hygric properties), the physical behavior of materials over time, and the effects of rain and solar radiation, are ignored.

When a material becomes saturated with water, the water fills the air pockets, even the microscopic ones, in the material. Because water is a poor insulator, this reduces the thermal resistance of the material. In addition, the moisture content is not a static condition; it can vary over time. Steady-state dew-point calculations are unable to consider moisture content of materials. A more sophisticated approach, *hygrothermal analysis,* has been developed in response to this. Hygrothermal analysis can be used to determine changes in the building envelope over time caused by the ability of component materials to transport moisture through capillary action, the effects of rain and solar radiation, and fluctuations in moisture absorption and temperature (Staube and Burnett, 2001).

WUFI® (Wärme und Feuchte instationär) is one of the available software packages for analyzing transient hygrothermal behavior of building envelopes (Kunzel et al., 2001). It is an analytical software program that simulates the combined heat and moisture transport through opaque exterior wall assemblies, including masonry walls, brick veneers, precast concrete cladded walls, and rainscreen assemblies. It was developed by the Fraunhofer Institute of Building Physics (IBP) in Germany, and is also available through the Oak Ridge National Laboratory as a research tool. By using the actual building orientation; the assumed interior environmental conditions; and temperature, precipitation, and relative humidity conditions based on historical weather data for a specific climate, WUFI can calculate the moisture content for different material layers in an assembly, as well as temperature gradients, relative humidity, and dew point. It can also be used to study long-term effects, such as the presence of moisture within the building envelope and the development of mold.

Avoiding condensation within the building enclosure, and thus avoiding the resulting degradation of building materials and the growth of mold and bacterial organisms, can help ensure a high level of building performance and improved indoor air quality. The following steps should be taken when performing a hygrothermal analysis:

- Build a computer model of the portion of the exterior wall to be analyzed
- Assign the properties and dimensions to the exterior wall materials
- Assign time increments for the calculation period
- Assign the environmental conditions (exterior and interior) and climate data
- Run the simulations and obtain results
- Interpret the data

ASHRAE, in its *Standard 160 Criteria for Moisture-Control Design Analysis in Buildings*, establishes the criteria for selecting analytic procedures, inputs, and outputs, and for evaluating the results (ASHRAE, 2009). To illustrate this analysis procedure, Figure 2-46 shows an example for a cool and humid climate, the same climate type used for our dew-point analysis method example (Figures 2-44 and 2-45). This facade assembly has the same components: interior gypsum board, cold-formed steel framing (and the cavity between the framing members), exterior gypsum sheathing, vapor barrier, expanded polystyrene insulation, air space, and brick.

Monitoring points are placed at different locations in the wall section, usually where one material meets another or where a material faces air. In Figure 2-46, those locations are the inside and outside faces of the interior gypsum board, framing cavity, exterior gypsum sheathing, vapor barrier, insulation, air space, and brick. For hygrothermal analysis, the properties of the materials within the building section must be known, because those properties, such as initial water content of materials, thermal resistance, density, porosity, specific heat capacity, and permeability, are factors in the modeling. Hygrothermal models such as WUFI typically include databases of materials and their properties, obtained from material tests and published sources; users can add new materials to the databases if the appropriate values are known.

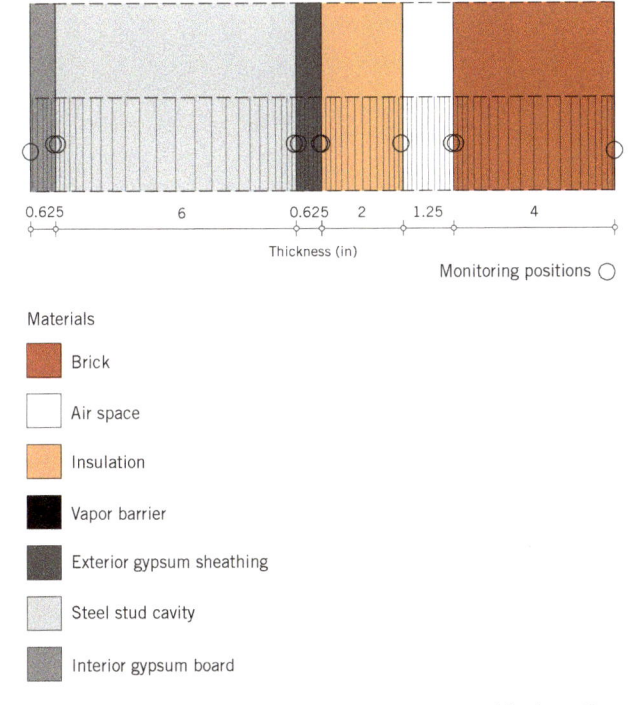

Figure 2-46 Materials and monitoring positions used for hygrothermal analysis.

For our sample model, the building is located in a cool, humid climate (zone 5A), characterized by cold winters and hot, humid summers. Controlling air and moisture movement in this climate zone is important, as large shifts in temperatures and humidity levels can cause moisture accumulation in exterior walls. The climate data are used to select temperature, relative humidity levels, solar radiation, and rain accumulation. Because this type of model allows transient analysis, the calculations consider hourly conditions over a specified time period, such as five or ten years. For our sample model, Figure 2-47 shows anticipated annual rainfall and solar radiation over a five-year period. Figure 2-48 shows exterior and interior temperatures and relative humidity conditions for the same five-year period. This is much different from the dew-point method, which can only look at an average set of conditions at just one point in time.

The results of the hygrothermal analysis can be shown as data points for material water content, temperature, and relative humidity for all material layers for every hour in the considered time period. Most of the materials initially have some level of moisture content, which is defined as the mass of water in a material per unit volume of dry material. For example, Table 2-10 shows results for a hygrothermal analysis of our

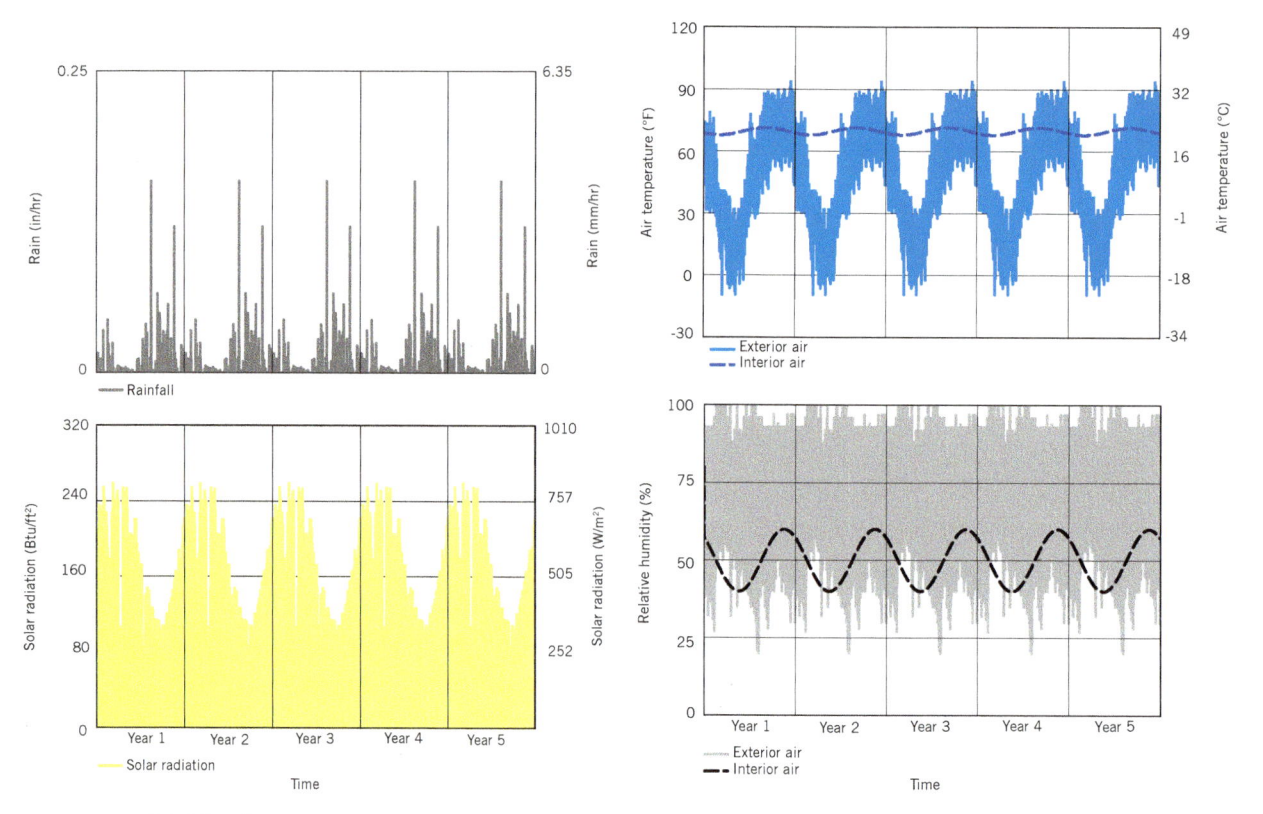

Figure 2-47 Rainfall and solar radiation data used in hygrothermal analysis.

Figure 2-48 Exterior and interior temperature and relative humidity data used in hygrothermal analysis.

sample exterior wall. Initial and final water content values are shown, along with the highest and lowest values identified during the time frame of the analysis. Note that for the materials outside the vapor barrier (brick, air cavity, and insulation), the water content increases over time. This is the result of rain absorption through the brick and vapor diffusion through the wall. In contrast, materials that are located on the inside of the vapor barrier (exterior gypsum sheathing, steel framing cavity, and interior gypsum board) become drier over time; in each case the highest water content is the same as the initial values. This demonstrates that the vapor barrier is effective in stopping vapor diffusion through the wall, and that moisture is not accumulating in the parts of the wall where evaporation or discharge through weep holes is not possible.

Table 2-10 Comparison of water content for a brick veneer exterior wall, considering combined heat and moisture transport over a five-year period.

Material layer	Initial water content (lb/ft^3)	Final water content (lb/ft^3)	Lowest water content (lb/ft^3)	Highest water content (lb/ft^3)
Brick	0.21	0.39	0.17	4.17
Air space	0.12	0.53	0.11	0.67
Insulation	0.02	0.03	0.01	0.03
Vapor barrier	0	0	0	0
Exterior gypsum sheathing	0.39	0.26	0.20	0.39
Steel stud cavity	0.12	0.05	0.03	0.12
Interior gypsum board	0.54	0.33	0.26	0.54

In a hygrothermal analysis, temperature, relative humidity, and dew point can also be determined for every monitored point in the assembly. Figure 2-49 shows results for temperature and dew-point changes at three monitoring positions of our sample wall—the inside brick surface, the inside face of the insulation layer, and the inside surface of the gypsum board—over the five-year calculation period. The bell curves show annual cyclical increases and decreases in temperature and dew point. Condensation will occur where the temperature curve falls below the dew-point curve. For the exterior surface, this is not a concern, as condensation will drain through the air cavity. For the interior material layers, however, the temperature curve must always be above the dew-point curve.

In the top graph, the temperature and dew-point curves at the interior brick surface are consistently close to each other. A review of the detailed results reveals that while the temperature is above the dew point in most cases, there are instances during very cold months where the temperature curve is at or below the dew-point curve. In those cases, vapor condenses on the interior (cavity) side of the brick, but the water drains down the air space until the flashing at the base of the cavity directs it to the weep holes. Figure 2-49 also shows that the temperature swings for this surface are greater than for the other material layers—not surprising, as the brick is outside the building insulation and is most exposed to the fluctuating outside conditions. The other two graphs in this figure show the temperature and dew-point curves for the interior sides of the insulation and the gypsum board. In both cases, the temperature curves are well above the dew point, so condensation should not occur on those surfaces.

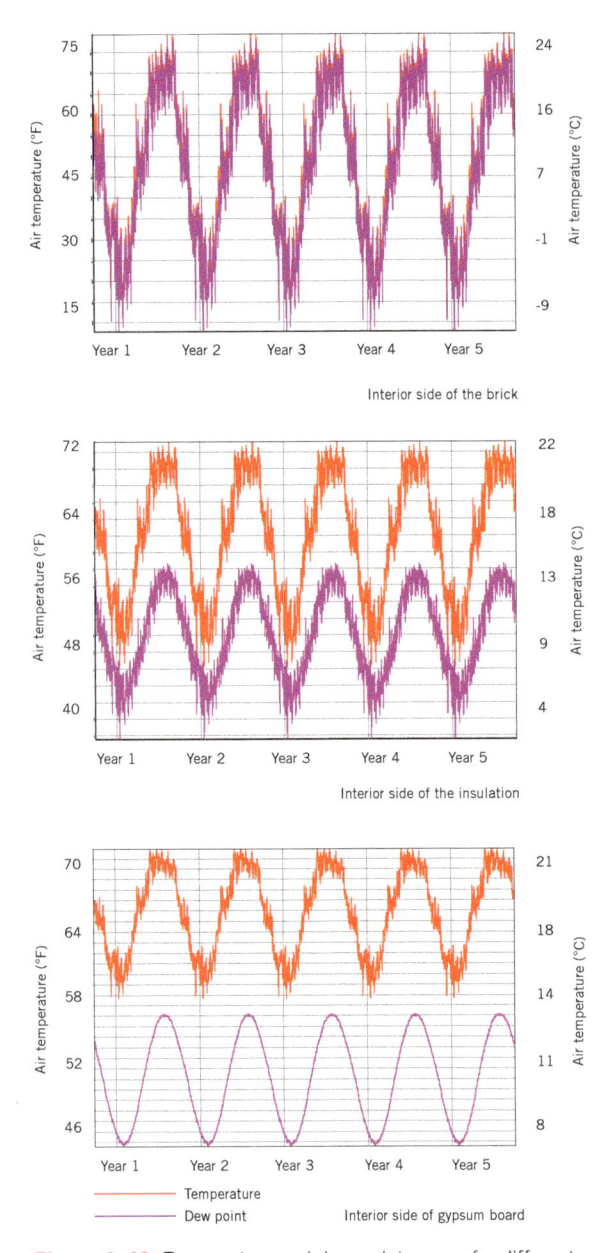

Figure 2-49 Temperature and dew-point curves for different monitoring points in hygrothermal analysis (interior side of brick, interior side of insulation, and interior surface of the wall).

WUFI can also be used to construct isopleth graphs that show the potential for mold growth. A mold-growth graph consists of relative hygrothermal (humidity and temperature) data values for all calculated time steps in the simulation, and two curved lines, or *isopleths*. These isopleths, designated as LIM I and LIM II, represent the "Lowest Isopleth for Mold"—the temperature and humidity conditions below which germination of mold species is not expected (Sedlbauer, 2002). LIM I is for materials that are biodegradable, such as wallpaper; LIM II is for porous materials, such as plaster, mineral building materials, some woods, and some insulating materials. Data values falling above the isopleths represent temperature and relative humidity conditions that favor germination of one or more mold species. In other words, if the majority of data values are above the LIM, mold growth might occur on susceptible materials. It is preferable that most, if not all, of the data points fall below the LIM. Figure 2-50 identifies hygrothermal conditions for the interior surface of our exterior wall example. It shows that all hygrothermal conditions are well below both isopleths. The hygrothermal data are represented in different colors to show how the isopleths change over time: at the start of the calculation, the color is yellow, and later points are shown in progressively darker shades of green, showing results for the intermediate calculations. The conditions at the end of the calculations are shown in black.

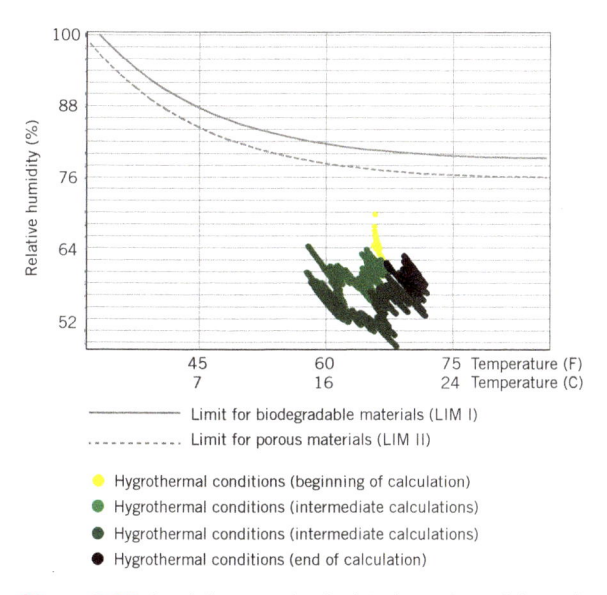

Figure 2-50 Isopleth curves for the interior surface of the wall.

Heat Transfer Analysis for Glazed Building Facades

The previous two sections focused on methods for analyzing heat and moisture transfer in opaque parts of building envelopes. Glazed building facades require a different approach for calculating thermal properties and for heat transfer analysis. As we saw in the earlier section on "Properties of Facade Materials and Components," to calculate the overall heat transfer coefficient (U-value) for a glazed facade, we have to determine the U-values for the center of glass, edge of glass, and frame conditions. Heat transfer in these types of facades can be analyzed using two-dimensional finite-element heat transfer models. For example, the Lawrence Berkeley National Laboratory has developed a computer software program called THERM, which can be used to study heat transfer through metal window frames and curtain walls (LBNL, 2011). THERM models the thermal gradient across the wall section using the material properties of components (heat transfer coefficients) and the temperature difference between the inside and outside environments.

The National Fenestration Rating Council (NFRC) describes methods for obtaining heat transfer coefficients in its publication *NFRC 100 Procedure for Determining Fenestration Product U-Factors* (NFRC, 2010). Table 2-11 shows the environmental conditions (outside and inside temperature, wind speed and direction, sky emissivity, and direct solar radiation) to be used for simulations and modeling when determining U-values of glazed building facades. These values are not dependent on building location or site.

Table 2-11 NFRC 100 environmental conditions.

Variables	IP (Imperial) units	SI (Metric) units
Outside temperature	0 °F	−18 °C
Inside temperature	70 °F	21 °C
Wind speed	123 mph	55 m/s
Sky temperature	0 °F	−18 °C
Sky emissivity	1.00	1.00
Direct solar radiation	0 Btu/ft^2	0 W/m^2

Properties of glazing can be calculated using WINDOW, another software program developed by the Lawrence Berkeley National Laboratory. WINDOW is interoperable with THERM. WINDOW can be used to calculate the solar heat gain coefficient (SHGC), shading coefficient (SC), visual transmittance (Tv), and summer and winter U-values for glazing units, as shown in Figure 2-51. To use WINDOW, designers select specific components of the glazing unit, including the layers of glass and type of gas between the glass layers, and WINDOW calculates its properties. As an example, we can use WINDOW to generate the following values for a triple-glazed, argon-filled glazing unit with two layers of low-e coating:

- U-value (winter): 0.122 Btu/h-ft^2-°F (0.6932 W/m^2-°K)
- U-value (summer): 0.125 Btu/h-ft^2-°F (0.7102 W/m^2-°K)
- SHGC: 0.297

- SC: 0.341
- Tv: 0.560

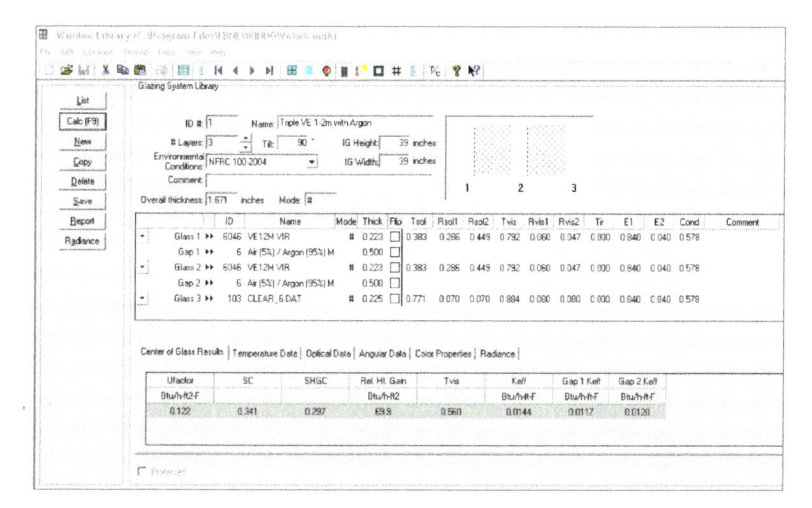

Figure 2-51 Calculation of glass properties for insulated glazing unit in WINDOW.

To obtain values for frames, a separate thermal analysis must be performed for each frame component. This is done through computer modeling in THERM. Exterior and interior conditions, the properties of the materials, and the configuration of each curtain wall component must be built into the model. To verify the results of the analysis, physical mockups of the curtain wall can be tested. If the system is only being modeled, and not physically tested, only half the widths of the frames are modeled. If the system will also be tested, then the frames are modeled as whole widths to match the physical mockup; half frames cannot be practically built or tested. Figure 2-52 shows a model of a thermally broken aluminum frame, with its calculated U-values. Table 2-12 shows calculated U-values for all frame vertical and horizontal components and at the edges of the glass.

THERM can also be used to find the thermal gradients across a curtain wall profile, as shown in Figure 2-53. Outdoor and indoor temperatures and relative humidity are selected to represent actual conditions for a specific building location. Review of climate data must be performed to determine appropriate seasonal exterior conditions. Interior operating temperatures can be assigned to interior surfaces of materials; the software calculates the thermal gradient using the heat transfer coefficients of individual components and the differences between interior and exterior conditions. Figure 2-53 shows the effectiveness of a triple-glazed, thermally broken system. The exterior mullion, mullion cap, and glass lite are at close to the outside temperature, while the interior mullion and inner lite are at room temperature.

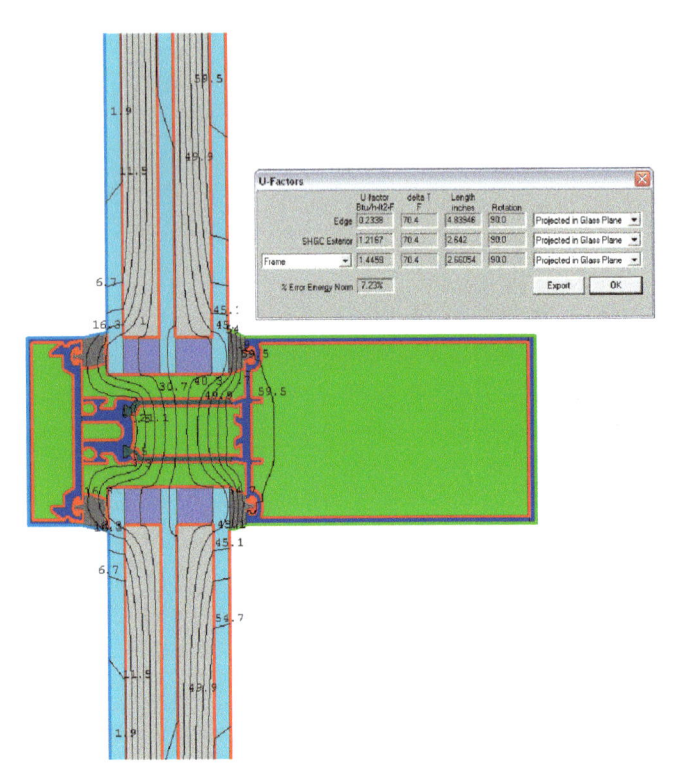

Figure 2-52 Calculation of U-values for frame and edge of glass using THERM.

Table 2-12 Results obtained by thermal simulations for curtain wall edge of glass and frame U-value for model shown in Figure 2-52.

Component	Edge-of-glass U-value (Btu/h-ft²-°F)	Frame U-value (Btu/h-ft²-°F)
Mullion	0.2338	1.4459
Head	0.2359	1.5711
Sill	0.2325	1.1726
Jambs		
Right jamb	0.2320	1.2706
Left jamb	0.2355	1.7040

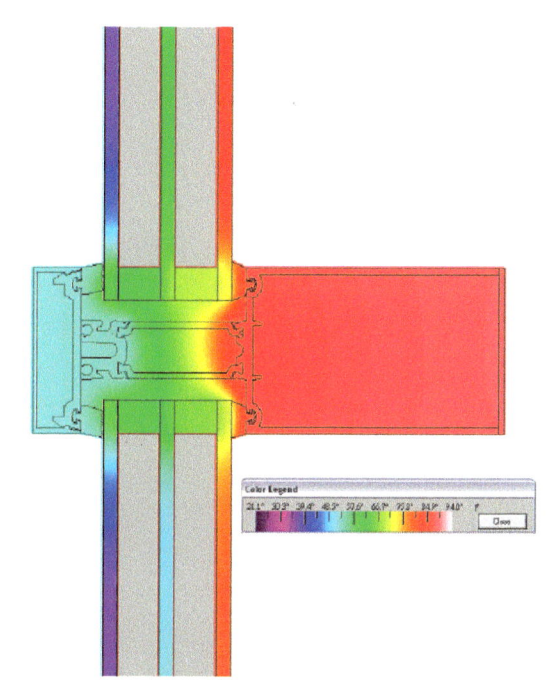

Figure 2-53 Thermal gradient across a curtain wall section.

CHAPTER SUMMARY

This chapter has shown how the design of sustainable facades must consider many factors, including environmental conditions, building orientation, fenestration design, and the properties of materials and facade components. The physical behavior of the facade is a major contributor to a building's energy use. Designing sustainable, high-performance facades starts with identifying the environmental and climatic factors acting on the building envelope, building orientation, facade orientation, and the ratio of glass to opaque wall. The next step is identifying the facade type, based on the program requirements, orientation, spatial organization, client's requirements, and desired aesthetic qualities. Designers must consider the characteristics of the materials and components, such as thermal and optical properties and embodied energy that go into the construction of a building's facade. A sustainable building design incorporates these elements, ensuring that design decisions are made that limit the negative environmental impacts of the building.

REFERENCES

ASHRAE. (2005). *Handbook of Fundamentals.* Atlanta, GA: American Society of Heating, Refrigerating and Air-Conditioning Engineers, Inc.

ASHRAE. (2007). *BSR/ASHRAE/IESNA 90.1-2007, Energy Standard for Buildings except Low-Rise Residential Buildings.* Atlanta, GA: American Society of Heating, Refrigerating and Air-Conditioning Engineers, Inc.

ASHRAE. (2009). *ASHRAE Standard 160: Criteria for Moisture-Control Design Analysis in Buildings.* Atlanta, GA: American Society of Heating, Refrigerating and Air-Conditioning Engineers, Inc.

ASTM. (2003). *ASTM E 2178-03 Standard Test Method for Air Permeance of Building Materials.* West Conshohocken, PA: ASTM International.

ASTM. (2005). *ASTM E 2357-05 Standard Test Method for Determining Air Leakage of Air Barrier Assemblies.* West Conshohocken, PA: ASTM International.

ASTM. (2010). *ASTM E 96-10 Standard Test Methods for Water Vapor Transmission of Materials.* West Conshohocken, PA: ASTM International.

Inventory of Carbon & Energy (ICE), Version 2.0. Retrieved from http://www.bath.ac.uk/mech-eng/sert/embodied/

ISO. (2006). *ISO/DIS 14040: Environmental Management—Life Cycle Assessment—Principles and Framework.* Geneva, Switzerland: International Standards Organization.

Kunzel, H., Karagiozis, A., and Holm, A. (2001). "A Hygrothermal Design Tool for Architects and Engineers (WUFI ORNL/IBD)." In H. Trechsel, ed., *ASTM Manual 40: Moisture Analysis and Condensation Control in Building Envelopes* (pp. 136–151). West Conshohocken, PA: American Society of Testing and Materials.

Lawton, M., Roppel, P., Fookes, D., Teasdale, A., and Schoonhoven, D. (2010). "Real R-Value of Exterior Insulated Wall Assemblies." *Proceedings of the BEST2 Conference.* Portland, OR: Building Enclosure Science and Technology.

LBNL. (2011). *THERM 6.3/WINDOW 6.3 NFRC Simulation Manual* (Mitchell, R., Kohler, C., Zhu, L., Arasteh, D., Carmody, J., Huizenga, C., and Curcija, D., LBNL-48255). Berkeley, CA: Lawrence Berkeley National Laboratory.

NFRC. (2010). *NFRC 100 Procedure for Determining Fenestration Product U-Factors.* Greenbelt, MD: National Fenestration Rating Council.

Sedlbauer, K. (2002). "Prediction of Mould Fungus Formation on the Surface of and Inside Building Components." PhD dissertation, Fraunhofer Institute for Building Physics.

Staube, J., and Burnett, E. (2001). "Overview of Hygrothermal Analysis Methods." In H. Trechsel, ed., *ASTM Manual 40: Moisture Analysis and Condensation Control in Building Envelopes* (pp. 81–89). West Conshohocken, PA: American Society of Testing and Materials.

CHAPTER 3

DESIGNING FOR COMFORT

What makes a facade "sustainable"? All facades create barriers between the exterior and interior environment, providing building occupants with thermally, visually, and acoustically comfortable spaces. Sustainable facades do more. They provide optimal levels of comfort using the least amount of energy. To achieve this high performance, designers need to consider many variables—thermal insulation, daylighting, solar shading, glare, acoustics, and indoor air quality—when designing facades for sustainable interior environments.

THERMAL COMFORT

Thermal comfort is defined by ASHRAE as "that condition of mind which expresses satisfaction with the thermal environment" (ASHRAE, 2004). Because it is a condition of mind, comfort is inherently based on one's experience and perception; there are large variations in physiological and psychological responses for different individuals. Few buildings are designed to meet the unique thermal comfort needs of a single person. Therefore, organizations such as ASHRAE have established standards for thermal comfort that apply to the majority of people most of the time.

Six primary variables affect thermal comfort: air temperature, air movement, humidity, mean radiant temperature, occupants' metabolic rate, and occupants' clothing. Although each of these variables can be separately measured, the human body responds to them holistically. When the design for interior space balances these variables correctly, the occupants will feel comfortable. These six variables have specific characteristics and effects on thermal comfort:

- *Indoor air temperature* affects the rate of heat loss from the skin. It can be controlled by changing the temperature of the air supplied to a space by the HVAC systems, by bringing outside air into a space, or by increasing or decreasing the amount of direct sunlight within a space by adjusting window shading devices. Although indoor air temperature can be measured precisely and objectively, occupants' comfort perception will differ depending on the outdoor air temperature, the amount of solar radiation at different times of day, and the type of activities being performed.

- *Moving air* affects thermal comfort in two ways: it conducts heat from a warm surface, such as skin, to the colder room air and surfaces; and it helps evaporation of perspiration from skin. The faster the air moves, the greater are these effects. Typically, the movement of air within a space cannot be controlled by the occupants. Therefore, to maintain their comfort, occupants respond by adjusting one of the variables they can control, such as the air temperature or their clothing.

- The measure of the amount of water vapor in the air is the *relative humidity (RH)*. It is given as a percentage of the actual vapor in the air compared to the maximum amount of vapor possible in fully saturated air for a certain temperature. Thus, a relative humidity of 100% describes air that is completely saturated by water vapor, and an RH of 0% describes air that is arid, or completely dry. Under humid conditions, the rate at which perspiration evaporates through skin is lower than under dry conditions. Because the human body uses evaporative cooling of the skin as its primary mechanism to regulate body temperature, people usually find overly humid air to be uncomfortable.

However, numerous health problems are caused by excessively dry indoor air, so a balance must be achieved. Depending on the air temperature, most people are comfortable with relative humidity levels ranging from 25% to 60%. The effect of relative humidity on a person's thermal comfort is usually less than that of air temperature and air movement across the skin. Typically, it cannot be controlled by the occupants.

- *Mean radiant temperature* is the measurement of the energy radiated by objects and surfaces. It is different from air temperature, and is perceived as heat on one's skin. Solar radiation from sunlight is one of the greatest sources of heat. Because radiant energy acts independently of air temperature, a room's occupants may feel discomfort from the radiant energy even though the air in the room is at a normally comfortable temperature. The effects of radiation can be minimized by any opaque object that blocks the radiation. In the case of solar radiation, window blinds may be used to block sunlight and create shade. However, if the blinds are inside the window glass, the material of the blinds will absorb some of the solar energy and radiate it into the room.

- *Metabolic rate* is the measure of the amount of energy, in calories, expended by a human body and the amount of internal body heat generated through thermogenesis. Metabolic rates can fluctuate depending on a person's physical characteristics and types of activities. The metabolic rate of a person engaged in strenuous exercise will be higher than that of a person sitting at a desk. Because of their different metabolic rates, each person will experience different sensations of comfort in the same environment.

- Clothing is the simplest form of personal insulation. It forms a barrier that creates a layer of trapped body heat between the skin and the clothing. This is the variable most within the control of an occupant. People have an expectation for how much clothing is appropriate for a particular type of space and activity. If they need to wear more or less clothing to feel comfortable, they will be dissatisfied with the thermal performance of the space.

Methods of Measurement

Thermal comfort is a perceived sensation, and therefore a subjective experience. Several methods have been developed to objectively measure occupants' satisfaction with interior environmental conditions. ASHRAE's Predicted Mean Vote (PMV) and Predicted Percentage of Dissatisfied (PPD) are calculation methods for statistically predicting the number of individuals who would express dissatisfaction with certain comfort conditions. The PMV index uses a seven-point, hot-to-cold thermal sensation scale, based on responses from a large number of people exposed to a certain environment. The PMV thermal sensation scale spans from −3 for a cold thermal sensation to +3 for a hot thermal sensation, with intermediate stages of −2 (cool), −1 (slightly cool), 0 (neutral), +1 (slightly warm), and +2 (warm). The PPD index predicts the percentage of people who are thermally dissatisfied, based on data derived from the PMV index. Figure 3-1 shows the relationship between PPD and PMV. PPD assumes that people who vote +3, +2, −2, and −3 in the PMV are thermally dissatisfied, and that the distribution of votes follows an inverse bell curve, with 0 at the center of the bell.

88 DESIGNING FOR COMFORT

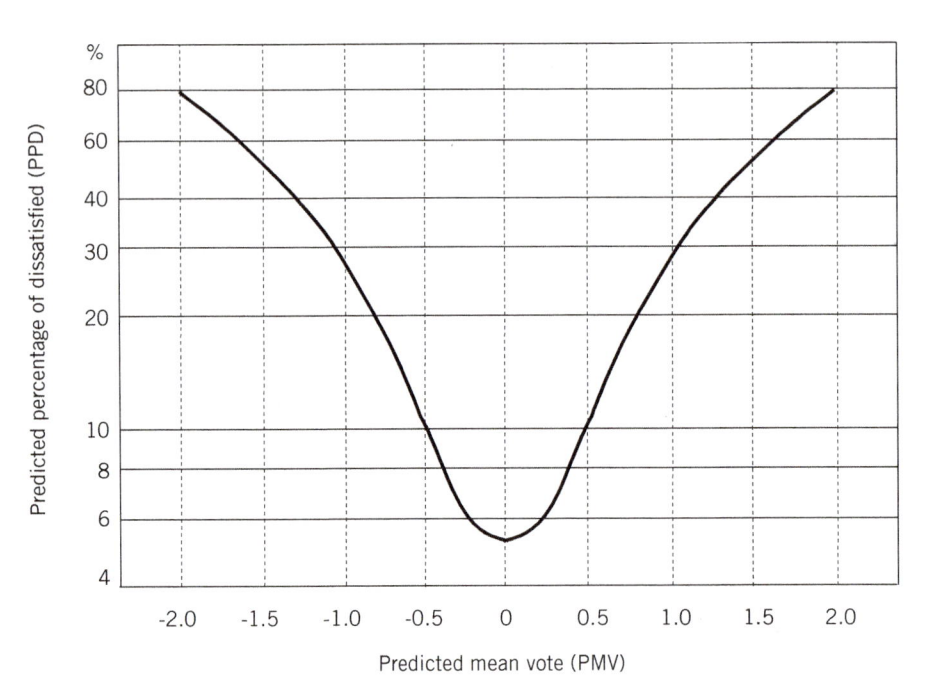

Figure 3-1 Relationship between PMV and PPD indices.

The PPD curve is represented by unitless numbers, with the number being the percentage of people who are thermally dissatisfied. ASHRAE Standard 55-2004 recommends that PMV values be between +0.5 and −0.5 for general conditions, which correspond to a PPD of 10 (i.e., 10% of the occupants are dissatisfied).

For naturally ventilated spaces, where occupants have some control over their environment (e.g., by opening or closing windows to alter air temperature and air movement), the ASHRAE standard provides an optional method for determining thermally acceptable conditions. Indoor operating temperatures can be adjusted up or down, depending on the mean monthly outdoor temperatures, while still maintaining acceptable comfort conditions. This is illustrated in Figure 3-2, which specifies ranges of operating temperatures for acceptable thermal comfort in naturally ventilated buildings. Higher operating temperatures are acceptable for climates with high mean monthly temperatures, significantly reducing energy consumption by mechanical systems. This allows for 10% of the occupants to experience whole-body thermal discomfort, and for an additional 10% to experience thermal discomfort for some part of their bodies. For example, if the mean monthly outdoor temperature is 95°F (35°C), the indoor operating temperatures can be relatively high, between approximately 75°F (24°C) and 87°F (30.5°C), and still satisfy 80% of the occupants. At the other extreme, if the mean monthly outdoor temperature is 50°F (10°C), the indoor operating temperatures can be relatively low, between approximately 64°F (17.5°C) and 77°F (25°C).

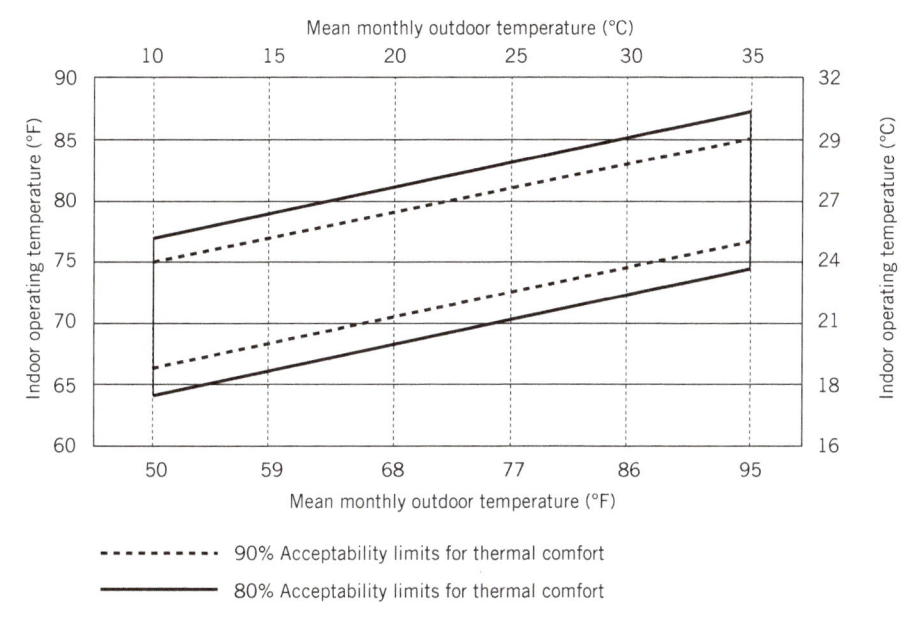

Figure 3-2 Acceptable operating temperatures for naturally conditioned spaces, according to ASHRAE Standard 55-2004.

These criteria can also be used for buildings with mixed-mode ventilation systems (i.e., natural ventilation, or facade openings, combined with HVAC systems). Mixed-mode buildings can be naturally ventilated with outside air through facade openings when environmental and climatic conditions are favorable and mechanically ventilated when conditions are not favorable. The goal of well-designed mixed-mode buildings is to reduce or eliminate energy consumption by fans and cooling systems when conditions permit natural ventilation.

The Center for the Built Environment (CBE) at the University of California at Berkeley (UCB) has developed a more advanced model for understanding and determining occupants' thermal comfort. It relies on complex relationships between environmental conditions and the physiological response of an occupant, who is represented in the model by a "thermal manikin" (Huizenga et al., 2001). In the CBE model, thermal comfort is related to the principles of human thermal regulation. To differentiate local thermal comfort, the thermal manikin can be monitored at an arbitrary number of body segments, such as head, chest, arms, and legs. Most applications use sixteen body segments. Figure 3-3 shows how the thermal manikin can be used to reflect characteristics of actual users, such as level of clothing, metabolic rate, and physiological properties. Convection, conduction, and radiation of heat between the manikin and the environment are considered in the calculations.

Thermal comfort

Solar radiation

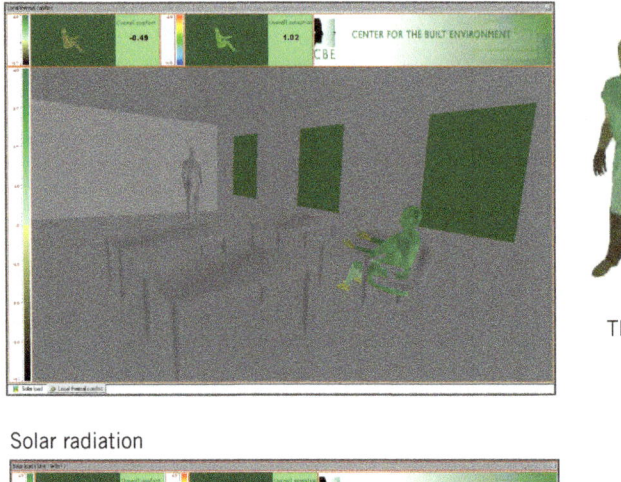

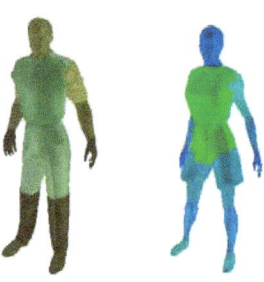

Thermal manikin response
(thermal comfort)

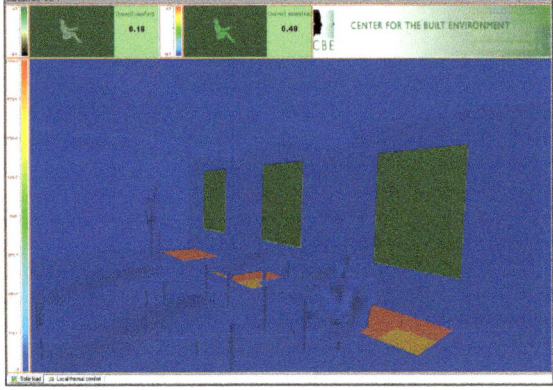

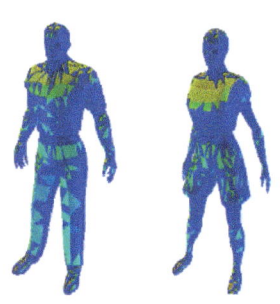

Thermal manikin response
(solar radiation)

Courtesy of Charlie Huizenga, Center for the Built Environment.

Figure 3-3 Thermal manikins and comfort responses.

The CBE model can be used to predict occupants' thermal comfort and thermal sensation indices. The *thermal sensation* index is similar to ASHRAE's PMV index, with "very hot" (+4) and "very cold" (−4) added to the ends of the scales. This accommodates extreme environments that may be encountered. Thus, the thermal sensation index is based on a nine-point scale: +4 (very hot), +3 (hot), +2 (warm), +1 (slightly warm), 0 (neutral), −1 (slightly cool), −2 (cool), −3 (cold), and −4 (very cold). The *thermal comfort* scale indicates whether the occupants are comfortable with their indoor environments, and the scale includes "just comfortable" (+0), "comfortable" (+2) and "very comfortable" (+4) on the positive axis, and "just uncomfortable" (−0), "uncomfortable" (−2) to "very uncomfortable" (−4) on the negative axis. This comfort scale differs from other methods for measuring thermal comfort by differentiating levels of comfort as positive or negative. This forces subjects to be explicit about whether their perceived thermal state falls in the overall category of "comfortable" or "uncomfortable" (Arens et al., 2006). Scales for both thermal comfort and thermal sensation are necessary, because knowing that occupants feel cool or warm does not necessarily tell us if they are comfortable or uncomfortable.

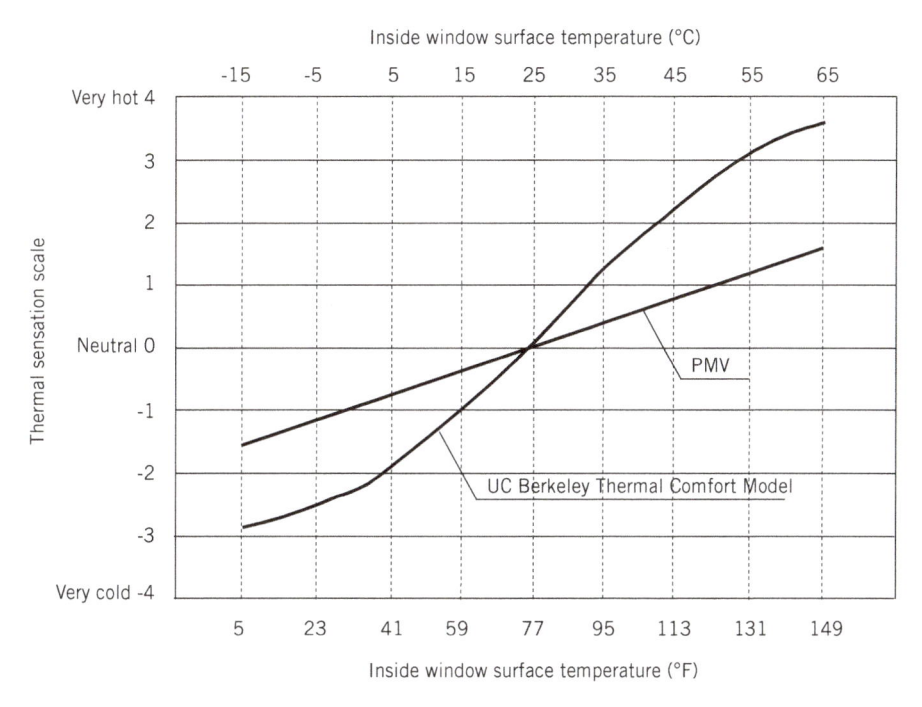

Figure 3-4 Comparison between PMV and CBE Thermal Comfort Model results (Adapted from Huizenga et al., 2006).

Figure 3-4 compares ASHRAE's PMV with the CBE Thermal Comfort Model for a specific condition. This comparison is based on an occupant sitting 3 feet (1 meter) from a window, and shows occupant's thermal sensation as the temperature of the glass surface gets hotter or colder (Huizenga et al., 2006). Both methods show that the occupant will be neutral at 0 when the window temperature is 77°F (25°C); however, the CBE Thermal Comfort Model is more responsive to the changes in glass temperature and its effects on thermal sensation, and can better predict local discomfort caused by the window.

Facade Design and Thermal Comfort

Of all the facade elements, windows have the largest thermal fluctuations. Windows are usually the coldest interior surfaces in cold weather and the warmest interior surfaces in warm weather. This is the case even for windows with high-performance glazing and thermally broken frames. As a result, facades with high window-to-wall ratios (WWRs) are more likely to affect the thermal comfort of occupants than those with low WWRs. This effect increases as occupants get closer to the window, and also depends on how active the occupants are. For example, occupants who spend most of the time seated close to the windows are more likely to feel discomfort than occupants seated farther away or moving within the space.

The optimal WWR should be based on the floor plan of a space, the occupants' positions in the space, and the types of occupant activities. Smaller WWRs should be used for spaces where occupants are typically close to the windows, especially for south-oriented facades. For example, in the design of commercial office spaces where the occupants are seated near windows, the WWR should not exceed 40%, and WWRs as low as 25% should be considered. For spaces where occupants do not spend a lot of time near windows, or for corridors and other circulation spaces, higher WWRs can be used with minimal effect on the occupants' thermal comfort. Window size is not always entirely the designer's choice; in some cases, such as hospital patient rooms, building codes or other standards may prescribe minimum window sizes.

The choice of facade glazing materials also influences occupants' thermal comfort. The effects are different for summer and winter. During winter, the thermal comfort effect is largely driven by inside window surface temperature, which is usually colder than the room it faces. Table 3-1 shows, for six common glazing types, the lowest outdoor temperature at which a person seated three feet (one meter) from a window would feel comfortable. The table shows that double-glazed, air-insulated, low-e glazing units are suitable for climates where winter exterior temperatures are above 21°F (−6°C), while triple-glazed, air-insulated, low-e glazing units can be used for temperatures as low as −18°F (−28°C).

During the summer, thermal comfort is driven by the combination of the inside surface temperature of the glass and the transmitted solar radiation through the glass. These in turn are significantly influenced by the construction of the glazing units, the material properties of the glass, and the effectiveness of shading elements used with the window. Table 3-1 shows, for the same six glazing types, the maximum amount of solar radiation on the surface of the glass before an occupant seated close to a window starts to feel uncomfortable. As we can see, spectrally selective double-glazed, air-insulated, low-e glazing units are the best choice for climates with high solar radiation. These types of glazing units have a light-to-solar-gain ratio of 1.25 or higher (i.e., they have high visual transmittance and low SHGC), allowing large amounts of daylight to enter the interior while blocking much of the solar heat.

Table 3-1 Glazing systems and winter and summer environmental conditions for meeting thermal comfort of occupants seated close to a window.

Glazing type	Winter — Minimum allowable outdoor temperature in °F (°C)	Summer — Maximum allowable solar radiation Btu/ft^2 (W/m^2)
Double-lite air-insulated IGU (clear)	45 (7)	150 (469)
Double-lite air-insulated IGU (low-e)	21 (−6)	165 (516)

Glazing type	Winter — Minimum allowable outdoor temperature in °F (°C)	Summer — Maximum allowable solar radiation Btu/ft² (W/m²)
Spectrally selective double-lite air-insulated IGU (low-e)	16 (–9)	342 (1,069)
Triple-lite air-insulated IGU (clear)	28 (–2)	146 (456)
Triple-lite air-insulated IGU (low-e)	–18 (–28)	196 (613)
Spectrally selective triple-lite air-insulated IGU (low-e)	–22 (–30)	323 (1,009)

Source: Huizenga et al., 2006.

The variation in window surface temperatures, and its effect on occupant comfort, can be tempered by changing the interior air temperature. The cooling or heating effect of cold or warm glass can be compensated for by raising or lowering the air temperature inside the space. Figure 3-5 shows how the interior air temperature affects the occupant comfort under a variety of glass temperatures, for occupants seated close to the windows. The four curves correspond to different glass temperatures, and each curve shows the interior air temperature that gives occupants sitting close to the glass the greatest comfort. For example, if the glass temperature is 50°F (10°C), occupants near the glass will be most comfortable with an interior air temperature of 78°F (26°C). For a glass temperature of 104°F (40°C), the highest level of comfort is reached with a room temperature of approximately 70°F (21°C).

Air movement can also have an effect on thermal comfort. Facades can cause two forms of undesirable air movement: induced air motion caused by cold interior window surfaces, and infiltration of outside air through gaps in the exterior enclosure. In general, the drafts affect thermal comfort. In the exceptional cases—for example, very tall windows with low-performance glass—a heater under the window sill may mitigate the effects of the draft. In a truly sustainable strategy for interior comfort, this type of glazing system should be properly designed and selected to preclude interior air induction.

Air infiltration can have a much more significant effect on comfort. Although facades cannot be built fully airtight, infiltration resistance can be achieved if the assembly is designed with an appropriate air barrier. Air leakage can be aggravated if the interior air pressures are significantly different from the exterior air pressure. These internal pressure differences can be created by the HVAC system or by the varying vertical air pressures in tall buildings (*stack effect*). Significant pressure differences between the interior and the exterior of the building can cause air to be driven through the facade if there are penetrations in the air barrier. This will result in outside air being pulled into the space or conditioned interior air being driven out of the building, requiring more internal air to maintain thermal comfort.

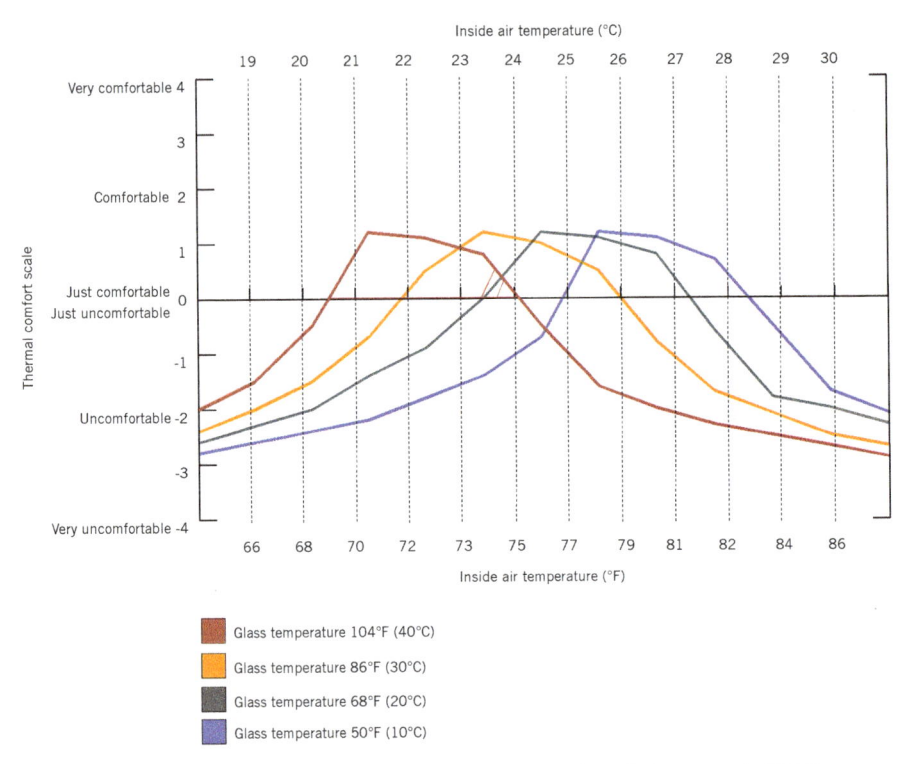

Figure 3-5 Thermal comfort and glass temperature (Adapted from Huizenga et al., 2006).

In summary, designers have four design strategies available to improve the thermal comfort of a building's occupants:

- Find the optimal window-to-wall ratio (WWR). In some conditions, it is better to have more windows or larger windows to bring in more daylight, whereas in other conditions it is better to have fewer or smaller windows for increased wall insulation and better acoustics. The optimal WWR strikes a balance between all thermal comfort factors and other factors that give the occupants the best overall comfort.

- Select glazing materials with the best performance characteristics, especially solar heat gain coefficient and U-value.

- Design shading elements to reduce interior solar heat gain during warm seasons, while allowing direct sunlight to provide warmth during cold seasons.

- Provide a facade assembly strategy that will be as airtight as possible, with all gaps sealed to limit uncontrolled movement of air through the facade. This will keep exterior air from penetrating the exterior wall and conditioned air within the interior space.

DAYLIGHT AND GLARE

Daylighting Strategies

Use of natural light has become an important strategy for improving buildings' overall energy efficiency. By providing occupants with natural light, reliance on artificial lighting to perform daytime activities is reduced. Because even energy-efficient light fixtures can generate significant amounts of heat, extensive use of daylighting can play a major role in reducing cooling loads.

Research has shown that the benefits of daylight extend beyond energy savings to include the positive physiological and psychological well-being of people. Exposure to natural light positively affects people's circadian rhythms, which can lead to higher productivity and greater satisfaction with the internal environment (Edwards and Torcellini, 2002). Different wavelengths and spectral distributions of light have different effects on the human body, and daylight, unlike most artificial light sources, includes the full spectral distribution of wavelengths needed for biological functions. For this reason, people subconsciously prefer daylight to any type of artificial lighting (Liberman, 1991). Studies have shown that in commercial office spaces, daylight promotes increased productivity, improved health of occupants, reduced absenteeism, and financial savings. In educational facilities, the benefits include improved student attendance and academic performance. Research also suggests that natural light in hospitals and assisted-living facilities improves the physiological and psychological states of patients and staff (Edwards and Torcellini, 2002).

Though few (if any) negative effects result from exposure to daylight, exposure to direct sunlight has both good and bad effects. For example, when the ultraviolet radiation in sunlight hits human skin, the skin produces the essential vitamin D. However, too much sunlight on skin can cause tissue damage. Window glass usually blocks most of the sun's ultraviolet radiation from reaching interior spaces.

Designers of naturally lit spaces need to consider the project's design goals and criteria, and its fixed and variable conditions. Design goals and criteria include subjective qualities, such as privacy and views to the outside, as well as objective and measurable qualities, such as energy use and the intensity of the daylight. They are set either by the project team (for example, views to the outside) or by prevailing codes, zoning ordinances, and standards. When considering visual comfort, designers need to think about illumination levels, daylight distribution, and protection against direct sunlight and glare. Integration of building systems is also important, because facades, lighting, shading elements, HVAC systems, and building controls must function together to have the largest effect on building performance. For example, spaces that use natural daylight for perimeter zones and control artificial lighting with photosensors and dimmers reduce the cooling loads for the HVAC system and, most likely, the sizes of mechanical equipment and ductwork.

Fixed conditions are outside the designer's control. They include the building's location and the climate, which determine, respectively, the position of the sun and the outdoor temperature, and the surrounding buildings, trees, topography, and other features that can affect daylight availability and views. Designers can control the variable conditions, such as building geometry and the design of the facade, including material properties, size and orientation of windows, and shading of windows. By understanding the fixed conditions, and carefully manipulating the variable ones, designers can create spaces that use daylighting to enhance occupants' visual comfort. Table 3-2 shows typical examples of fixed and variable conditions.

Table 3-2 Daylight design considerations.

Design goals and criteria	Fixed and variable conditions
Visual comfort	Climate (fixed)
Illuminance	Daylight availability
Daylight distribution	Temperature
Exposure to direct sunlight	Site and location (fixed)
Glare	Latitude
Visual characteristics	Local daylight availability
Views to the outside	Exterior obstructions and surrounding buildings
Daylight quality: color, brightness	Ground reflectance
Privacy	
Building energy use/costs	Room and fenestration properties (variable)
Codes and standards	Geometry
Systems and products	Material properties and reflectance
Integration of systems: facade, lighting, shading, HVAC, and controls	Fenestration size and orientation
	Shading system
	Lighting system (variable)
	Light fixture properties
	Ambient and task lighting
	Controls
	Occupants' activities (fixed)

People experience visual comfort when they have the right amount of light—natural or artificial—to perform their tasks. *Illuminance* measures the intensity of perceived light on a surface. The units of measure for illuminance are foot-candles (fc) in the imperial system and lux in the SI, or metric, system (1 fc = 10.764 lux). The Illuminating Engineering Society recommends ranges of illuminance levels for different types of spaces and tasks, which are published in the *IESNA Lighting Handbook* (IESNA, 2011). For example, public spaces with dark surroundings require from 2 to 5 fc (20 to 50 lux); work areas where visual tasks are occasionally performed require from 10 to 20 fc (100 to 200 lux); and spaces where detailed visual tasks are performed for prolonged periods of time require from 200 to 500 fc (2,000 to 5,000 lux).

Humans perceive differences in light levels through logarithmic, rather than arithmetic, progressions. Therefore, a change from 25 to 50 fc would appear to be the same increase in light as a change from 50 to 100 fc, as in both cases the amount of light is doubled. Similarly, an increase of 25 foot-candles would appear greater when the light changes from 25 to 50 fc (a 100% increase) than with a change from 50 to 75 fc (a 50% increase).

The orientation and WWR of a building influence the availability of natural light for interior spaces. Analyzing daylight availability during the different seasons is an important part of the design process for high-performance sustainable facades. Lighting simulation software programs, such as Radiance, developed by the Lawrence Berkeley National Laboratory, can be used to simulate and study different design options. The following case study demonstrates the procedure and results. The building under consideration is a research facility, consisting primarily of laboratories and offices. It is located in a mixed, humid climate (zone 4A). Figure 3-6 shows two of the facades, along with the projected shadows from a neighboring building, on June 21 and December 21. In this case study, we compare two interior laboratory spaces. Both spaces have ribbon windows on the long northeast-facing facade, and Laboratory 1 also has floor-to-ceiling windows on the short northwest-facing facade. The window-to-wall ratios are 65% for Laboratory 1 and 55% for Laboratory 2.

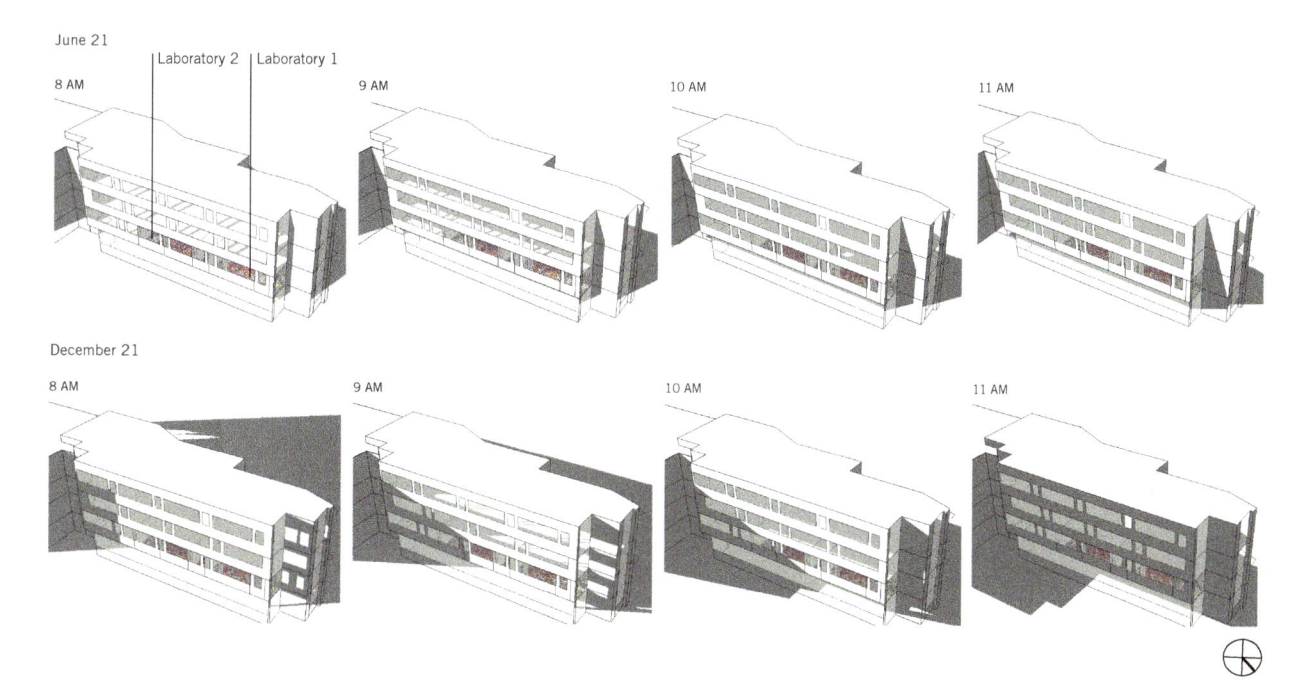

Figure 3-6 Facade orientation, location of laboratories, and projected shadows.

Using the Lawrence Berkeley National Laboratory's Radiance software, simulations were performed for both of these laboratories. Figure 3-7 compares the daylight levels for the two laboratory spaces on June 21 at 10:00 a.m., showing floor plans and three-dimensional views of the daylight distribution within the interior spaces. The recommended illumination level for laboratories is 50 fc (560 lux). Laboratory 1 has higher daylight levels than Laboratory 2 as a result of its higher WWR; it has adequate light levels even at the inside wall. Laboratory 1 also has a pronounced "hot spot" in the corner next to the full-height windows. Laboratory 2 has lower, but more uniform, daylight levels than Laboratory 1. At roughly halfway into the room, daylight levels fall below the recommended illumination level.

Figure 3-8 shows daylight levels for the two laboratory spaces on December 21. Daylight levels during the winter are significantly less than during the summer, due to lower exterior illumination levels during winter for this location. They drop below the recommended levels at 9 feet (approximately 3 meters) from the windows in Laboratory 1 and 6 feet (2 meters) in Laboratory 2.

The primary energy-related design objective of a daylighting system is to provide as much usable daylight as deep in a building's interior as possible. The secondary objective of daylighting is energy conservation. As a rule of thumb, the depth of the interior daylighting zone in a room is twice the height of the window. Sustainable strategies for improving natural light levels provide ways of increasing that depth without increasing the amount of glazing.

Light shelves have been successfully and economically used to expand the daylighting zone. *Light shelves* are horizontal fins mounted to the inside of the window framing, usually at least 80 inches above the floor to comply with building codes and accessibility requirements. During winter months, when the height of the sun is low, sunlight can pass above the light shelf to provide radiant warmth to the interior spaces. During summer months, when the sun is higher in the sky, the direct sunlight is blocked by the light shelf. However, the sunlight "bounces" off the top surface of the light shelf to hit the ceiling of the space, and then bounces again deep within the space, as shown in Figure 3-9. This effectively increases the daylighting zone using indirect light with minimal or no direct sunlight penetrating the building. A light shelf can be nothing more than a light-colored painted surface, or it can be more sophisticated. The top surface can be covered with prismatic aluminized films to increase reflectivity. The shelf can be shaped into compound geometries tailored for specific solar altitudes, or the shelf can be moveable and adjusted seasonally to provide the optimal patterns of reflected light. Sloped ceilings can further enhance the bounced indirect light effect.

Translucent glazing materials can be used to provide filtered, uniform, and glare-free daylight. By combining transparent vision glass at eye level with translucent glass above and below, designers can enhance the daylighting while giving occupants views to the outside.

DAYLIGHT AND GLARE 99

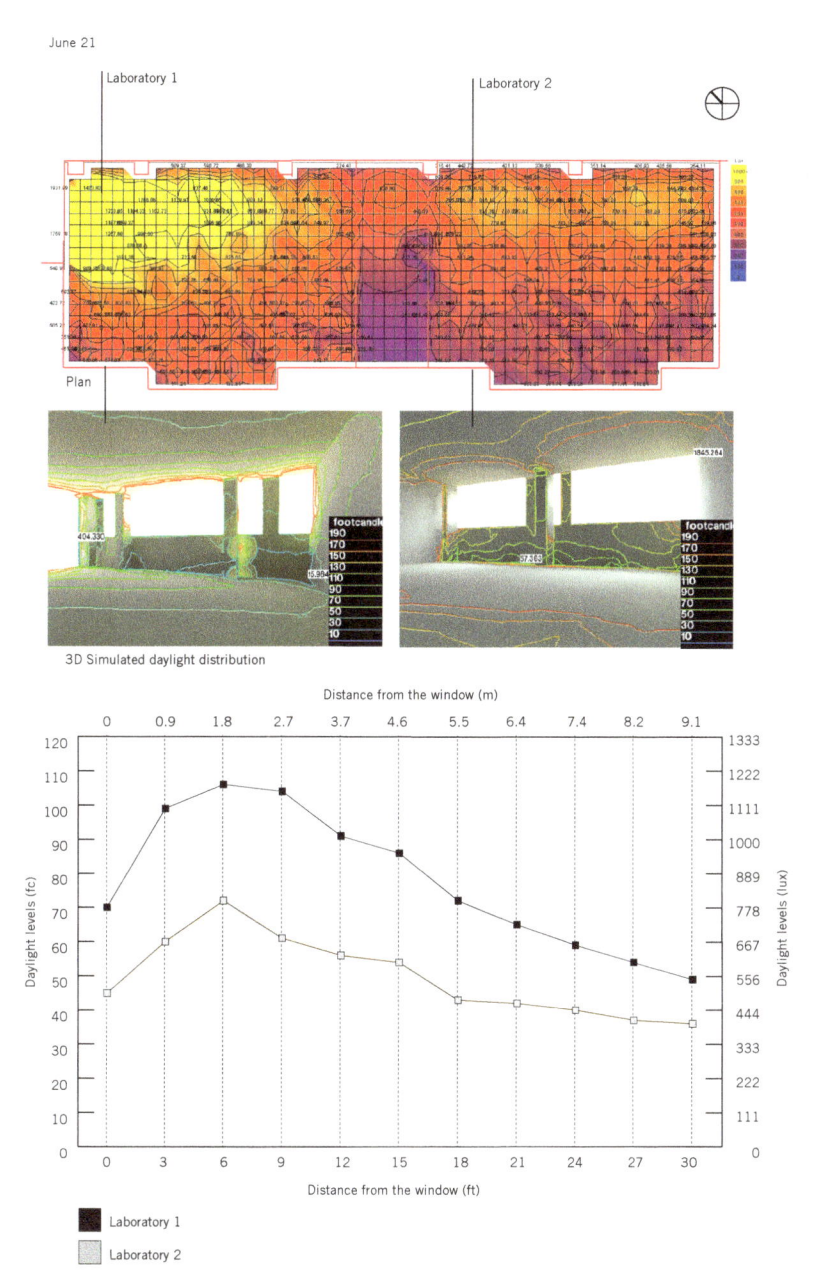

Figure 3-7 Daylight levels for two spaces on June 21 at 10:00 a.m.

100   DESIGNING FOR COMFORT

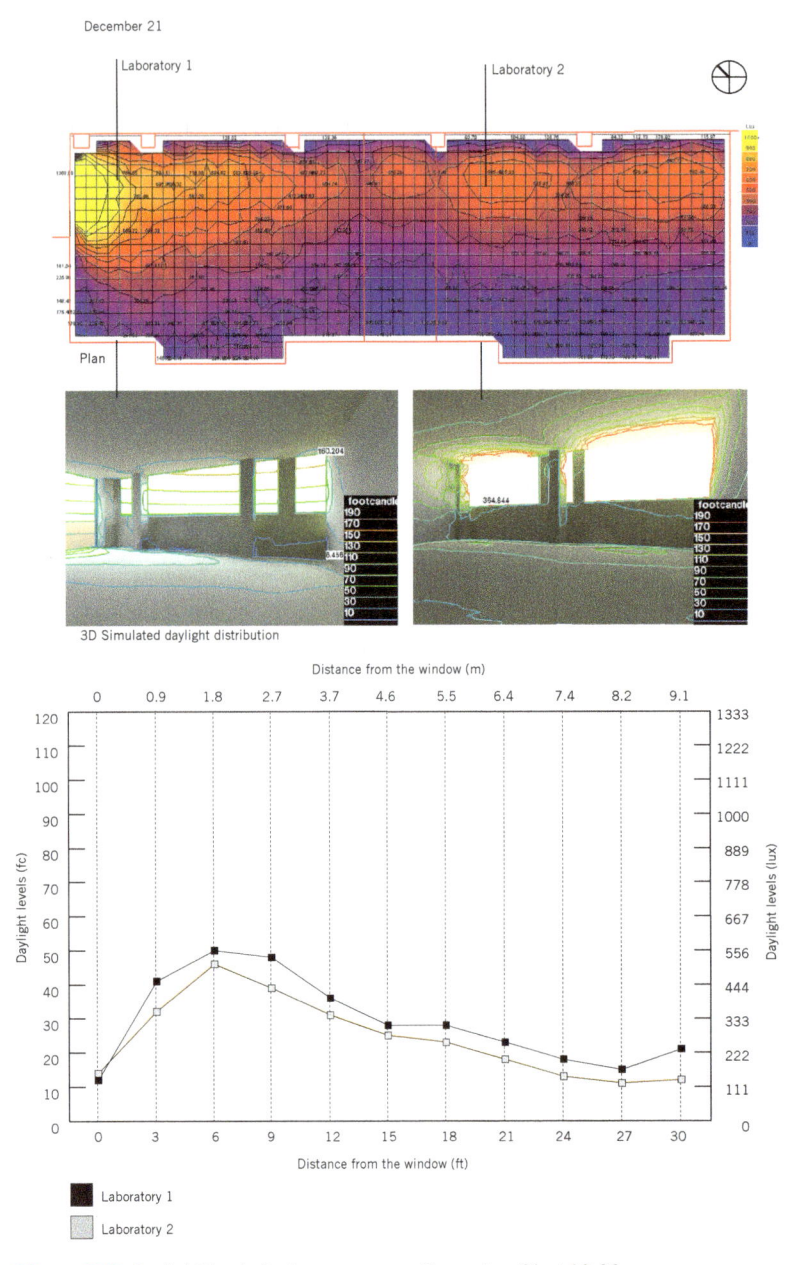

Figure 3-8 Daylight levels for two spaces on December 21 at 10:00 a.m.

DAYLIGHT AND GLARE 101

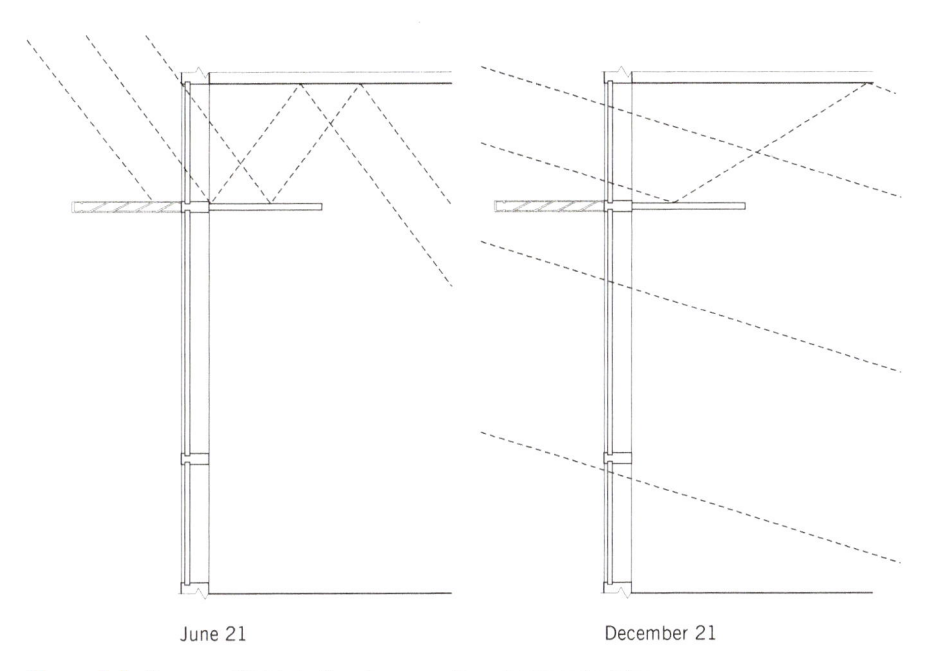

June 21 December 21

Figure 3-9 Diagram of light shelf performance in summer and winter.

Diffuse light guiding systems

Lightshelf Anidolic integrated system

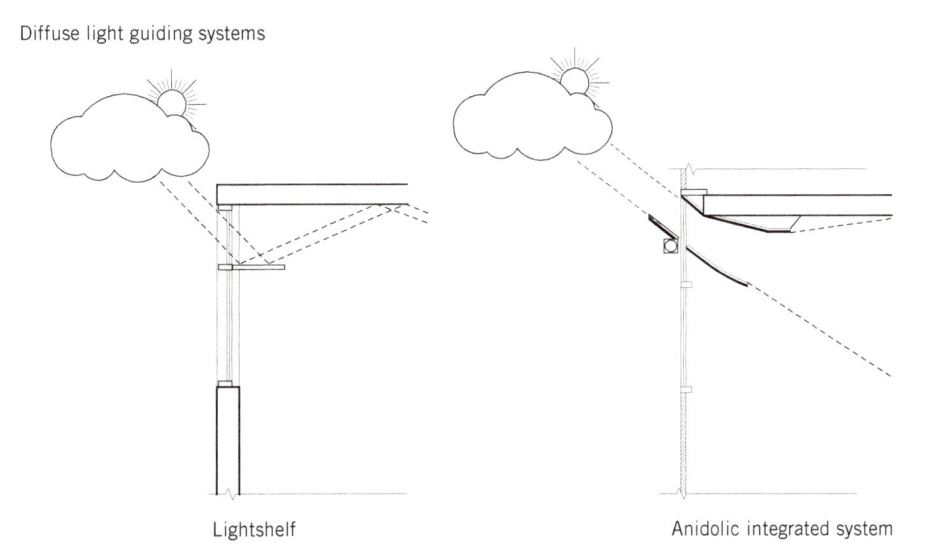

Figure 3-10 Diagram showing daylight facade strategies for locations with predominantly cloudy sky conditions (Adapted from Ruck et al., 2000).

A successful daylighting strategy depends on how much daylight reaches the building envelope. Locations with predominantly cloudy skies require different daylighting strategies from those with mostly clear skies. Figure 3-10 shows strategies that are effective in locations where cloudy skies predominate. Large windows located high and equipped with light shelves can be effective. Where clear skies predominate, strategies that control direct sunlight, such as reduction of window size and the use of shading elements, should be applied. Figure 3-11 shows effective strategies in these locations. Table 3-3 lists different strategies and their applicability for various sky conditions, climates, and design criteria.

Case study 3-1 illustrates how facade design options affect interior daylight levels, and how light shelves or other light-redirecting mechanisms can enhance the daylighting of interior spaces.

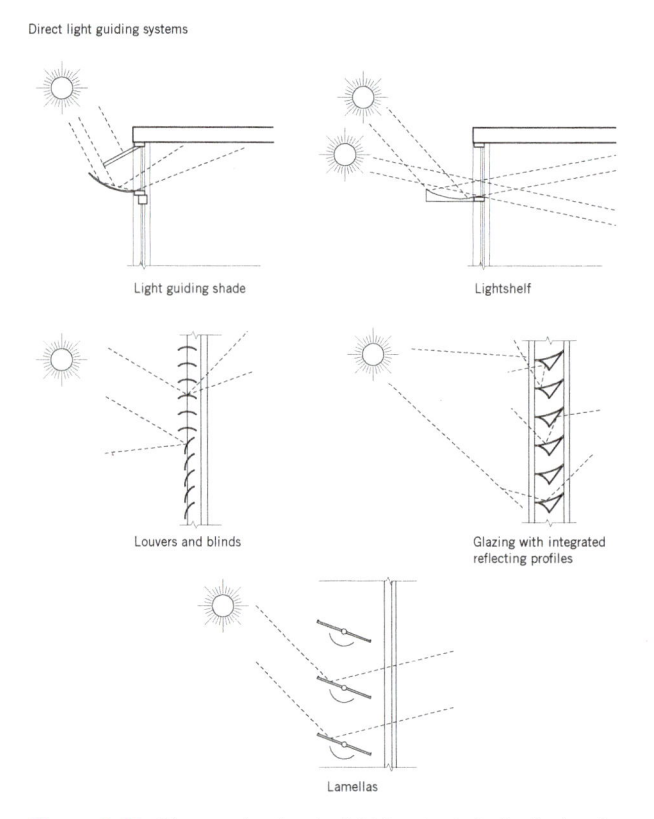

Figure 3-11 Diagram showing daylight facade strategies for locations with predominantly sunny sky conditions (Adapted from Ruck et al., 2000).

Table 3-3 Applicability of different daylight facade strategies.

Type	Strategy	Climate	Location of system	View to the outside	Light redirection into interior	Uniform illumination	Energy saving potential	Glare	Need for solar tracking
System for locations with predominately diffuse light	Light shelf	Temperate climates with cloudy skies	Windows above eye level	+	+	0	0	0	No
	Anidolic integrated systems	Temperate climates	Windows	+	+	+	+	−	No
System for locations with predominately direct sunlight	Light guiding shade	Hot and sunny	Windows above eye level	+	+	0	0	+	No
	Louvers and blinds	All climates	Windows	0	+	+	+	+	No
	Light shelf for redirecting light	All climates	Windows at eye level	+	+	+	+	0	No
	Glazing with reflecting profiles	Temperate climates	Windows	0	0	0	0	0	No
	Lamellas	Temperate climates	Windows	0	0	0	0	0	Yes

Legend: + Excellent   0 Average   − Poor

Source: Ruck et al., 2000.

The building is a hospital located in climate zone 4A (mixed, humid). The curtain wall design used for the south and southwest facades is shown in Figure 3-12. These facades enclose an interior public space that is used as a waiting area and a circulation corridor.

The curtain wall materials are low-e insulating vision glass, opaque spandrel glass, and low-e insulating fritted glass. An external horizontal shading element is attached to the curtain wall mullions above eye level. Figure 3-13 shows how the horizontal sunshade reduces incident solar radiation along the south facade. Because fritted glass reduces daylight due to its lower visual transmittance, several different daylighting strategies were investigated as a method to increase the daylight levels without increasing the amounts of incident solar radiation. The considered strategies included a light shelf, modified ceiling geometry, and variation in the placement of spandrel areas and fritted glass.

104   DESIGNING FOR COMFORT

1 Fritted glass
2 Horizontal shading device
3 Vision glass
4 Spandrel

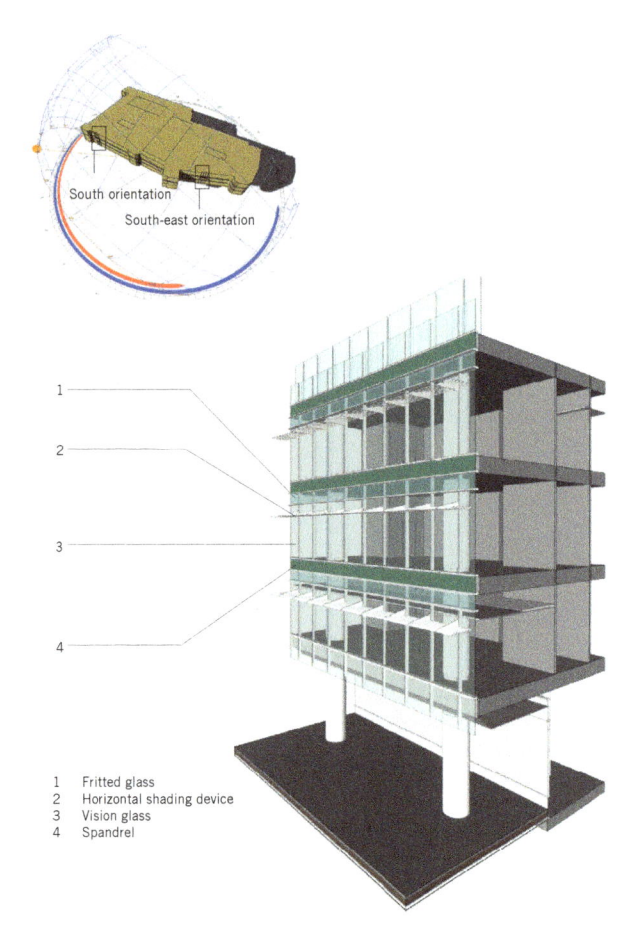

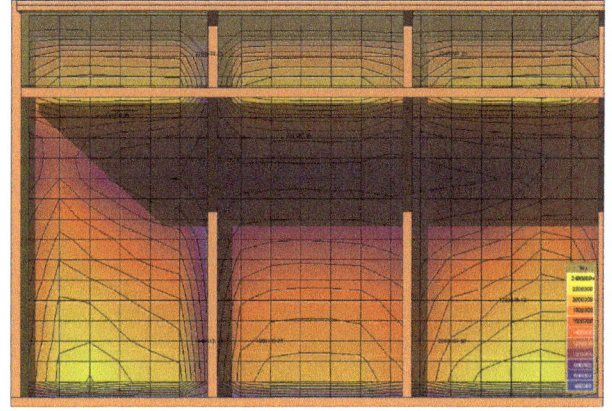

Figure 3-12 Facade design (south and southwest orientation).

Figure 3-13 Effects of horizontal shading device on incident solar radiation (south facade).

Three design scenarios were analyzed for their effects on daylighting (Figure 3-14). The constants in all three options are the floor-to-floor height, the depths of the mullion extrusions, the depth of the room, and the exterior horizontal sunshade. The characteristics of different scenarios are as follows:

- Option 1: Curtain wall with fritted glass at the upper portion of the facade, and the interior space with a level ceiling

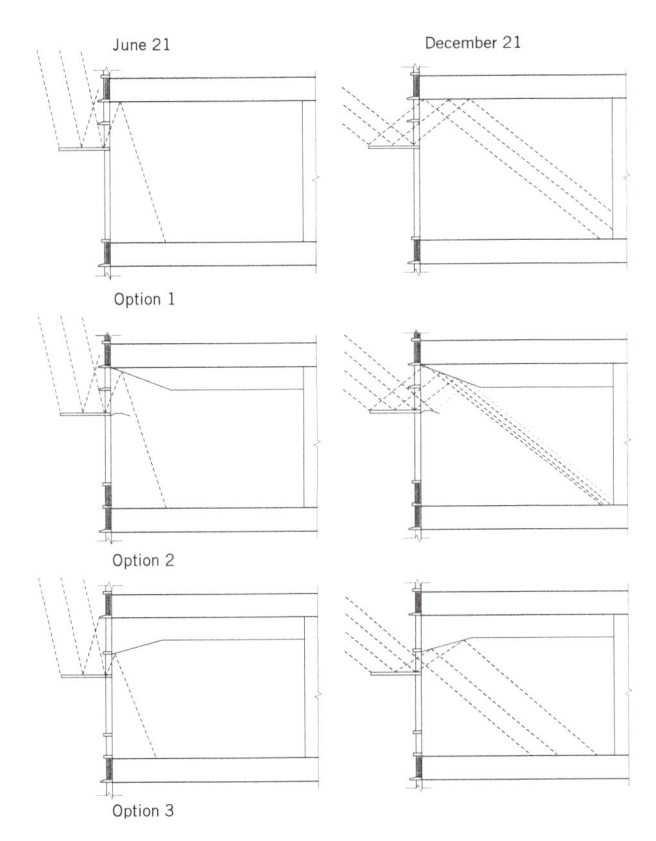

Figure 3-14 Diagrams of simulated options.

- Option 2: Curtain wall with a 1-foot (0.3-meter) deep interior aluminum light shelf, spandrel glass below sill height, and the interior space with a ceiling sloping down from the curtain wall into the interior space
- Option 3: Curtain wall with fritted glass near the floor finish, and the interior space with a ceiling sloping up from the curtain wall into the interior space

Summer and winter daylight levels were simulated and analyzed for these three options using the Radiance simulation program. The results for the south-oriented facade are shown in Figures 3-15 (summer conditions) and 3-16 (winter conditions). Figures 3-17 and 3-18 show results for the southeast-oriented facade.

106   DESIGNING FOR COMFORT

June 21
South facade

Option 1

Option 2

Option 3

Figure 3-15 Daylight levels during summer conditions for south-oriented facade (June 21, noon).

December 21
South facade

Option 1

Option 2

Option 3

Figure 3-16 Daylight levels during winter conditions for south-oriented facade (December 21, noon).

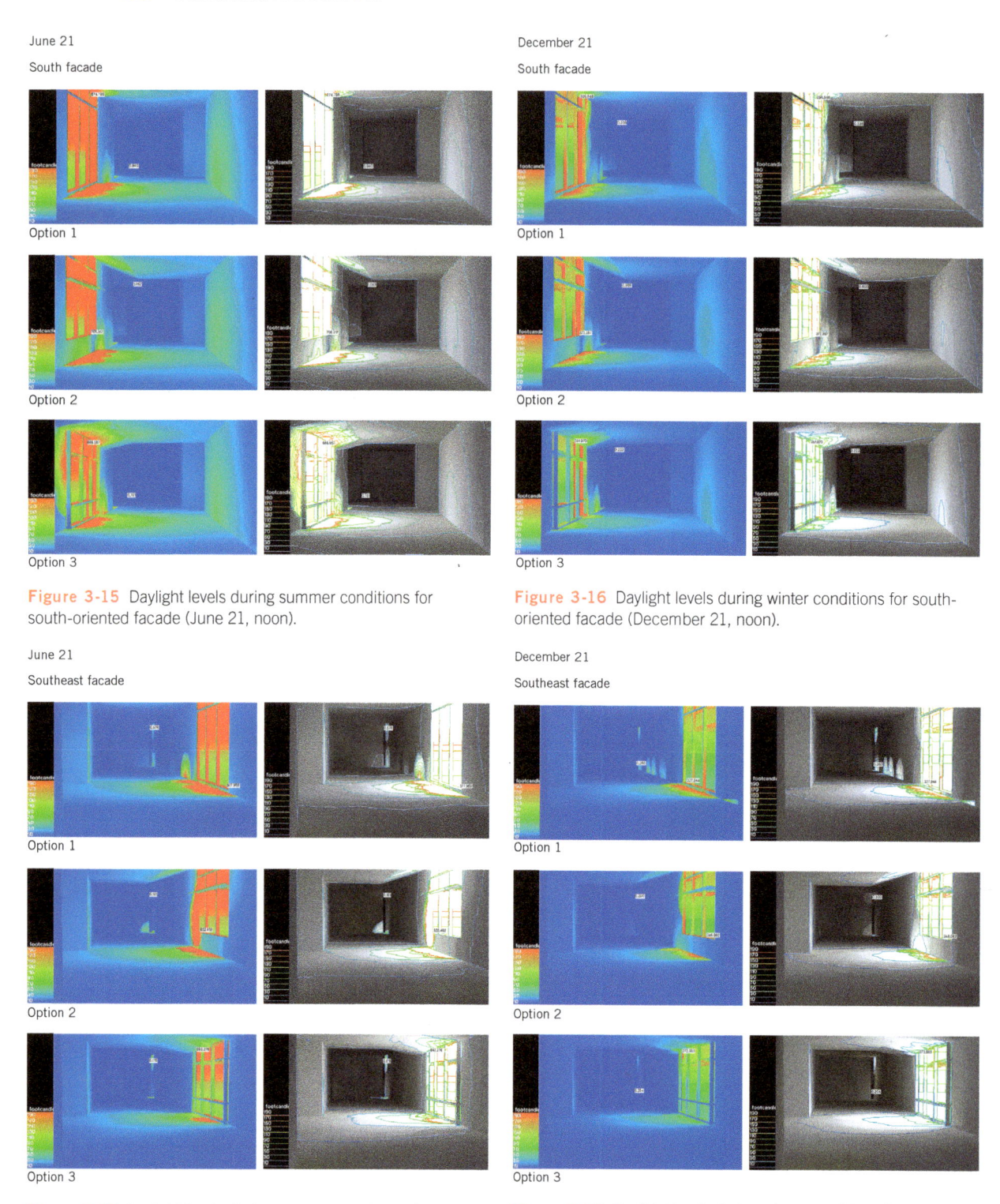

June 21
Southeast facade

Option 1

Option 2

Option 3

Figure 3-17 Daylight levels during summer conditions for southeast-oriented facade (June 21, noon).

December 21
Southeast facade

Option 1

Option 2

Option 3

Figure 3-18 Daylight levels during winter conditions for southeast-oriented facade (December 21, noon).

DAYLIGHT AND GLARE   107

The light shelf used in Option 2 and the sloped ceiling used for Option 3 both increase daylight levels compared to Option 1. Because Option 2 has a smaller vision area than Option 1, the light shelf and the ceiling sloping down from the curtain wall are good strategies for reducing solar heat gain without negatively affecting the available daylight in the interior space. Option 3, with a ceiling sloping up from the curtain wall and with fritted glass placed at the lower portion of the curtain wall, is also a good strategy for increasing the daylight levels, improving distribution of light, and reducing potentials for glare.

CASE STUDY 3.1 CENTERS FOR DISEASE CONTROL AND PREVENTION, NATIONAL CENTER FOR ENVIRONMENTAL HEALTH

The Environmental Health Laboratory Building at the Centers for Disease Control and Prevention is an example of balancing the aesthetic and environmental objectives of the facade design. It is located in Atlanta, Georgia (climate zone 3A). The building's program includes a variety of functions, including laboratories, offices, conference rooms, and circulation, each having its own daylighting needs. Each facade is designed to balance those needs with its orientation. As a result, there is considerable variation in the design of each facade (Figure 3-19).

Figure 3-19 Building facade enclosing (from left to right) laboratories, atrium, and offices.

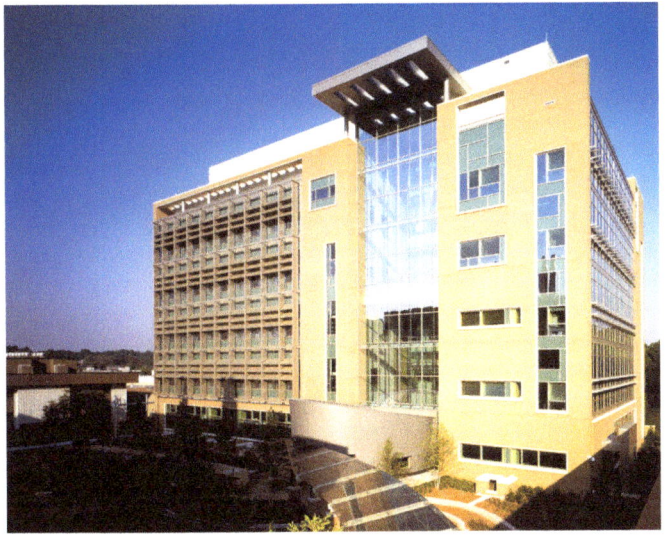

Courtesy of Nick Merick © Hedrich Blessing

A five-story atrium separates the laboratories and the offices. Sloped ceilings in the open laboratories bounce daylight deep into the interior spaces, as shown in Figures 3-20 and 3-21. The facade uses exterior vertical shades and horizontal louvers to control solar heat gain and glare.

108 DESIGNING FOR COMFORT

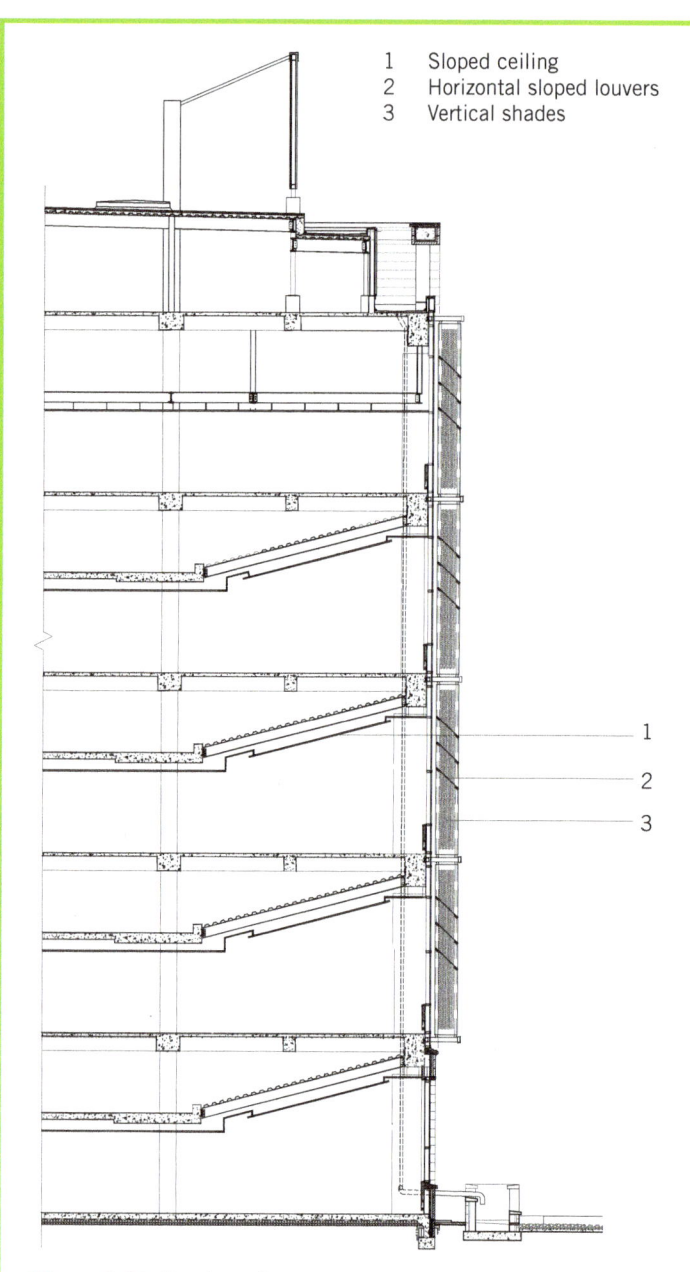

1 Sloped ceiling
2 Horizontal sloped louvers
3 Vertical shades

Figure 3-20 Exterior wall section.

Figure 3-21 Sloped lab ceiling as a method to increase daylight levels.

Glare

Glare is caused when there are areas of relatively intense brightness compared with other darker areas within the field of view. Glare, like thermal comfort, is a subjective physiological response, but it can cause visual discomfort to occupants. It can also impair people's performance. The human eye can function well across a wide range of illumination levels, but not if an area of extreme brightness is present in the field of view. Good daylighting design controls glare while providing sufficient light for visual performance.

Two methods for measuring glare are the Unified Glare Rating (UGR), developed by the International Commission on Illumination (CIE), and Visual Comfort Probability (VCP), developed by the Illuminating Engineering Society of North America. Both have been developed primarily for artificial lighting rather than for daylighting, but are used in computer simulation programs for glare analysis. UGR and VCP can be predicted using the daylighting simulation software Radiance.

The UGR identifies visual discomfort, and is calculated by a formula that takes into account the position and brightness of each potential glare source, as well as the position of the viewer and angle of sight. CIE has the following recommendations for acceptable ranges (CIE, 1995):

Comfort zone:

- Imperceptible: < 10
- Just perceptible: 13
- Perceptible: 16
- Just acceptable: 19

Discomfort zone:

- Unacceptable: 22
- Just uncomfortable: 25
- Uncomfortable: > 28

VCP is an estimate of the percentage of people who would feel comfortable in a given visual environment. For example, a VCP value of 75 indicates that 75% of the occupants would be satisfied with their visual environment. It is based on an empirical prediction assessment, and considers the number of lighting sources and their locations, the background luminance, the room size and shape, the surface reflectance of materials, the illuminance levels, the observer's location and line of sight, and the differences in glare sensitivity for different individuals.

Methods for controlling glare start with the proper sizing of windows, as large areas of glass often result in uncontrolled brightness and unwanted glare. However, small punched openings in otherwise opaque walls can create contrasting bright spots that are uncomfortable to look at. Translucent, light-diffusing glass can be effective in reducing glare. Light shelves, light monitors, and other methods for redirecting daylight can also help reduce glare.

To show the relationship between available daylight, room dimensions, orientation, neighboring buildings, and glare, we use the following case study (Figures 3-22 to 3-25). Figure 3-22 shows two laboratory spaces along the southwest facade of a building. Both laboratories have small, equally spaced punched windows with interior light shelves. In plan, both spaces are deep and narrow. Recommended illuminance levels for these types of spaces are between 60 and 150 fc (667 and 1667 lux).

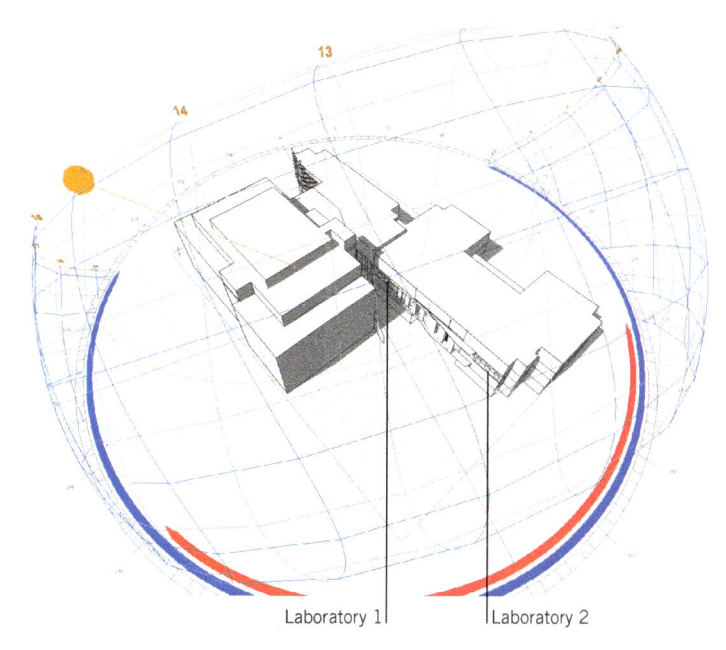

Figure 3-22 Location of laboratories.

First, we determine the daylight levels in the two spaces. Figure 3-23 shows simulated daylight levels on June 21 at 2:00 p.m. Because both spaces are approximately the same size, face the same direction, and have similar window configurations, it would be expected that these spaces would have similar daylighting patterns. However, an adjacent building partially blocks sunlight from reaching the facade of Laboratory 1, seen in Figure 3-22. Therefore, the daylight levels in this space are less than those in Laboratory 2, and never quite reach the recommended light levels. Laboratory 2 has much higher daylight levels near the windows, but has a significant drop-off as the distance from the windows increases; daylight falls below recommended light levels at around 9 feet (2.7 meters).

Figure 3-24 shows daylight levels for both laboratories on December 21 at 2:00 p.m. Laboratory 1 has usable daylight up to 3 feet (0.9 meter) from the windows, while Laboratory 2 has usable daylight up to around 6 feet (1.8 meters) from the windows.

What are the effects of glare? High contrasts in light levels between windows and opaque surfaces can cause glare, and Figure 3-25 shows the interior views used to calculate UGR and VCP ratings. Calculations were performed for 2:00 p.m. and 5:00 p.m. on June 21, and for 2:00 p.m. on December 21. Results are shown in Table 3-4.

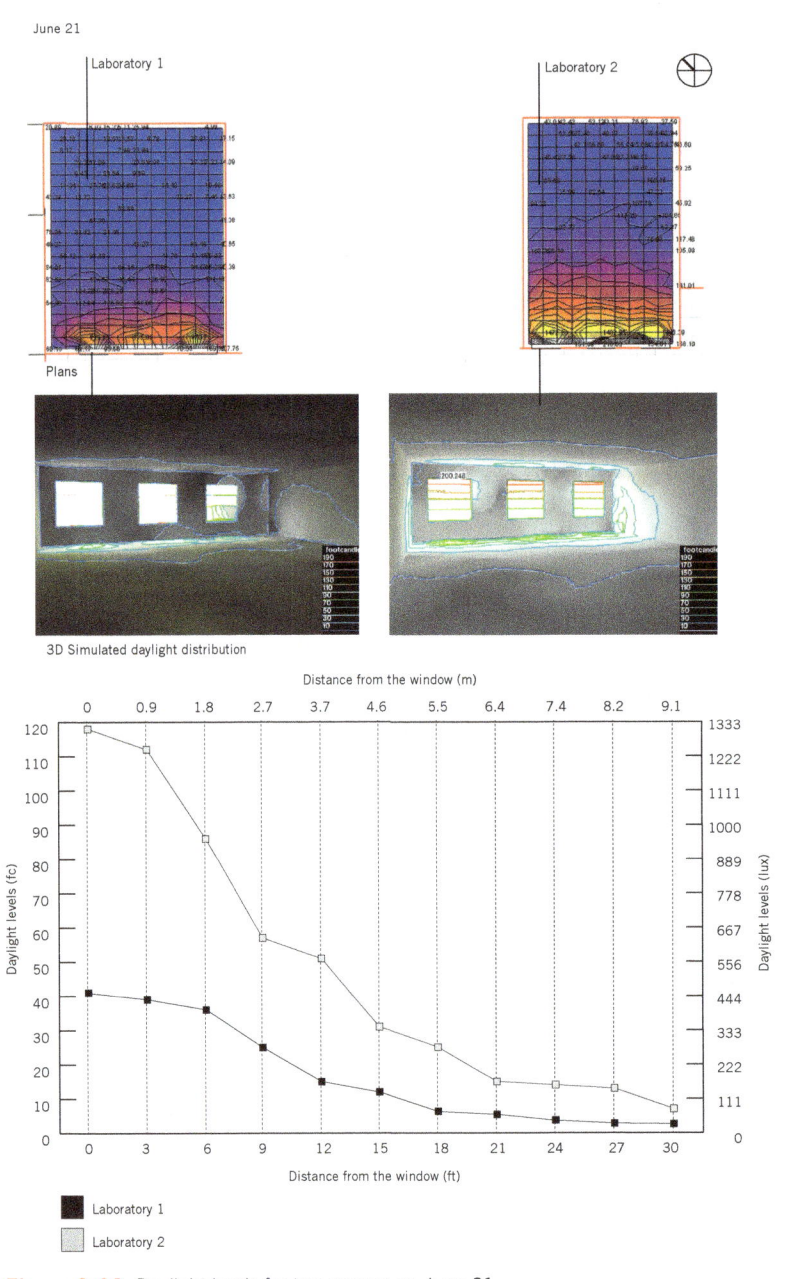

Figure 3-23 Daylight levels for two spaces on June 21.

DAYLIGHT AND GLARE   113

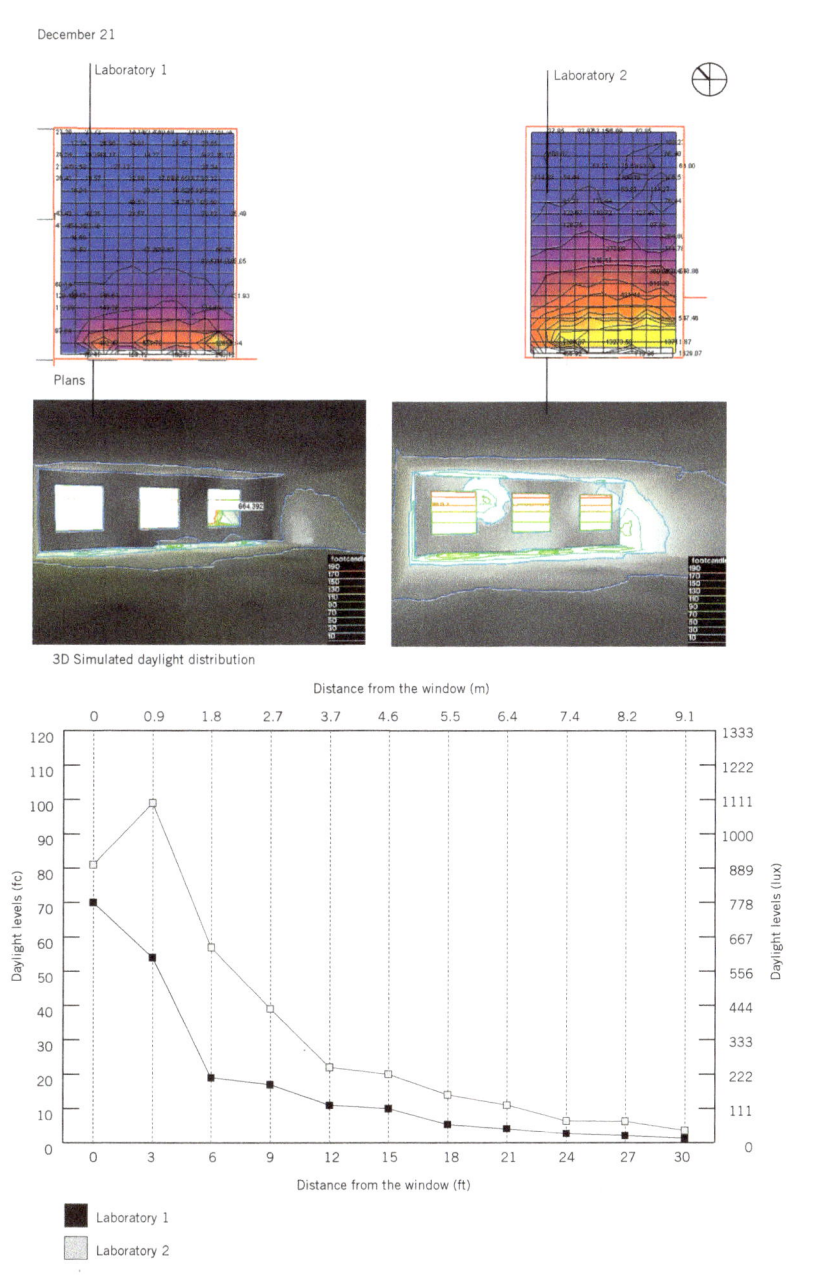

Figure 3-24 Daylight levels for two spaces on December 21.

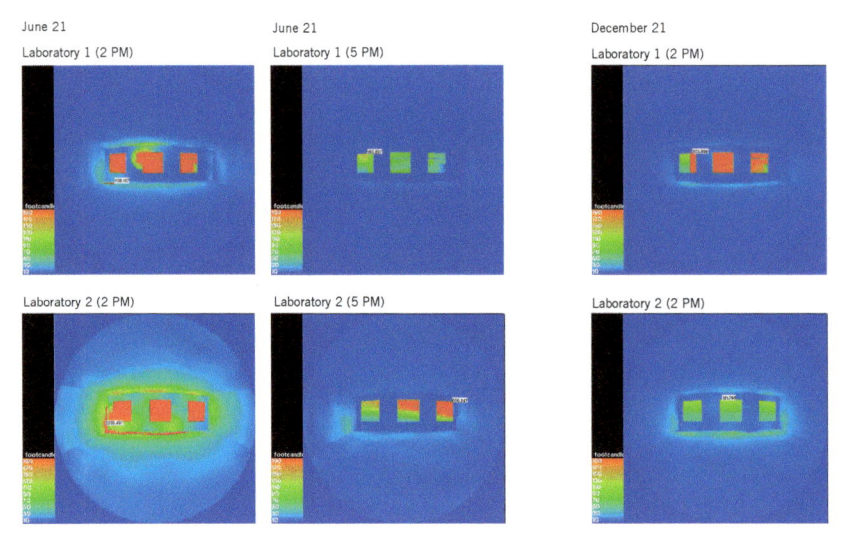

Figure 3-25 Fish-eye perspective of the interior spaces used to determine glare potential.

Table 3-4 Glare indices for the two spaces shown in Figure 3-25.

	Laboratory 1			Laboratory 2		
Glare	June 21 (2:00 p.m.)	June 21 (5:00 p.m.)	December 21 (2:00 p.m.)	June 21 (2:00 p.m.)	June 21 (5:00 p.m.)	December 21 (2:00 p.m.)
UGR index	27.5	22.8	26.9	23.3	23.5	15.4
VCP index	9.3	35.3	11.6	12.8	21.1	66.4

The glare analysis shows that occupants in both of these spaces would find the glare uncomfortable at certain times. The deep, narrow geometry of the rooms and the small sizes of the windows relative to the opaque walls contribute to this. On June 21 at 2:00 p.m., Laboratory 1, with a UGR of 27.5, is near the uncomfortable end of the discomfort zone. Only 9.3% of occupants would be satisfied with the visual conditions. Visual conditions improve slightly during the late afternoon hours, with the UGR decreasing to a still-unacceptable 22.8. The VCP index indicates that less than half of the occupants (35.3%) would be satisfied with the visual conditions. The UGR for Laboratory 2 at the same date and time is 23.3, which falls within the discomfort zone. This is confirmed by a VCP index of 13%, indicating that few of the occupants would be satisfied.

The glare analysis for the winter months tells a different story. Laboratory 1's UGR for December 21 at 2:00 p.m. is 26.9, still deep in the discomfort zone. The VCP tells us that less than 12% of the occupants will be satisfied with the visual conditions. In contrast, Laboratory 2 shows considerable improvement. With a UGR of 15.4, the space is well within the comfort zone, with a noticeable but acceptable level of glare. The VCP index of 66.4% shows that roughly two-thirds of the occupants would be satisfied with the visual conditions.

Why the big difference between the two spaces in winter? Quite simply, a neighboring building blocks sunlight from Laboratory 1. In the summer months, the sun is high enough for sunlight to pass over the obstruction and reach the Laboratory 1 windows. In the winter, however, the obstruction blocks most of the lower-angle sunlight. Were it not for the obstruction, Laboratory 1's winter daylighting and glare levels would probably be similar to those of Laboratory 2.

This case study illustrates how room geometry, window size and orientation, exterior obstructions, and seasonal changes affect daylighting and the potential for glare.

ACOUSTIC COMFORT AND AIR QUALITY

Acoustics

Good acoustic design should attenuate unwanted noise and enhance desired sounds. External sources of noise, such as traffic, factories, and airline flight paths, can affect occupants' acoustic comfort. However, not all noise is undesirable. People unconsciously use ambient sounds to orient themselves within a building, to help make themselves aware of the time of day, and to provide "white" background noise for speech privacy (Reffat and Harkness, 2001). Therefore, they prefer interior environments that are relatively quiet, but not absolutely free of ambient sounds. The normal acoustic environment of an occupied space is a combination of sounds from multiple sources, such as air diffusers, equipment (refrigerators, computers, telephones, etc.), music, voices (from within the space or from adjacent spaces), and the external environment. As long as those sounds do not become obtrusive, and the occupants are not consciously aware of them, the ambient sounds may be acceptable.

There are a number of established methods for evaluating the acoustic quality of an interior space. These are shown in Table 3-5. Each method evaluates a different aspect of acoustic performance, and not all of them are relevant to facade design.

Table 3-5 Acoustic comfort factors for interior spaces.

Acoustic comfort factors	Description	Metric
Background (ambient) noise level	Amount of noise generally distributed within the interior space	dB
Noise criteria	Relative loudness of a space	NC levels
Sound transmission class for walls, partitions, floors	Ability of wall, partition, or floor assembly to block airborne sound	STC

Acoustic comfort factors	Description	Metric
Impact insulation class rating for floors and ceiling assemblies	Ability of floors or ceilings to block impact sounds traveling through the structure	IIC
Outdoor-indoor transmission class	Ability of exterior enclosure assemblies to block airborne sound	OITC
Noise reduction coefficient	Sound-absorption efficiency rating for different materials	NRC

The sound transmission class (STC) rating system is one way to represent the acoustic experience of an occupant in a room. Partition and floor assemblies are tested to determine their STC ratings. STC is a measure of acoustic performance for a range of frequencies (125 to 4,000 Hz) that encompass most everyday interior sounds, particularly human speech. The International Building Code specifies that walls, partitions, and floor and ceiling assemblies between dwellings, and between dwellings and public spaces, should have an STC rating of 50 or more for airborne sound (ICC, 2012). Impact insulation class (IIC) rating is similar to STC; however, it represents the transmission of impact sounds through the structure, particularly floors or ceilings.

The STC rating system was introduced in 1970, and has become the standard tool for the acoustic design of interior partitions and floor assemblies. However, because the system is based on the mid- and high-frequency sounds associated with human speech and normal household activities, it has proven inadequate for low-frequency exterior sounds. ASTM, in its E413 standards that govern STC ratings, states that the STC classification method is not appropriate for some sound sources, such as motor vehicles, aircraft, and trains (ASTM, 2010).

Another method for evaluating the acoustic performance of constructed assemblies, the Outdoor-Indoor Transmission Class (OITC), was introduced in 1990 specifically for normal exterior sounds—particularly those generated by an aircraft taking off, a nearby railroad, or a busy freeway (i.e., planes, trains, and automobiles). The OITC's range of frequencies, from 80 to 4,000 Hz, includes all the STC frequencies, as well as lower frequencies. Like the STC ratings, the OITC system uses a single number to rate the acoustic performance of a product or an assembly of materials. For both STC and OITC, the higher the number, the better a product or assembly will perform acoustically.

Calculations to determine OITC ratings must be based on carefully controlled laboratory or field tests of a product or assembly. Many manufacturers of standard windows, doors, curtain walls, insulation, and joint seals provide OITC ratings for their products. However, custom systems and assemblies often must be tested, either in an acoustic testing facility or in the field, to determine their OITC ratings.

For high-performance facades, ASHRAE recommends a composite OITC of at least 40. Fenestration areas should have an OITC rating of at least 30 (ASHRAE, 2009).

Designers can follow these general principles to improve the acoustic performance of a facade:

- Increase the mass of the materials. In general, the more massive a material is, the higher the sound transmission loss will be.
- Match the resonant frequency of the materials to the predominant sound waves. When the frequency of the sound waves matches the resonant frequency of the materials, energy is absorbed, resulting in higher sound transmission loss.
- Increase the width of air spaces.
- Provide acoustic breaks. Similar to thermal bridges, solid materials that bridge across air spaces will help sound waves pass through a wall. Acoustic breaks will hamper sound transmission.
- Fill air spaces in opaque walls with insulation materials with desired thermal and acoustic performance ratings.
- Use layers of different materials. This will create discontinuities in the wall, making it more difficult for sound waves to move from one material to the next.
- Finally, and perhaps most basically, seal air leaks in the wall assembly. Air leaks give sound waves a continuous path through a single medium (air) from the outside to the inside.

Some of these principles apply only to opaque walls. For glazed facades, designers have other strategies available for improving acoustic performance:

- Thicker glass will increase the mass that the sound waves have to pass through. However, unless unusually thick glass is required for other reasons (ballistic resistance, for instance), this approach is not an economical way to significantly improve acoustic performance. Increasing the thickness of the glass from ¼ inch to ½ inch will increase the OITC from 29 to 33, and the STC from 31 to 36.
- Laminated glass will improve the acoustic performance of single-glazed windows. The laminated inner layer creates a discontinuity of materials that dampens the sound vibrations. A nominal ¼-inch lite of laminated glass, consisting of two layers of ⅛-inch glass and a 0.060-inch-thick laminate interlayer, will have an OITC of 32 and an STC of 35.
- Standard air-filled insulating glass units will perform better than most single-glazed windows (1-inch-thick insulating unit with ½-inch air space will have an OITC of 26–28 and an STC of 31–33).
- Using laminated glass for one or both lites in a 1-inch-thick, air-filled insulating unit will further increase its acoustic performance. With one lite of ¼-inch laminated glass, the OITC of the insulating unit increases to 28–30, and the STC increases to 34–36. When both lites are ¼-inch laminated glass, the OITC and STC increase to 29–31 and 37–39, respectively.

- Triple-glazed insulating units, with the middle lite being either glass or a laminate membrane, will further enhance the acoustic performance.
- When the insulating unit is constructed with a "soft" separation between the lites of glass, the acoustic performance will be improved.
- Adding a secondary interior lite of glass, separated from the outer insulating unit by a substantial air space, will result in still better acoustic performance. An assembly consisting of a standard 1-inch insulating unit, a 2-inch air space, and an inner lite of 1/4-inch glass will have an OITC of 32–35 and an STC of 42–44. When laminated glass is used for one lite of the insulating unit and for the single interior lite, the OTC is 35–37 and the STC is 44–46.

Most of these measures to improve a facade's acoustic performance will also improve its thermal performance.

With buildings that use natural ventilation to reduce energy consumption, we can expect more sound to pass through the exterior walls than if the walls were fully sealed. For naturally ventilated buildings, higher indoor noise levels should be allowed (Field, 2008). Research indicates that internal noise levels of up to 65 dB (equivalent to normal conversation 3 feet away) may be acceptable (Ghiaus and Allard, 2005). Calculations can predict the amount of exterior noise that passes through the building facade, including noise coming from openings for natural ventilation. If the predictions show that acceptable acoustic comfort will not be met, attenuating elements, such as acoustic louvers and white noise generators, can be incorporated into the design (De Salis et al., 2002).

Emerging facade technologies, such as double-skin glass facades, can improve the acoustic performance of an exterior wall. For a detailed discussion of double-skin facades, see Chapter 4.

Air Quality

Acceptable *indoor air quality* (IAQ) is defined as indoor air that has no contaminants at harmful concentrations and that satisfies at least 80% of the occupants (ASHRAE, 2007).

IAQ affects the health and comfort of building occupants, and is an integral design element for sustainable, high-performance buildings. The sources of unacceptable air quality include microbial contaminants (such as mold and bacteria), gases (including carbon monoxide, radon, and volatile organic compounds), and particulates and other air pollutants, all of which can affect occupants' health. Acceptable IAQ is dependent on many building systems, such as HVAC systems, air-mixing techniques, interior finish materials, and building operations. However, because air infiltration and leakage through the building envelope can affect IAQ, it must be considered when designing the facade.

Air infiltration occurs when the exterior air enters through cracks in the facade. The amount of infiltration will depend on the air pressures across the facade. This can be mitigated by sealing openings and providing air barriers within the assembly. Well-designed and correctly installed air barriers will prevent the movement of air through the exterior wall assembly. Air barriers control the airflow between unconditioned and conditioned spaces, and are intended to resist air-pressure differences, stack effect, and wind loads. They should be impermeable to airflow, and must be continuous over the entire building envelope to be effective in blocking air movement. Air barriers keep airborne pollutants from reaching interior spaces. No exterior wall, however, can ever be designed or constructed to be completely airtight. Some incidental leakage is expected; performance specifications for exterior wall assemblies should specify a maximum allowable air infiltration that is consistent with industry standards.

CHAPTER SUMMARY

In this chapter, we discussed how occupants' comfort should be one of the criteria when designing sustainable, high-performance facades. The objective for any sustainable facade is to provide occupants with thermal, visual, and acoustic comfort while using the least possible energy. Therefore, understanding the principles involved, the methods of measurement, and the available design strategies becomes crucial during the design process.

REFERENCES

Arens, E., Zhang, H., and Huizenga, C. (2006). "Partial- and Whole-body Thermal Sensation and Comfort, Part I: Uniform Environmental Conditions." *Journal of Thermal Biology,* Vol. 31, No. 1–2, pp. 53–59.

ASHRAE. (2004). *ASHRAE Standard 55-2004 Thermal Environmental Conditions for Human Occupancy.* Atlanta, GA: American Society of Heating, Refrigerating, and Air-Conditioning Engineers.

ASHRAE. (2007). *ANSI/ASHRAE Standard 62-1-2007 Ventilation for Acceptable Indoor Air Quality.* Atlanta, GA: American Society of Heating, Refrigerating, and Air-Conditioning Engineers.

ASHRAE. (2009). *ANSI/ASHARE/USGBC/IES Standard 189.1 for the Design of High-Performance Green Buildings.* Atlanta, GA: American Society of Heating, Refrigerating, and Air-Conditioning Engineers.

ASTM. (2010). *ASTM E 412-10 Classification for Rating Sound Insulation.* West Conshohocken, PA: ASTM International.

CIE. (1995). *CIE 117-1995 Discomfort Glare in Interior Lighting.* Vienna, Austria: International Commission on Illumination.

De Salis, M., Oldham, D., and Sharples, S. (2002). "Noise Control Strategies for Naturally Ventilated Buildings." *Building and Environment,* Vol. 37, No. 5, pp. 471–484.

Edwards, L., and Torcellini, P. (2002). *A Literature Review of the Effects of Natural Light on Building Occupants* (NREL/TP-550-30769). Golden, CO: National Renewable Energy Laboratory.

Field, C. (2008). "Acoustic Design in Green Buildings." *ASHRAE Journal,* Vol. 50, No. 9, pp. 60–70.

Ghiaus, C., and Allard, F., eds. (2005). *Natural Ventilation in the Urban Environment: Assessment and Design.* London, UK: Earthscan.

Huizenga, C., Hui, Z., and Arens, W. (2001). "A Model of Human Physiology and Comfort for Assessing Complex Thermal Environments." *Building and Environment,* Vol. 36, pp. 691–699.

Huizenga, C., Zhang, H., Mattelaer, P., Yu, T., Arens, E., and Lyons, P. (2006). *Window Performance for Human Thermal Comfort* (Final Report to the NFRC). Berkeley, CA: Center for the Built Environment, University of California.

ICC. (2012). *2012 International Building Code.* Country Club Hills, IL: International Code Council.

IESNA. (2011). *IESNA Lighting Handbook,* 10th ed. New York, NY: Illuminating Engineering Society of North America.

Liberman, J. (1991). *Light Medicine of the Future.* Santa Fe, NM: Bear & Co.

Reffat, R., and Harkness, E. (2001). "Environmental Comfort Criteria: Weighting and Integration." *Journal of Performance of Constructed Facilities*, Vol. 15, No. 3, pp. 104–108.

Ruck, N., Aschehoug, O., Aydinli, S., Christoffersen, J., Courret, G., Edmonds, I., Jakobiak, R., Kischkoweit-Lopin, M., Klinger, M., Lee, E., Michel, L., Scartezzini, J., and Selkowitz, S. (2000). *Daylight in Buildings: A Source Book on Daylighting Systems and Components.* Berkeley, CA: Lawrence Berkeley National Laboratory and International Energy Agency (IEA) Solar Heating and Cooling Programme and Energy Conservation in Buildings & Community Systems Programme.

CHAPTER 4

EMERGING TECHNOLOGIES IN FACADE DESIGNS

Since the middle of the nineteenth century, innovation in building forms and functions has relied on advances in building science, materials, and technology. New or improved building materials have offered great opportunities for innovation in architectural expression and design. Advances in metallurgy have allowed steel and aluminum to be economical options for building facades. Raised floors for ventilation and wiring, originally developed for computer rooms and other equipment-oriented spaces, are now commonly used in a variety of occupancies. The combination of lighter-weight materials, new technology, and an ever-increasing emphasis on balancing low construction costs with high performance has led to the development of the exterior curtain wall as one of the most efficient and affordable cladding solutions.

Recent developments in facade technology are following three general trends. The first is in small-scale methods: coatings, thin films, advanced glazing technologies, and advanced materials developed to improve facade performance at the micro level. The second is toward large-scale innovations, such as double-skin facades. The third trend is the increased integration of energy-generation components into the building skin. With each of these trends, the functional performance goals are the same: separating the indoor and outdoor environments, mitigating adverse external environmental effects, and maintaining internal occupant comfort conditions with minimum energy consumption. In this chapter, we look at some of these new and emerging technologies that are available or under development.

EMERGING MATERIALS AND TECHNOLOGIES

Advanced Facade Materials

ETFE (ethylene tetrafluoroethylene) is a Teflon®-coated fluoropolymer material blown or extruded to form large, durable sheets. ETFE is resistant to degradation by ultraviolet (UV) light and atmospheric pollution. To address different use conditions, it can be manufactured as single-ply sheets or double- or triple-ply air-filled "pillows." ETFE is low-maintenance, recyclable, and, when compared to glass, extremely lightweight. In itself, as a single-sheet material, ETFE has very poor thermal and acoustic performance and should not be used in facade applications. However, in the double- and triple-ply configurations it has excellent thermal properties, because the air trapped between the layers acts as an insulator. The air-filled pillows are maintained at constant air pressures relative to wind loads by pumps, letting the skin adjust in response to the varying loads. ETFE is not a fabric and cannot be used as a self-supporting tensile structure. Instead, the pressurized air holds the pillows intact. A secondary structure, usually consisting of aluminum extrusions, steel rods, or steel cables, is needed to support the pillows. Figure 4-1 shows triple-ply air-filled ETFE pillows with a supporting structure.

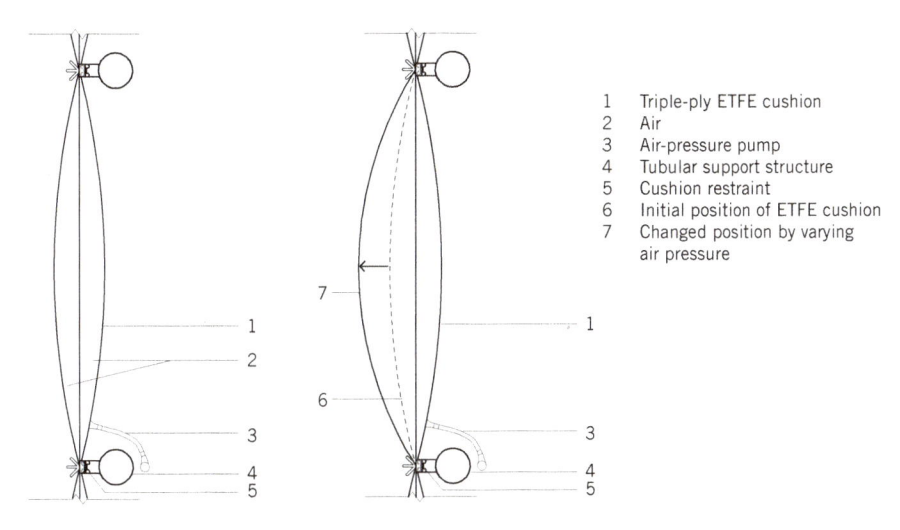

Figure 4-1 Diagram of triple-ply ETFE cushion, supported by tubular extrusions, and changing position of exterior ply by varying air pressure.

1. Triple-ply ETFE cushion
2. Air
3. Air-pressure pump
4. Tubular support structure
5. Cushion restraint
6. Initial position of ETFE cushion
7. Changed position by varying air pressure

ETFE is a combustible material; however, it is inherently low in flammability because of the presence of fluorine in its chemical composition. This makes the ETFE material self-extinguishing. Because it is normally in tension, ETFE softens and ultimately fails at temperatures above 390°F (200°C) (LeCuyer, 2008).

ETFE does not block exterior sound well, as it is composed of very thin membranes. Impact noise, such as heavy rain striking the surface, is transferred to the interior. For some building occupancies, such as recreational facilities, pools, or atriums, this may not be a problem. However, in libraries, museums, and other spaces where acoustics are important, this can be a concern. Nets or meshes placed over the external surface of ETFE cushions can be used to acoustically dampen the impact sounds.

ETFE is typically manufactured as a transparent material to admit light into interior spaces. To reduce solar heat gain, opaque frit (as dots, stripes, or other patterns) can be printed on the membranes. The denser the frit pattern, the greater the shading provided by the ETFE. By applying carefully aligned patterns on the exterior and the intermediate membranes of a three-ply system, and by varying the internal air pressures within the pillows, varying amounts of shading can be achieved. Figure 4-2 shows how this works. The right-hand diagram shows the pillow configuration during sunny conditions. The air pressure of the inner pillow chamber is much greater than that of the outer chamber, so the intermediate membrane almost touches the exterior membrane. The opaque patterns are aligned so that in this configuration, most of the sunlight is blocked. In the left-hand diagram, when the sunlight is not intense (e.g., overcast or partly cloudy days), the air pressures of the inner and outer chambers are adjusted to pull the intermediate membrane away from the exterior membrane, allowing daylight to pass through the patterns of opaque coating and enter the interior spaces.

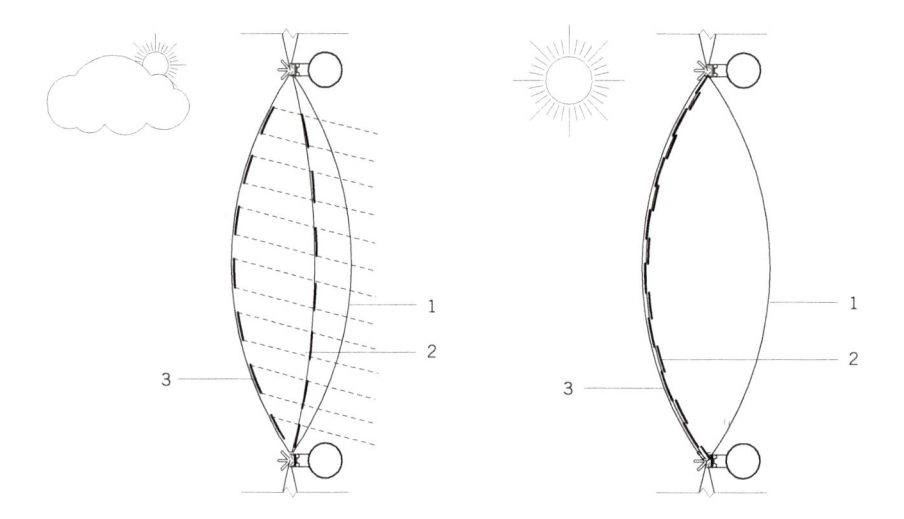

1   Interior membrane of triple-ply ETFE cushion
2   Intermediate membrane with frit pattern
3   Exterior membrane of triple-ply ETFE cushion with frit pattern

Figure 4-2 Diagram showing varying shading patterns achieved by changing air pressure in ETFE triple-ply membranes with printed opaque patterns.

Aerogels are synthetic solids that consist almost entirely of air. They have the lowest density among all known solids. Because of their low density, aerogels have extremely low thermal conductivity, and thus are ideal for applications where high thermal insulation is needed. Commercial glazing products using aerogel inserts are currently available. In some of these products, the aerogel is integrated with polycarbonate sheets to form a translucent cladding material. In others, silica aerogel in granular form fills the spaces between the glass lites of insulating units (Figure 4-3) or within the cavities of channel glass. Aerogel is hydrophobic (i.e., moisture resistant) and noncombustible, with good acoustic properties. Thermal resistance of aerogel-filled glazing, with U-values between 0.10 Btu/hr-ft^2-°F (0.57 W/m^2-°K) and 0.18 Btu/hr-ft^2-°F (1.00 W/m^2-°K), is superior to that of standard insulating glazing units, which rarely achieve U-values less than 0.25 Btu/hr-ft^2-°F (1.43 W/m^2-°K). Silica aerogel is translucent, making it an excellent way to bring diffuse daylight into interior spaces. However, this translucence makes it inappropriate for vision glass.

Vacuum-insulated glazing units provide improved thermal resistance compared to standard air- or gas-filled insulated glazing units. These units use a vacuum between two lites of glass to raise the assembly's thermal resistance. There is virtually no conduction or convection of heat between the two lites, because there is no gas to act as a medium for heat transfer. A low-e coating on the #2 or #3 glass surfaces significantly reduces the radiation of heat through the glass. With little heat transfer from conduction, convection, or radiation, vacuum-insulated glazing units can achieve U-values of less than 0.10 Btu/hr-ft^2-°F (0.57 W/m^2-°K).

EMERGING MATERIALS AND TECHNOLOGIES 125

The vacuum between the two lites of glass places them under negative pressure, pulling them toward each other. To counteract this, a grid of spacers is placed between the lites, as seen in Figure 4-4. These spacers, or pillars, are made of material with low conductivity, and are spaced several inches from each other in both directions. Vacuum-insulated glazing units are typically thin (between ¼ inch and ½ inch), making them ideal where high-performance glazing has to be installed in existing frames—a situation common for building retrofit projects.

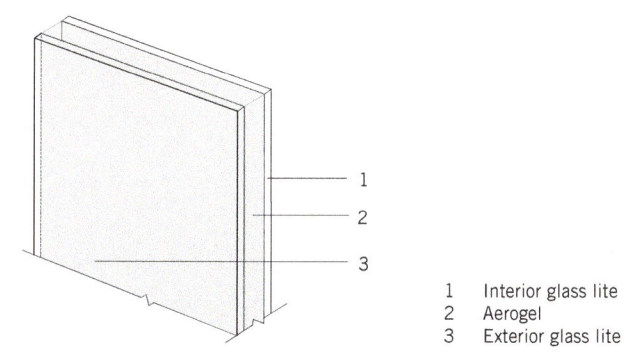

1 Interior glass lite
2 Aerogel
3 Exterior glass lite

Figure 4-3 Diagram of glazing unit with integrated aerogel insulation.

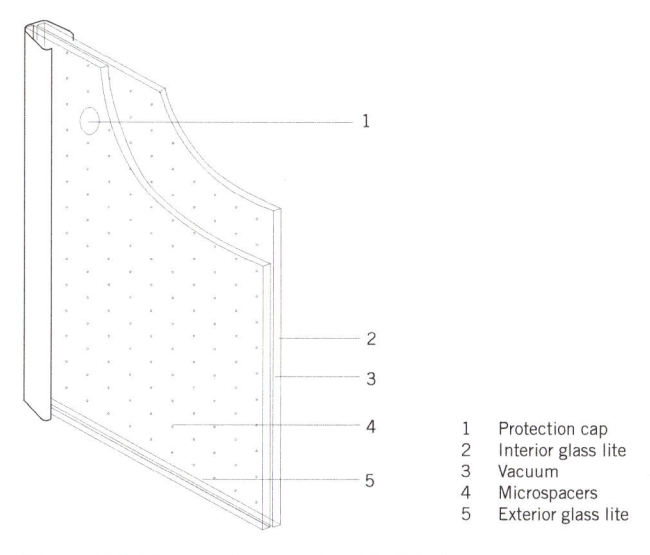

1 Protection cap
2 Interior glass lite
3 Vacuum
4 Microspacers
5 Exterior glass lite

Figure 4-4 Diagram of vacuum-insulated glazing unit.

Vacuum-insulated panels (VIPs) are an emerging class of insulating materials. They consist of a core of insulation material (usually silica or glass fiber) enclosed in an airtight, vacuum-sealed film envelope. VIPs have up to one-seventh the thermal conductivity of conventional insulation materials (Wang et al., 2007). VIPs are not finished materials, so they should be used within opaque facade elements or behind curtain wall spandrels. Because VIPs have such good insulating qualities, their use can decrease the thickness of an exterior wall without harming its thermal performance.

Smart Materials

Living organisms are able to adapt to changing conditions in the environment. Advances in physical and material sciences have led to the development of smart materials that mimic living organisms by physically responding to variable exterior and interior acoustical, lighting, and environmental conditions (Spillman et al., 1996).

There are various types of smart materials: shape memory alloys, fiber optic sensors, electrically activated materials (piezoelectric, electrostrictive, magnetostrictive, electrorheological, thermoelectric, and electrochromic), phase change materials, self-cleaning materials, and photovoltaics. Some of these smart materials are applicable for facades and are commercially available. These include facade-integrated photovoltaics, electrochromic glass, self-cleaning materials, phase change materials, and fiber optics.

Other materials are still in the development stage, or not applicable to facades. For example, piezoelectric materials, which produce electricity from applied pressure, have little application for facades. Thermoelectric materials, which convert temperature to electricity and vice versa, are commercially available, but their use for facades is still mostly in the research phase. The amount of energy typically produced by thermoelectric materials is relatively low and thus would not have a significant impact on the overall building's energy use.

Electrochromic glass incorporates a film that changes its opacity when electrical voltage is applied. For example, clear electrochromic glass can change to a dark tint, as seen in Figure 4-5. The glass can maintain that tinted shade without additional electricity. To return the glass to its transparent state, voltage is applied again. Darkening (and lightening) occurs from the edges, moving inward, and can take several minutes. This type of glass provides dynamic shading control for the building. Visual transmittance ranges from around 60% (for clear state) to 4% (tinted state). The solar heat gain coefficient (SHGC) changes from 0.48 in the clear state to 0.09 in the tinted state. With this type of glass, the energy consumption of the building can be reduced despite the use of energy to change the tint of the glass.

Suspended particle device (SPD) glass consists of a thin film of liquid crystals suspended in a transparent conductive material and laminated between two layers of glass. By applying voltage, the amount of light passing through the glass can be controlled. In the SPD's normal, nonelectrified state, these liquid crystals are randomly arranged; light is scattered between the crystals to give the glass a translucent appearance.

EMERGING MATERIALS AND TECHNOLOGIES   127

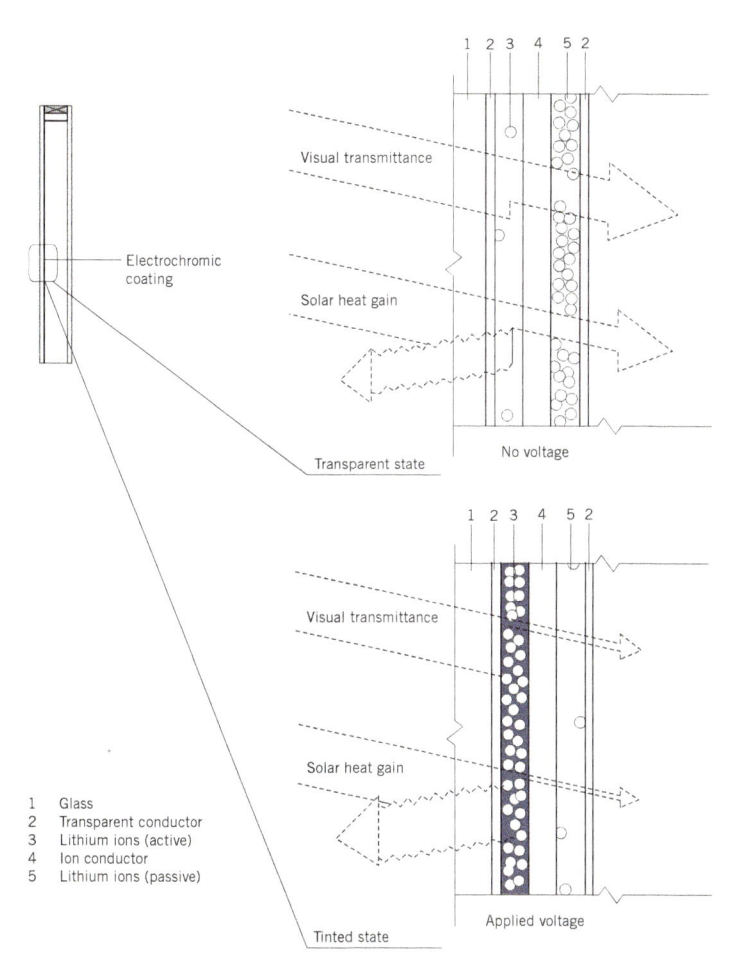

Figure 4-5 Electrochromic glass diagram.

1 Glass
2 Transparent conductor
3 Lithium ions (active)
4 Ion conductor
5 Lithium ions (passive)

When voltage is applied, the crystal particles align, allowing light to pass through the material and make it transparent, as seen in Figure 4-6. SPD glass is typically used for privacy control in interior spaces; the time required to switch between translucent and transparent states is almost instantaneous. However, the effects on energy savings are not significant, and this technology is not a recommended application for exterior building envelopes.

128 EMERGING TECHNOLOGIES IN FACADE DESIGNS

1. Glass
2. Transparent conductor
3. Suspension liquid/film
4. Suspended particle devices

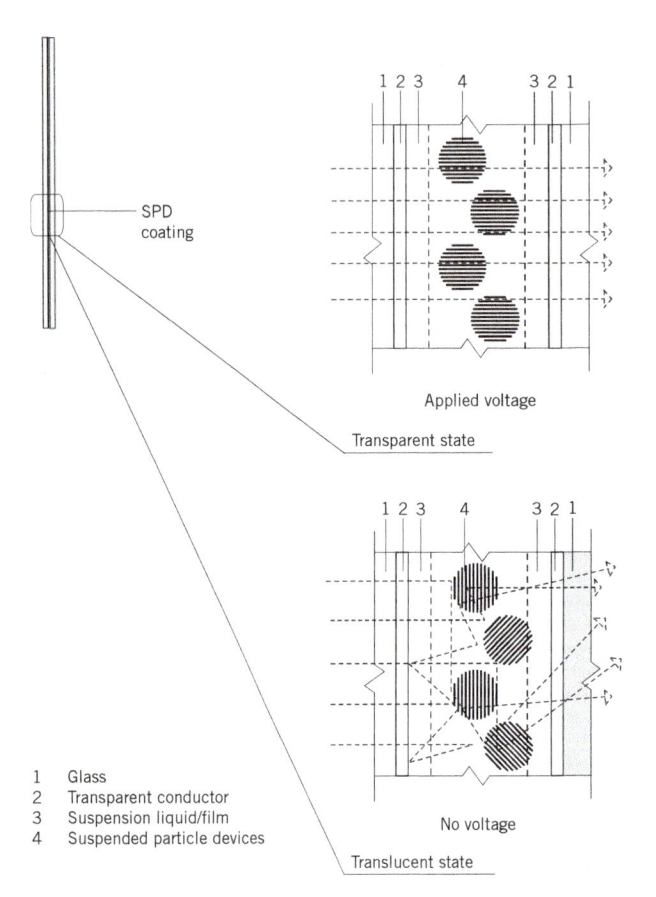

Figure 4-6 SPD glass diagram.

Self-cleaning glass typically uses a thin film of titanium dioxide on the #1 or exterior surface as a photo-catalytic coating. *Photocatalysts* are compounds that use the UV bands of sunlight to facilitate a chemical reaction. When exposed to sunlight, the titanium oxide triggers a strong oxidation process that converts noxious organic and inorganic substances into harmless compounds. The self-cleaning process on glass involves two stages, as seen in Figure 4-7. In the photocatalytic stage, organic dirt breaks down when the glass is exposed to sunlight. Next, in the hydrophilic stage, rain washes the dirt from the glass by picking up the loose particles. This is an effective way of keeping glass clean without high maintenance costs. However, in drought-prone locations with low precipitation, the second stage may require some intervention and maintenance. Research has shown that self-cleaning glass also helps in reducing air pollutants in dense urban areas (Chabasa et al., 2008).

1   Glass
2   Photocatalytic coating
3   UV light
4   Rain

Stage 1: Photocatalytic stage
Stage 2: Hydrophilic stage

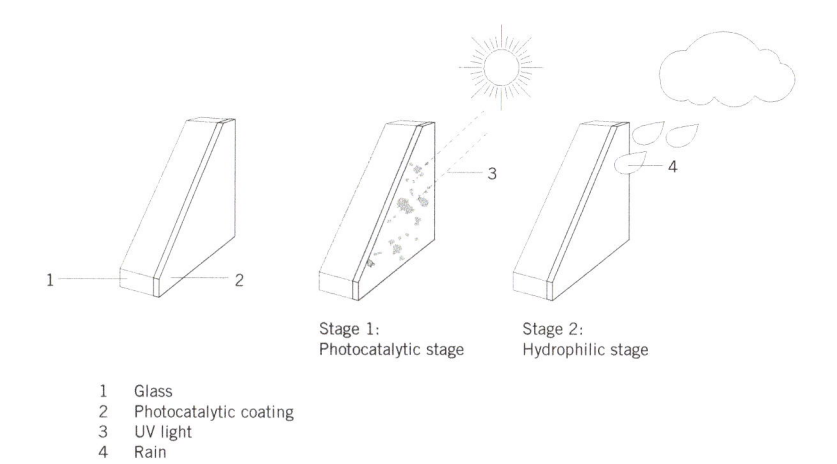

Figure 4-7 Diagram showing the two steps in the self-cleaning process for glass with photocatalytic coating.

Self-cleaning is not limited to glass. Titanium dioxide can be applied to other types of materials, such as concrete, to provide the self-cleaning effect. Concrete with photocatalytic cement produces self-cleaning concrete panels that remove pollutants from the air; however, photocatalytic cement does not have an effect on the strength of concrete (Cassar, 2004).

Phase-change materials (PCMs) are solid at room temperatures, but liquefy at higher temperatures, absorbing and storing heat in the process. PCMs are either organic (i.e., waxes) or inorganic (i.e., salts). When PCMs are incorporated into the building envelope, they can absorb high exterior temperatures during the day and dissipate the heat to the interior at night. PCM products, such as triple-insulated glazing units (IGUs) with integrated PCM, are commercially available. These IGUs consist of four layers of glass and three insulating gaps (shown in Figure 4-8). Within the outermost gap is a prismatic pane. Inert gas fills the two outer gaps, and a PCM encapsulated within transparent polycarbonate containers fills the inside gap. This type of IGU acts as a passive heat source. During the winter months, the prismatic pane allows low-angle sunlight to pass through the glass layers and heat up the PCM. This causes the PCM to liquefy and give off heat to the interior. During summer months, the prismatic pane acts as a barrier, reflecting high-angle solar rays back to the outside, allowing the PCM to stay in its solid form. Insulating properties of this type of glazing unit are very high, with published U-values for commercial products of 0.08 Btu/hr-ft^2-°F (0.48 W/m^2-°K). Visual transmittance for a solid-state PCM is between 0% and 28%, with an SHGC as low as 0.17 and as high as 0.48. Liquid-state PCM will have a visual transmittance from 4% to 45%, with an SHGC as high as 0.48 or as low as 0.17. In either its solid or liquid state, a PCM makes the glazing unit translucent, so this material is not appropriate where views to the outside are desired.

130   EMERGING TECHNOLOGIES IN FACADE DESIGNS

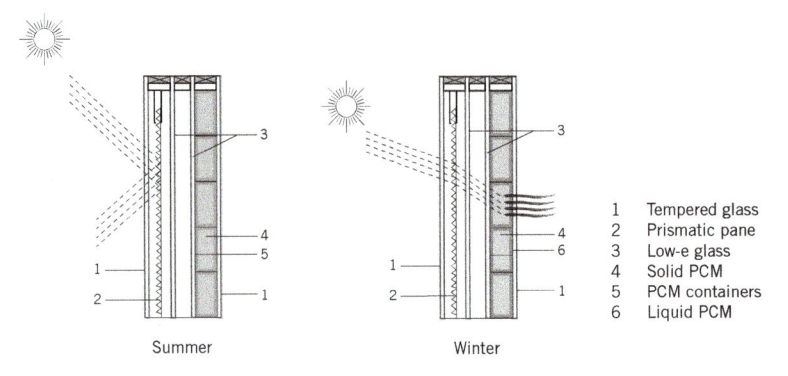

1 Tempered glass
2 Prismatic pane
3 Low-e glass
4 Solid PCM
5 PCM containers
6 Liquid PCM

Figure 4-8 Diagram of triple-insulated glazing unit with integrated PCM.

Photovoltaic (PV) glass integrates crystalline solar cells or amorphous thin films that generate energy from light. With photovoltaic glass, the PVs are integrated into laminated or double-glazed units. There are two general types of PV glass: semitransparent and opaque (Figure 4-9). Semitransparent PV glass is similar to patterned ceramic frit, allowing some light to penetrate through the glass while giving occupants views to the outside. Opaque PV glass uses solid PVs, and is appropriate for spandrels and other nonvision areas of the facade. A section later in this chapter discusses in more detail the use of PVs in facades for energy generation, and their performance.

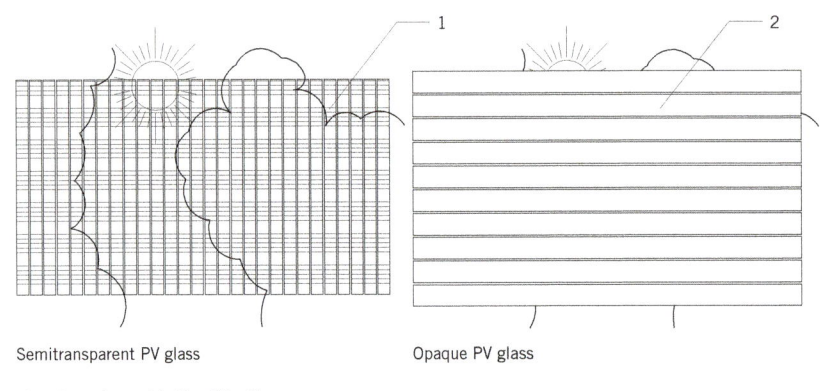

1 Amorphous thin-film PV cells
2 Crystalline PV cells

Figure 4-9 Semitransparent and opaque PV glass.

Table 4-1 compares the advanced and smart glazing materials discussed in these first two sections with standard high-performance glazing products (in this case, double-glazed, air-filled, low-e glazing units).

Table 4-1 Comparison of commercially available emerging facade glazing materials with standard high-performance products.

Material	Solar Control	Insulation	Daylight	Glare Control	Maintenance	View to exterior	Lifetime
Aerogel insulation within insulated glazing unit	0	+	+	+	0	—	0
Vacuum-insulated glazing unit	0	+	0	0	0	0	—
Electrochromic glass	+	0	0	+	0	0	0
SPD glass	0	0	0	+	0	—	0
Translucent state Transparent state	0	0	0	+	0	0	0
Self-cleaning glass	0	0	0	0	+	+	0
PCM in insulated glazing unit	+	+	0	+	0	—	+
PV glass (semitransparent)	+	0	0	+	0	—	0

Legend: + Improved performance   0 Similar performance   — Lower performance

Advances in material science and engineering may introduce to the market new categories of self-healing materials, including polymer composites, metal composites, and reinforced self-healing concrete, if current research is successful (White et al., 2001; Kuang et al., 2008; Asanuma, 2000). These materials incorporate healing agents or embedded shape-memory alloy wires that respond to and repair cracks in the material. How does this work? The self-healing polymer composites contain microcapsules of polymer healing agents. As a crack develops within the material, microcapsules along the crack are ruptured, releasing the polymer. When the polymer comes into contact with catalysts embedded in the material, it solidifies and bonds the crack. A similar concept applies to metal composites and self-healing concrete. These emerging materials would revolutionize building facades, as they would allow materials to repair themselves without the need for human assistance.

CASE STUDY 4.1 PRINCESS NORA BINT ABDULRAHMAN UNIVERSITY FOR WOMEN ACADEMIC COLLEGES

Princess Nora Bint Abdulrahman University for Women is an 86-million-square-foot (8-million-sm) academic campus in Riyadh, Saudi Arabia (climate zone 1B). The design of the campus considered several important factors: understanding and responding to the local climate, incorporating cultural character into the design, using materials that are sensitive to local construction techniques, maintaining scalable proportions, and creating urban spaces.

The Academic Colleges consist of nine buildings located at the heart of the campus. Being located in the hot, arid climate of Saudi Arabia, most of the outdoor spaces and facades of the buildings are exposed to direct sunlight and have to be shaded. Employing a cost-effective shading system that is easy to construct and is made of readily available materials was an appropriate design approach for the Academic Colleges, as seen in Figure 4-10.

Figure 4-11 shows the two layers of the typical exterior wall assembly: an aluminum curtain wall system with an intricate shading system outside of it. The curtain wall system is straightforward, with high-performance vision glazing and insulated shadow boxes at columns and spandrels. The innovative part of the assembly is the shading system, which consists of panelized glass-fiber-reinforced concrete (GFRC) screens supported by structural steel members.

Figure 4-10 Courtyard shading.

EMERGING MATERIALS AND TECHNOLOGIES

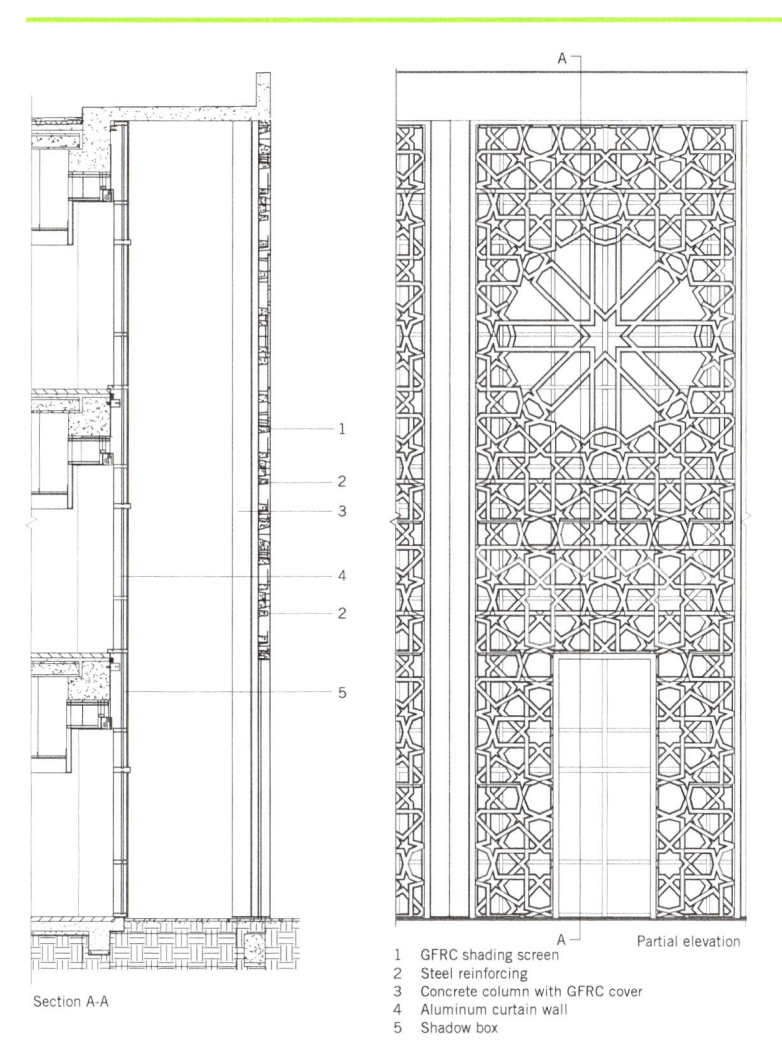

1 GFRC shading screen
2 Steel reinforcing
3 Concrete column with GFRC cover
4 Aluminum curtain wall
5 Shadow box

Section A-A
Partial elevation

Figure 4-11 Exterior wall section and elevation.

Introduced to the construction industry in the 1970s, GFRC is a composite building material, consisting of high-strength glass fibers embedded in a cementitious matrix of Portland cement, water, aggregates, and additives. The glass fibers reinforce the concrete, similar to steel reinforcement in conventional reinforced concrete. This reinforcement gives the finished material higher flexural and tensile strengths, allowing it to be used in applications that seek very thin profiles. GFRC is lightweight and durable, and can be cast into various shapes and forms.

134 EMERGING TECHNOLOGIES IN FACADE DESIGNS

Figure 4-12 Section perspective.

The GFRC panels for the Academic Colleges were shaped into intricate geometric patterns based on traditional Islamic architecture (Figure 4-12). These panels not only create a cultural architectural expression for the campus, but also provide shade for the curtain wall and visual privacy for the occupants. The nine Academic Colleges are covered by approximately 800,000 ft^2 (74,000 sm) of the shading screens, resulting in an overall reduction in building energy consumption of 3.5% and a 13% reduction in heat gain on the exterior envelopes. Furthermore, because the GFRC shading panels were light in weight, carbon emissions associated with their transportation to the site were reduced.

DOUBLE-SKIN FACADES

All the facades we have discussed so far are variations of single-skin facades. A *single-skin facade* consists of a single exterior wall system, which may use double lines of defense against water and air infiltration with double- or triple-glazed windows.

Double-skin facades are fundamentally different; they consist of distinct exterior and interior glazed wall systems, separated by a ventilated air cavity. The cavity creates a thermal buffer between the interior and exterior environments. The air cavity can be ventilated by natural convection caused by warm air naturally rising, by mechanical devices, or by a hybrid mode that combines the two. In some double-skin facade designs, the air cavity is interrupted vertically or horizontally (or both) by solid or perforated partitions. Selection of the type of the glazing, the width and partitioning of the air cavity, and the ventilation mode depends on climate, building orientation, and design requirements.

Double-skin facades are classified according to ways the air cavity is partitioned (the facade type), the ventilation mode, and the airflow pattern, as seen in Figure 4-13. These three variables can be combined in numerous ways for a wide variety of design possibilities.

Double-skin facade type	Ventilation mode	Airflow pattern
Box window	Natural	Exhaust air
Corridor		Supply air
Shaft box	Mechanical	Static air buffer
		External air curtain
Multistory	Hybrid	Internal air curtain

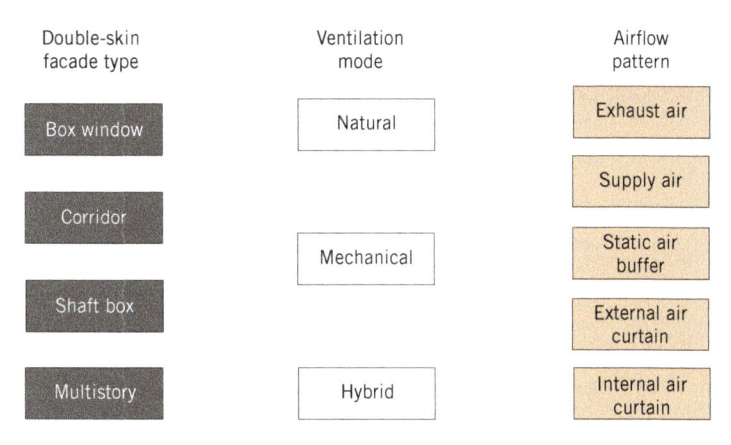

Figure 4-13 Classification of double-skin facades.

Basic double-skin facade types include:

- *Box window facades*, which have horizontal partitions at each floor level, as well as vertical partitions between windows. Each air cavity is typically ventilated naturally.
- *Corridor facades*, which have uninterrupted horizontal air cavities for each floor level, but are physically partitioned at the floor levels. All three ventilation modes are possible.
- *Shaft box facades*, which are similar to corridor facades, but use vertical shafts for natural stack-effect ventilation. Hybrid-mode ventilation is often used for this facade type.
- *Multistory facades,* which have uninterrupted air cavities the full height and width of the facade. All three ventilation modes can be used.

Diagrammatic elevations, sections, and plans for these four types of double-skin facade are shown in Figures 4-14 to 4-17.

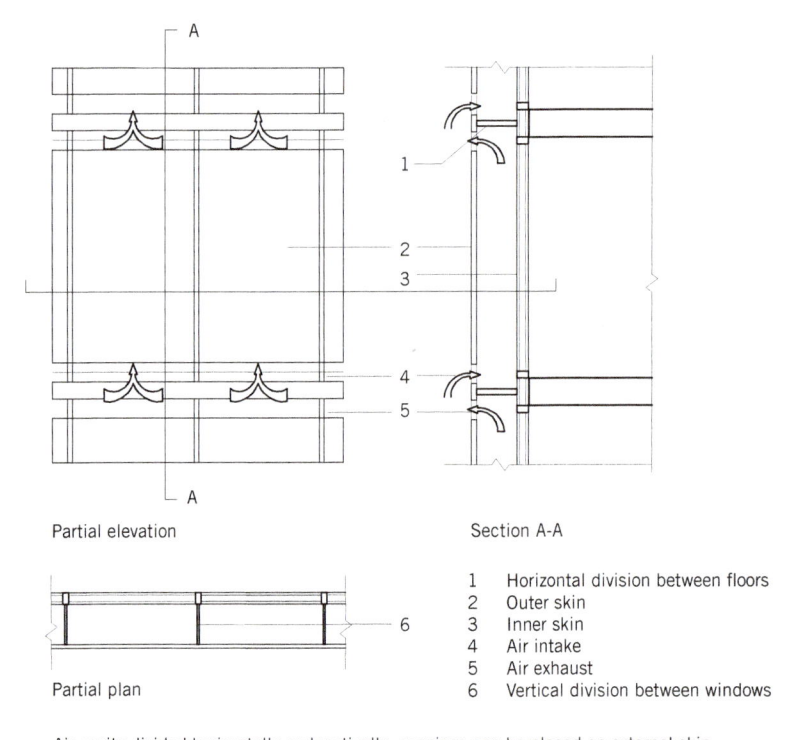

Partial elevation

Section A-A

Partial plan

1. Horizontal division between floors
2. Outer skin
3. Inner skin
4. Air intake
5. Air exhaust
6. Vertical division between windows

Air cavity divided horizontally and vertically, openings can be placed on external skin
Each window requires own air intake and exhaust openings

Figure 4-14 Box window double-skin facade.

Selection of the double-skin ventilation mode (natural, mechanical, or hybrid) should be based on building location (i.e., climate zone). The approach to partitioning should be based on cost, functional requirements, and number of floors. Natural ventilation of the air cavity works best in temperate or cold climates; mechanical ventilation may be required for hot climates. Hybrid systems will often use natural ventilation during the colder winter months and mechanical ventilation during hot summer months, making this mode applicable for mixed climates.

Different airflow patterns are shown in Figure 4-18, and depend on the location of air intake and exhaust.

Many design decisions related to double-skin facades depend on the selection of the facade type, the ventilation mode, and the airflow pattern. For example, the kinds of glazing units used for the interior and exterior skins depend in part on the ventilation mode. If the facade is naturally ventilated, insulating double-glazed units are usually used for the inner skin to provide a thermal barrier and single-glazed units for the exterior skin to ensure that the stack effect occurs. When mechanical ventilation is used, the opposite is usually the case: the insulating units are used for the outer skin and single glazing for the inner skin. When shading devices are used, they are typically placed between the two skins to limit the solar gain within the cavity.

Partial elevation

Section A-A

1 Horizontal division between floors
2 Outer skin
3 Inner skin
4 Air intake
5 Air exhaust

Partial plan

Air cavity divided horizontally
Each floor requires own air intake and exhaust openings

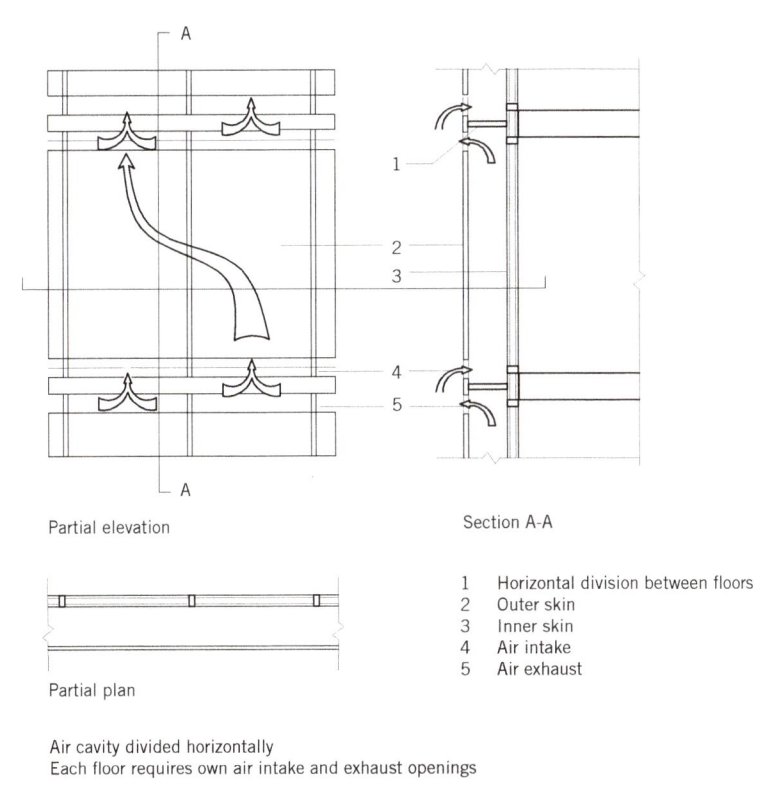

Figure 4-15 Corridor-type double-skin facade.

Initial costs of double-skin facades are higher than for single-skin facades. However, when designing sustainable facades, life-cycle costs for the life of the building should be taken into consideration. After energy consumption costs are evaluated for the life of the building, higher first-cost designs may result in lower overall costs. This does not take into account other advantages of double-skin walls that are more difficult to price, such as wind-load reduction, reduced glare, and improved acoustic performance.

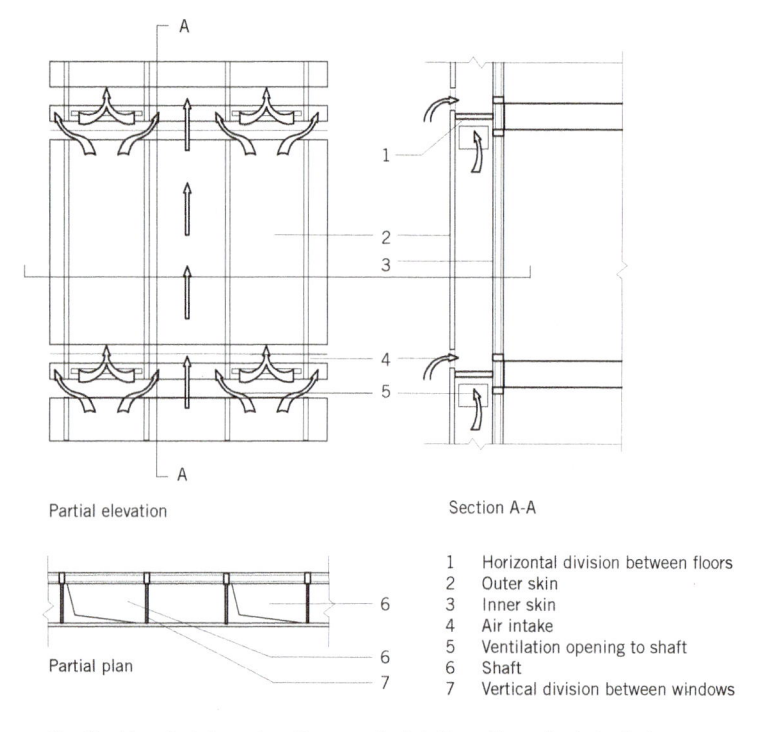

Partial elevation

Section A-A

Partial plan

1   Horizontal division between floors
2   Outer skin
3   Inner skin
4   Air intake
5   Ventilation opening to shaft
6   Shaft
7   Vertical division between windows

Combined boxed window and continuous vertical shaft used to create stack effect
Ventilation permitted over several floors

Figure 4-16 Shaft box double-skin facade.

The majority of double-skin facades to date have been used for buildings in temperate and cold climates. However, some buildings in warm, hot and arid, and hot and humid climate types are successfully using double-skin facades. Many of these buildings incorporate natural or hybrid-mode ventilation, integrated movable shading devices, hybrid ventilation systems, and different airflow patterns (Blomsteberg, 2007; Badinelli, 2009, Tanaka et al., 2009; Haase et al., 2009).

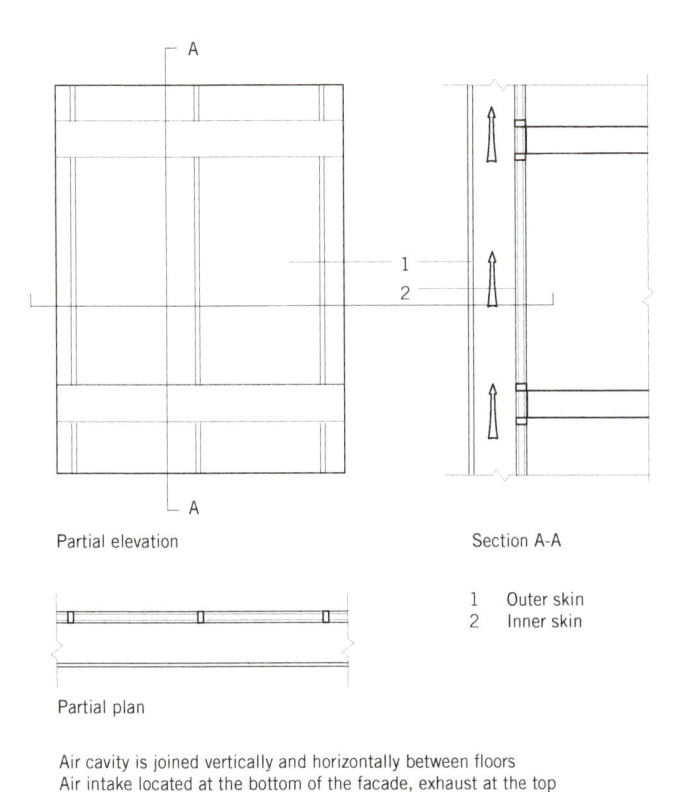

Partial elevation

Section A-A

1   Outer skin
2   Inner skin

Partial plan

Air cavity is joined vertically and horizontally between floors
Air intake located at the bottom of the facade, exhaust at the top

Figure 4-17 Multistory double-skin facade.

EMERGING TECHNOLOGIES IN FACADE DESIGNS

In the following subsections, we will look at the criteria and methods used for selecting the type of double-skin facade, for analyzing its characteristics and properties, and for selecting design strategies for specific climate zones.

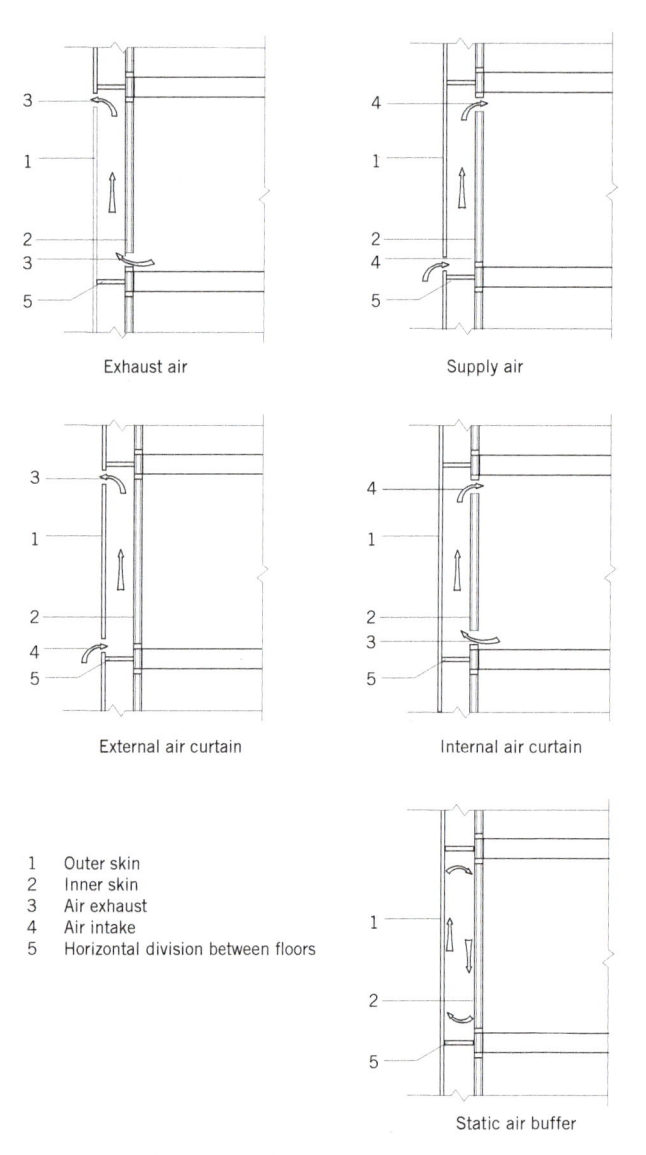

Exhaust air

Supply air

External air curtain

Internal air curtain

1 Outer skin
2 Inner skin
3 Air exhaust
4 Air intake
5 Horizontal division between floors

Static air buffer

Figure 4-18 Diagram of different airflow patterns in double-skin facades.

Double-Skin Facades in Hot and Arid Climates

Facades that consist mostly of vision glass are the major concern for energy consumption in hot and arid climates (Askar et al., 2001). Traditional techniques for providing comfortable living and working spaces in this type of environment include massive walls that keep interiors cool during the days. At night, when the outdoor air is cool, the stored heat is released to the interior spaces. Windows are positioned to allow natural ventilation, but shaded to prevent direct sunlight from entering the interior. With modern single-skin facade technology, designers have a number of high- and low-tech strategies to choose from to manage energy consumption. They can provide shading devices at windows to admit daylight but block direct sunlight. They can orient rooms and provide operable windows to encourage air currents to ventilate inhabited spaces. They can employ passive strategies (ducts, wind towers, and shafts) to promote air circulation. And they can use evaporative cooling to extract heat from the interior. A well-designed single-skin facade can perform well in this demanding climate. Can a double-skin facade perform better?

Figure 4-19 compares five facade scenarios—two single-skin and three double-skin facades—for a hot and arid climate (Aksamija, 2009). The graph shows monthly energy consumption for an office space facing south. The constants include building location; dimensions of the office space, orientation, occupancy of the office space, equipment and lighting loads; and window-to-wall ratio. The variables are the facade type, the air cavity dimensions, and the types of glazing. All three double-skin scenarios are multistory facades with shading blinds within the mechanically ventilated air cavity.

The figure shows that during summer months, double-skin walls perform about as well as single-skin walls. However, the double-skin facade's ability to insulate and trap heat allows it to outperform single-skin facades during winter months. For overall annual reduction of energy consumption, the two double-skin facades with smaller cavity depths and low-e or reflective coatings will perform better than the other three facades. This suggests the following strategies for the design of double-skin walls in hot and arid climates:

- *Air cavity:* During summer months, double-skin walls with smaller air cavities perform slightly better than those with larger air cavities. During July and August, the hottest months, neither performs noticeably better than the single-skin facades. In winter, however, the double-skin facades with narrower air cavities outperform both single-skin walls and the double-skin wall with the larger cavity.

- *Ventilation mode:* Because all three double-skin walls in the study used mechanical ventilation, the figure does not tell us if natural or hybrid ventilation would be better. However, with the majority of consumed energy being for cooling, there are possible advantages to using hybrid ventilation. Hot and arid climates have extreme temperature shifts from day to night. Because of the diurnal change between hot daytime temperatures and cold nighttime temperatures, mechanical system would be most effective during the day and natural ventilation during the night.

- *Shading:* Traditional construction techniques for hot and arid climates teach us the importance of blocking direct sunlight from entering the interior. Roof overhangs can provide protection against

142   EMERGING TECHNOLOGIES IN FACADE DESIGNS

solar heat gain for one- or two-story buildings. For taller buildings, double-skin facades with shading devices inside the air cavity can give effective protection against direct sunlight.

- *Glazing*: The amount of vision glass and the type of glazing have a significant effect on energy consumption. Reducing the amount of vision glass will reduce cooling loads in this climate, and selecting low-e or reflective glazing can decrease cooling loads during hot summer months.

Although double-skin facades are not often used in hot and arid climates, this analysis shows that a well-designed double-skin facade can perform at least as well as a well-designed single-skin facade. Whether the energy savings over the building's lifetime justify the additional costs of double-skin construction can be determined only by analyzing the data for a specific project.

Base model 1: single-skin facade with low-e glazing
Base model 2: single-skin facade with triple glazing
Double-skin facade with 3 ft (1 m) air cavity and low-e glazing
Double-skin facade with 4.5 ft (1.5 m) air cavity and low-e glazing
Double-skin facade with 3 ft (1 m) air cavity and reflective glazing

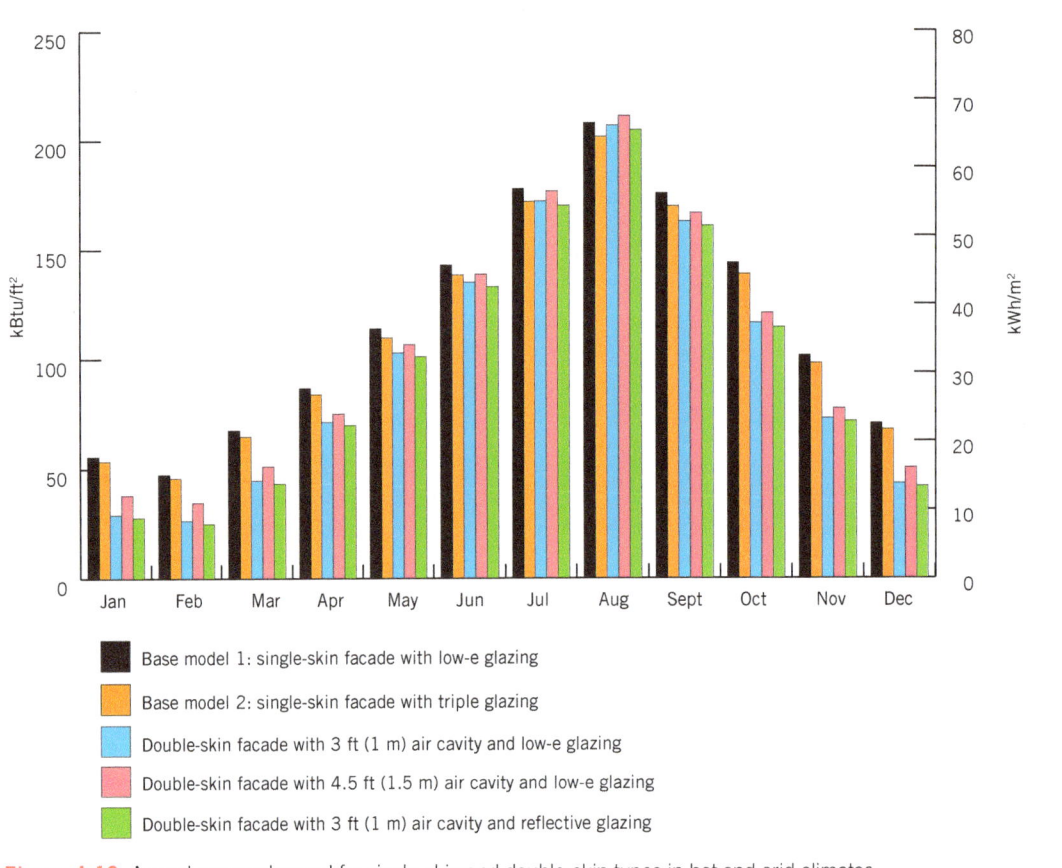

Figure 4-19 Annual energy demand for single-skin and double-skin types in hot and arid climates.

Double-Skin Facades in Cold Climates

Substantial research has been done on the performance of double-skin walls in cold and temperate climates (Stec et al., 2005; Poirazis, 2006). Double-skin walls generally perform well in these climates because of their inherent thermal insulation properties. During the winter months, the air cavity provides an effective thermal barrier. During the summer, ventilation of the cavity removes hot air and keeps the interior spaces cooler.

Figure 4-20 compares five facade scenarios and their annual energy consumption in a cold climate (Aksamija, 2009). Four are variations of double-skin facades (DS-1 through DS-4), and one, acting as the base model, is a single-skin facade (SS-1). Constants for all scenarios are the building location, the interior space (an office facing south), occupancy schedules, and equipment and lighting loads. The

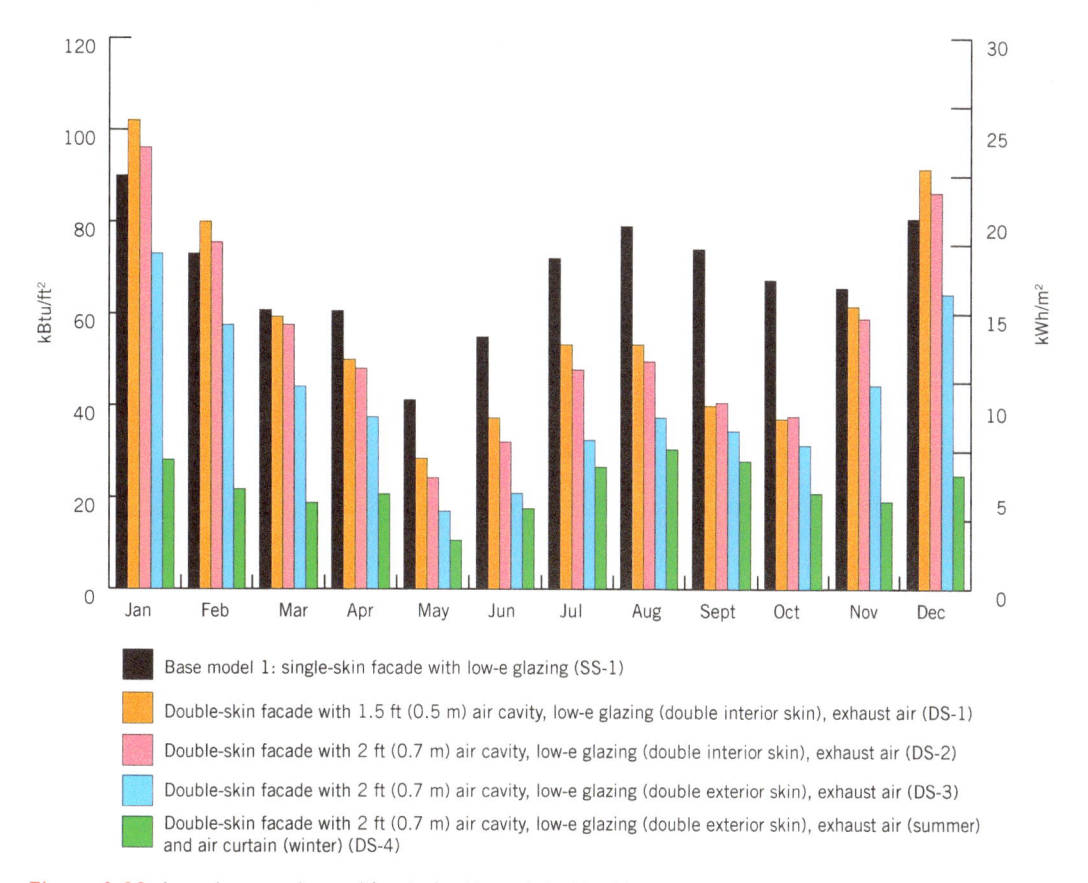

■ Base model 1: single-skin facade with low-e glazing (SS-1)
■ Double-skin facade with 1.5 ft (0.5 m) air cavity, low-e glazing (double interior skin), exhaust air (DS-1)
■ Double-skin facade with 2 ft (0.7 m) air cavity, low-e glazing (double interior skin), exhaust air (DS-2)
■ Double-skin facade with 2 ft (0.7 m) air cavity, low-e glazing (double exterior skin), exhaust air (DS-3)
■ Double-skin facade with 2 ft (0.7 m) air cavity, low-e glazing (double exterior skin), exhaust air (summer) and air curtain (winter) (DS-4)

Figure 4-20 Annual energy demand for single-skin and double-skin types in cold climate.

variables include air cavity dimensions for the double-skin facades, placement of the double-glazed skin (on the interior or exterior side of the air cavity), and the airflow pattern. For all the double-skin scenarios, natural ventilation, supported by stack effect and a rooftop fan, is used to ventilate the air cavity. One of the double-skin facades (DS-4) uses the air cavity as an air curtain: the control dampers at the base of the cavity are closed during winter, so that the still air between the two skins acts as an insulator.

We can first compare the single-skin facade (SS-1) with two of the double-skin facades (DS-1 and DS-2). Each of the double-skin facades uses insulating low-e glazing for its interior skin. The air cavity is 1.5 feet (0.5 m) wide for DS-1 and 2 feet (0.7 m) wide for DS-2. From December through February, the single-skin facade (SS-1) performs better than DS-1 and DS-2. All three facades perform about the same in March and November. For the remainder of the year, however, both double-skin walls perform significantly better than SS-1. Annual energy demand for DS-1 and DS-2 is approximately 17% and 24%, respectively, less than for SS-1. Because the only difference between DS-1 and DS-2 is the width of the air cavity, we can see that this variable has a significant effect on energy demand.

The next step is to look at the other two double-skin facades, DS-3 and DS-4. Both of these facades have 2-foot-wide air cavities. There is only one difference between them: DS-4 uses a ventilated cavity during the summer months and an air curtain during the winter months, whereas DS-3 ventilates its cavity all year round. Compared to SS-1, both DS-3 and DS-4 perform significantly better every month of the year (they also outperform DS-1 and DS-2 every month). Annual energy demand for DS-3 is 64% less than for SS-1, while DS-4's energy demand is 72% less than that of SS-1. Use of air curtain airflow pattern during the winter months clearly has an enormous effect on reducing a building's energy loads.

In summary, in cold climates, double-skin facades will likely perform better than single-skin facades. Among the double-skin facades, those with wider air cavities will perform better than those with shallower cavities. Having the double glazing on the exterior side of the air cavity improves the performance of the double-skin system. Finally, double-skin facades that combine ventilated cavities during summer with air curtains of entrapped air during winter performed the best of all the analyzed facades. Therefore, we can make these general recommendations for the design of double-skin facades in cold climates:

- *Air cavity:* Wider air cavities perform significantly better than shallower ones. In addition, cavities that are less than two feet wide are difficult to access for maintenance.

- *Ventilation mode and airflow pattern:* Because a large portion of consumed energy in cold climates goes toward heating, there are advantages to trapping air in the cavity to improve insulation and reduce heat loss to the outside. Although the primary concern in cold climates is the heating demand, the summer cooling loads must still be considered. During summer months, the air cavity must be ventilated to protect it from overheating.

- *Glazing:* Double-glazing the exterior skin rather than the interior skin can significantly reduce overall energy consumption.

DOUBLE-SKIN FACADES 145

CASE STUDY 4.2 CASE WESTERN TINKHAM VEALE UNIVERSITY CENTER

Tinkham Veale University Center is located on the Case Western Reserve University campus in Cleveland, Ohio (climate zone 5A). The west facade of the building encloses a double-height student lounge and common space, as seen in Figure 4-21. The facade consists entirely of vision glass, to provide a visual connection between the interior and exterior.

Figure 4-21 West facade of the Tinkham Veale University Center.

The west-facing double-skin facade was designed to control light and heat gain throughout the year. Two mechanisms are used to control these factors: roller shades and ventilation of the air cavity between the two skins. The two-story double-skin wall includes radiometer-controlled roller shades that deploy when direct sunlight strikes the facade. The shades automatically lower to a level sufficient to block direct sunlight, but will not drop below 7 feet (2.1 m) above the floor so that views are preserved. The shades operate in all seasons to control solar heat gain.

146 EMERGING TECHNOLOGIES IN FACADE DESIGNS

The air cavity uses a hybrid ventilation mode, combining natural and mechanical ventilation. The ventilation system consists of dampers at the bottom of the facade, and axial fans and another set of dampers at the top, as seen in Figures 4-22 and 4-23. The system operates differently in the summer and the winter to achieve different ends; therefore, airflow patterns vary from season to season.

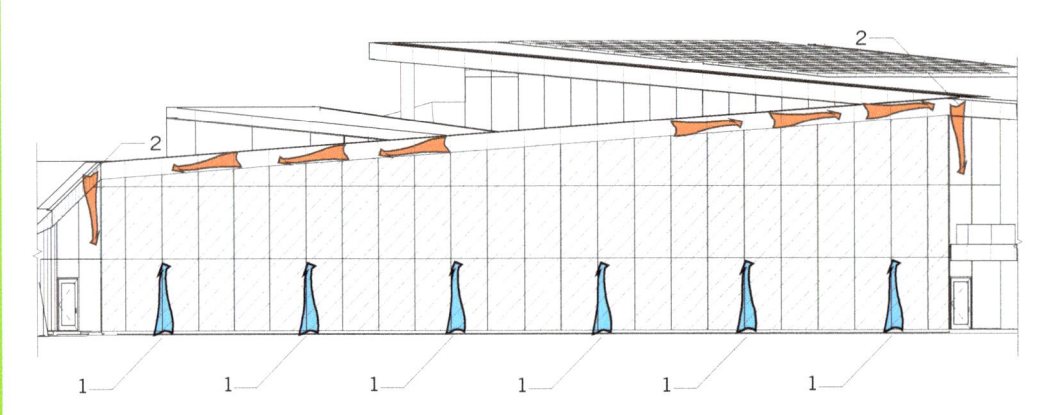

1 Air intake through the dampers
2 Exhaust air through the axial fans

Figure 4-22 West elevation and ventilation of the air cavity.

During the summer months, the facade uses an exhaust air-curtain flow pattern (Figure 4-23). This keeps the air temperature in the cavity within 30°F (10°C) of the outdoor air temperature. As a result, the cavity does not impose additional heat loads on the building. When the temperature in the cavity exceeds a predetermined temperature differential, both sets of dampers open and the fans move outdoor air through the cavity to equalize the temperature, as seen in Figure 4-24. Once the differential has been reduced to a preset level, the dampers close and the fans stop.

Winter operation employs a static air-buffer flow pattern, thus creating a mass of warm air in the cavity that mitigates heat loss to the exterior. This is achieved by closing both sets of dampers, trapping air in the cavity and allowing it to be heated by the sun. The preheating is not required to properly heat the adjacent spaces, but it will allow the building's mechanical system to deliver less heat when the conditions are right.

Because of the double-skin glazing system used in the west facade, the cooling and heating load is reduced by 58.8% during the peak summer and winter times when compared to a high-performance single-skin facade, as seen in Figure 4-25. The figure compares different facade design options and their effects on peak energy loads.

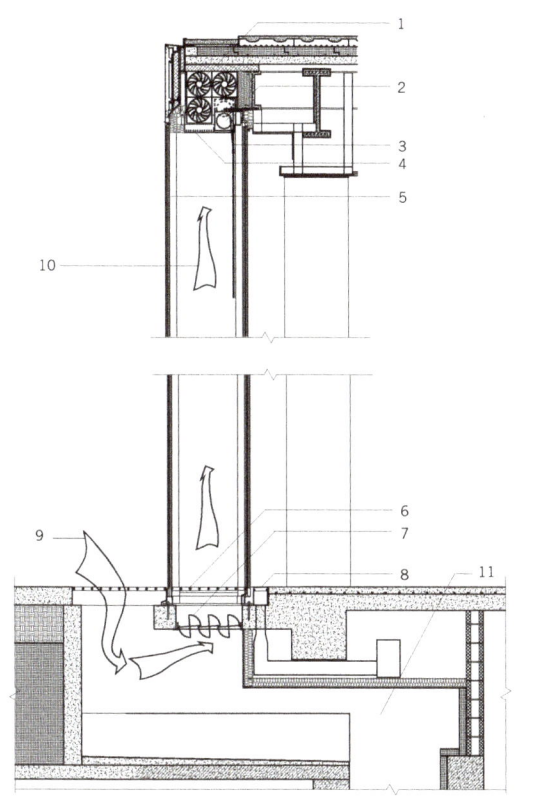

1. Axial fans
2. Roller shade housing
3. Roller shade with guide wire
4. Continuous aluminum bar grille
5. Curtain wall system
6. Stainless steel cross bars at the bottom
7. Automated dampers
8. Continuous linear floor grille
9. Air intake during summer to ventilate the double-skin cavity
10. Ventilated air to go through the axial fan space and exit the building
11. Air intake for an existing underground garage

Figure 4-23 Double-skin wall section, ventilation system, and air intake through the dampers.

148 EMERGING TECHNOLOGIES IN FACADE DESIGNS

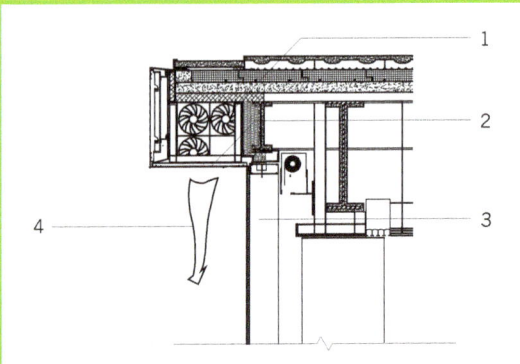

1. Axial fans
2. Continuous aluminum bar grille
3. Curtain wall system
4. Air ventilated out

Figure 4-24 Double-skin ventilation system and exhaust through the axial fans at the edges of the west elevation.

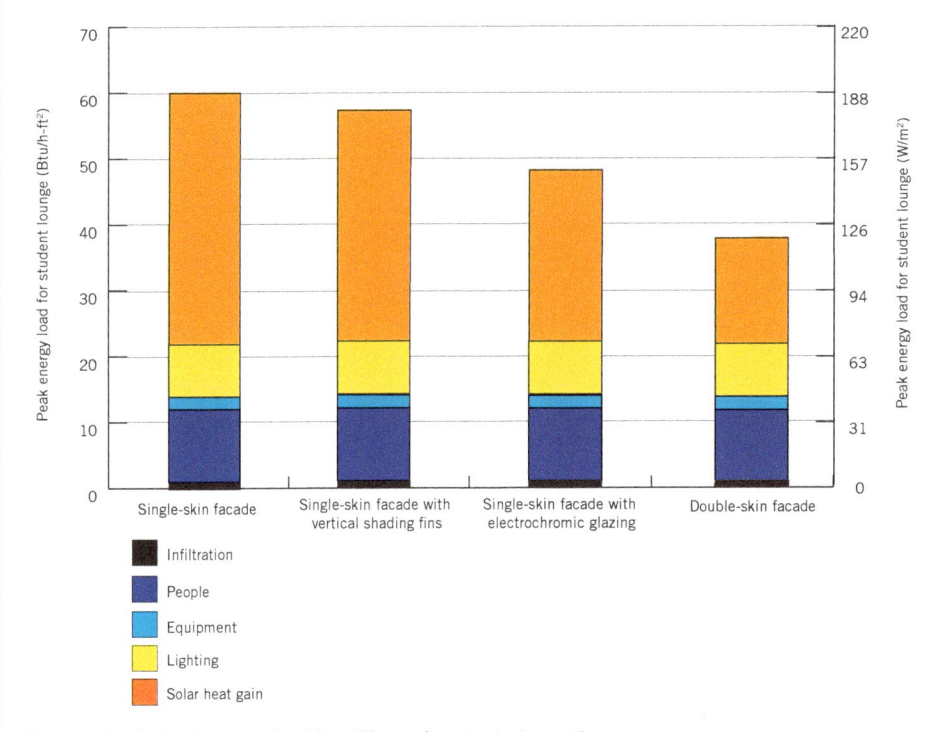

- Infiltration
- People
- Equipment
- Lighting
- Solar heat gain

Figure 4-25 Peak energy load for different facade design options.

FACADES AS ENERGY GENERATORS

Alternative energy sources, such as solar and wind power, are increasingly used in buildings. There are two categories of solar energy: passive and active. Passive solar energy is either heat or radiation that is directly produced by sunlight hitting the building's exterior materials. For example, using exterior materials with large thermal capacities, heat from the sun can be absorbed into the material during the day and dissipated to the building's interior at night. With active solar energy, devices such as solar collectors and photovoltaic (PV) panels heat fluids or generate electricity. Facades can be designed to take advantage of both forms of solar energy. Other alternative energy sources are less used in facade applications, so this section focuses only on energy generation from the sun.

Solar air heating systems and *solar dynamic buffer zone (SDBZ) curtain walls* are two examples of emerging passive solar energy systems for facades. Solar air-heating systems usually consist of a secondary skin made of solar collecting materials, such as dark-colored perforated metal, that preheat air entering the building, as seen in Figure 4-26. This skin can be installed several inches outside the exterior wall, creating a shallow air cavity of naturally heated air. They are different from the double-skin facades discussed in the preceding section since opaque materials are used. This system can be coupled with the HVAC system to deliver the heated air directly to the interior. During summer months, the warm air is exhausted to the exterior, and dampers can be used to stop the flow of warm air to the interior. Solar air-heating systems are designed to supplement rather than replace conventional heating systems. Solar dynamic buffer zone curtain walls also use preheated air, but use spaces within the spandrel areas of curtain walls instead of exterior air cavities (Richman and Pressnail, 2009).

Photovoltaics are among the most commonly used active energy-generation systems for facades. There are two types of facade-integrated PV modules: thin films and solid cells. The first consists of thin films of interconnected solar cells, which convert visible light into electricity, sandwiched between glass panes. Thin-film cells can be integrated into almost any facade surface, such as shading devices, spandrels, and vision glass. Solid solar cell modules can be integrated with spandrel areas or shading devices. The performance and aesthetic appearance of the PVs depend on their type, their size, and their position relative to the sun's path.

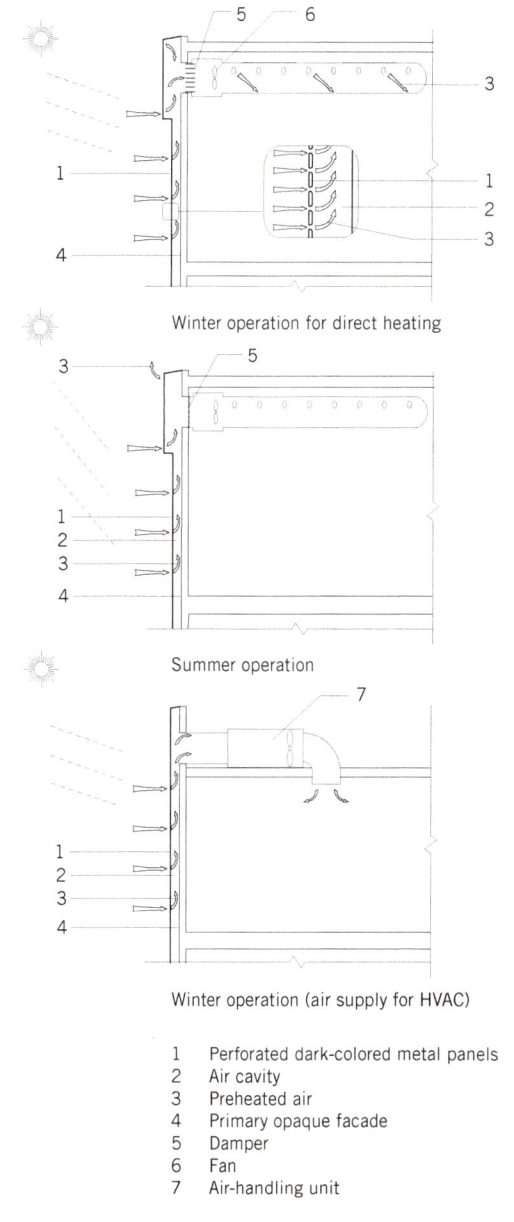

Winter operation for direct heating

Summer operation

Winter operation (air supply for HVAC)

1 Perforated dark-colored metal panels
2 Air cavity
3 Preheated air
4 Primary opaque facade
5 Damper
6 Fan
7 Air-handling unit

Figure 4-26 Solar air-heating system diagram and modes of operation.

Monocrystalline silicon cells are uniform in color and structure, and the most conventional types of cells used in PV modules. Their efficiency, measured as a percentage of solar energy converted into electric energy, is typically no more than 20% under the best conditions. *Polycrystalline silicon cells* have non-uniform surface structure and color, with visible variations in the silicon structure. Polycrystalline cells generally have lower costs and lower efficiencies than monocrystalline cells. *Amorphous silicon cells* use hydrogenated amorphous silicon, with only a few microns of material needed to absorb the incident light. Because they can be deposited on both rigid and flexible substrates, thin films typically use this type of cell. Manufacturing costs for amorphous cells are relatively low, but their efficiencies are also low, typically no more than 7%. The advantage of amorphous thin films in facade applications is that they work equally well in shade and in sunlight. Monocrystalline and polycrystalline cells require direct sunlight to achieve their highest efficiencies. Their energy production is reduced if they are shaded; not oriented to receive the maximum amount of sun; or covered by snow, sand, or dust.

Photovoltaics generate the most energy when the plane of the PVs is perpendicular to the sun's rays. To find the position that maximizes the effectiveness of the PV panels over the course of a year, two factors must be considered: orientation in plan and inclination angle. The ideal orientation in the northern hemisphere is directly south, and in the southern hemisphere is directly north. Deviation from this ideal orientation to the east or west results in lower energy production.

The other factor is the inclination angle. For PVs to be most effective, they should be inclined to face the sun. This angle is determined by the height of the sun in the sky, which in turn is determined by the latitude of the building site. A useful rule of thumb is that PV panels should be tilted at an angle equal to the latitude.

To illustrate this concept, Figures 4-27 to 4-29 compare total available solar radiation with the incident radiation (the radiation that strikes the PV panel) for planar surfaces with different inclination angles, one matching the latitude and the other at 90° (i.e., vertical). Figure 4-27 shows the average hourly solar radiation for a location along the 42° latitude in the northern hemisphere. Figure 4-28 shows hourly incident solar radiation for a surface facing directly south, with 42° inclination (to match the latitude). This surface receives most of the available radiation during the summer months. Figure 4-29 shows incident solar radiation for a vertical surface, such as a curtain wall (inclination of 90°). The vertical surface receives most of the available solar radiation during winter months and only a small amount during the summer. For a building at this latitude to generate the largest amount of energy through solar radiation, both inclined and vertical photovoltaic panels are needed. For example, PV panels integrated with inclined shading devices would capture the summer solar radiation, while PVs mounted to unshaded vertical walls would capture the low-angle winter sunlight.

Figure 4-30 compares energy production for a PV system located on a site along 42°N latitude and facing directly south. The PV system consists of 10,000 ft^2 (930 m^2) of high-efficiency polycrystalline silicon panels. The graph shows monthly energy generation for four scenarios, with panel inclination angles of 42°, 20°, 0°, and 90°. Consistent with our rule of thumb, the highest annual output is achieved by inclining panels to an angle equal to the latitude. Decreasing the inclination to a 20° angle results in decreased energy output during summer months and increased output during winter months. The output for panels placed on a flat horizontal surface is lower during the entire year compared to the optimal angle. Placement on a vertical surface results in the lowest level of energy production. Designers should be aware that PVs mounted to vertical facades are inefficient for generating energy.

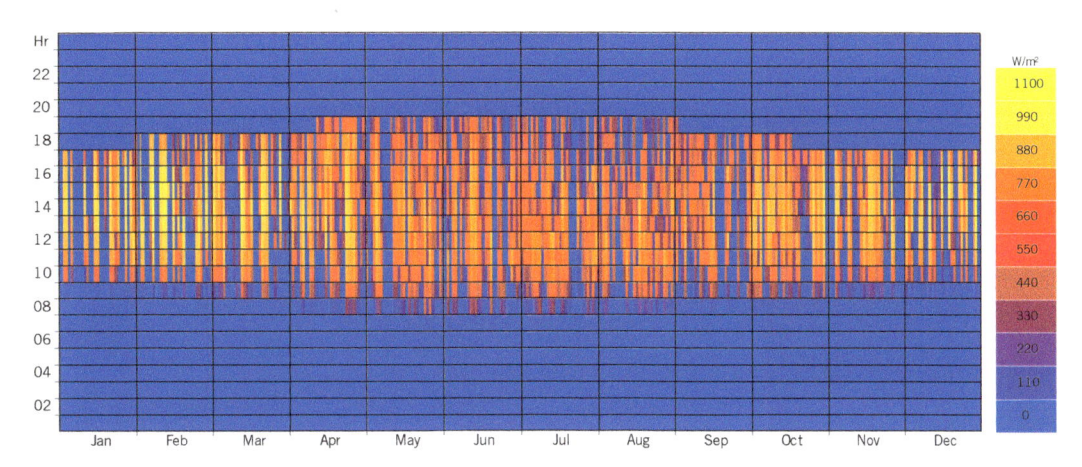

Figure 4-27 Hourly available solar radiation (location along 42°N latitude).

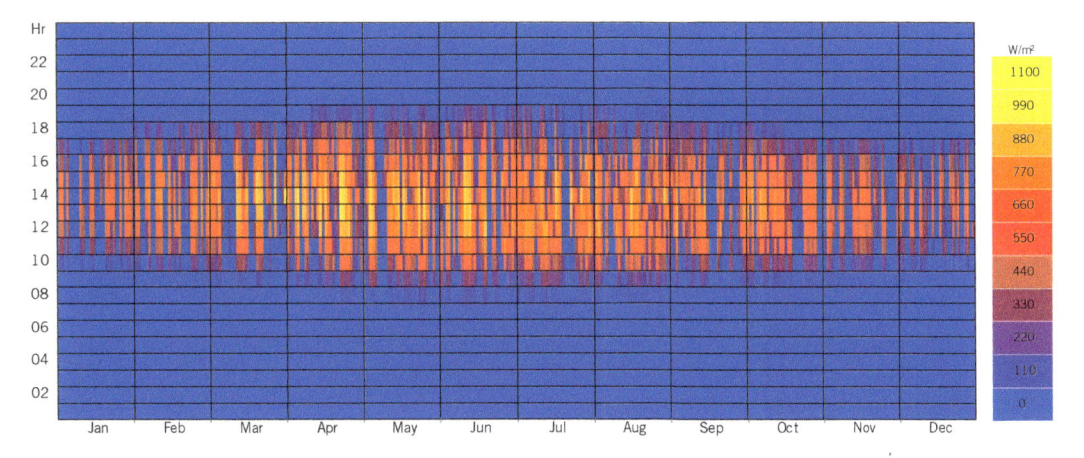

Figure 4-28 Incident solar radiation on a south-facing surface with 42° inclination angle (at 42°N latitude).

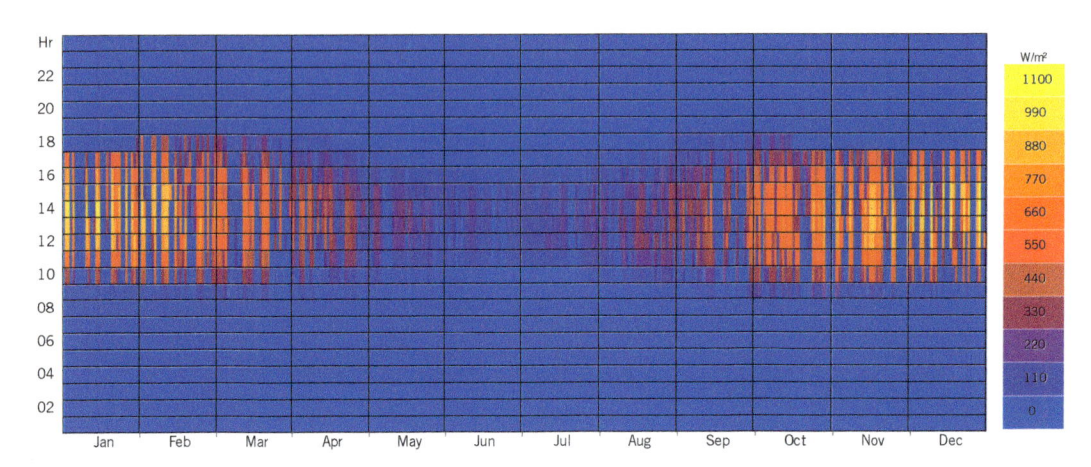

Figure 4-29 Incident solar radiation on a south-facing surface with 90° inclination angle (at 42°N latitude).

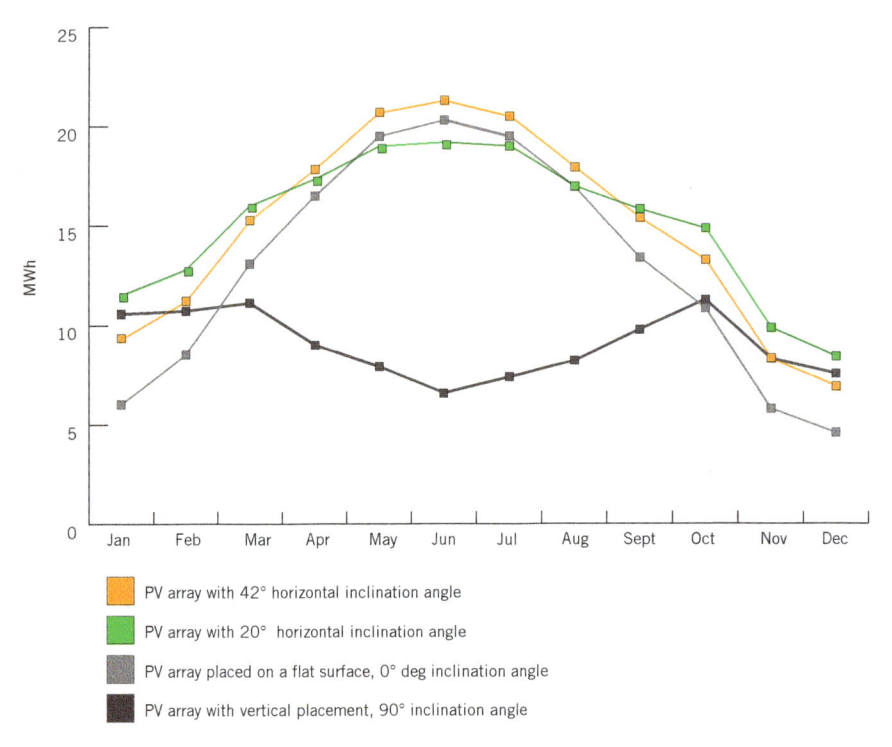

Figure 4-30 Annual energy output for PV panels with different inclination angles.

A way around this problem is to position the PVs on inclined shading elements, or to integrate them with vertical shading elements that are able to rotate and follow the position of the sun. Figure 4-31 compares the energy output for PV panels mounted on fixed vertical surfaces with the energy output for an equal area of PVs mounted to movable vertical shading devices that track the path of the sun. Integrating PVs into movable shading devices improves the energy generation, but not as much as inclining the PVs.

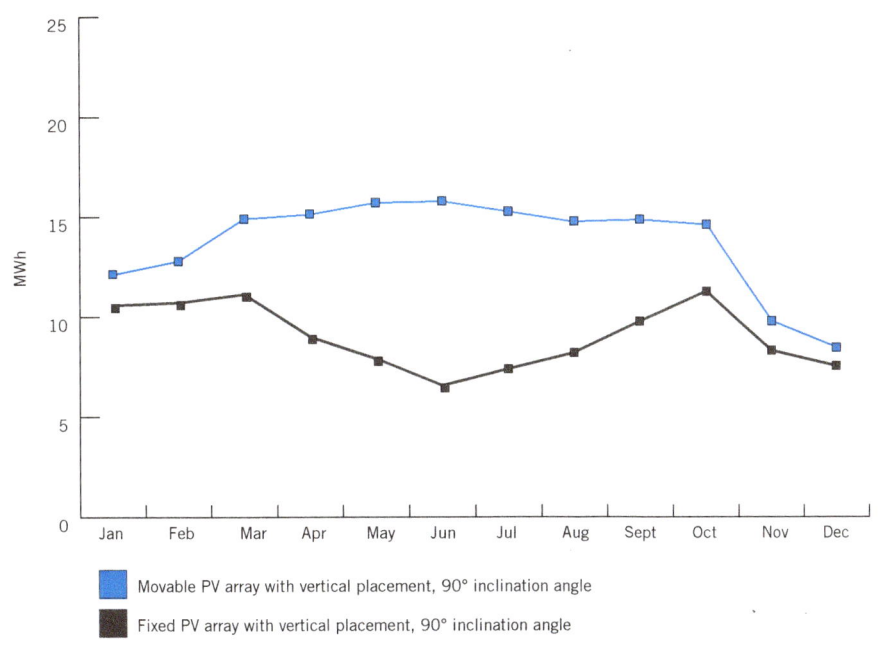

■ Movable PV array with vertical placement, 90° inclination angle
■ Fixed PV array with vertical placement, 90° inclination angle

Figure 4-31 Annual energy output for facade-integrated PV panels.

CONTROL SYSTEMS FOR FACADES

In the future, facades will respond intelligently to changes in their environment. Interactive, dynamically controlled facades will include systems that moderate their performance as the outdoor and indoor conditions change, and will allow adjustments by individual occupants. The facade components will sense changes in the exterior environment and respond to them automatically by adjusting solar gain, daylighting, heat loss, and ventilation. Smart building controls, building automation systems, and occupant-operated controls will be integrated to achieve the greatest energy savings. Systems that allow occupants to have control over their local indoor environment, using individual control mechanisms that are integrated with reliable automated controls, are a solution ensuring that each occupant is comfortable.

Control systems for "intelligent" facades should accept inputs from a wide range of building sensors, both wired and wireless, to satisfy energy and occupant comfort criteria. Currently, low-cost sensors and Internet-based communication protocols are feasible methods for controlling facade components. Facades are typically divided into zones focused on the same function, such as control of shading devices. For example, each building orientation would be a different zone, with control mechanisms (such as lowering blinds on the east side of the building during morning hours) appropriate to each zone. Where a building shape may generate specific wind and sun conditions (for example, a courtyard within a building), several zones can be defined for the same facade with specific sensors and control mechanisms.

Facade control systems include thermal storage, natural ventilation, integration of facade and lighting systems, and control of shading devices and internal shades. Building automation systems that track key facade performance metrics over time, provide comparisons to archived performance data, and employ fault detection and automated repairs to correct faults are the future of the emerging facade technologies.

The control systems for facades must have real-time sensing capabilities to keep track of changing environmental conditions, such as temperature, relative humidity, solar position, cloud cover, and wind (Figure 4-32). These control systems will use predictive algorithms to foresee the possible short-term changes in the environment. Moreover, thermal storage, natural ventilation, and integration of facade and lighting systems are crucial for energy savings opportunities. Fully integrated "intelligent" systems that sense occupancy patterns, adjust lighting, automatically move shading devices, and adjust HVAC systems can significantly reduce energy use.

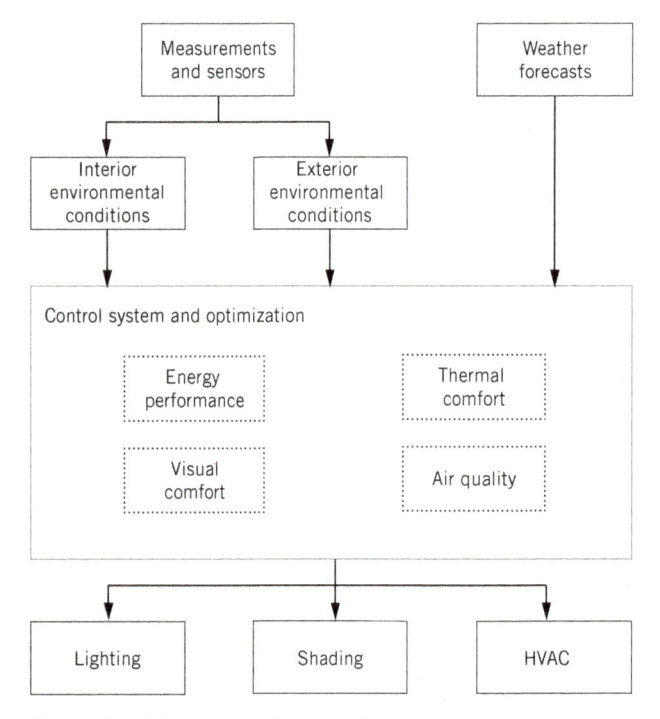

Figure 4-32 Conceptual diagram of facade control system.

CHAPTER SUMMARY

New developments in materials, systems, and information technology are changing the aesthetic and functional characteristics of building facades. Intelligent, sustainable materials, as well as systems integration, provide new design opportunities for architects and engineers. The design potential for facades to reduce building energy consumption while improving occupant comfort are increasingly linked to material selections, production technology, and adaptive construction processes. These emerging technologies offer radical changes to the built environment in terms of energy use, thermal behavior, performance, and aesthetics. Emerging technologies will change the ways in which buildings are designed and operated. By using intelligent materials, sustainable facades, and intelligent building operations, designers will positively affect the way humans live.

REFERENCES

Aksamija, A. (2009). "Context Based Design of Double Skin Facades: Climatic Considerations during the Design Process." *Perkins+Will Research Journal,* Vol. 1, No. 1, pp. 54–69.

Asanuma, H. (2000). "The Development of Metal-Based Smart Composites." *Journal of the Minerals, Metals and Materials Society,* Vol. 52, No. 10, pp. 21–24.

Askar, H., Probert, S. D., and Batty, W. J. (2001). "Windows for Buildings in Hot Arid Countries." *Applied Energy,* Vol. 70, pp. 77–101.

Badinelli, G. (2009). "Double Skin Facades for Warm Climate Regions: Analysis of a Solution with an Integrated Movable Shading System." *Building and Environment,* Vol. 44, pp. 1107–1118.

Blomsteberg, A., ed. (2007). *BESTFAÇADE: Best Practices for Double Skin Facades* (EIE/04/135/S07).

Cassar, L. (2004). "Photocatalysis of Cementitious Materials: Clean Buildings and Clean Air." *Materials Research Society Bulletin,* May, pp. 328–331.

Chabasa, A., Lombardoa, T., Cachierb, H., Pertuisotb, M. H., Oikonomoub, K., Falconec, R., Verita, M., and Geotti-Bianchinic, F. (2008). "Behaviour of Self-Cleaning Glass in Urban Atmosphere." *Building and Environment*, Vol. 43, pp. 2124–2131.

Haase, M., Marques da Silva, F., and Amato, A. (2009). "Simulation of Ventilated Facades in Hot and Humid Climates." *Energy and Buildings,* Vol. 41, No. 4, pp. 361–373.

Kuang, Y., and Ou, J. (2008). "Self-Repairing Performance of Concrete Beams Strengthened Using Superelastic SMA Wires in Combination with Adhesives Released from Hollow Fibers." *Smart Materials and Structures,* Vol. 17, pp. 1–7.

LeCuyer, A. (2008). *ETFE: Technology and Design*. Berlin, Germany: Birkauser Verlag.

Poirazis, H. (2006). *Double Skin Facades: A Literature Review* (IEA SCH Task 34, ECBCS Annex 43 Report).

Richman, R., and Pressnail, K. (2009). "A More Sustainable Curtain Wall System: Analytical Modeling of the Solar Dynamic Buffer Zone (SDBZ) Curtain Wall." *Building and Environment,* Vol. 44, pp. 1–10.

Spillman, W., Sirkis, J., and Gardiner, P. (1996). "Smart Materials and Structures: What Are They?" *Smart Materials and Structures,* Vol. 5, pp. 247–254.

Stec, W., and van Paaseen, A. (2005). "Symbiosis of the Double Skin Facade with the HVAC System." *Energy and Buildings,* Vol. 37, No. 5, pp. 461–469.

Tanaka, H., Okumiya, M., Tanaka, H., Yoon, G., and Watanabe, K. (2009). "Thermal Characteristics of a Double-Glazed External Wall System with Roll Screen in Cooling Season." *Building and Environment,* Vol. 44, pp. 1509–1516.

Wang, X., Walliman, N., Ogden, R., and Kendrick, C. (2007). "VIP and Their Applications in Buildings: A Review." *Proceedings of the Institution of Civil Engineers, Construction Materials,* Vol. 160, No. CM4, pp. 145–153.

White, S. R., Sottos, N. R., Geubelle, P. H., Moore, J. S., Kessler, M. R., Sriram, S. R., Brown, E. N., and Viswanathan, S. (2001). "Autonomic Healing of Polymer Composites." *Nature,* Vol. 409, pp. 794–797.

CHAPTER 5

CASE STUDIES

CASE STUDIES

Buildings are not self-contained mechanisms functioning independently from their surrounding natural systems. Nor can we be indifferent to the effects that buildings have on the local and global environment. Sustainable facades are integral parts of environmentally sensitive, high-performance buildings—and such buildings require careful planning, design, construction, and operation. In the previous chapters, we discussed various ways of achieving sustainable, high-performance facades. In this chapter, we look in depth at case studies of architectural projects that illustrate how those strategies can be implemented.

The case-study projects illustrate four ways to approach sustainable facade design:

- Building orientation
- Tectonic sun exposure control
- External shading elements
- Facade materials and wall assemblies

BUILDING ORIENTATION AND FACADE DESIGN

Arizona State University Interdisciplinary Science & Technology Building

The Interdisciplinary Science & Technology (IST) Building at the Arizona State University is located in Tempe, Arizona, which is characterized as a hot and arid climate (IECC zone 2B or "Bwh" in the Koppen classification). Figure 5-1 shows average daily temperatures, thermal comfort zone, and available solar radiation for each month. Hot and sunny conditions prevail much of the year in this location; therefore, the major objectives for the facade design were mitigating adverse solar radiation and using passive design strategies to provide a comfortable interior environment for the occupants.

The IST Building (Figures 5-1 to 5-12) is sited in one of the most dense and pedestrian-oriented areas of the campus. The building provides laboratory modules for biochemistry, biology, microbiology, and molecular biology research, as well as analytic and computer laboratories. The laboratory components of the building are arranged in an L-shaped configuration, with the short part running in the east-west direction along the north side of the site, and the long part running in the north-south direction along the west side of the site. The building's massing reflects its program: simple rectilinear elements along the north and west sides hold the laboratories and support functions, while the eastern wing houses office spaces. Core facilities and vertical transportation are located at the intersection of the two parts.

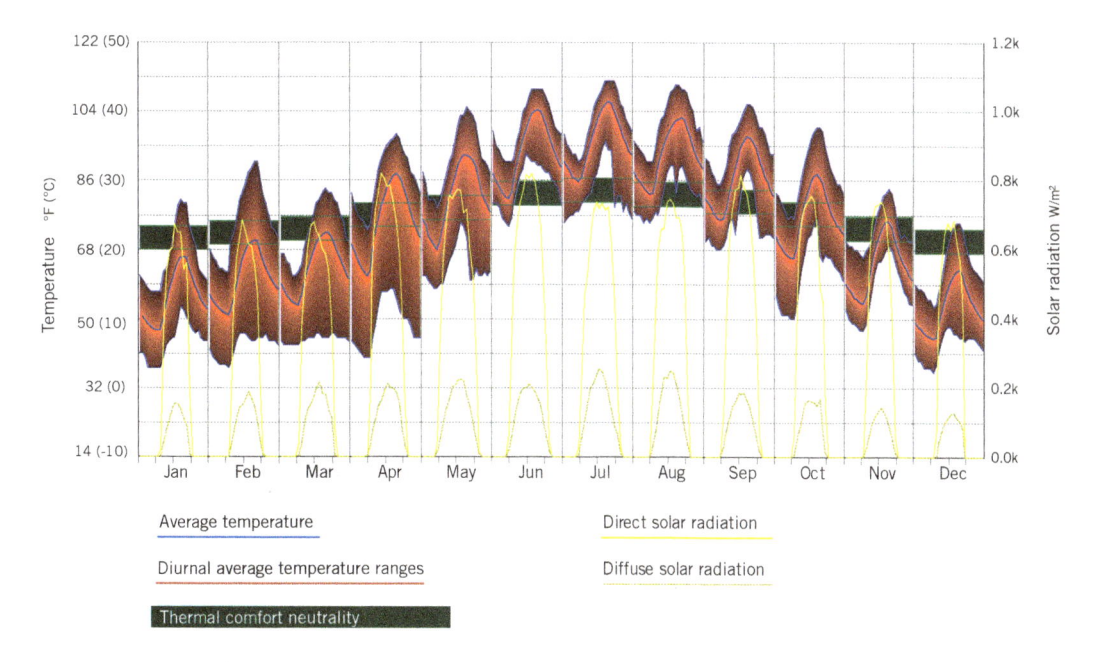

Figure 5-1 Typical exterior temperature conditions.

The building's form, along with its massing of solids and voids, responds directly to its site and solar orientation. The north-south orientation of the building was dictated by the constraints of the site. However, a number of design strategies were used to make the building efficient and environmentally responsive. The building was pushed to the western edge of the site to provide enough space for a courtyard between the east and west wings, as seen in Figure 5-2. The east wing was positioned and shaped to capture the prevailing winds, which cool the courtyard and the adjacent paseo (plaza).

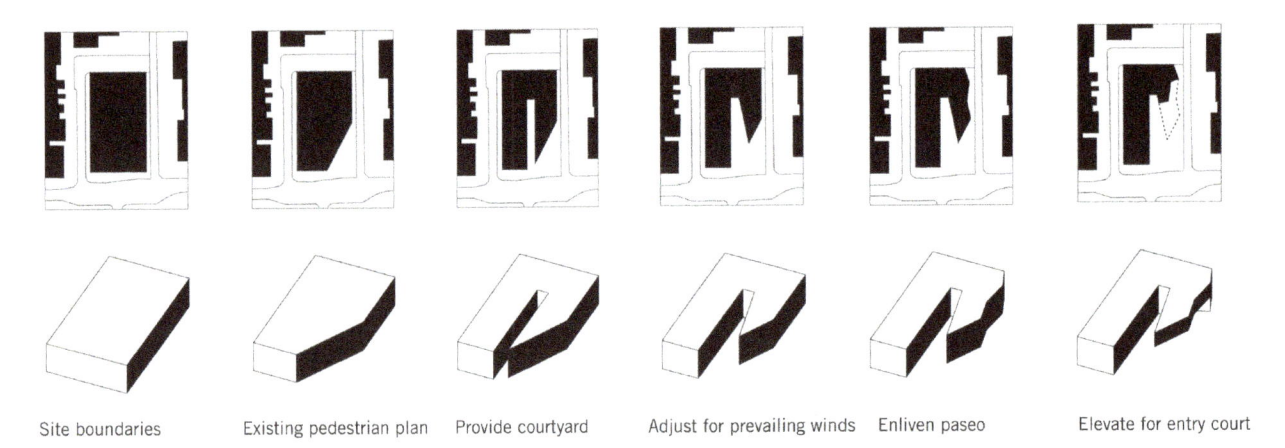

| Site boundaries | Existing pedestrian plan | Provide courtyard | Adjust for prevailing winds | Enliven paseo | Elevate for entry court |

Figure 5-2 Building massing and components.

The orientation of the facades directly influenced their design. The north facade is flush, with large, unshaded windows allowing daylight to penetrate deep into interior spaces. The south facades of the east and west wings incorporate deep overhangs (seen in Figure 5-5), as horizontal shading elements are best suited for this orientation. The south facades also have vertical shading elements to minimize glare and prevent low-angle sunlight from penetrating into the interior during morning and afternoon hours. The east facades of the east and west wings have high-performance glazing and horizontal metal louvers, as seen in Figures 5-6 and 5-7. The louvers, shown in Figure 5-8, block unwanted solar radiation, especially in the morning, and reduce glare, while allowing the labs to benefit from natural light and views out to the courtyard and paseo.

The west facade, shown in Figure 5-9, consists primarily of cast-in-place concrete with few windows, and uses thermal mass as a passive sustainable design strategy. Most appropriate for locations with extreme day-to-night temperature swings, this design approach uses walls made of thermally massive materials, such as masonry or concrete, to absorb the daytime solar energy. At night, much of this energy radiates to the building's interior, providing free nighttime heat. Laboratory support spaces, which are often unoccupied, are located along this side of the building. Vertical extruded fins shade conference rooms and break rooms, the few spaces along this facade with windows.

BUILDING ORIENTATION AND FACADE DESIGN 161

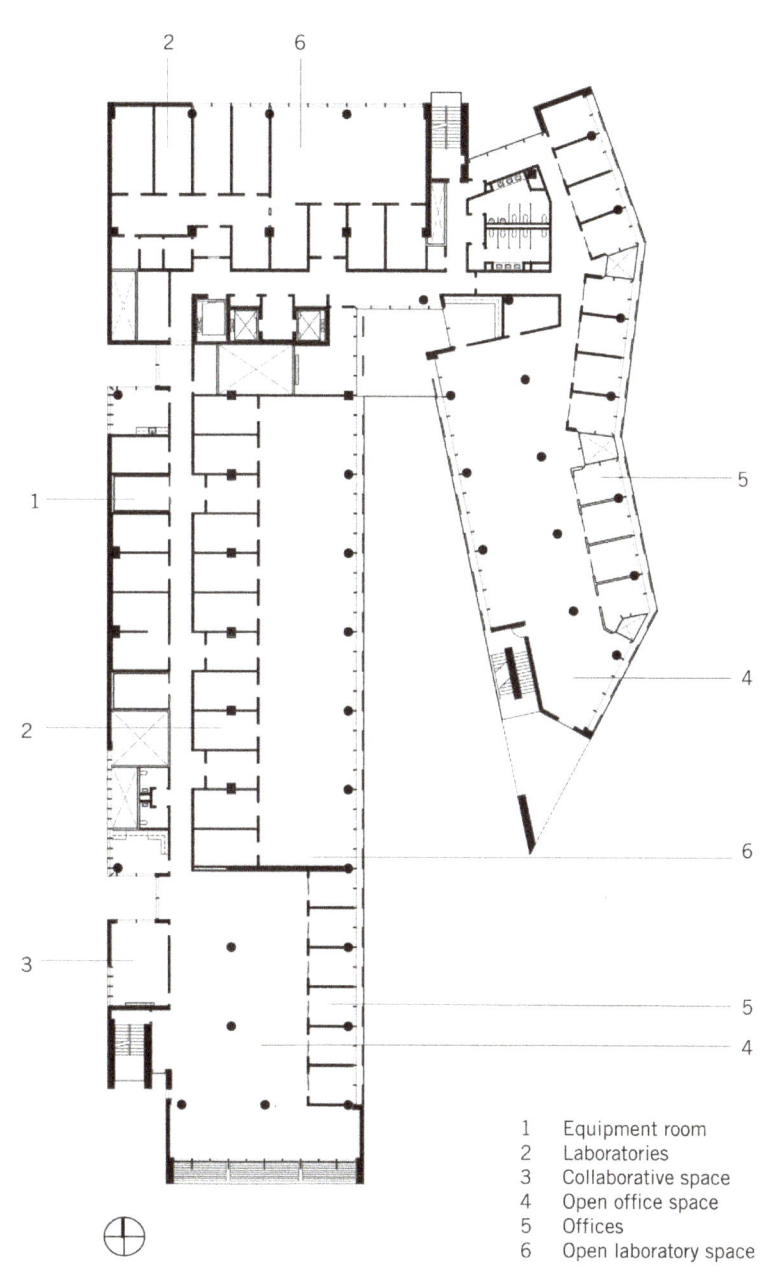

1 Equipment room
2 Laboratories
3 Collaborative space
4 Open office space
5 Offices
6 Open laboratory space

Figure 5-3 Typical floor plan.

Figure 5-4 Exterior view from the south.

Courtesy of Steinkamp Photography

BUILDING ORIENTATION AND FACADE DESIGN   163

Figure 5-5 View from the south.

Figure 5-6a, Figure 5-6b East facade.

164 CASE STUDIES

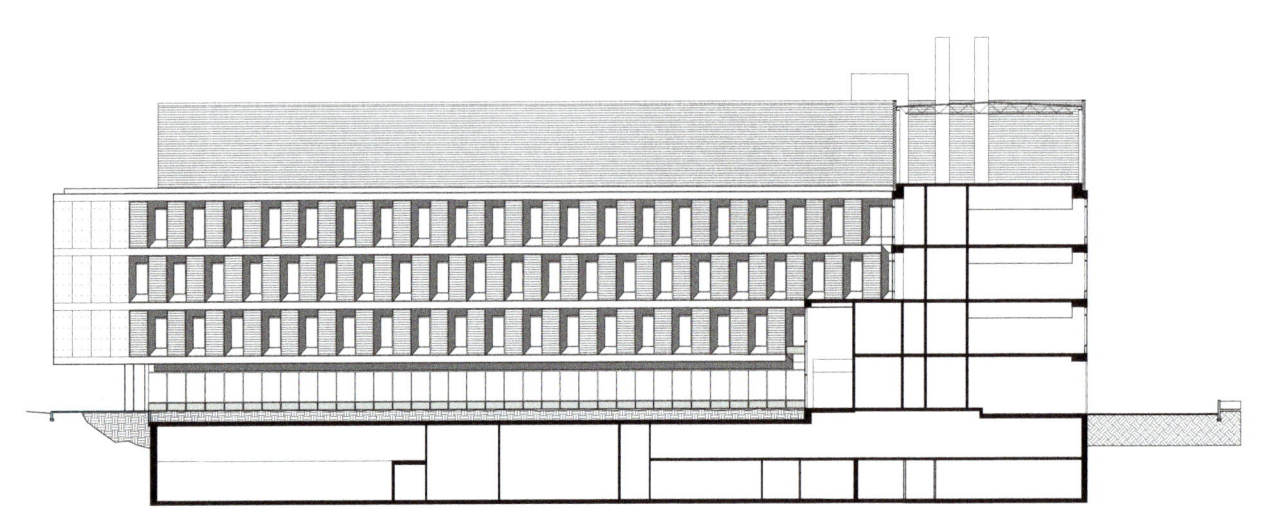

Figure 5-7 East facade of the west wing (elevation).

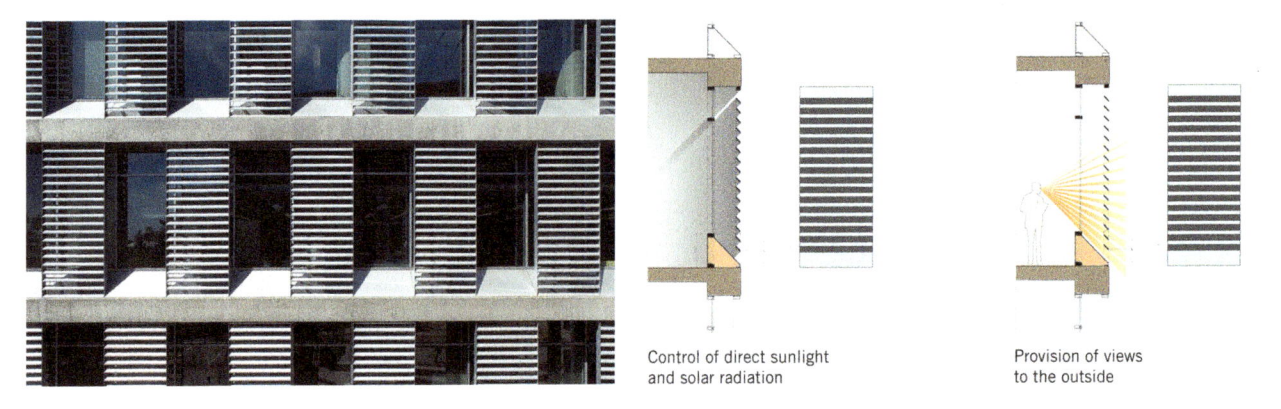

Control of direct sunlight
and solar radiation

Provision of views
to the outside

Figure 5-8a, Figure 5-8b East facade shading elements.

Other energy reduction strategies include low-e glazing, high-efficiency lighting, occupancy sensors, daylight harvesting, after-hours ventilation rate setbacks, variable volume airflow for all areas, and electronic linear Venturi fume hood and laboratory airflow control valves. Daylight is provided to all regularly occupied spaces, including the nuclear magnetic resonance suite in the building's basement. Figures 5-10 and 5-11 show interior spaces with direct access to daylight. Digital controls were integrated with lighting and mechanical systems for all areas, allowing scheduling of occupied and unoccupied periods.

BUILDING ORIENTATION AND FACADE DESIGN 165

Figure 5-9 West facade.

Figure 5-10 Interior laboratories and daylight.

Figure 5-11 Circulation space and daylight.

The designers studied sunscreen options for the south and east facades to maximize views and minimize sunlight penetration. Daylight simulations were used to study varying window and shading configurations. For example, Figure 5-12 shows daylight simulations for three design options for the south facades. All three options use floor-to-ceiling glazing. The first option has a horizontal overhang. The second option adds horizontal louvers to Option 1. The third option adds vertical shading elements to Option 2, to reduce potential glare during early morning and late afternoon hours. The final design used the horizontal overhangs of Option 1 plus the vertical shading of Option 3 to block solar radiation and reduce glare.

South facade (December 21)

Option 1: Overhang (morning)

Option 2: Overhang and horizontal louvers (noon)

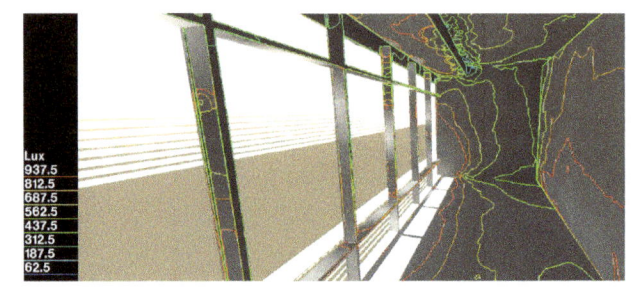

Option 3: Overhang, horizontal louvers, and vertical fins (afternoon)

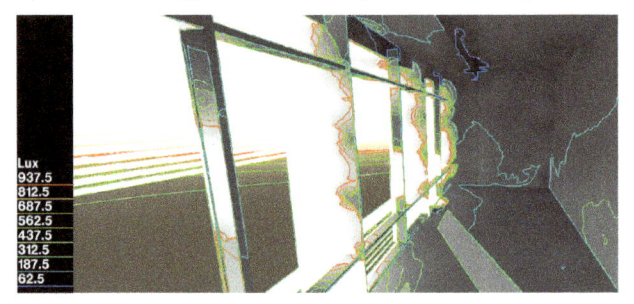

Figure 5-12 Daylight simulations for south-facing facade.

These passive design strategies based on the orientation of the building facades were successful in minimizing energy consumption for the IST Building, and for providing thermally and visually comfortable spaces for the occupants. With its low annual energy consumption, the building exceeded the ASHRAE 90.1 energy standard requirements by 31%, and was awarded LEED Gold certification by the U.S. Green Building Council.

Center for Urban Waters

The Center for Urban Waters (Figures 5-13 to 5-26) is a laboratory building dedicated to hydrologic research. The facility is shared by the City of Tacoma Environmental Services Department, the University of Washington, and the Puget Sound Partnership, a Washington state agency. The facility is primarily used for studying and analyzing water samples from the waterways of Tacoma and surrounding areas. It is also used for educational activities. The program includes laboratories, offices, conference rooms, an exhibit center, a cafeteria, and related building services.

Tacoma is located in a region with a mixed marine climate (IECC zone 4C, or "Cfb" in the Koppen classification). Figure 5-13 shows average daily temperatures, thermal comfort zone, and available solar radiation for each month. We can see from the chart that cool temperatures are predominant during winter months, while generally mild temperatures prevail for the rest of the year. This temperate climate zone allows cooling by natural ventilation, and the relatively mild winters and low solar radiation suggest that a moderate amount of glazing on the south and west orientations will not negatively affect a building's energy performance. Most buildings in this climate type are heating-dominated. However, because of the type of research performed and the equipment used in this facility, the Center for Urban Waters is a cooling-dominated building.

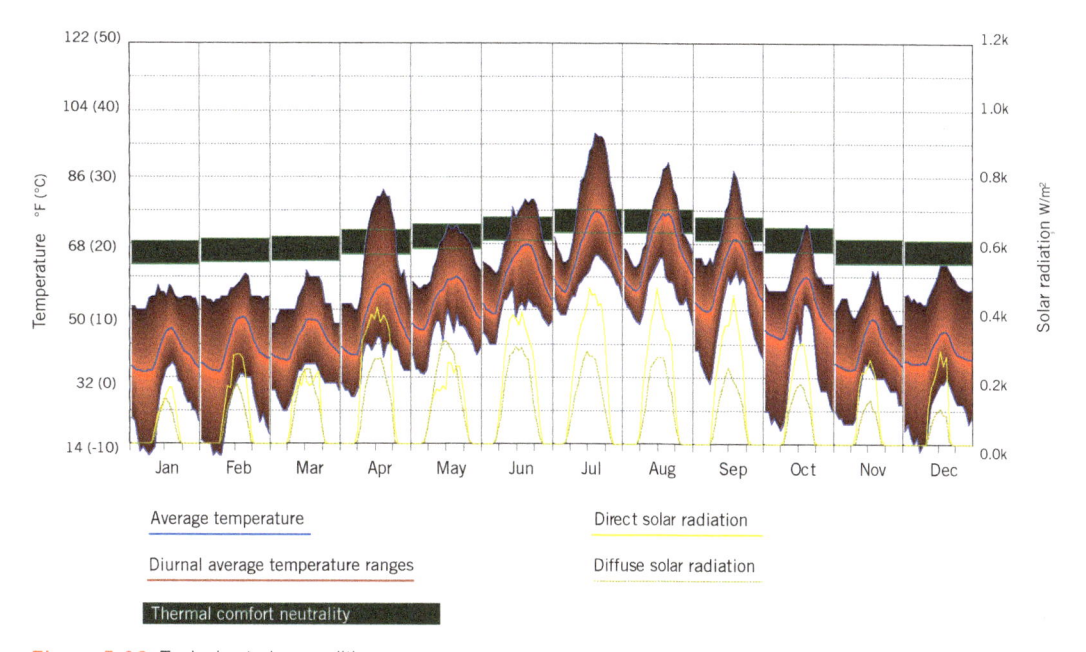

Figure 5-13 Typical exterior conditions.

The Center for Urban Waters is on a long and narrow site along the industrial waterfront of the Thea Foss Waterway. The geometry of the site led to a narrow building design, oriented roughly north and south. This design was able to maximize the daylighting of the interior spaces and to use natural ventilation to reduce the building's energy loads. Figure 5-14 shows the building in relation to the waterfront and the neighboring industrial structures.

The building design uses passive sustainable design strategies, which are strongly influenced by the site's orientation. The major programmatic elements are grouped into two zones: a laboratory zone facing inland and an office zone along the waterway. Because of the programmatic requirements of the research activities, the laboratories require mechanical ventilation. Locating them adjacent to the industrial neighborhood, with its reduced opportunities for fresh air, was a practical response to the site.

In contrast, natural ventilation for the office spaces was considered highly desirable. By facing the waterway—a source of fresh air—the offices benefit from natural ventilation. The office spaces on the north end of the building, with the laboratories to the east, use single-sided natural ventilation. At the south end of the building, where the offices have west and east exposures, natural cross-ventilation is provided. Operable windows in the west and south facades allow occupants to control the amount of natural ventilation. Landscaping was used to create a buffer zone to the east of the offices, keeping out air and noise produced by the neighboring industrial activities.

Solar orientation was also a factor in the design of the west and south facades. The glazed curtain wall on the south facade uses horizontal shading elements to block midday sun, while providing unobstructed views to the water. Figure 5-16 shows natural ventilation and shading strategies.

The best views from the building are along the west facade, overlooking the waterway. The western exposure, however, also receives the greatest solar heat gain. Early designs for this facade included a glass curtain wall protected by vertical sunshades—a reasonable and sustainable approach, but one that proved too costly. Instead, an aluminum rainscreen with punched high-performance windows was developed. The designers studied two materials for the opaque parts of the facade: composite panels, in which a resin core is sandwiched between layers of light-gauge aluminum; and formed heavy-gauge aluminum panels. Both materials would perform well, but a life-cycle analysis showed that the composite panels would be more difficult to recycle at the end of the building's useful life.

BUILDING ORIENTATION AND FACADE DESIGN 169

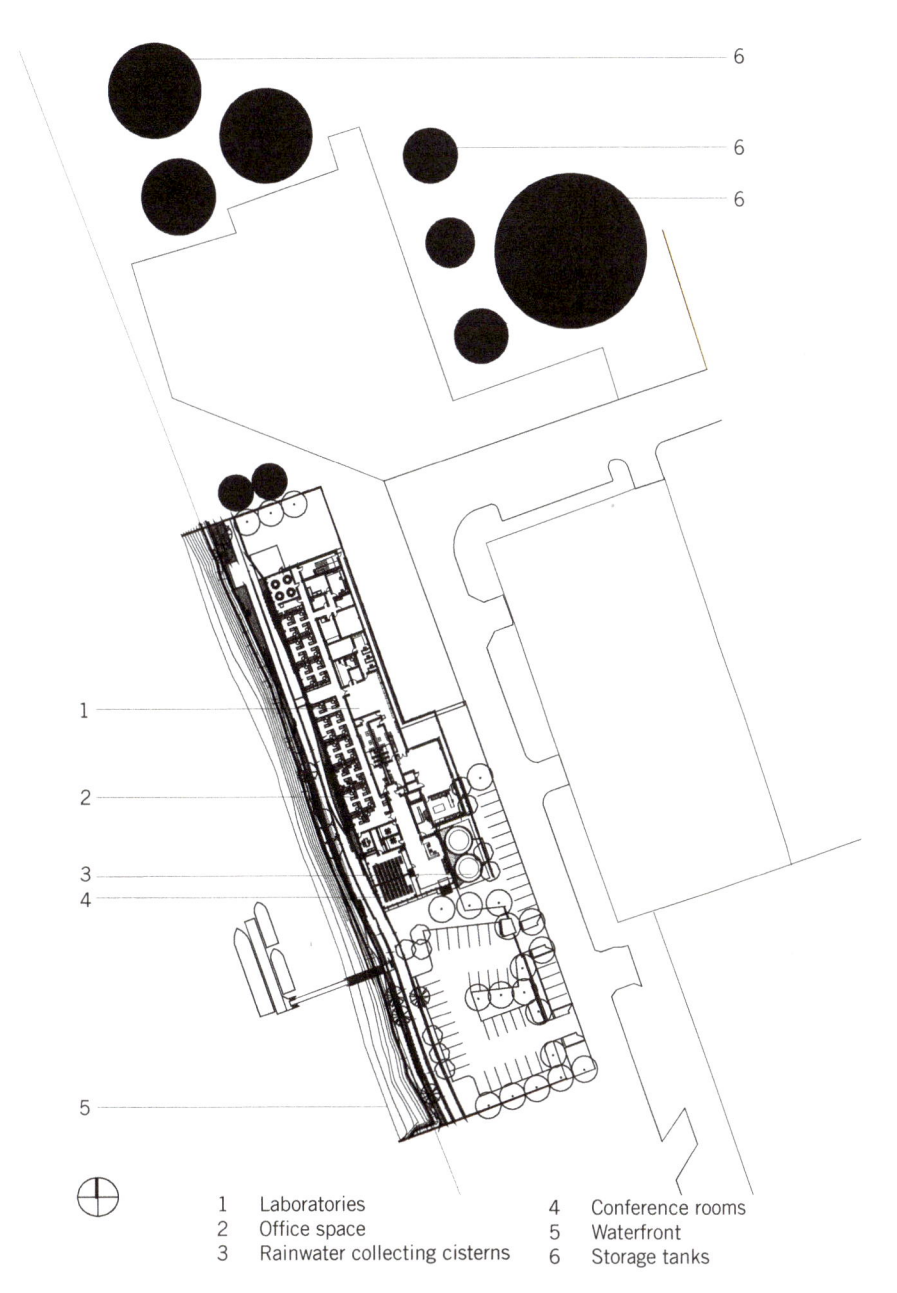

1 Laboratories
2 Office space
3 Rainwater collecting cisterns
4 Conference rooms
5 Waterfront
6 Storage tanks

Figure 5-14 Center for Urban Waters site and typical floor plan.

170   CASE STUDIES

Courtesy of Benjamin Benschneider/OTTO

Figure 5-15 Site context, with the Thea Foss Waterway in the foreground and Mt. Rainier in the background.

To compensate for the loss of the vertical sunshades, the designers integrated a system of automated exterior blinds into the west facade. Similar to venetian blinds typically used for interiors, the closed blinds prevent solar heat gain within the building during afternoon hours. When open, the blinds also allow passive solar heating. The exterior wall section in Figure 5-19 shows the exterior blind assembly. When the sun is shining on the west facade, the blinds are in the down position, with the blades either open or closed. When the sun is not on the west side, or when the wind is unusually strong, or at night, the blinds are in the up position, housed in a pocket behind the rainscreen facade.

In some rooms, such as conference rooms, floor-to-ceiling windows with exterior blinds are used to provide expansive views. Elsewhere, such as at the typical open offices, windows are limited to narrow glazed slots to optimize energy performance. The west facade also has high clerestory windows above the vision windows. There are no exterior blinds at these clerestory windows; instead, interior translucent-resin light shelves at the sills of the windows block direct sunlight and bounce daylight deep into the rooms (Figure 5-20).

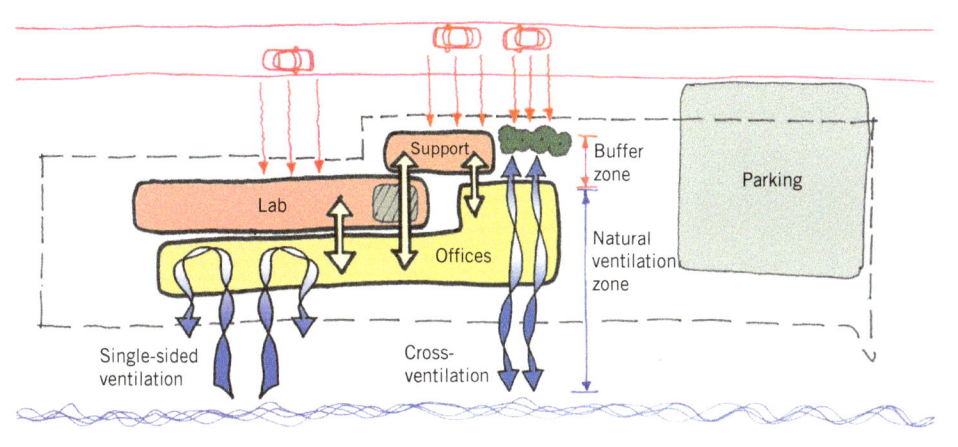

BUILDING ORIENTATION AND FACADE DESIGN   171

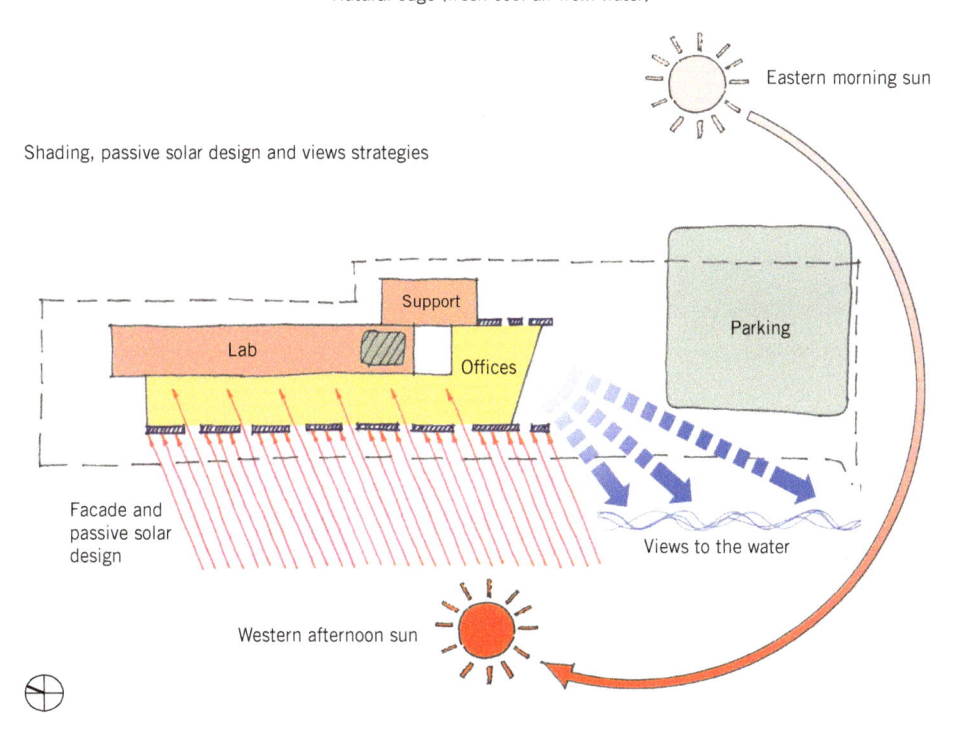

Figure 5-16 Building orientation and passive design strategies.

172   CASE STUDIES

Figure 5-17 Exterior view of the south and west facades.

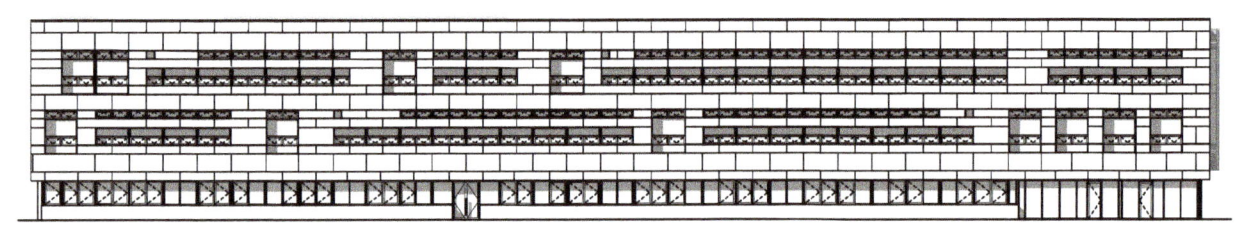

Figure 5-18 West elevation.

BUILDING ORIENTATION AND FACADE DESIGN   173

Light-shelf detail

Exterior blinds pocket detail

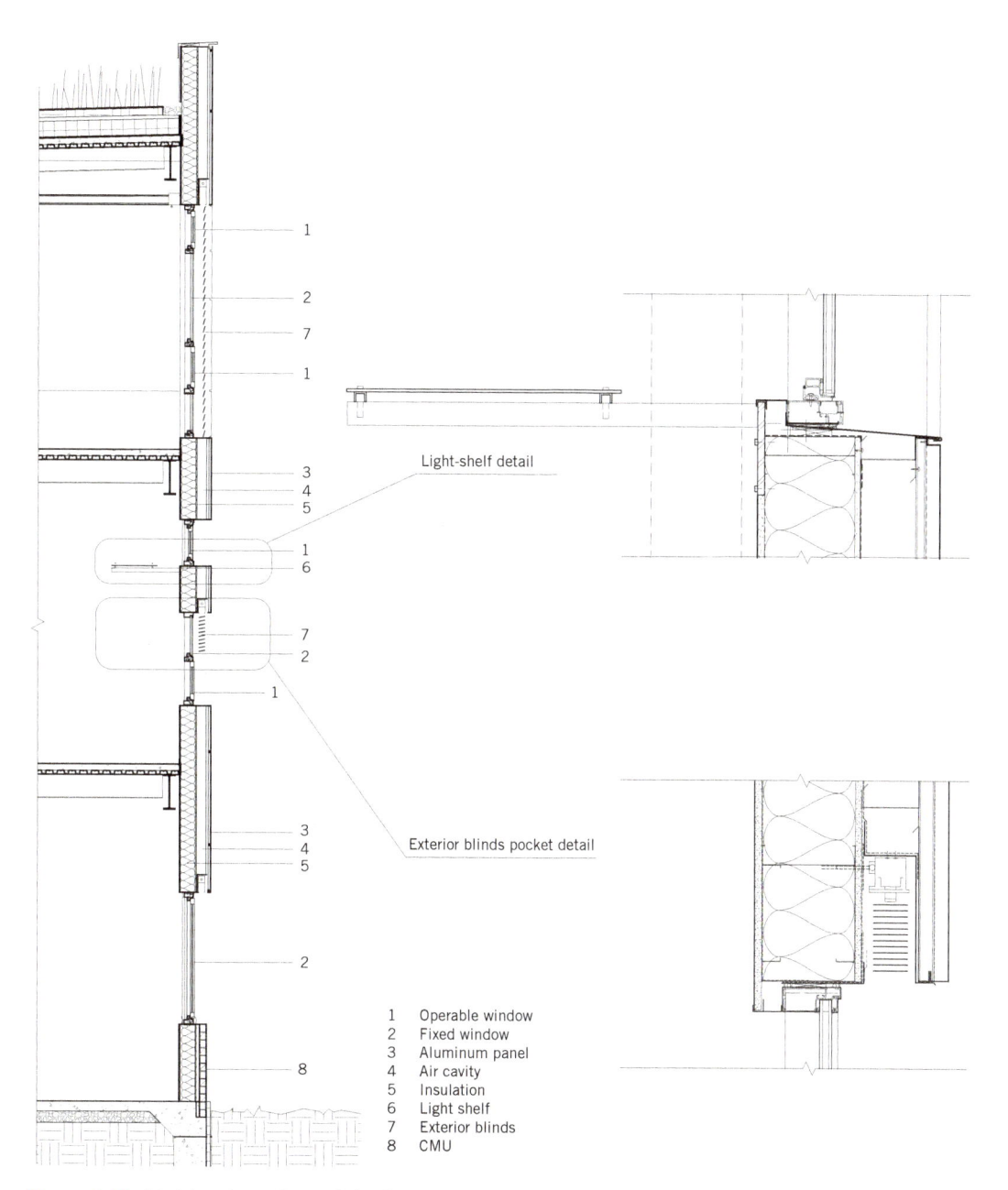

1 Operable window
2 Fixed window
3 Aluminum panel
4 Air cavity
5 Insulation
6 Light shelf
7 Exterior blinds
8 CMU

Figure 5-19 West facade section and details.

Figure 5-20 Light shelf along the west facade.

On the east facade, a rainscreen made of horizontal corrugated metal panels faces the industrial side of the site. Covering the upper half of the second- and third-level slot windows are perforated corrugated metal screens. These screens help control early morning sun and reduce potential glare, while maintaining views and maximizing daylighting (Figure 5-24).

Only on the south facade is curtain wall used (Figure 5-17). Fixed exterior horizontal sunshades, made of 16-inch- (406-mm-) deep perforated aluminum plates, are supported by tapered aluminum outriggers (shown in Figure 5-21). Vertical spacing of the sunshades is 12 inches (305 mm). The curtain wall projects outward along the second and third levels at the southeast corner, forming a canopy that protects the main entrance. This portion of the south facade does not have external shading elements, but a ceramic frit applied to the glass reduces direct solar exposure (Figure 5-22). Even with the fritted glass, the spaces behind this part of the curtain wall experience a wider temperature range than spaces with the horizontal sunshades. Therefore, spaces with lower criteria for thermal comfort and glare, such as breakout rooms, were planned for these locations (Figure 5-23).

Figure 5-21 South curtain wall facade and horizontal shading elements.

The north facade continues the east facade's corrugated metal rainscreen. This facade was designed to provide high thermal resistance. Therefore, the windows were kept small. Sun shading elements were not needed for this orientation (Figure 5-25).

The overall window-to-wall ratio (WWR) for all four facades is low, around 32%. Glass selection was based on the orientation of the windows and the functional requirements of the interior spaces. The vision areas for all facades consist of double-glazed, air-insulated glazing units, with a low-e coating applied to the exterior surface of the interior lite (surface #3). Curtain wall spandrels consist of insulated glazing units made of green-tinted float glass, sandblasted to a white-line finish on the inner surface of the exterior lite (surface #2), with a colored frit pattern on the inner surface of the interior lite (surface #3). The opaque areas of the facades were designed for an average thermal resistance of R-19 hr-ft^2-°F/Btu (3.36 m^2-°K/W).

176 CASE STUDIES

Figure 5-22 Fritted glass along the south facade.

Courtesy of Benjamin Benschneider/OTTO

Figure 5-23 Interior space and south facade.

Courtesy of Benjamin Benschneider/OTTO

Figure 5-24 East facade and metal panel rainscreen.

Courtesy of Benjamin Benschneider/OTTO

Figure 5-25 North facade.

Courtesy of Benjamin Benschneider/OTTO

BUILDING ORIENTATION AND FACADE DESIGN   177

Besides the high-performance facade design, the Center for Urban Waters incorporates other energy-efficiency and sustainability strategies, including vegetated roofs, stormwater collection, water reuse, use of recycled and reclaimed materials, geo-exchange wells, radiant heating and cooling, and a heat-recovery system in the laboratories and office spaces (Figure 5-26).

As a result, the modeled energy consumption indicated a 36% energy-use savings, compared to an ASHRAE 90.1 baseline building. The Center's Energy Usage Intensity (EUI) is 81 kBtu/ft^2 (256 kWh/m^2), compared to 123 kBtu/ft^2 (388 kWh/m^2) for the baseline. Measurement and verification systems installed in the building track actual building performance and inform users of the real-time energy use. The Center for Urban Waters was completed in 2010, and achieved LEED Platinum certification by the U.S. Green Building Council.

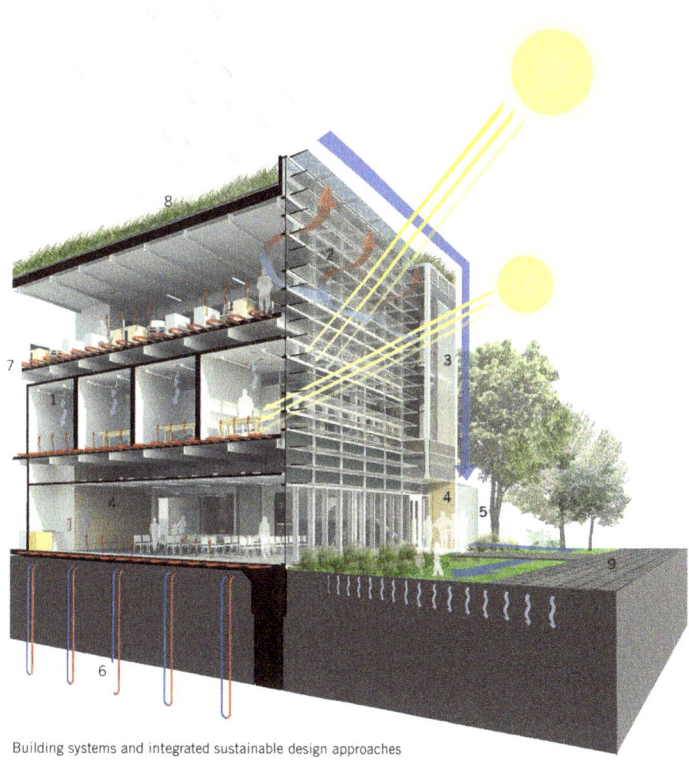

Building systems and integrated sustainable design approaches

1 Operable windows and fans
2 Fixed horizontal shading elements
3 Fritted glass
4 Salvaged wood
5 Rainwater collecting cisterns
6 Geo-exchange wells
7 Radiant floors
8 Green roof
9 Permeable pavers

Figure 5-26 Sustainable design strategies.

TECTONIC SUN EXPOSURE CONTROL

Kuwait University College of Education

Kuwait University College of Education (Figures 5-27 to 5-38) is located in Shadadiyah, Kuwait. Figure 5-27 shows average daily exterior temperatures and solar radiation conditions for this location for each month. The climate is characterized as very hot and dry (IECC zone 1B or Koppen classification "Bwh"). Large daily swings in temperature are common between the night and day. The summer months are unbearably hot and arid—it has been described as the world's hottest urban climate—while the winter months have relatively mild conditions. These seasonal variations challenged the design team to find innovative ways to provide a comfortable environment for the building's occupants while maintaining relatively low energy use.

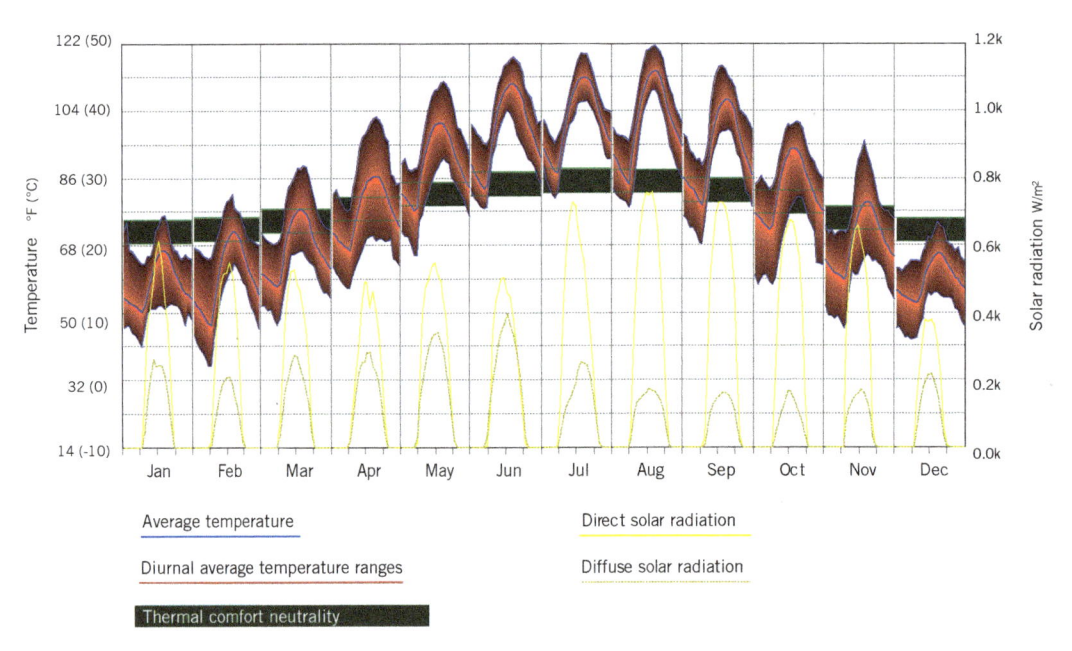

Figure 5-27 Typical exterior environmental conditions.

Kuwait University College of Education is part of a master plan for the Sabah Al-Salem University City. Three criteria were the primary driving forces for the design solution:

- A strong, individual identity for the College of Education building
- A student-centered environment that fosters a community of learning
- A highly sustainable design that provides daylight to all classrooms, offices, and main circulation spaces

TECTONIC SUN EXPOSURE CONTROL   179

Figure 5-28 Kuwait College University College of Education exterior view.

The five-story rectangular building consists of a perimeter zone of modular classrooms and administrative spaces surrounding an inner core of major assembly spaces and outdoor courtyards. A free-form, glass-enclosed "boardwalk" is carved into the building's perimeter. This primary building circulation path provides access to the auditorium, cafeteria, learning resource center, faculty lounge and dining, and courtyards. Figure 5-29 shows the relationship between the boardwalk and the other spaces. The interplay of the building's solids and voids as the sloping boardwalk path is carved into its mass defines the architectural identity of the College of Education. Four central garden courtyards provide daylight and views to the learning spaces that surround and overlook them.

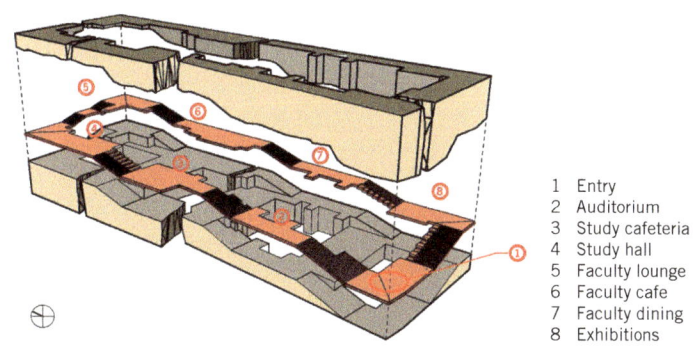

1 Entry
2 Auditorium
3 Study cafeteria
4 Study hall
5 Faculty lounge
6 Faculty cafe
7 Faculty dining
8 Exhibitions

Figure 5-29 Building circulation diagram.

180 CASE STUDIES

The site constraints required that the long elevations of the College of Education face east and west. A self-shading facade protects the building's interiors from the intense solar radiation while maintaining views for its occupants. Inspired by traditional Kuwaiti patterned screens, the facade was designed using three-dimensional modeling and visualization software. Solar analysis was performed to understand incident solar radiation (Figure 5-30). Because the master plan has identified future buildings on the east and west sides of the College of Education, these buildings were anticipated in the analysis (in Figure 5-30, the neighboring building to the west appears as a dashed-line box). The results showed increased values along the top portion of the west facade, and lower values near the bottom. The north and south facades are not shaded by the surrounding buildings; this is reflected in the uniform north-facade incident solar radiation in Figure 5-30.

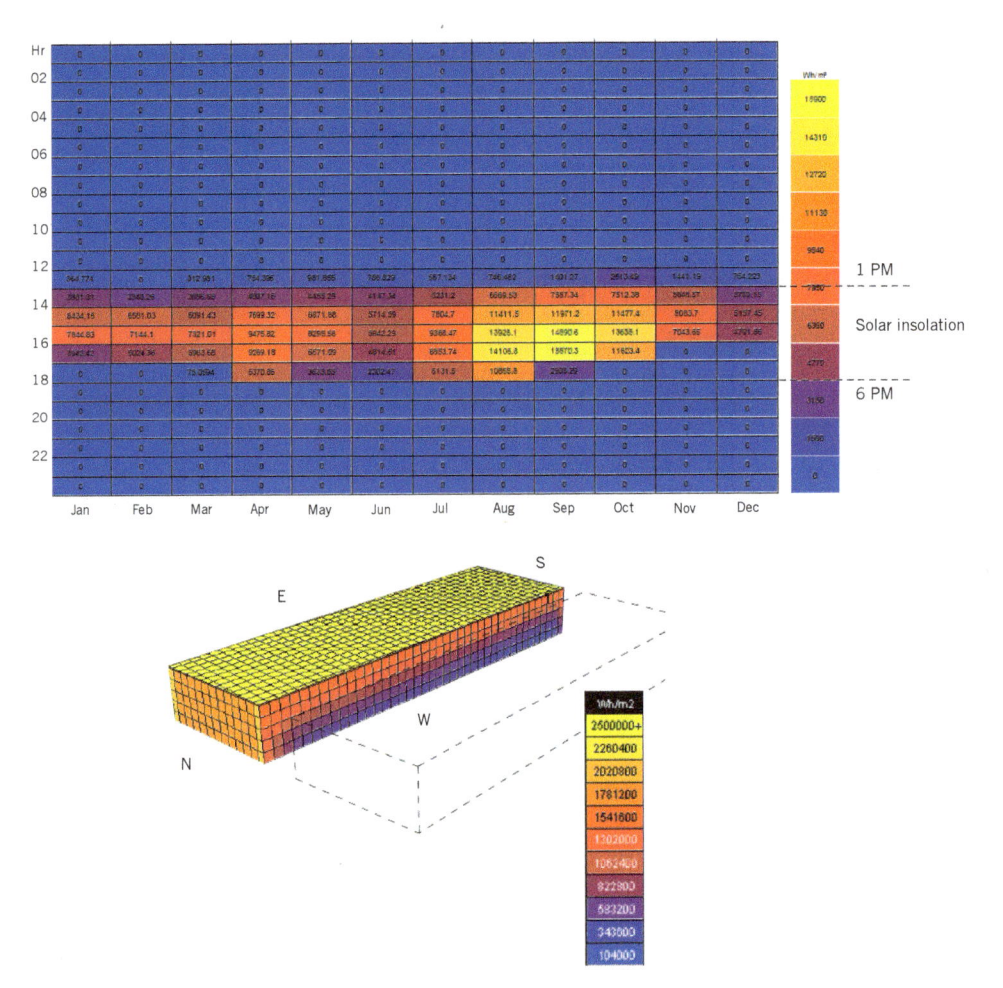

Figure 5-30 Total monthly incident solar radiation on the west facade (top) and solar radiation analysis on different facades (bottom).

TECTONIC SUN EXPOSURE CONTROL

The complex geometry of the facade uses integral shading elements, set at the optimal cutoff angles, to shade the building from intense solar radiation, as seen in Figure 5-31. Also, the depth of the curtain wall varies, from deeper at the building's top to narrower at the bottom, to provide shading for the areas where it is most needed, along the top portion of the building's east and west facades.

1 Shading glass fins
2 Glass-fiber-reinforced concrete (GFRC)
3 Steel skeleton
4 Glazing
5 Rigid insulation
6 Batt insulation

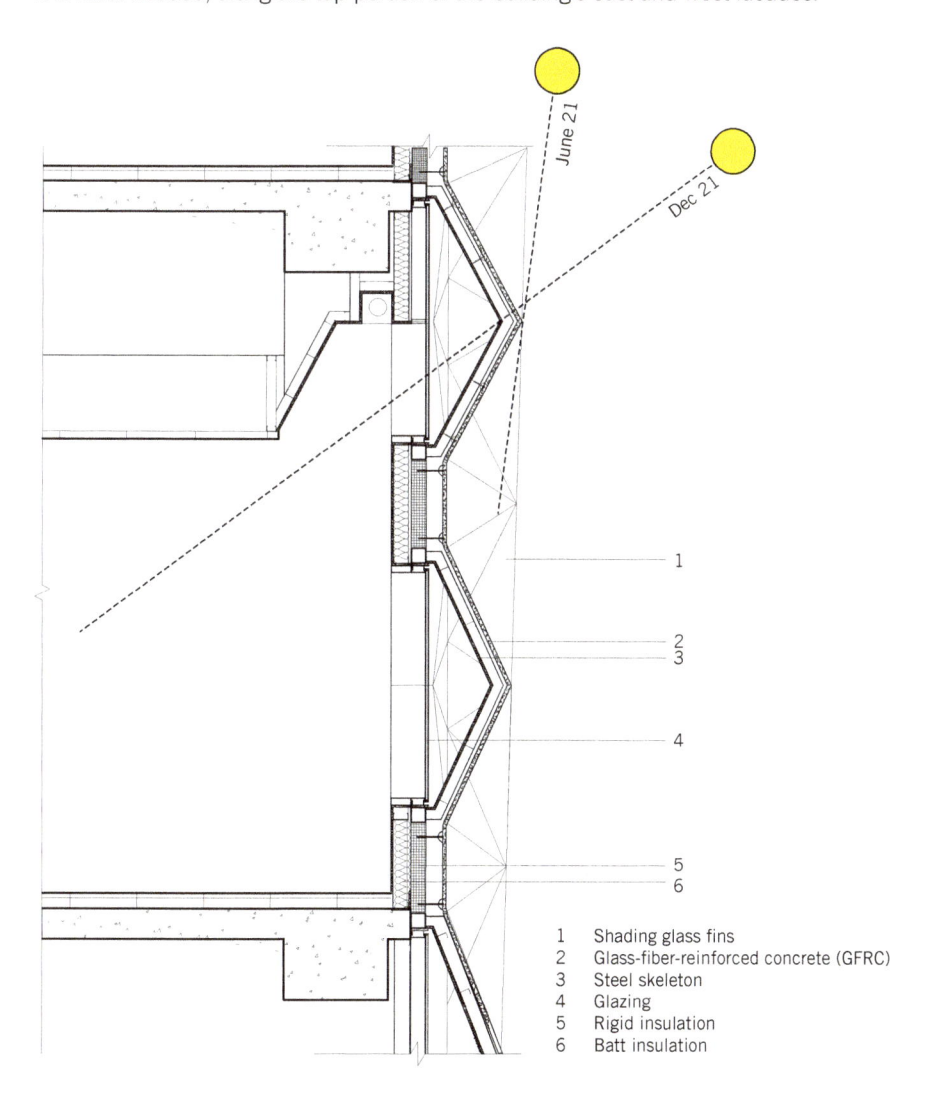

Figure 5-31 Self-shading facade geometry.

CASE STUDIES

Several layers form the self-shading exterior skin, as seen in Figures 5-32 and 5-33. The following are the major components of the facade:

- Shading fins are constructed of two layers of tempered laminated glass, with a ceramic frit between the glass layers. These shades reduce direct solar radiation and transmitted solar heat gain, thus reducing cooling loads for the HVAC system. These translucent planes also direct diffuse light into the interior spaces and reduce glare at the exterior wall (Figure 5-34).

- The opaque parts of the facades are panels made of glass-fiber-reinforced concrete (GFRC), a lightweight and thin (less than 1 inch or 2.5 cm thick) material.

- The galvanized steel skeleton provides a lightweight, structurally efficient support for the GFRC panels. Its low weight results in low superimposed loads on the building's structural system.

- Low-e insulating glass is used to reflect radiant infrared light and to reduce cooling loads. Operable windows on the east and west facades allow natural ventilation during milder seasons. These diamond-shaped windows, similar in shape to the fixed windows of the facade, use a pivoting mechanism to open and close.

- Insulation behind the GFRC minimizes heat transfer between the exterior and interior environment.

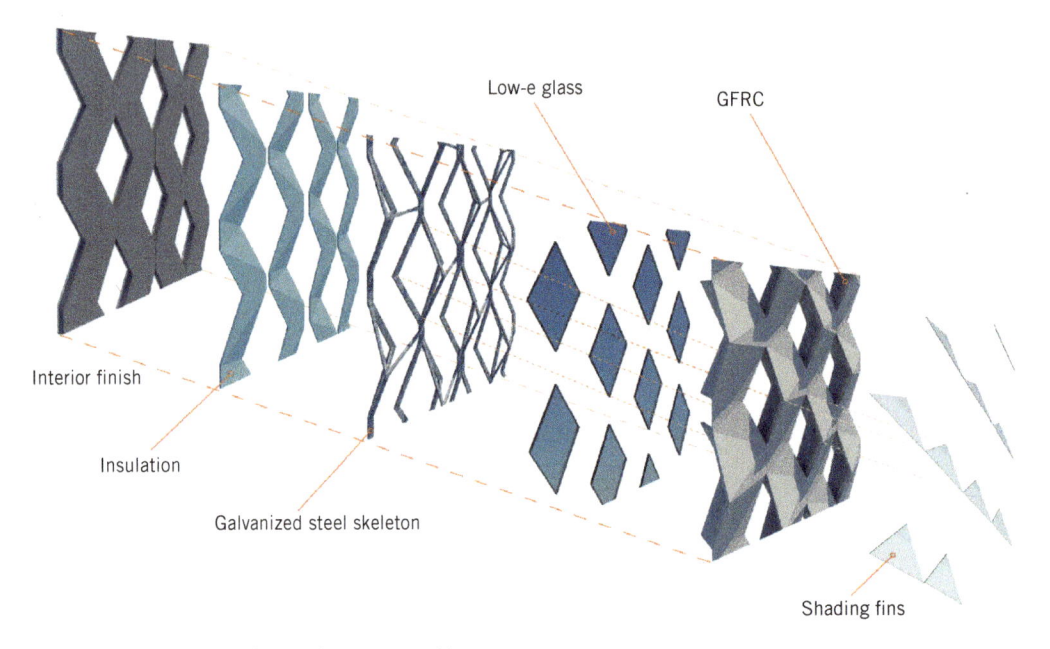

Figure 5-32 Diagram of major facade assembly components.

Section A-A

Partial west elevation

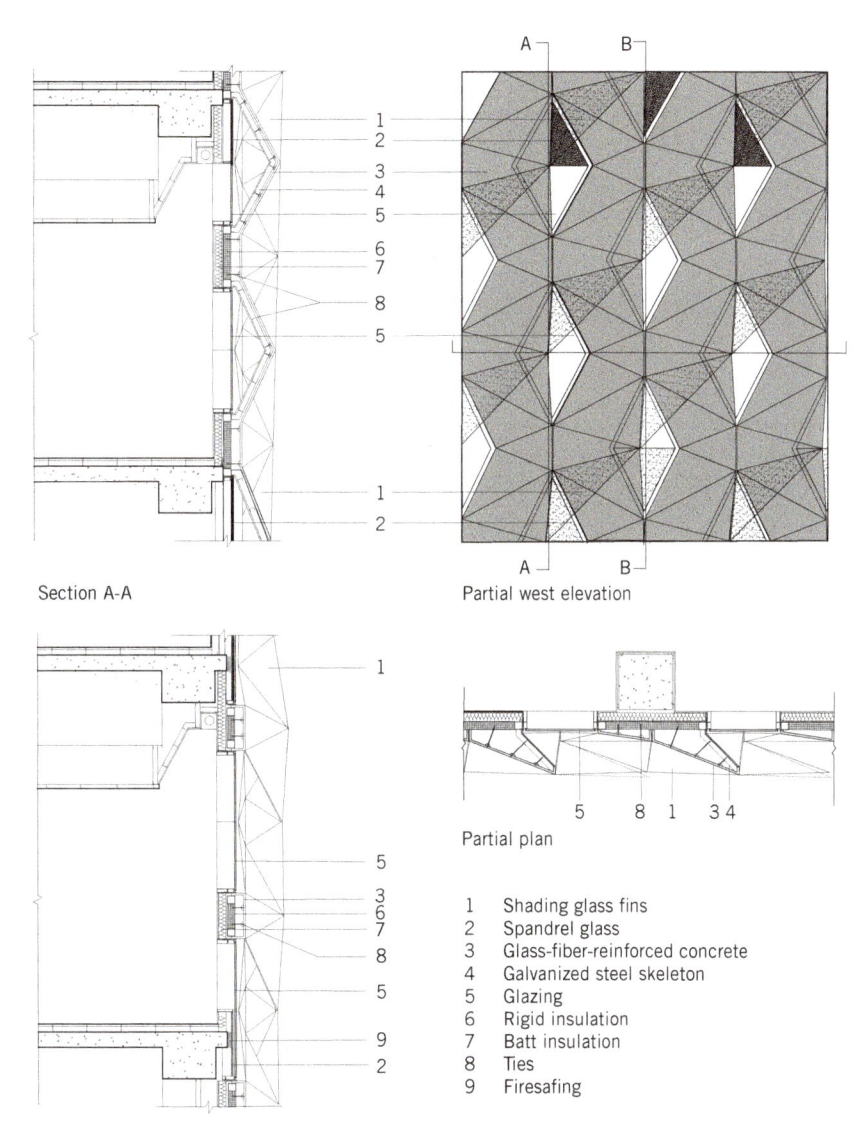

Partial plan

1 Shading glass fins
2 Spandrel glass
3 Glass-fiber-reinforced concrete
4 Galvanized steel skeleton
5 Glazing
6 Rigid insulation
7 Batt insulation
8 Ties
9 Firesafing

Section B-B

Figure 5-33 Partial west elevation, plan, and sections.

184 CASE STUDIES

The self-shading curtain wall uses shading and filtering mechanisms to protect the building from the harsh sun and to provide sufficient daylight for interior spaces. Figure 5-34 shows a daylight simulation study that compares two options for the west facade, with and without the translucent glass fins. The light levels without the glass fins are significantly higher than with the fins. This would likely cause uneven distribution of daylight and could cause visual discomfort and glare. By filtering the light before it enters the interior space, the glass fins provide even distribution. Figures 5-35 to 5-37 show the translucent glass fins, and how they provide shading.

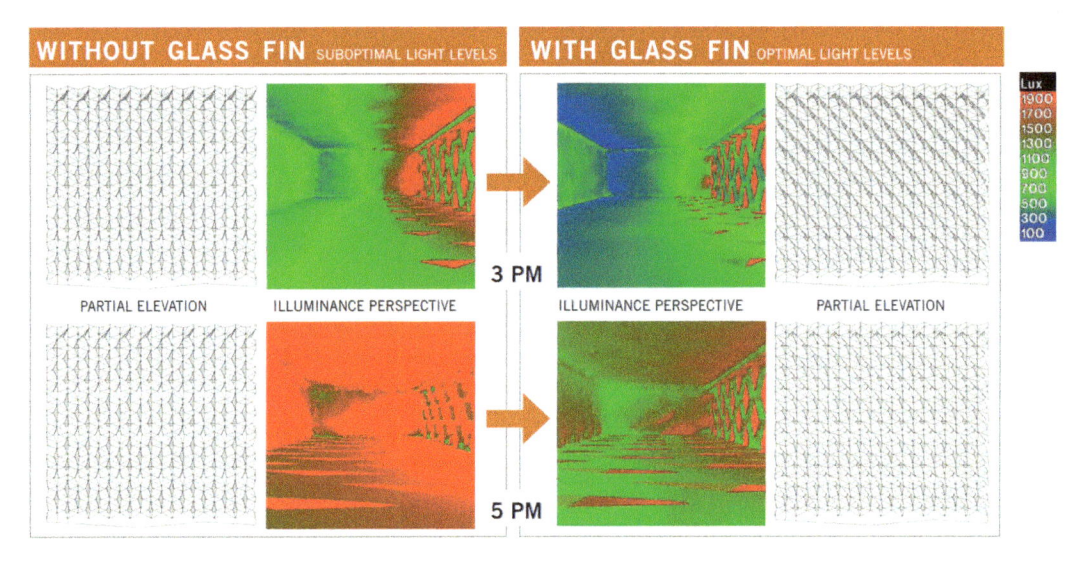

Figure 5-34 Daylight simulations result for the west facade (June 21).

Figure 5-35 Glass fins.

TECTONIC SUN EXPOSURE CONTROL   185

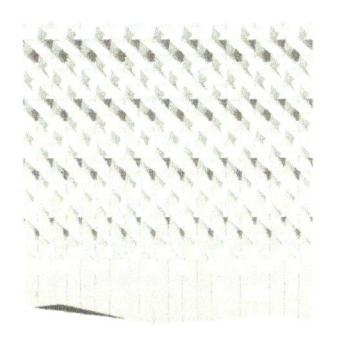

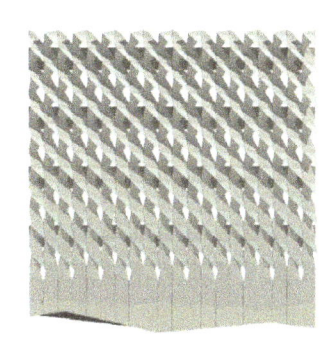

June 21   May/September 21   December 21

Figure 5-36 Shading study.

Figure 5-37 Physical model.

Figure 5-38 GFRC panel mockup.

Energy modeling performed during design indicated that the facade design, along with other energy-efficient design strategies, would reduce the building's energy consumption by 21% compared to a baseline building prescribed by the ASHRAE 90.1-2004 standard. The facade design would also eliminate 82% of the solar heat gain. Kuwait University College of Education is expected to achieve LEED Gold rating by the U.S. Green Building Council when completed in 2014.

King Abdullah Financial District Parcel 4.01 Building

When complete, the King Abdullah Financial District (KAFD), located in Riyadh, Saudi Arabia, will be the largest financial center in the Middle East. The master plan for this 160-hectare development includes high-rise commercial buildings and high- and low-rise residential buildings, as well as mixed-use buildings, infrastructure, transportation, and open green spaces.

The climate is very hot and dry (IECC climate zone 1B or Koppen classification "Bwh"). Figure 5-39 shows climatic conditions, including average daily exterior temperatures, thermal comfort zone, and available solar radiation. Days are hot most of the year, but are extremely hot from April through October. Solar radiation is high during the entire year, requiring sustainable buildings to incorporate passive design strategies to protect interior spaces from solar radiation and to reduce cooling loads.

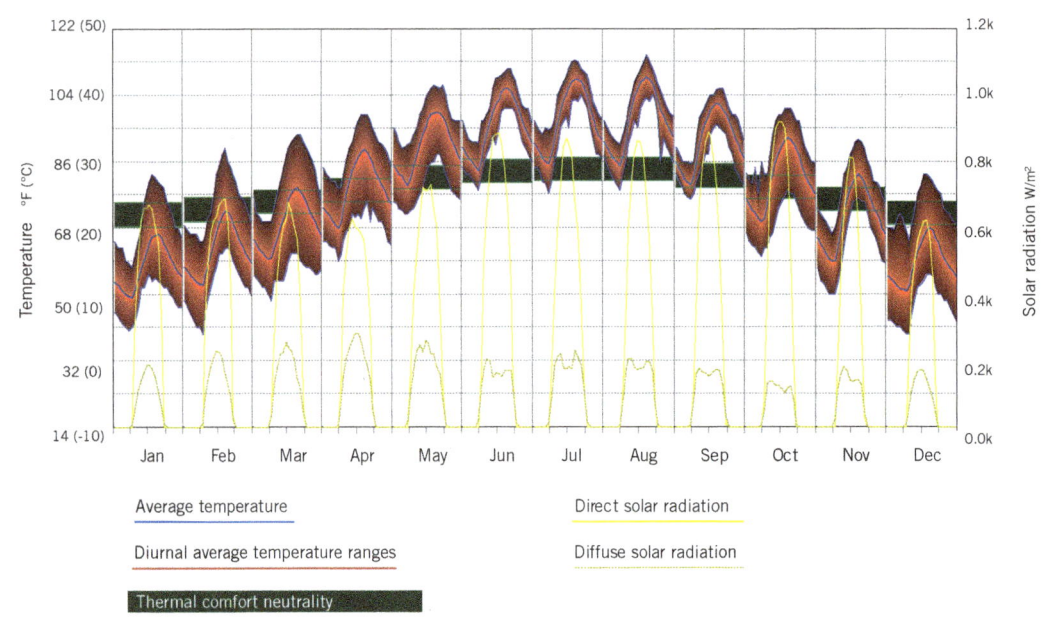

Figure 5-39 Typical exterior conditions.

Our case-study building is located on Parcel 4.01, just north of the central part of the district (Figures 5-40 to 5-54). Figure 5-40 shows the entire district master plan, and the relationship of this building's site to adjacent green spaces, freeways, and buildings.

1 KAFD 4.01
2 Greenway
3 West part of the development
4 Highway
5 East part of the development

Figure 5-40 KAFD Parcel 4.01 site plan.

Two important design elements dominate the master plan. Running north-south, adjacent to the four-lane ring road, is a west-facing "urban wall" of high-rise buildings. This wall defines the western edge of the development's eastern portion. Running east-west is an urban greenway that crosses over the ring road to link the eastern part of the development with the smaller western part. The KAFD 4.01 site is at the northeast corner, where these elements intersect. The master plan required that the building continue the urban wall south to the greenway, and that the building footprint extend to the northwest, northeast, and southwest corners of the site.

In addition to the explicit master plan requirements, the site imposed other constraints on the building design. Established traffic patterns on adjacent streets limited the options for vehicular access to the site. Pedestrian access is primarily from the north, east, and south. A planned monorail will connect the south and east sides of the site, and the landscaped greenway will provide a focus for views from within the building. Figure 5-41 shows the site analyses for several of the site constraints, including site access, security, location of open space, and pedestrian and vehicular circulation.

Figure 5-41 Site requirements diagrams.

Another important factor in the design of KAFD 4.01 is its program, which includes commercial offices, retail space, and residential units. Figure 5-42 shows the massing of the building—a thirteen-story tower with a two-story south wing—and the stacking of its program elements. Retail spaces occupy the Ground Level and Level 01, offices occupy Levels 02 through 07, and residential units are on Levels 09 through 12. Levels 08 and 13 house mechanical equipment; Level 13 also has rooftop terraces. Below grade are five parking levels.

The building's orientation, massing, and distinctive shape, shown in Figure 5-43, are responses to the need to control solar radiation. Figure 5-44 shows the east and north facades, while Figure 5-45 shows east facade. Figure 5-46 shows solar radiation on the site, indicating that the intersection point between

TECTONIC SUN EXPOSURE CONTROL   189

the east and west part of the development receives the greatest amounts of solar radiation. The eastern part of the development benefits from the close spacing of individual buildings; this provides shading for this area. Because there are no neighboring building to shade the west and south parts of the KAFD 4.01 site, the building's form and facade were designed to minimize solar radiation along these orientations.

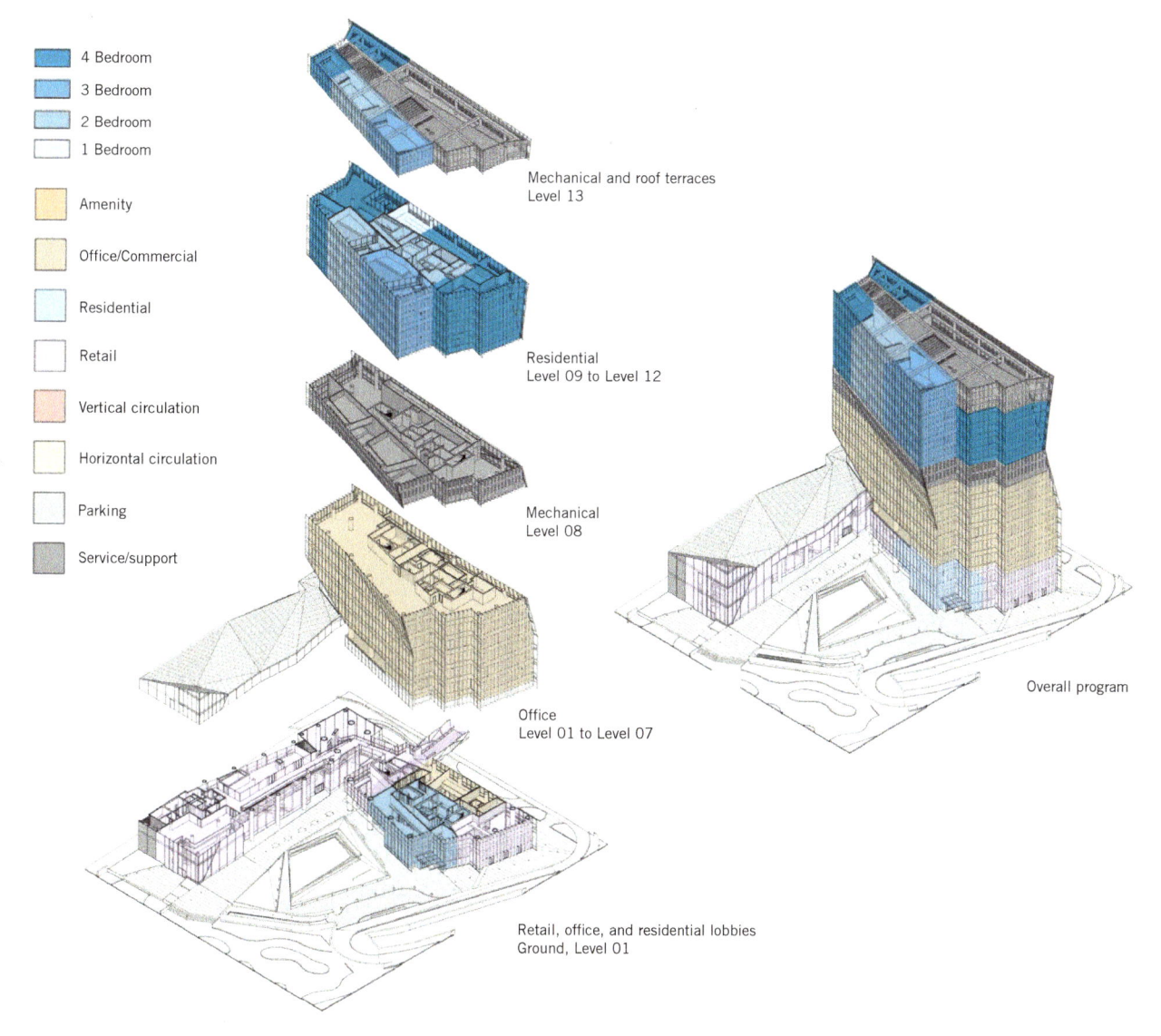

Figure 5-42 KAFD 4.01 program.

Figure 5-43 KAFD 4.01 south and west facades.

Figure 5-47 shows the position of the sun during summer and winter months. The footprint of the building's tower is an irregular rectangle, with the long sides facing north and south and the short sides facing east and west. The design of the tower's facades and its geometry are direct responses to the incident solar radiation. Figure 5-48 compares a flat south facade with the self-shading south facade designed for the building, demonstrating that the facade's irregular geometry reduces incident solar radiation.

TECTONIC SUN EXPOSURE CONTROL 191

Figure 5-44 KAFD 4.01 north and east facades.

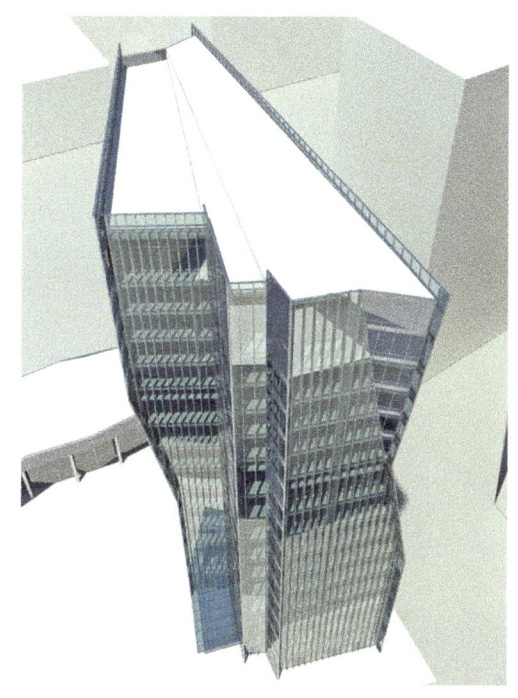

Figure 5-45 KAFD 4.01 east facade.

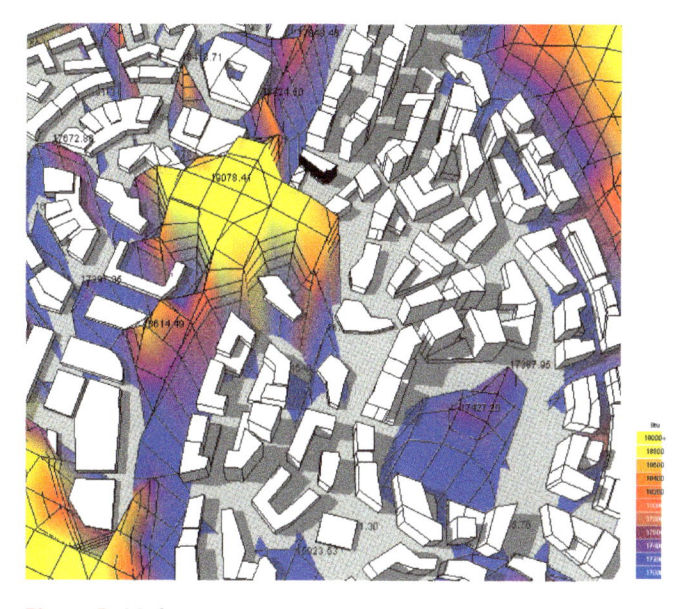

Figure 5-46 Solar radiation on the site.

192 CASE STUDIES

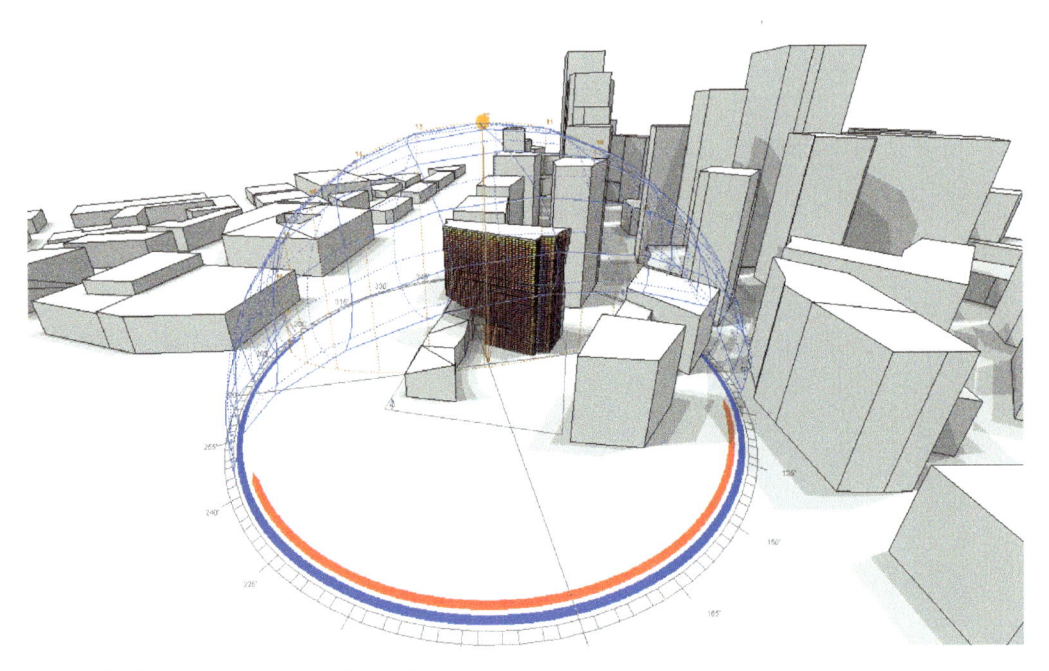

Figure 5-47 Solar radiation along the south facade.

Solar radiation: flat south facade

Solar radiation: self-shading south facade

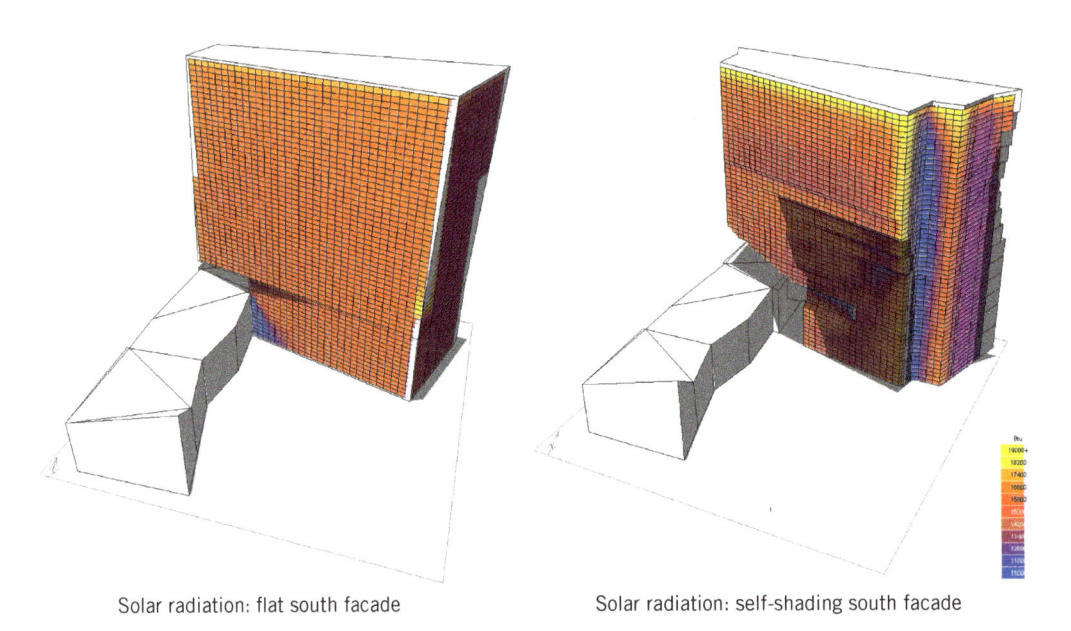

Figure 5-48 Incident solar radiation comparison for flat south facade and self-shaded form.

KAFD 4.01 has two basic types of exterior wall: a custom curtain wall with glass mullions supported by a steel frame for the lower two stories, and a thermally broken unitized aluminum curtain wall for the tower. The master plan limited transparent glass to 40% of the total exterior wall area, and required that the privacy of the residential occupants be considered in the building design. To comply with these requirements and still provide as much vision glass as possible, vision glass was coated with a pattern of ceramic frit. As the portion of glass coated with frit is not transparent, the overall window-to-wall ratio could be as high as 56% and still comply with the master plan requirements. Table 5-1 shows a detailed breakdown of window-to-wall ratios for each facade. Deep vertical fins at each mullion on the east and west facades provide privacy and shading from direct sunlight for the people living in the residential units.

Table 5-1 Window-to-wall ratios (WWR) for all tower facades.

Facade orientation and components	Area ft² (m²)	Areas Level 2 and above Transparent glass area ft² (m²)	Area of glass with 40% frit coverage ft² (m²)
East			
Vision glazing	7,672 (713)	7,672 (713)	
Opaque panels	6,122 (569)		
Louvers	1,076 (100)		
Total east facade	14,870 (1,382)	7,672 (713)	
		WWR = 52%	
South			
Vision glazing	20,939 (1,946)	20,939 (1,946)	12,847 (1,194)
Opaque panels	9,200 (855)		
Metal slab edge covers	3,992 (371)		
Total south facade	34,131 (3,172)	20,939 (1,946)	12,847 (1,194)
		WWR = 61%	WWR = 38%
West			
Vision glazing	3,788 (352)	3,788 (352)	
Opaque panels	2,496 (232)		
Louvers	570 (53)		
Metal slab edge covers	226 (21)		
Total west facade	7,080 (658)	3,788 (352)	
		WWR = 54%	

Facade orientation and components	Area ft² (m²)	Areas Level 2 and above Transparent glass area ft² (m²)	Area of glass with 40% frit coverage ft² (m²)
North			
Vision glazing	17,991 (1,672)	17,991 (1,672)	11,190 (1,040)
Opaque panels	11,793 (1,096)		
Louvers	22 (2)		
Metal slab edge covers	4,207 (391)		
Total north facade	34,013 (3,161)	17,991 (1,672) WWR = 53%	11,190 (1,040) WWR = 33%
All building facades	90,094 (8,373)	50,390 (4,683) WWR=56%	35,497 (3,299) WWR=39%

High-performance, low-e double glazing was used for all facades. Three glass types, with visual transmittance values of 25%, 45%, and 69%, were specified. All insulated glazing units were filled with argon to improve performance. The three glazing types had center-of-glass U-values of 0.19 Btu/h-ft²-°F (1.1 W/m²-°K). Most of the glazing for the tower facades used the glass type with the lowest visual transmittance (25%), as those facades would receive the highest levels of solar radiation. The glass type with 45% visual transmittance was used on parts of the east tower facade. The glass type with the highest visual transmission (69%) was used for the retail areas on the first two levels, as they would be exposed to the least solar radiation. Figure 5-49 shows the images of the three glass types, as well as the graduated frit pattern used on the north and south facade glazing.

A number of passive design strategies were incorporated into the design of the facades. The east, south, and west facades are "warped," with parts of the curtain walls sloping outward as they rise higher. The warped facades allow the upper floors of the building to shade parts of the facades below, so the building shades itself. Figure 5-50 shows a wall section through part of the warped curtain wall along the south orientation.

Each facade orientation required a different design solution. The longest sides of the building face north and south, while the short sides face east and west. During the summer months, when the sun is high, solar radiation on the south facade is mostly blocked by the warped facade above; the remaining sunlight is mitigated by the high-performance glazing and the gradient frit patterns. The vertical fins on the east and west facades, shown in Figures 5-51 and 5-52, block early morning and afternoon sun, and provide privacy to occupants of the residential units. Figure 5-53 shows a partial section of the north facade curtain wall.

TECTONIC SUN EXPOSURE CONTROL   195

North and south vision glass (Tv=25%)

East and west vision glass (Tv=45%)

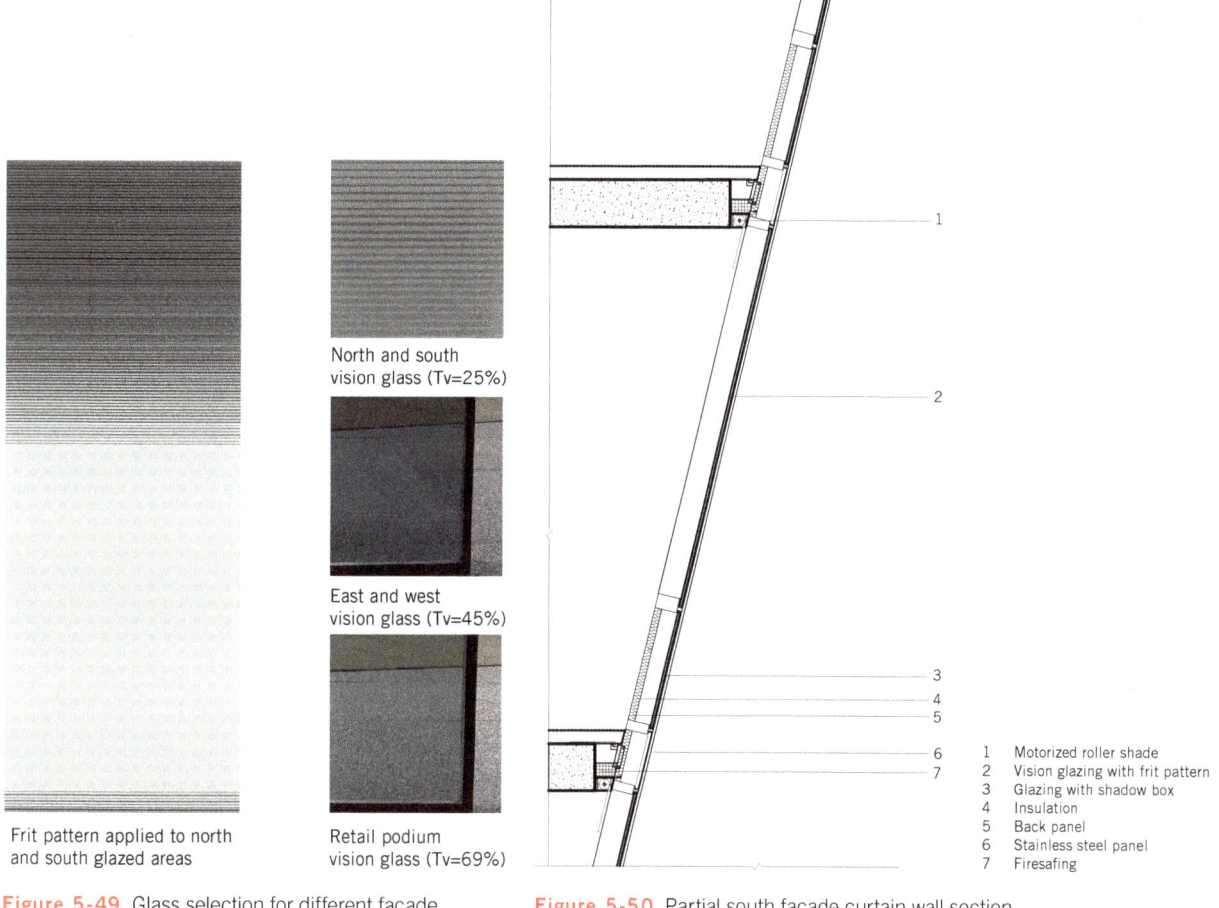

Retail podium vision glass (Tv=69%)

Frit pattern applied to north and south glazed areas

Figure 5-49 Glass selection for different facade orientations.

Figure 5-50 Partial south facade curtain wall section.

1 Motorized roller shade
2 Vision glazing with frit pattern
3 Glazing with shadow box
4 Insulation
5 Back panel
6 Stainless steel panel
7 Firesafing

Daylight harvesting was another important strategy for reducing the building's energy loads. The long, narrow floor plates of the tower allow large areas of each floor to be naturally lit. Occupancy sensors and daylight dimming controls, integrated with the main building management system, are positioned throughout the perimeter zones to control artificial lighting.

CASE STUDIES

Partial axonometric

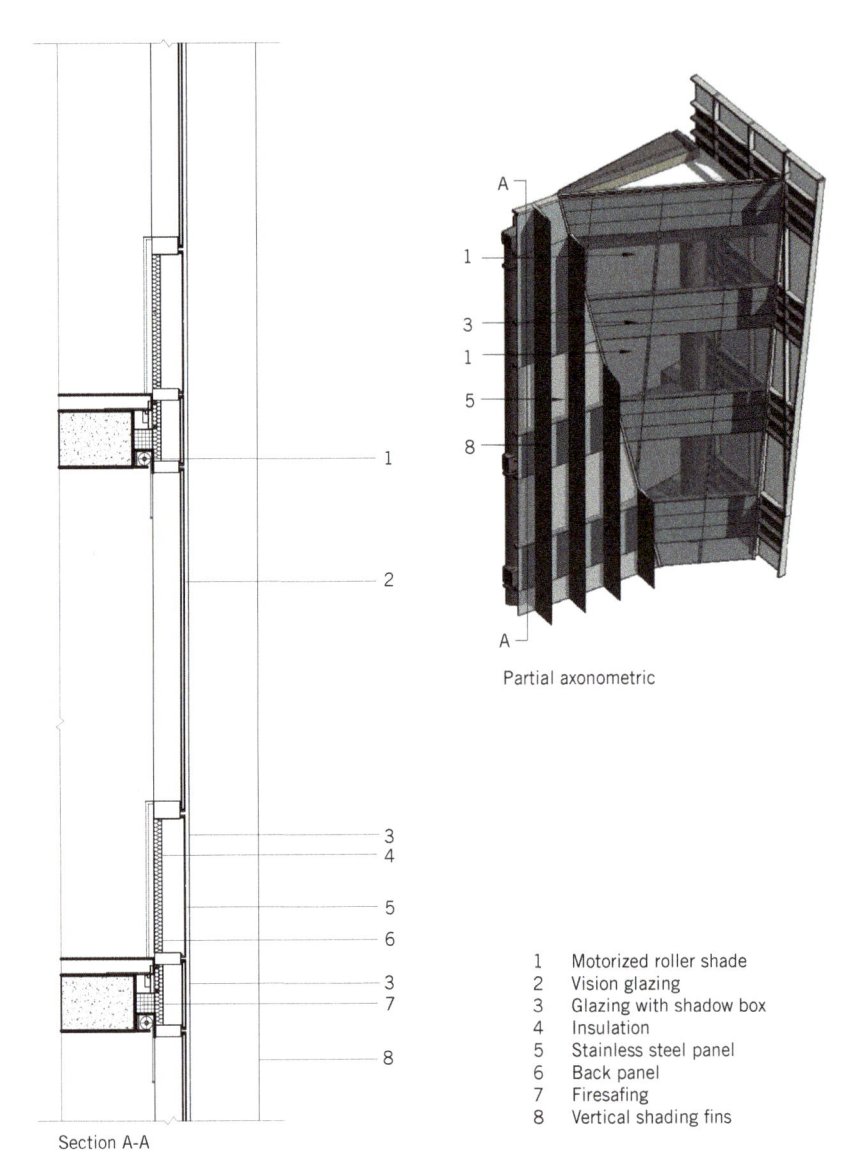

1 Motorized roller shade
2 Vision glazing
3 Glazing with shadow box
4 Insulation
5 Stainless steel panel
6 Back panel
7 Firesafing
8 Vertical shading fins

Section A-A

Figure 5-51 Partial east facade curtain wall section and axonometric view.

TECTONIC SUN EXPOSURE CONTROL   197

Section A-A

Partial axonometric

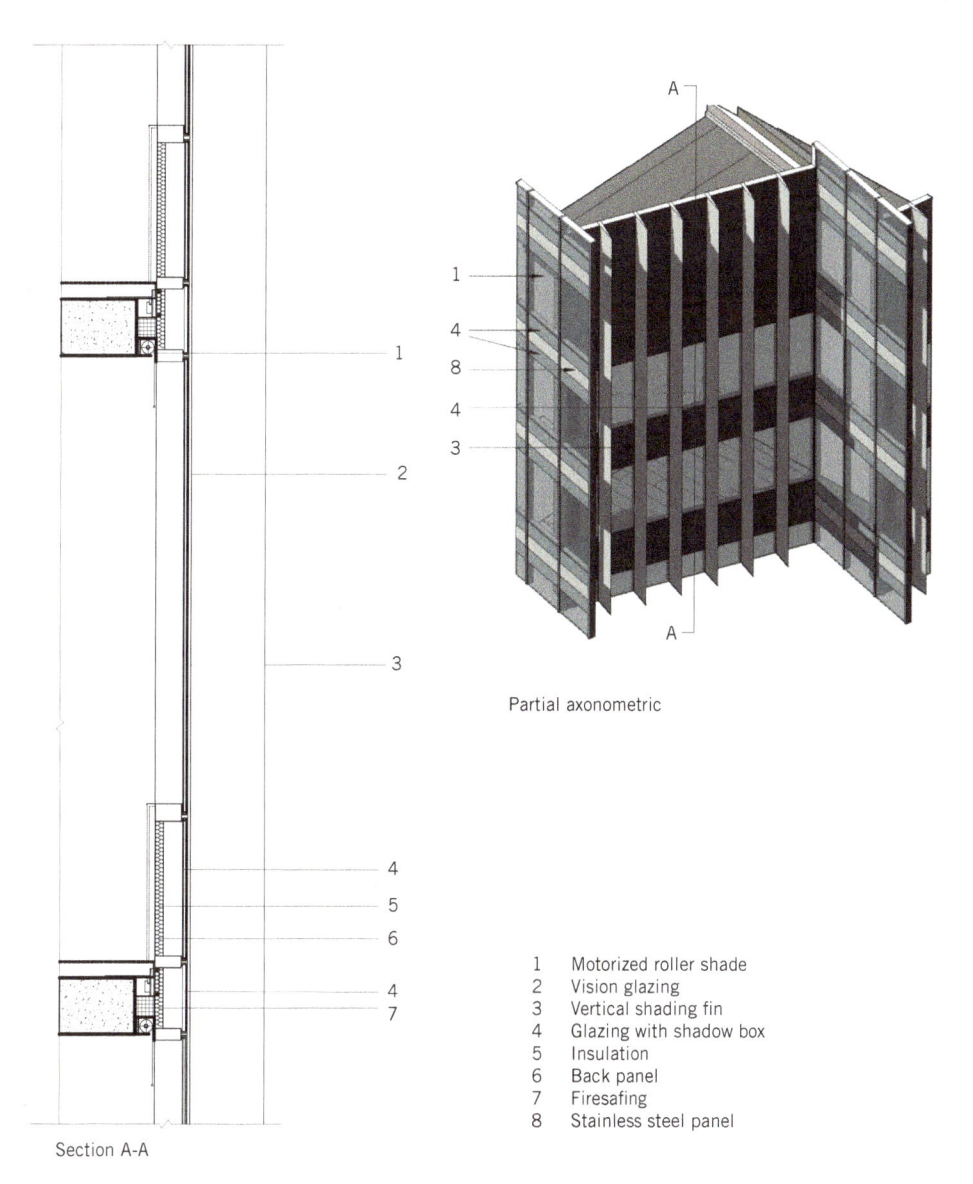

1 Motorized roller shade
2 Vision glazing
3 Vertical shading fin
4 Glazing with shadow box
5 Insulation
6 Back panel
7 Firesafing
8 Stainless steel panel

Figure 5-52 Partial west facade curtain wall section and axonometric view.

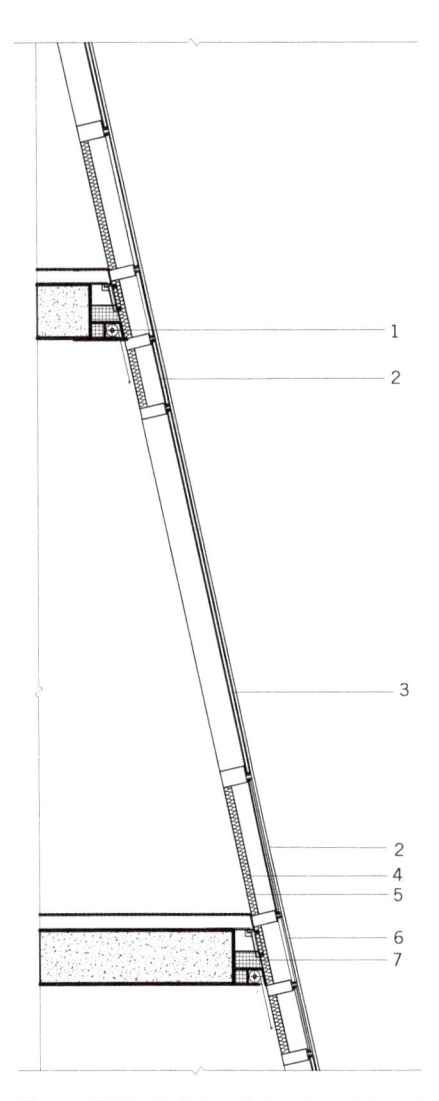

1 Motorized roller shade
2 Glazing with shadow box
3 Vision glazing with frit pattern
4 Insulation
5 Back panel
6 Stainless steel panel
7 Firesafing

Figure 5-53 Partial north facade curtain wall section.

Preliminary energy modeling performed during design indicated that the overall energy savings for KAFD 4.01 would be approximately 11% compared to the ASHRAE 90.1-2007 standard baseline. The energy modeling also indicated that cooling loads would be reduced by 12%, fan loads by 42%, and heating loads by 57%.

Full-size mockup performance tests were conducted for typical portions of the south facade. The tests included resistance to wind and impact loads, air infiltration under static pressure, and water penetration under static and dynamic pressures. Figure 5-54 shows the facade mockup that was used for the testing procedures, and the static water penetration test in progress.

KAFD 4.01 is an example of an integrated approach to facade design. All the elements of the building—form, massing, glazing, and shading devices—are used as passive strategies to control solar exposure. The building's innovative geometry resulted in a partially self-shading skin on the critical south facade, as well as an aesthetically distinctive architectural form.

Figure 5-54a, Figure 5-54b Facade performance mockup testing.

King Abdullah Financial District Parcel 4.10 Building

Our next case study project is also part of the King Abdullah Financial District in Riyadh, Saudi Arabia (Figures 5-55 to 5-64). The Parcel 4.10 building (KAFD 4.10) is located in the north part of the district, four buildings north of KAFD 4.01, as seen in Figure 5-55.

1 KAFD 4.10
2 Greenway
3 West part of the development
4 Highway
5 East part of the development

Figure 5-55 Site plan and location of KAFD 4.10.

As was the case with KAFD 4.01, the climate is very hot and dry, with extremely high temperatures and solar radiation throughout the summer months (Figure 5-39). Sustainable design was a key requirement for the entire KAFD development. This had a significant effect on the form and skin treatment for KAFD 4.10. Both of our KAFD case-study projects, Buildings 4.01 and 4.10, respond to the same environmental conditions. However, because of their different sites and program requirements, they have quite different forms and different facade designs.

Master plan requirements and site constraints jointly influenced KAFD 4.10's form and massing. Some of the requirements were the same as for Building 4.01. For instance, the west facade had to fit in with the west-facing "urban wall" along the ring road. Particular to this site was the requirement that the north and south facades align with those of the two neighboring buildings to form a unity in the massing of the three buildings. A required plaza adjoins similar plazas north and east of the site. The building massing and envelope design also had to be sensitive to solar orientation and provide sufficient shading while optimizing views and daylighting.

The building consists of two towers, a residential tower oriented north-south and a commercial tower oriented east-west, forming an L-shaped plan. Figure 5-56 shows the facade treatment of the north and west facades of the office tower, and the west facade of the residential tower. A public plaza in the northeast corner of the site is framed by the towers. The west face of the residential tower forms part of the urban wall, while the south facade of the commercial tower aligns with the south facade of the building to the east. The towers shade the outdoor spaces on the site from direct sunlight.

Figure 5-56 Residential and office towers for KAFD Parcel 4.10, view from northwest.

KAFD 4.10 is a mixed-use building, with retail spaces in the lower floors (extending beyond the footprint of the towers), and the commercial and residential functions above. The office tower consists of fifteen floors; the residential tower comprises twenty-three floors, the top three of which span over the office tower. The longest sides of the office tower face north and south, and the longest sides of the residential tower face east and west, as seen in Figure 5-57.

1. Plaza
2. Retail
3. Office tower core
4. Office spaces
5. Residential tower core
6. Residential spaces
7. Roof garden

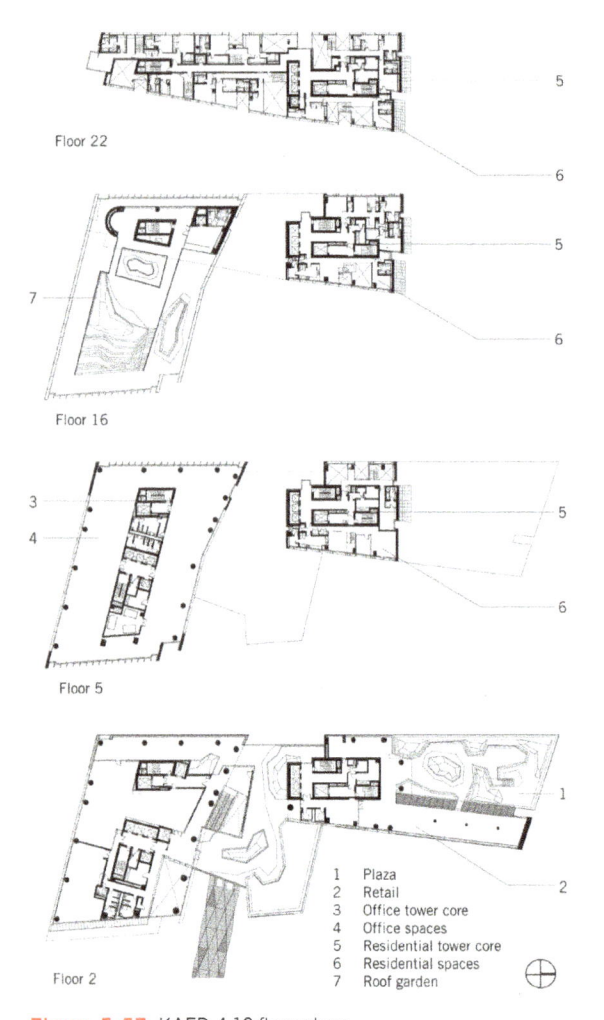

Figure 5-57 KAFD 4.10 floor plans.

Figure 5-58 shows the variety of exterior wall systems that make up the facades of KAFD 4.10. Because the east and west sides of both towers offer the best views of surrounding areas, those facades have higher window-to-wall ratios than the north and south facades. The large areas of vision glass provide daylight and views for the occupants, while external shading devices keep heat gain as low as possible. For the east and west facades of the office tower, deep vertical aluminum fins shade the interior from most direct sunlight. For its east and west facades, the residential tower uses an aluminum curtain wall with deep extrusions and a combination of transparent and fritted glass to provide daylight, views, and shading.

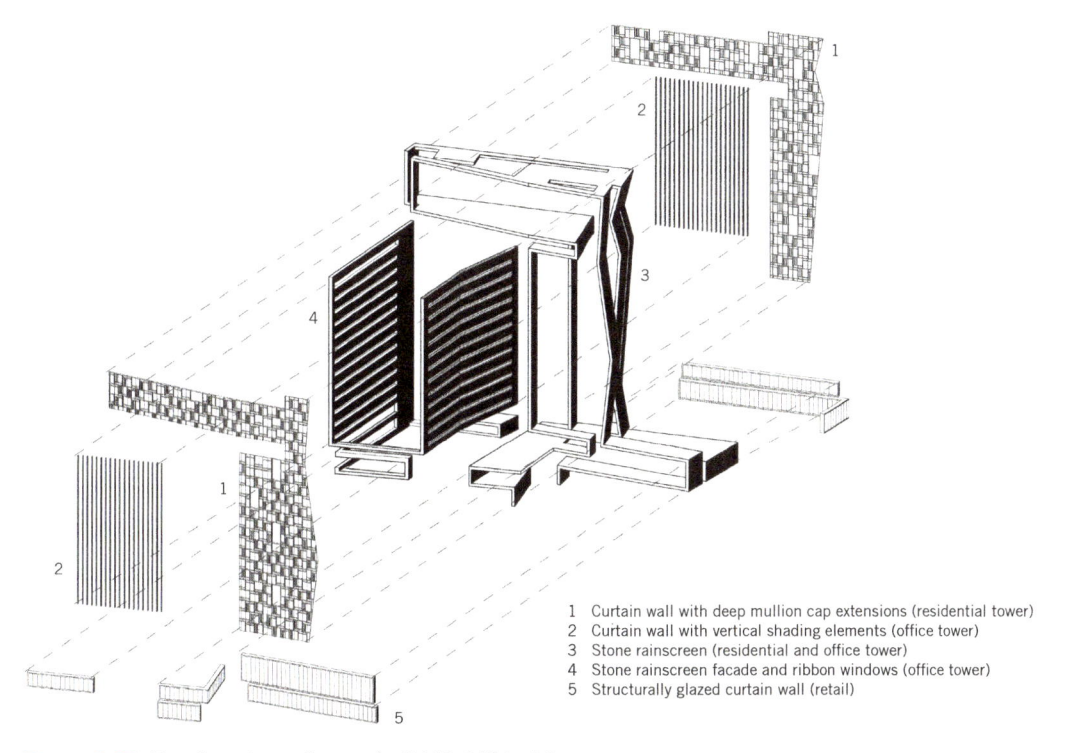

1 Curtain wall with deep mullion cap extensions (residential tower)
2 Curtain wall with vertical shading elements (office tower)
3 Stone rainscreen (residential and office tower)
4 Stone rainscreen facade and ribbon windows (office tower)
5 Structurally glazed curtain wall (retail)

Figure 5-58 Facade systems diagram for KAFD 4.10 building.

On the north and south elevations of the office tower, continuous horizontal windows within a stone veneer rainscreen allow views to the outside; horizontal stone shading devices above the windows block direct sunlight and bounce daylight into the interior spaces. The north and south elevations of the residential tower are also clad with stone veneer rainscreens.

The components of these systems are described in more detail as follows:

- East and west facades of the residential tower consist of a unitized aluminum curtain wall with tinted, low-e-coated, insulated glazing units. Glazed shadow boxes (spandrel glass with insulated metal back panel) are at the spandrel areas (Figure 5-59).

- North and south facades of the office tower consist of a rainscreen system with natural stone cladding, an air cavity, insulation, and an air-and-vapor barrier, all supported by reinforced concrete walls. Horizontal aluminum strip windows are at each floor. Horizontal stone-clad sunshades are near the tops of the strip windows, as seen in Figure 5-60.

204 CASE STUDIES

Partial axonometric

Shading device detail

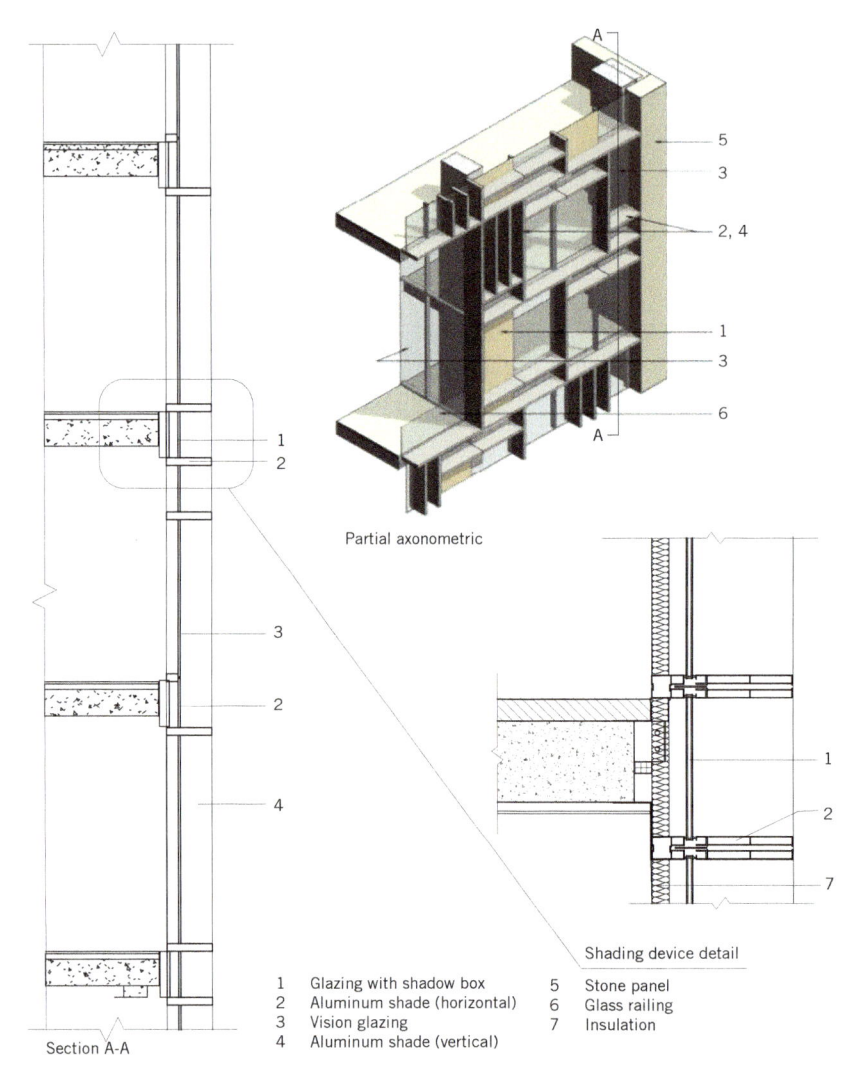

1	Glazing with shadow box	5	Stone panel
2	Aluminum shade (horizontal)	6	Glass railing
3	Vision glazing	7	Insulation
4	Aluminum shade (vertical)		

Section A-A

Figure 5-59 East and west facade curtain wall section, partial axonometric, and detail of the horizontal shading device (residential tower).

- East and west facades of the office tower consist of a unitized aluminum curtain wall with four-sided structural silicone glazing; tinted, low-e, insulated glazing units; custom-profile vertical aluminum fins; and glazed shadow boxes at the spandrel areas. Figure 5-61 shows a section and a shadow box detail of the office tower's west facade.

TECTONIC SUN EXPOSURE CONTROL   205

Stone-clad sun shade detail

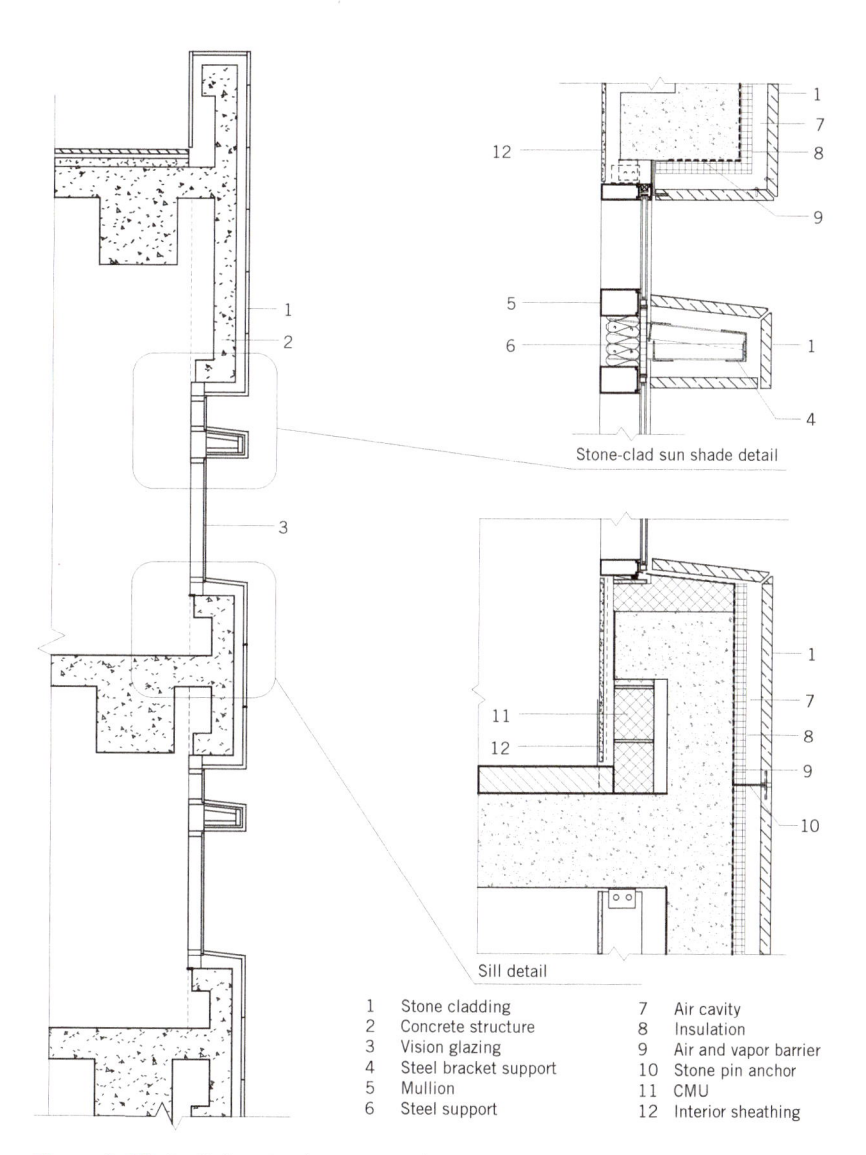

Sill detail

1	Stone cladding	7	Air cavity
2	Concrete structure	8	Insulation
3	Vision glazing	9	Air and vapor barrier
4	Steel bracket support	10	Stone pin anchor
5	Mullion	11	CMU
6	Steel support	12	Interior sheathing

Figure 5-60 South facade rainscreen section, partial axonometric, and detail (office tower).

- North and south facades of the residential tower consist of a rainscreen system and a curtain wall. The rainscreen is made of natural stone cladding, an air cavity, insulation, and an air-and-vapor barrier, all supported by inclined reinforced concrete walls (Figure 5-62). Figure 5-63 shows section and detail of the curtain wall, which constitutes a small percentage of the north and south facades.
- Retail space facades consist of a stick-built curtain wall system.

206 CASE STUDIES

Shadow box detail

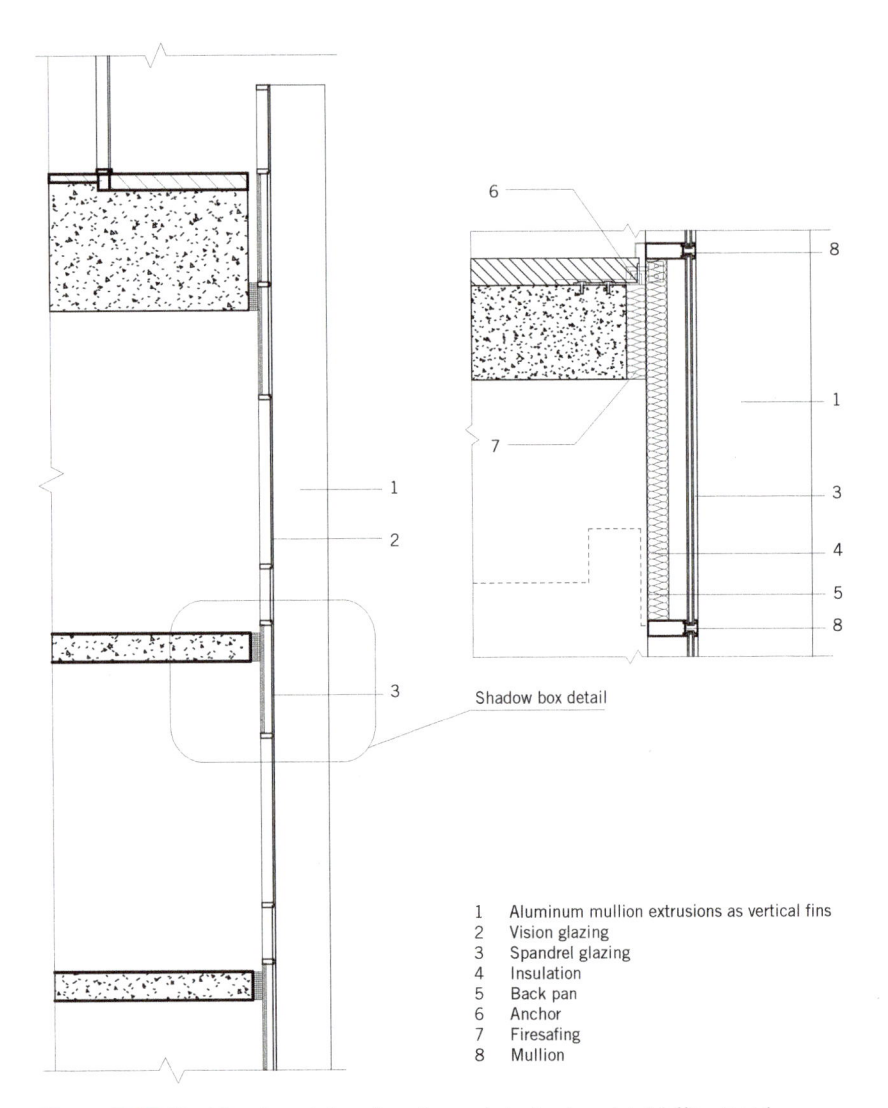

1 Aluminum mullion extrusions as vertical fins
2 Vision glazing
3 Spandrel glazing
4 Insulation
5 Back pan
6 Anchor
7 Firesafing
8 Mullion

Figure 5-61 West facade curtain wall section and shadow box detail (office tower).

TECTONIC SUN EXPOSURE CONTROL   207

Partial axonometric

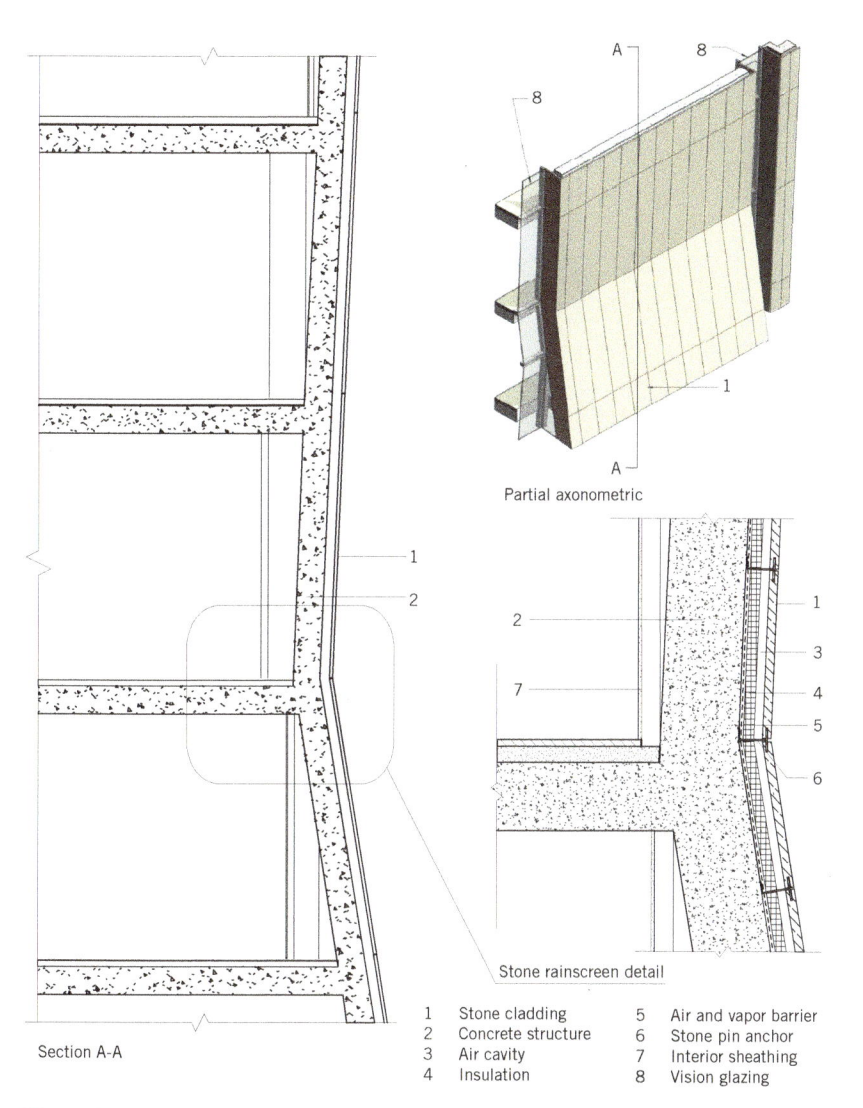

Stone rainscreen detail

Section A-A

1 Stone cladding
2 Concrete structure
3 Air cavity
4 Insulation
5 Air and vapor barrier
6 Stone pin anchor
7 Interior sheathing
8 Vision glazing

Figure 5-62 North facade rainscreen section, partial axonometric, and detail (residential tower).

208　CASE STUDIES

Partial axonometric

Curtain wall detail

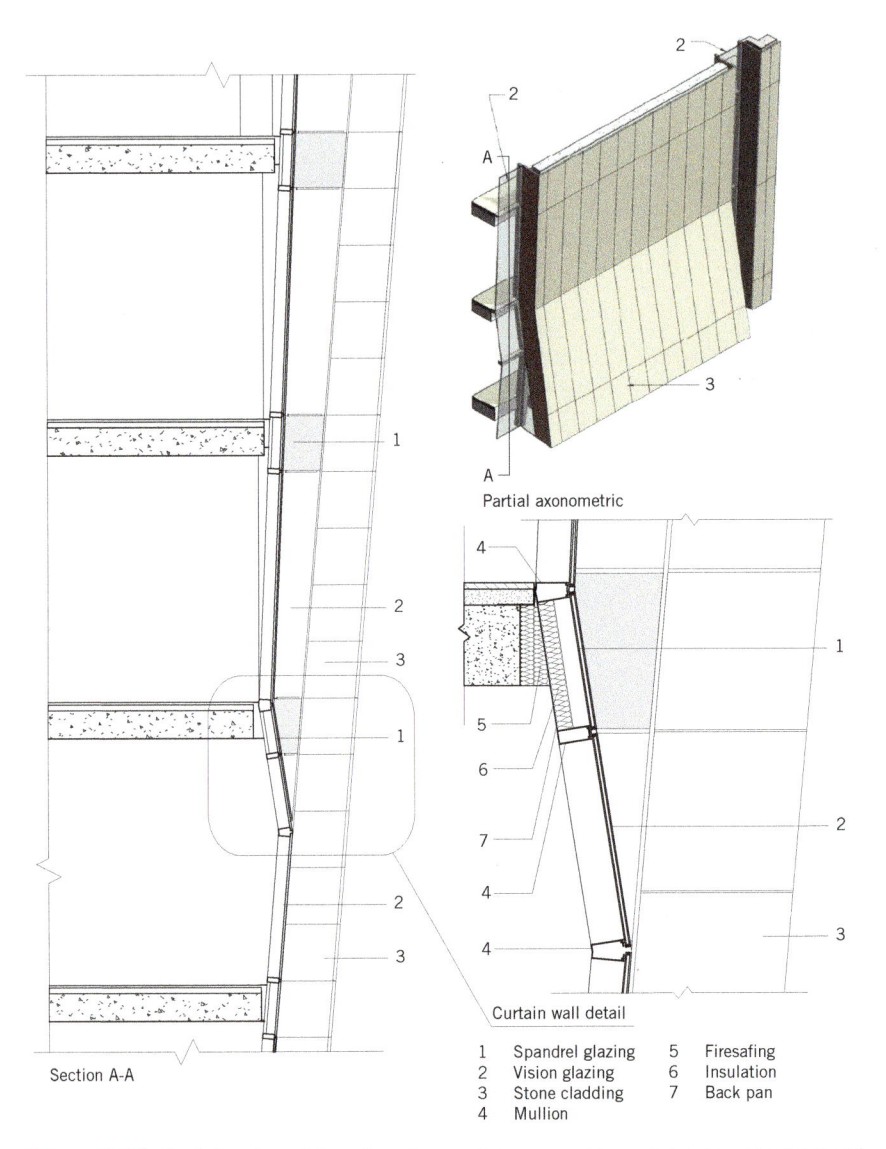

Section A-A

1　Spandrel glazing
2　Vision glazing
3　Stone cladding
4　Mullion
5　Firesafing
6　Insulation
7　Back pan

Figure 5-63 North facade curtain wall section, partial axonometric, and detail (residential tower).

The master plan guidelines for the building's facade treatment required that no more than 40% of the overall wall surfaces be transparent. Table 5-2 lists window-to-wall ratios for all facades. The overall WWR for the entire building is 40.8%.

Table 5-2 Window-to-wall ratios for all facades.

Facade orientation	Transparent glass (no frit)	Glass with 20% frit coverage	Glass with 80% frit coverage	Total transparent area	Total facade area	Transparency percent
Office Tower						
East	7,866 (731)			7,866 (731)	16,775 (1,559)	47%
South	9,695 (901)			9,695 (901)	27,642 (2,569)	35%
North	8,974 (834)			8,974 (834)	28,277 (2,628)	32%
West	8,242 (766)			8,242 (766)	17,722 (1,647)	47%
Residential Tower						
East	19,153 (1,780)	1,033 (96)	420 (39)	20,186 (1,876)	29,988 (2,787)	67%
South	2,367 (220)			2,367 (220)	17,958 (1,669)	13%
North	2,217 (206)			2,217 (206)	21,412 (1,990)	10%
West	16,667 (1,549)	473 (44)	248 (23)	17,140 (1,593)	29,762 (2,766)	58%
Total building facades				77,354 (7,189)	189,537 (17,615)	40.8%

Facade areas without retail podium ft² (m²)

Full-size mockups of portions of the east facades, shown in Figure 5-64, were tested to verify their performance. Performance testing included resistance to wind and impact loads, air and water penetration under static pressures, and water penetration under dynamic pressures.

Energy modeling conducted during the design phases indicated that the overall energy savings for KAFD 4.10 would be approximately 15% compared to the ASHRAE 90.1-2007 baseline. The energy model also showed that cooling loads would be reduced by 18%, interior lighting loads by 27%, and heating loads by 50%.

Figure 5-64 Facade performance mockup testing.

EXTERNAL SHADING ELEMENTS

University of Texas Dallas Student Services Building

The University of Texas Dallas (UTD) Student Services Building is located in a hot climate (IECC zone 2B or Koppen classification "BSh"). Figure 5-65 shows annual average daily temperatures in relation to thermal comfort zone for this location, as well as the available solar radiation. Summer months are generally hot and sunny, while the other seasons are relatively mild. Therefore, the summer conditions were the primary concern for the facade design.

The building site was determined by the campus master plan, which had three overarching planning principles: defining the social heart of the campus through a central mall, integrating the pedestrian corridor with adjacent buildings, and using indigenous landscaping. The UTD Student Services Building is located along the main pedestrian corridor. Its overall form is rectangular, with its longer sides facing north and south (Figure 5-66).

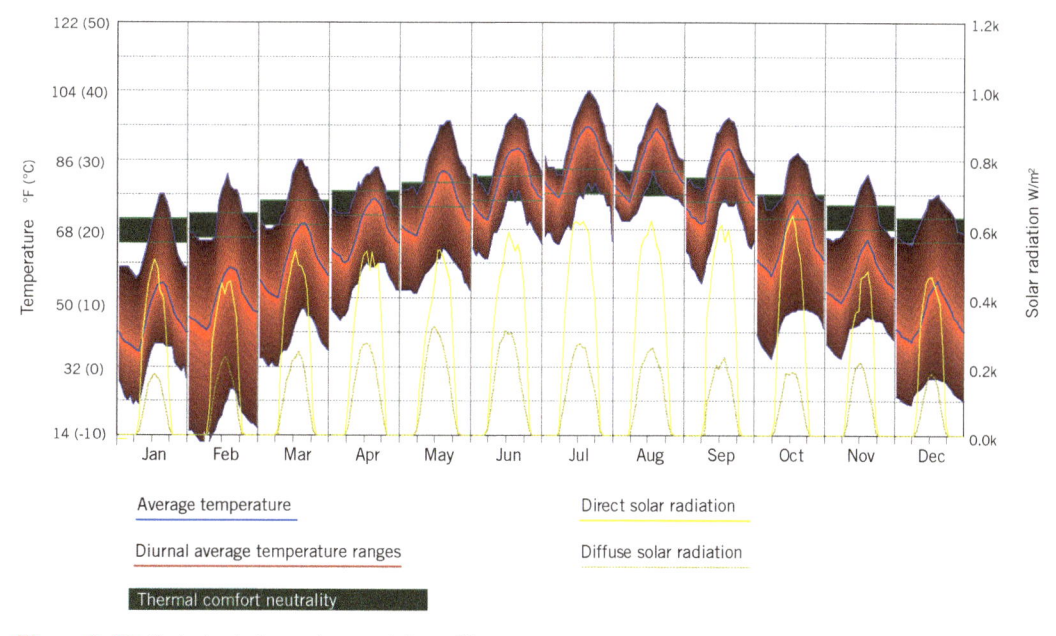

Figure 5-65 Typical exterior environmental conditions.

212   CASE STUDIES

1 UTD Student Services Building
2 Central mall
3 Pedestrian corridor

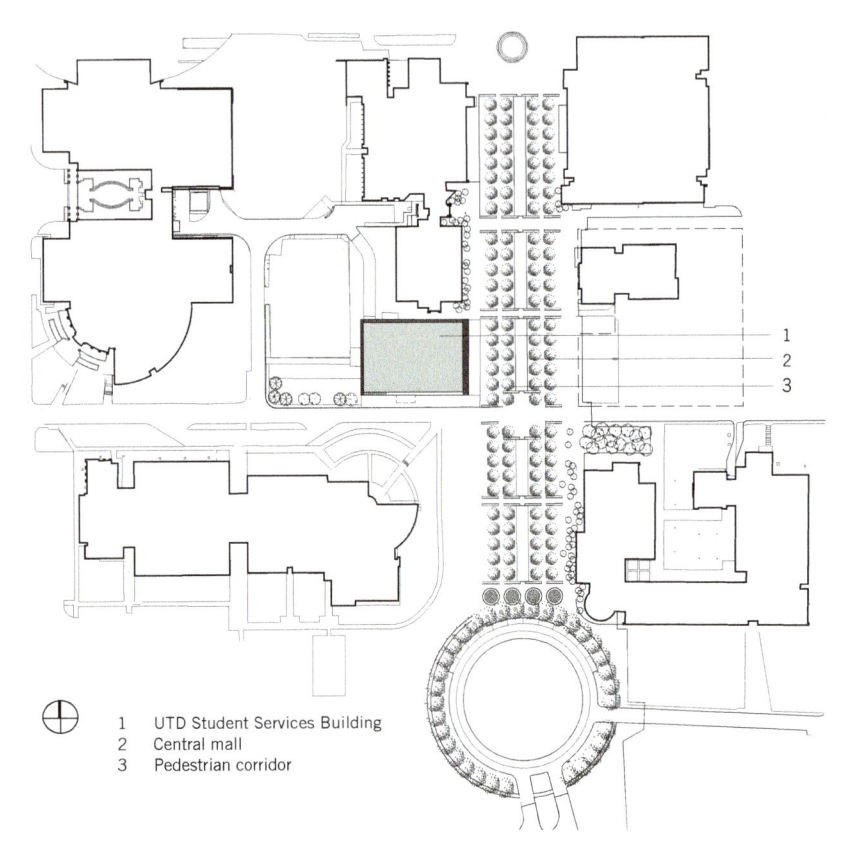

Figure 5-66 Site plan.

The University of Texas Dallas wanted the new Student Services Building to have a distinctive design, readily identifiable on campus. In addition, the building had to be at least 50% more energy-efficient than the average of all the other buildings on campus, but at a comparable construction cost. To accomplish these goals, the design team developed an approach to shading the building's facades that makes the building look quite different from the surrounding buildings. Figures 5-67 to 5-69 show the south and east facades and the exterior shading devices that create a distinctive design of this building.

The program for the four-story Student Services Building includes spaces for student enrollment, health services, counseling, financial aid, student registration services, and a career center. Figure 5-70 shows floor plans for the ground and third floors. The external shading elements fully wrap the second and third floors on the east, west, and south facades, and partially on the north elevation. Three internal atriums provide daylight to interior spaces. Figure 5-71 includes a longitudinal section through the building showing these three atriums, and a diagram showing their volumetric distribution within the building and their relationship to the facade shading elements. Figures 5-72 and 5-73 show interior views of the atriums. The combination of solar shading and internal light harvesting limits solar heat gain, and provides three-quarters of the interior spaces with daylight. Almost all of the normally occupied spaces have views to the outside.

EXTERNAL SHADING ELEMENTS 213

Figure 5-67 Exterior view (south and east facades).

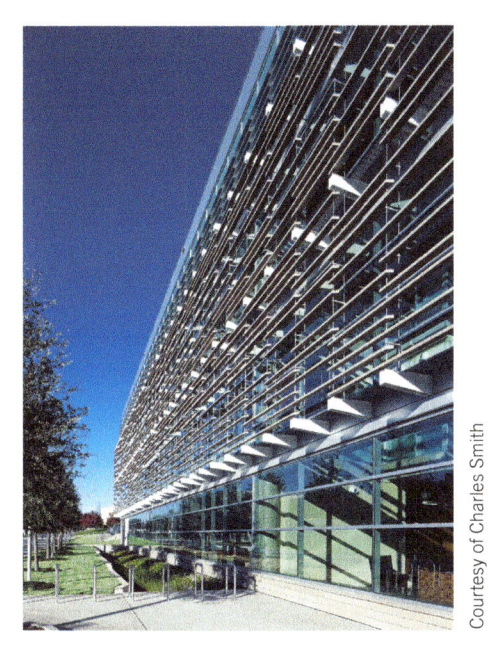

Figure 5-68 Exterior view of UTD Student Services Building (south facade).

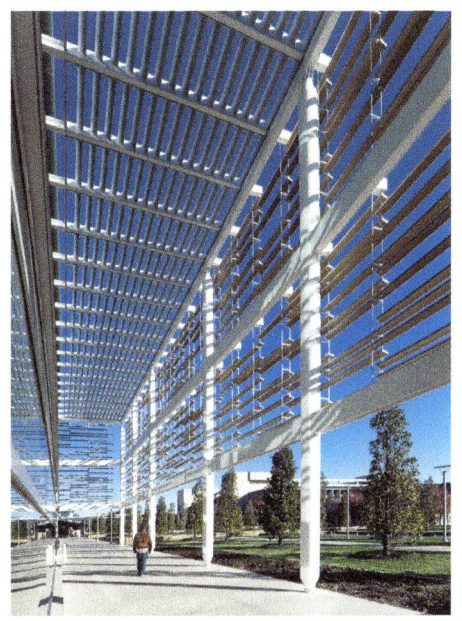

Figure 5-69 Exterior shading along the east facade.

214   CASE STUDIES

All four sides of the building are enclosed by a curtain wall. The east, west, and south facades (and part of the north facade) are wrapped by an exterior assembly of shading devices supported by the curtain wall. The shading system consists of horizontal terra-cotta louvers and vertical stainless steel rods. A partial elevation and an axonometric view of the south facade (Figure 5-74) show how the density and pattern of the shading elements vary.

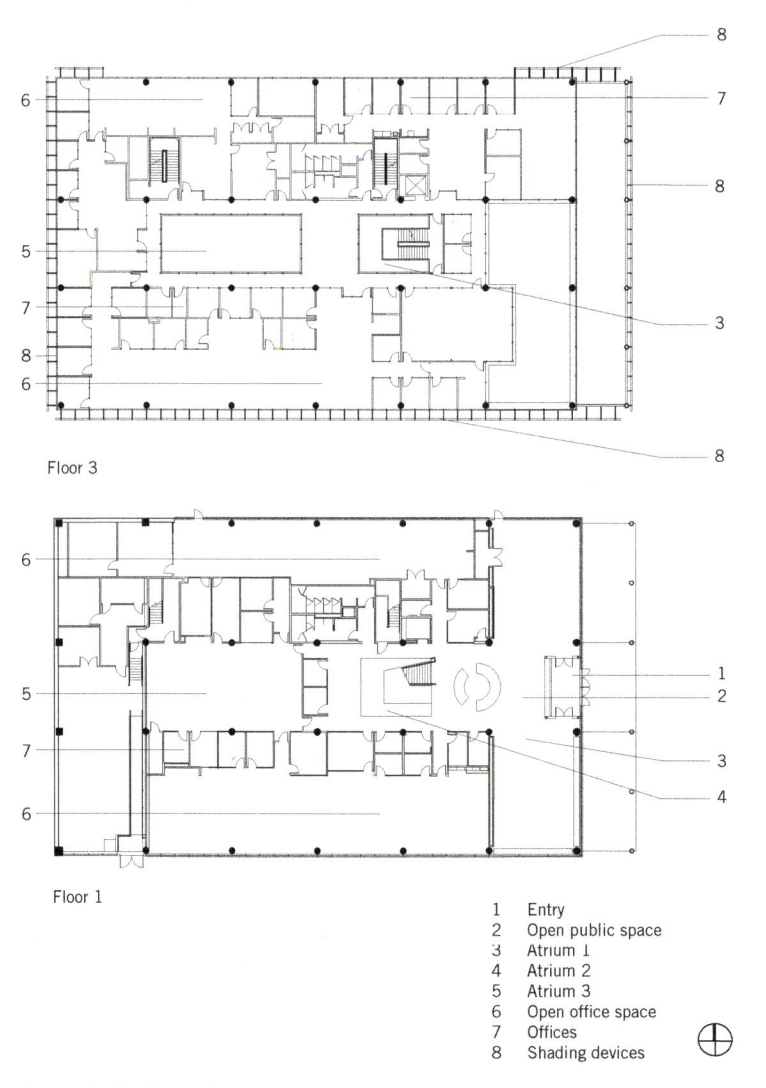

Floor 3

Floor 1

1 Entry
2 Open public space
3 Atrium 1
4 Atrium 2
5 Atrium 3
6 Open office space
7 Offices
8 Shading devices

Figure 5-70 Floor plans.

EXTERNAL SHADING ELEMENTS 215

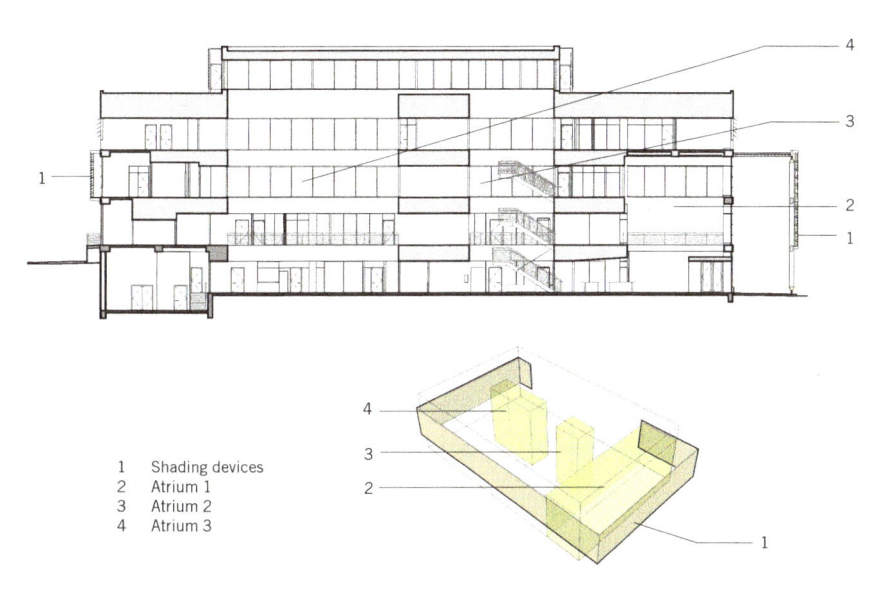

1 Shading devices
2 Atrium 1
3 Atrium 2
4 Atrium 3

Figure 5-71 Building section and internal atriums.

Figure 5-72 Central large atrium.

Figure 5-73 Southeast atrium and lobby.

Figure 5-75 shows the components of the shading elements. Horizontal terra-cotta blades are supported by pairs of vertical stainless steel rods spaced every 5 feet (1.5 m) along the facades. These vertical rods are attached to horizontal outriggers projecting from the building face at the floor levels. Because terra cotta has little tensile strength and cannot span between the vertical rods on its own, each blade is reinforced along its entire length with two horizontal stainless steel rods in hollow cylindrical cores. The advantages of terra cotta are its very low thermal conductivity, as well as natural sourcing of the material. Extruded aluminum plates at each end secure the horizontal rods to the vertical rods, and terra-cotta end caps finish the ends of each blade. Regularly spaced horizontal braces tie the pairs of vertical rods together to control deflection, as shown in Figures 5-76 and 5-77.

The building also incorporates other sustainable design strategies not related to the facade. Roof-mounted solar hot water collection panels provide all of the building's hot water needs. Reductions in water demand and the use of rainwater harvesting significantly reduce the building's use of potable water. Recycled and low-emitting materials were used throughout. Indoor air quality and carbon dioxide levels are monitored by the building management and control system, which improves interior comfort conditions.

The objective of designing a sustainable, energy-efficient, and cost-effective building was accomplished. The building was constructed approximately 10% under budget. Its operating energy costs were reduced by 63% compared to the average of the other campus buildings. The energy consumption reduction determined by design-phase energy modeling was 41% compared to the baseline building specified by the ASHRAE 90.1-2004 Standard. The UTD Student Services Building received LEED Platinum certification from the U.S. Green Building Council, the first such certification in the University of Texas system.

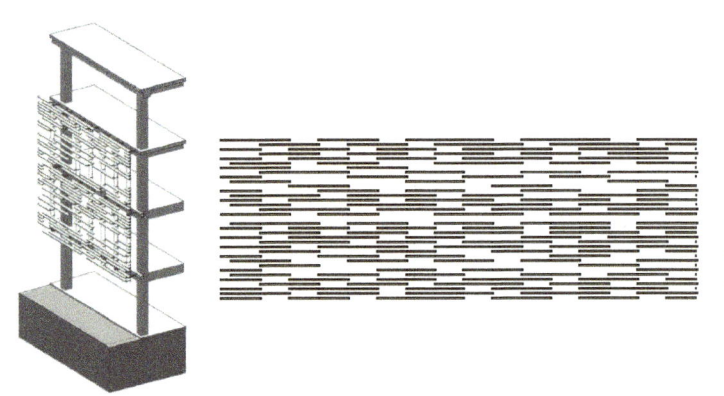

Figure 5-74 Axonometric view and partial elevation along the south facade.

1. Terra-cotta blade
2. Vertical stainless steel rod
3. Horizontal stainless steel threaded rod
4. Extruded aluminum end plate
5. Terra-cotta end cap

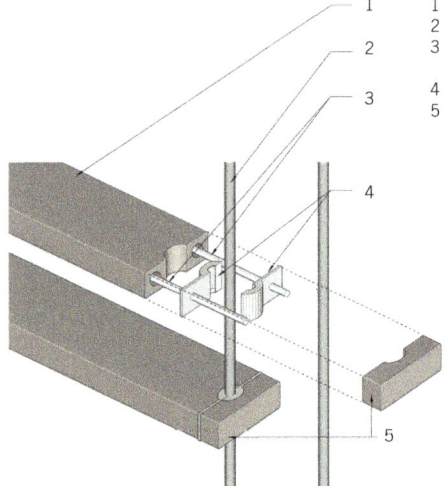

Figure 5-75 Terra-cotta shade diagram.

Figure 5-76 View to the outside showing terra-cotta shading system and varying density of shading elements.

Figure 5-77 View to the outside from an office space, showing the outriggers at the floor levels and the steel rod bracing.

FACADE MATERIALS AND WALL ASSEMBLIES

Bigelow Laboratory for Ocean Sciences

Bigelow Laboratory for Ocean Sciences, located in East Boothbay, Maine, is a new research campus on 64 acres of forested hills overlooking the Damariscotta River as it flows into the Atlantic Ocean. Its coastal climate is characterized as cool and humid (IECC zone 5A or "Dfb" in the Koppen classification system). Figure 5-78 shows annual daily temperatures and available solar radiation, as well as the average thermal comfort zone. The winter months are very cold with relatively low solar radiation, while spring and fall seasons are mild. Summers are hot (except for June, which has significantly lower daily temperatures than May or July), with high relative humidity levels due to the site's proximity to the ocean. Facades in this climate zone should be designed with high levels of thermal resistance. Passive solar heating can be a benefit in winter, but windows should be shaded against solar heat gain during the summer.

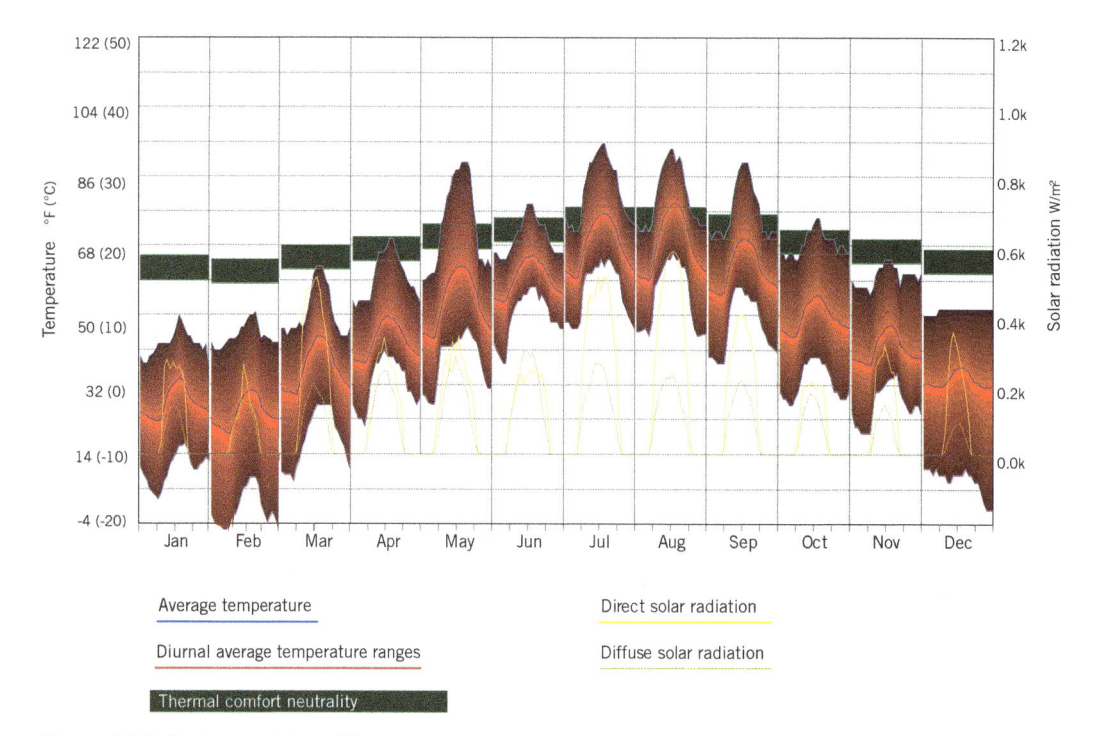

Figure 5-78 Environmental conditions.

FACADE MATERIALS AND WALL ASSEMBLIES 219

The overall master plan for the campus consists of five major components: four research wings, a "Commons" area of collaborative spaces connecting the wings, a shore facility, and future buildings for educational outreach, research, and housing for visiting researchers and students (Figures 5-79–5-89). The research component includes laboratory and research spaces for air–sea interactions, marine optics, ocean biogeochemistry, flow cytometry and single-cell genomics, algal culturing, microbiology, molecular biology, and remote sensing and observing of the ocean. Figure 5-79 shows the components and phases of the master plan. The site infrastructure, three research wings, part of the Commons, and the shore facility and pier for research vessels were completed at the time of this writing.

Sensitive treatment of the site was an important design consideration. The site components, including infrastructure and buildings, were carefully positioned to limit the disturbance to the natural habitat. Stormwater is managed by using native bioswales to mitigate runoff from the roofs. A bio-retention pool controls and cleans stormwater from the road and parking area.

Site infrastructure
Bigelow Center for Blue Biotechnology
Center for Ocean Biogeochemistry and Climate Change
Center for Ocean Health
Future research building
Future administration, educational facilities, and housing

1 Main entry
2 Central plant
3 Commons
4 Research wings
5 Shore facility
6 Future buildings for educational outreach
7 Future student residences
8 Future education wing
9 Future research wing
10 Future cottages for visiting scientists

Figure 5-79 Site plan and phases of the development.

Figure 5-80 Two research wings under construction.

The laboratory wings are oriented along an approximate east-west axis, with the long sides of each wing facing north and south, as can be seen in Figure 5-81. The spacing between research wings allows daylight to reach all occupied spaces, and low-angle solar radiation to provide some passive heating during the winter months. Solar positions during the different seasons, particularly the low winter sun, were used to determine the distance between the buildings. Along the south facade of each wing, large windows allow greater penetration of light into the interior environment. Figure 5-82 shows a view of the south facade from the interior Commons area.

Because the building has to contend with cold winters and hot summers, particular care was taken to design facades that combine improved thermal performance with extensive daylighting of interior spaces. Each facade uses passive design strategies to thermally respond to its orientation. The south facades have large punched windows with horizontal overhangs that block solar radiation during the summer months, but allow sunlight to penetrate during the winter months and provide passive heating. The north facades have lower window-to-wall ratios, with smaller windows and large areas of well-insulated opaque walls to provide improved thermal performance. Exterior materials were chosen for their resistance to the high levels of salt in the marine environment air. For example, zinc panels have a natural surface patina that can withstand salt without additional coatings, so they were selected as one of the primary opaque wall materials. Figure 5-85 shows a partial south elevation and exterior wall plan and sections. The components of this assembly include:

- Interlocking preweathered zinc tiles, supported by vertical and horizontal "Z" furring spaced 2.5 feet (760 mm) apart
- Semi-rigid mineral fiber insulation (3 in./76 mm thick)
- Sheet air-and-vapor barrier adhered to sheathing
- Fiber-reinforced sheathing (0.63 in./16 mm thick)
- Spray-foam insulation (3 in./76 mm thick) within a 6-inch (152 mm) steel stud cavity
- Interior sheathing (0.63 in./16 mm thick)

FACADE MATERIALS AND WALL ASSEMBLIES   221

1. Main entry
2. Commons
3. Office
4. Laboratory
5. Conference room
6. Remote Sensing and Ocean Observation Laboratory
7. Outdoor courtyard
8. National Center for Marine Algae and Microbiota
9. Cafe
10. Central plant
11. Mobile laboratory

Figure 5-81 First-level floor plan.

Figure 5-82 Interior view from the Commons area showing the zinc siding and horizontal sunshades of the south facade, and the curtain wall of the east and west facades.

Figure 5-83 Southeast corner of a research wing.

Figure 5-84 East facade curtain wall with shading devices and wood panels.

FACADE MATERIALS AND WALL ASSEMBLIES 223

1	Zinc panels
2	Semi-rigid insulation
3	Exterior sheathing
4	Spray-foam insulation
5	Interior sheathing
6	Shading devices
7	Vision glazing
8	Composite wood panel
9	Support for shading devices

Section A-A Section B-B Partial plan

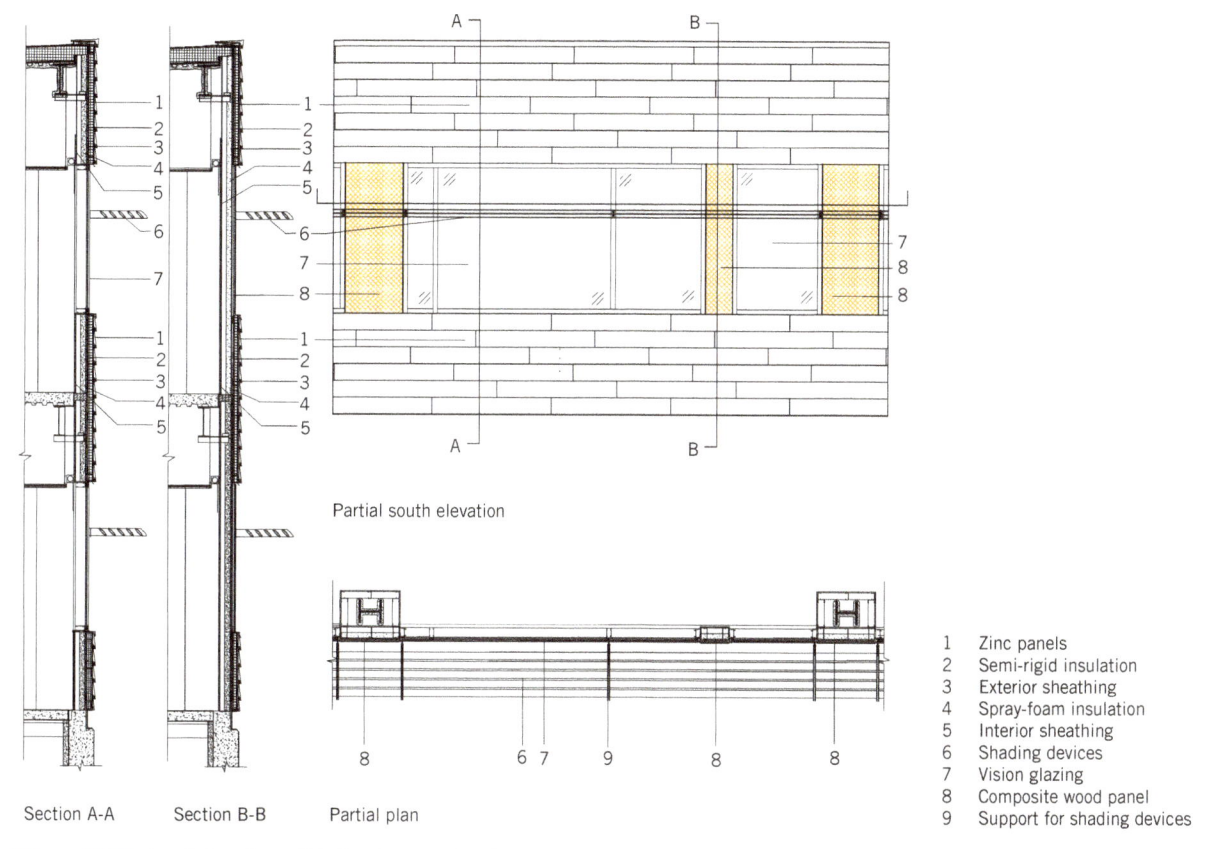

Figure 5-85 South facade partial elevation, partial plan, and sections.

The thickness of the exterior wall is 12 inches (305 mm). The windows consist of thermally broken aluminum mullions and low-e, argon-filled IGUs, with a U-value of 0.24 Btu/h-ft^2-°F (1.36 W/m^2-°K) and an SHGC of 0.38. Between the punched windows are resin-impregnated composite wood panels. With three inches (76 mm) of spray-foam insulation, these opaque wall areas have a U-value of 0.058 Btu/h-ft^2-°F (0.33 W/m^2-°K). The 30-inch- (760-mm-) deep overhang consists of five aluminum blades, angled to block high summer sun, shown in Figure 5-86.

1	Zinc panels	9	Interior sheathing
2	Vertical "Z" furring	10	Ceiling tile
3	Semi-rigid insulation	11	Internal roller shade
4	Horizontal "Z" furring	12	Mullion
5	Air-and-vapor barrier	13	Shading blade
6	Exterior sheathing	14	Support for shading devices
7	Spray-foam insulation	15	Vision glazing
8	Steel stud cavity		

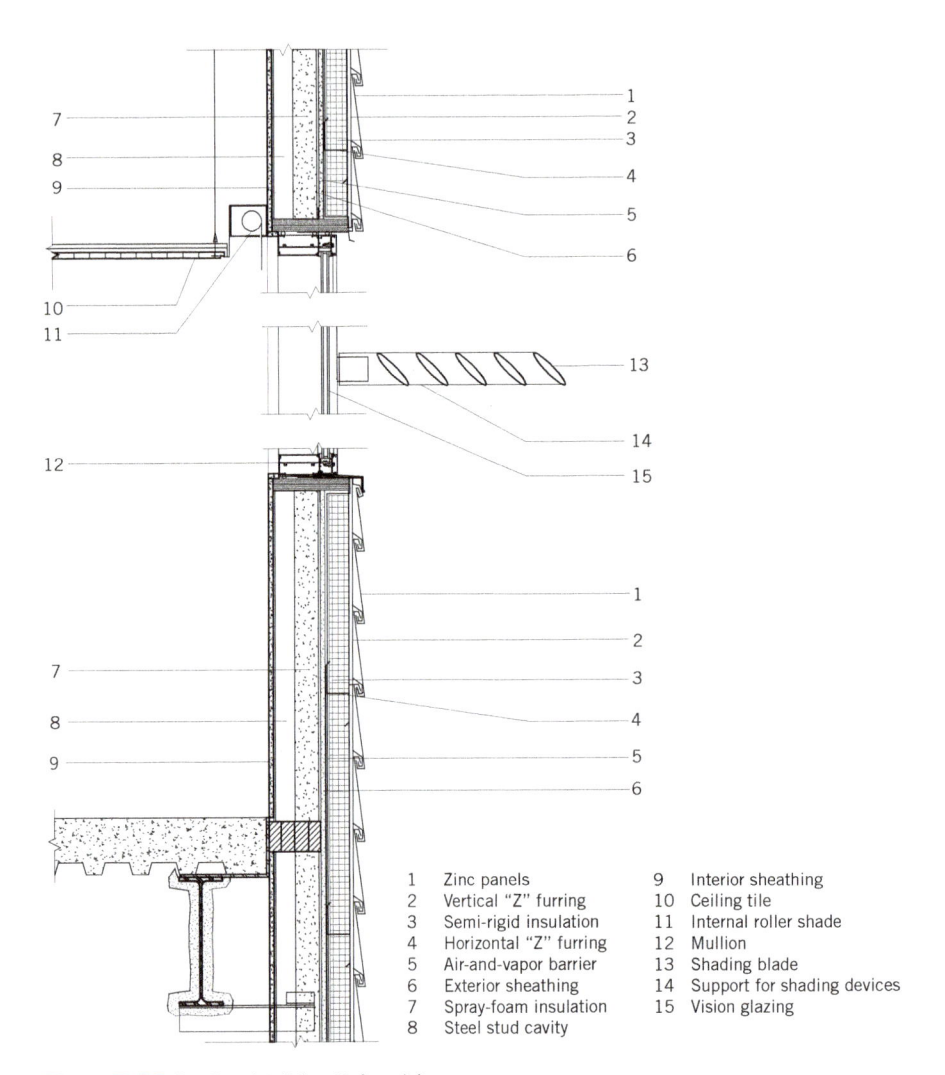

Figure 5-86 Section detail (south facade).

The west facade consists of three facade types: (1) zinc panels for the stairway enclosure and the open collaborative space, (2) curtain wall for the entry space, and (3) composite wood panels and curtain wall for the remaining areas. Figure 5-89 shows a partial west elevation and wall section, where composite resin wood panels are integrated into the curtain wall. The thickness of the opaque part of the exterior wall is 9 inches (230 mm) overall, with these components:

- Composite wood panels (0.38 in./10 mm thick)
- Semi-rigid mineral fiber insulation (2 in./50 mm thick)
- Sheet air-and-vapor barrier adhered to sheathing
- Fiber-reinforced sheathing (0.63 in./16 mm thick)
- Spray-foam insulation (3 in./76 mm thick) within a 4-inch (100 mm) steel stud cavity
- Interior sheathing (0.63 in./16 mm thick)

The curtain wall consists of thermally broken aluminum frames; low-e, argon-filled IGUs; and insulated spandrel areas at the upper portion of the curtain wall. The overall U-value of this facade is 0.062 Btu/h·ft^2-°F (0.35 W/m^2-°K).

Figure 5-87 North facade showing partial view of the cafe.

Figure 5-88 Interior view of an office space, located along the northeast corner.

CASE STUDIES

The facade design, as well as numerous other sustainable and energy-efficient design strategies, resulted in an overall energy-model savings of 53%, compared to the ASHRAE 90.1-2007 baseline building. At the time of writing, Bigelow Laboratory for Ocean Sciences is targeting LEED Gold certification from the U.S. Green Building Council.

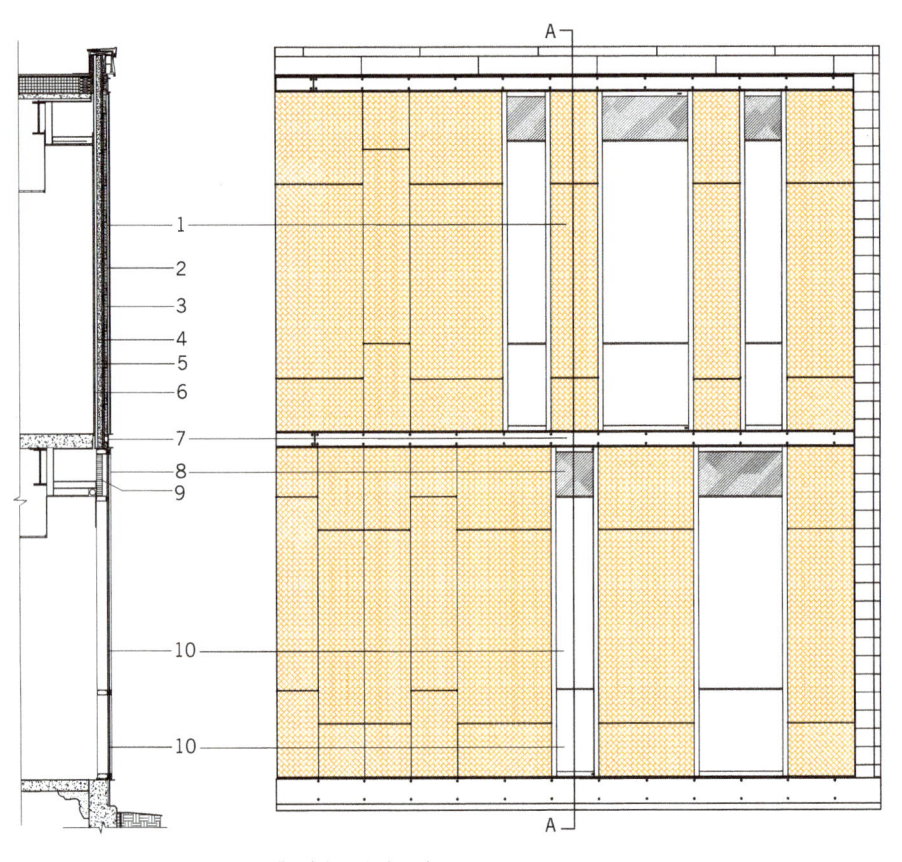

Section A-A   Partial west elevation

1. Composite wood panel
2. Semi-rigid insulation
3. Exterior sheathing
4. Spray-foam insulation
5. Stud cavity
6. Interior sheathing
7. Channel reveal
8. Spandrel glazing
9. Insulation
10. Vision glazing

Figure 5-89 Partial west elevation and exterior wall section.

APPENDIX

CASE STUDIES INDEX

CHAPTER 2

CASE STUDY 2.1:
Vincent Triggs Elementary School, Clark County Elementary Prototype (Las Vegas, Nevada)

Building Size: 86,400 sf (8,030 sm)

Completion: 2010

Architect of Record: John A. Martin & Associates–Nevada

Architectural Firm: Perkins+Will

    Managing Principal: Wendell Vaughn

    Project Manager: Eric Brossy de Dios

    Project Architects: Tinka Rogic, Seth Sakamoto

Client: Clark County School District

Structural Engineer: John A. Martin & Associates–Nevada

MEP Engineer: IBE (Ideas for the Built Environment)

General Contractor: Roche Construction

CASE STUDY 2.2:
Hector Garcia Middle School (Dallas, Texas)

Building Size: 175,000 sf (16,260 sm)

Completion: 2007

Architectural Firm: Perkins+Will

    Managing Principal: Peter Brown

    Project Designers: Rusty Walker, Carol Cumbie

    Project Manager: Patrick Glenn

    Project Architect: Patrick Glenn

    Education Planners: Peter Brown and Patrick Glenn

    Project Team: Andy Craigo, Justin Parscale, Mark Walsh

Client: Dallas Independent School District

Structural Engineer: APM & Associates/LA Fuess Partners

MEP Engineer: Basharkhah Engineering

Civil Engineer: APM & Associates

Landscape Architect: Berkenbile+Craig

AV/IT/Security Consultant: Datacom Design Group
Roofing Consultant: Amtech Building Sciences
Commissioning Agent: AIR Engineering
General Contractor: Satterfield & Pontikes

CASE STUDY 2.3:
Kendal Academic Support Center, Miami Dade College (Miami, Florida)

Building Size: 120,000 sf (11,150 sm)
Completion: 2012
Architectural Firm: Perkins+Will
    Design Principal: Pat Bosch
    Managing Principal: Gene Kluesner
    Project Designers: Angel Suarez, Denise Gonzales, Ruben Ramos
    Project Manager: Carlos Chiu
Client: Miami Dade College

CHAPTER 3

CASE STUDY 3.1:
Centers for Disease Control and Prevention, National Center for Environmental Health (Atlanta, Georgia)

Building Size: 145,000 sf (13,480 sm)
Completion: 2005
Architectural Firm: Perkins+Will
    Design Principal: Manuel Cadrecha
    Project Designer: David Rogers
    Managing Principal: Daniel Watch
    Project Architect: Deepa Tolat
Client: Centers for Disease Control and Prevention
Structural Engineer: Stanley D. Lindsey & Associates
MEP Engineer: Newcomb & Boyd Engineers
General Contractor: Gilbane Building Company

CHAPTER 4

CASE STUDY 4.1:
Princess Nora Bint Abdulrahman University for Women Academic Colleges (Riyadh, Saudi Arabia)

Building Size: 5,500,000 sf (511,111 sm)

Completion: 2011

Architect of Record: Dar Al-Handasah

Architectural Firm: Perkins+Will
> Design Principal: Pat Bosch
> Project Designers: Angel Suarez, Lincoln Linder, Yong Lee
> Technical Principal: George Valcarcel
> Managing Principal: Gene Kluesner
> Senior Project Architect: Gustavo Alfonso
> Project Architect: Damian Ponton
> Project Team: John Hoffman, Terence Ruffin, R. Dennis, A. Bragner, Y. Ikorou, Y. Diaz, J. Bernal

Client: Dar Al Handasah–Cairo

Construction Managers: Saudi Oger, Saudi Binladin Group

CASE STUDY 4.2:
Tinkham Veale University Center, Case Western Reserve University (Cleveland, Ohio)

Building Size: 89,500 sf (8,320 sm)

Completion: 2013

Architectural Firm: Perkins+Will
> Design Principal: Ralph Johnson
> Managing Principals: Mark Jolicoeur, Ken Rohlfing
> Programming/Planning Principal: Jeff Stebar
> Project Designers: Bryan Schabel, David Sheehan
> Senior Project Architect: Mark Walsh
> Project Architect: Jason Flores
> Project Team: Ben Sporer, Dennis Blaul, Marc Nunes, Lauren Prickett, Max Adams, Daniel Ferrario, Laura Lyndgaard, Alex Wu

Client: Case Western Reserve University
Structural Engineer: Thornton Tomasetti
MEP Engineer: Affiliated Engineers, Inc.
Civil Engineer: KS Associates
General Contractor: Donley's

CHAPTER 5

Interdisciplinary Science & Technology Building, Arizona State University (Tempe, Arizona)

Building Size: 175,169 sf (16,272 sm)
Completion: 2006
Architectural Firm: Perkins+Will
    Design Principal: Ralph Johnson
    Managing Principal: Michael Smith
    Project Designers: Bryan Schabel, Cengiz Yetken
    Project Manager: John Becker
    Project Architect: Lewis Wood
    Project Team: Scott Allen, Bill Berger, Yong Cai, Mary Guerrero, Jeff Olson, Cesar Pineda, Michele Sainte-Starbuck, Lynette Tedder, Mariah Walters
Client: Arizona State University
Associate Architect: Dick & Fritsche Design Group
Structural Engineer: KPFF Consulting Engineers
MEP Engineer: Bard, Rao + Athanas Consulting Engineers, Inc.
Landscape Architect: Logan Simpson Design, Inc.
Sustainability Consultant: Battle McCarthy
General Contractor: Gilbane Building Company

CASE STUDIES INDEX

Center for Urban Waters (Tacoma, Washington)

Building Size: 51,000 sf (4,740 sm)

Completion: 2010

Architectural Firm: Perkins+Will

    Design Principal: Kay Kornovich

    Project Manager: Dan Seng

    Project Team: Tony DeEulio, Devin Kleiner

Client: NDC Housing and Economic Development Corporation

Primary Tenant: City of Tacoma, Environmental Services Division

Developer: Lorig Associates, LLC

Structural and Civil Engineer: AHBL, Inc.

MEP Engineer: WSP Flack+Kurtz

Landscape Architect: Swift and Company

Commissioning: Rushing Company

General Contractor: Turner Construction Company

Kuwait University College of Education (Shadadiyah, Kuwait)

Building Size: 1,200,000 sf (111,520 sm)

Completion: Projected 2014

Architectural Firm: Perkins+Will

    Design Principal: Anthony Fieldman

    Managing Principal: Michael Kihn

    Technical Principal: Calvin Smith

    Project Team: Kamalrukh Katrak, Scott Kirkham, Ming Leung, Dutch Osborne, Dennis Park, Edward Stand, Junghee Sung, Minho Yang, Scott Yocom

Interior Design: Perkins+Will

Client: Kuwait University

Structural Engineer: Dar-Al Handasah

MEP Engineer: Dar-Al Handasah

Energy and Daylight Modeling Consultant: Atelier Ten

General Contractor: Turner Projacs, Construction Managers

King Abdullah Financial District Parcel 4.01 Building (Riyadh, Saudi Arabia)

Building Size: 166,576 sf (15,481 sm)

Completion: 2013

Architectural Firm: Perkins+Will

    Design Principal: David Hansen

    Senior Project Designer: Curt Behnke

    Managing Principal: Michael Palmer

    Senior Project Architect: James Giebelhausen

    Project Architect: Jason Sachs

    Project Team: Dan Figatner, Matt Booma, Sarah Wood, Bradon Biederman, Tara Rejniak

Client: Rayadah Investment Company

Structural Engineer: Dar Al-Handasah

MEP Engineer: Dar Al-Handasah

General Contractor: Saudi Binladin Group

King Abdullah Financial District Parcel 4.10 Building (Riyadh, Saudi Arabia)

Building Size: 385,563 sf (35,820 sm)

Completion: 2013

Architectural Firm: Perkins+Will

    Design Principal: Ralph Johnson

    Senior Project Designer: Ron Stelmarski

    Managing Principal: Michael Palmer

    Senior Project Architect: James Giebelhausen

    Project Architect: Jason Sachs

    Project Team: John Kitson, Mila Cuk, Scott Dansereau, Bruce Werner, Aashit Shah, Rebecca Cox

Client: Rayadah Investment Company

Structural Engineer: Dar Al-Handasah

MEP Engineer: Dar Al-Handasah

General Contractor: Saudi Binladin Group

University of Texas Dallas Student Services Building (Dallas, Texas)

Building Size: 74,343 sf (6,909 sm)

Completion: 2010

Architectural Firm: Perkins+Will

    Design Principal: Peter Busby

    Senior Project Designer: Ryan Bragg

    Project Designer: Ashwin Toney

    Managing Principal: Richard Miller

    Senior Project Manager: Dwight Burns

    Project Architect: Daniel Day

    Industrial Designer: Soren Schou

    Project Architect: Daniel Day

    Project Team: Paul Cowcher, Sean Garman, Harley Grusko, Herman Kao, Elke Latreille, Blair McCarry, Fred Pena, Terry Salinas, Nathan Shuttleworth

Client: The University of Texas at Dallas

Structural Engineer: Jaster Quintanilla

MEP Engineer: Infrastructure Associates

General Contractor: Hill & Wilkinson

Bigelow Laboratory for Ocean Sciences (East Boothbay, Maine)

Building Size: 65,000 sfGSF (6,040 smGSM)

Completion: 2012

Prime Consultant: WBRC Architects & Engineers

Associate Architectural Firm: Perkins+Will

    Managing Principal/Planning Principal: Gary Shaw

    Project Designer: Patrick Cunningham

    Senior Project Architect: Andre Goetze

    Project Team: Anthony Paprocki, Madaline Hale, Maryam Katouzian

Client: Bigelow Laboratory for Ocean Sciences

Structural Engineer: WBRC Architects & Engineers

MEP Engineer: WBRC Architects & Engineers

Construction Manager: Consigli Construction, Inc.

INDEX

A

Acoustics, 115–118
Acoustic comfort, 8–9, 115–118
Active energy-generation systems, 149–153. *See also* Photovoltaic (PV) glass; Photovoltaic (PV) panels
Advanced facade materials, 122–126
Aerogels, 25, 52, 124, 125
Air barriers, 67, 119
Air cavity:
    brick veneer facades, 40, 41
    Case Western Tinkham Veale University Center, 146
    double-skin facades, 135, 137, 141–148
    rainscreen facades, 47, 48
Airflow, 42, 66–67, 135, 137, 140, 144
Air infiltration, 93, 118–119
Air-insulated glazing units, 92–93, 175
Air leakage, 18, 67, 93
Air movement, thermal comfort and, 86, 93, 94
Air pollution:
    ETFE and, 122
    indoor air quality, 118
    self-cleaning materials, 128, 129
Air quality, 118–119, 216
Alternative energy, facades as source of, 149–153
Aluminum curtain-wall system:
    Bigelow Laboratory for Ocean Sciences, 225
    Center for Urban Waters, 174
    King Abdullah Financial District Parcel 4.01 Building, 193
    King Abdullah Financial District Parcel 4.10 Building, 202–205
    Princess Nora Bint Abdulrahman University for Women Academic Colleges, 132
Aluminum mullions, 50, 57, 223
Ambient sounds, 115, 116
American Society of Heating, Refrigerating and Air-Conditioning Engineers (ASHRAE):
    building performance metrics, 11
    climate classification system, 6–8
    Energy Standard for Buildings except Low-Rise Residential Buildings, 10–11
    hygrothermal analysis guidelines, 75
    OITC recommendations, 116
    R-value recommendations, 11–12
    SHGC recommendations, 13–14
    thermal comfort measurement, 87–89
    U-value recommendations, 12–13
Amorphous silicon PV cells, 150
Amorphous thin PV films, 130
Anidolic lighting, 101
Argon-gas-filled IGUs, 52, 59, 80
    Bigelow Laboratory for Ocean Sciences, 223, 225
    King Abdullah Financial District Parcel 4.01 Building, 194
Arizona State University Science & Technology Building (Tempe, Arizona), 159–167, 231
ASHRAE, *see* American Society of Heating, Refrigerating and Air-Conditioning Engineers
ASHRAE 90.1 energy standard:
    Arizona State University Science & Technology Building, 167
    Bigelow Laboratory for Ocean Sciences, 226
    Center for Urban Waters, 177
    King Abdullah Financial District Parcel 4.01 Building, 198
    King Abdullah Financial District Parcel 4.10 Building, 210
    Kuwait University College of Education, 186
    University of Texas Dallas Student Services Building, 216
ASTM standards:
    acoustic comfort, 116
    air barriers, 67
    air leakage, 67
    vapor barriers, 68
Atriums, 212, 215
Axial fans, 146–148

B

Batt insulation, 55, 56, 58, 181, 183
Bigelow Laboratory for Ocean Sciences (East Boothbay, Maine), 218–226, 234
Box window double-skin facades, 136–138
Brick cavity walls, 39–41
Brick ties, 57, 58, 70
Brick veneer facades:
    dew-point analysis, 70–73
    elements of, 40
    hygrothermal analysis, 77–78
    R-values, 55–56
Building orientation, *see* Orientation

C

Case Western Tinkham Veale University Center (Cleveland, Ohio), 145–148, 230–231
Cast-in-place concrete, 41, 65, 160
Centers for Disease Control and Prevention, National Center for Environmental Health (Atlanta, Georgia), 107–109, 229
Center for the Built Environment (CBE), 89–91
Center for Urban Waters (Tacoma, Washington), 167–177, 231–232
Ceramic frit:
    back-coated glass, 53
    Center for Urban Waters, 174
    components, 52
    King Abdullah Financial District Parcel 4.01 Building, 193
    Kuwait University College of Education, 182
    solar heat gain reduction, 25, 61
Channel glass, 124
CIE (International Commission on Illumination), 109
Circadian rhythms and daylight, 95
Cladding:
    aerogel inserts, 124
    concrete facades, 41

embodied energy of, 65–66
rainscreen facades, 47, 48
Clerestory windows, 170
Climates, 2–14
    classification systems, 3–8
    defined, 3
Climate-specific design:
    design strategies, 9–14
    environmental considerations and design criteria, 8–9
    guidelines for facades, 8–14
CMU wall, *see* Concrete masonry unit wall
Coatings, glass, 52. *see also* Frit/fritted glass; Low-emissivity coatings
Comfort, designing for, 86–119
    acoustic comfort, 115–118
    air quality, 118–119
    daylight and glare, 95–115
    thermal comfort, 86–94
Composite wood panels, 168, 223, 225, 226
Concrete:
    cast-in-place, 41, 65, 160
    glass-fiber-reinforced, 132–135, 182, 183, 185
    insulating concrete blocks, 41
    insulating concrete forms, 41
    precast panels, 18, 24, 41–47, 63, 65, 66
    self-cleaning, 129
    thin-shell precast panels, 44–45
Concrete facades, 41–42
Concrete masonry unit (CMU) wall, 40, 41, 55, 56, 65
Condensation, 68, 77
Control systems, 153–154
Corridor double-skin facades, 136, 137
Courtyards, 23, 160, 179
Curtain walls:
    Bigelow Laboratory for Ocean Sciences, 222, 224, 225
    Center for Urban Waters, 168, 174, 175
    daylighting, 103–105, 107
    defined, 48
    energy consumption in mixed humid climates, 62
    glazed facades, 48–54
    Hector Garcia Middle School, 38
    King Abdullah Financial District Parcel 4.01 Building, 193–198
    King Abdullah Financial District Parcel 4.10 Building, 202–205
    Kuwait University College of Education, 181, 184
    materials and components, 48

opaque areas, 52–54
origins of, 18
Princess Nora Bint Abdulrahman University for Women Academic Colleges, 132
thermal performance, 50
University of Texas Dallas Student Services Building, 214
U-values for, 59–60

D

Daylight:
    Arizona State University Science & Technology Building, 164
    Bigelow Laboratory for Ocean Sciences, 220
    and facade design strategies, 8, 10
    and glare, 111
    Kuwait University College of Education, 179
    University of Texas Dallas Student Services Building, 212
Daylight harvesting, 164, 195, 212
Daylighting:
    Bigelow Laboratory for Ocean Sciences, 220
    Center for Urban Waters, 168
    design strategies, 95–109
    King Abdullah Financial District Parcel 4.10 Building, 201
    and orientation, 22
Daylight simulations, 166, 184
Daylight studies, 43
Desiccated air space, 51
Design guidelines, climate-specific, 8–14
Dew point, 69, 77, 78
Dew-point analysis, 69–73
Dew-point temperature, 68, 69
Diffusion (vapor), 67
Double glazing, 51, 117, 175, 194
Double-skin facades, 135–148
    Case Western Tinkham Veale University Center, 145–148
    in cold climates, 143–148
    elements of, 135–140
    in hot and arid climates, 141–142
    peak energy load, 147, 148

E

Electrochromic glass, 126, 127
Embodied energy, 62–66
Emerging technologies, 122–155
    advanced facade materials, 122–126
    control systems for facades, 153–154

double-skin facades, 135–148
facades as energy generators, 149–153
smart materials, 126–131
Energy codes, 10–11. *See also* ASHRAE 90.1 energy standard
Energy conservation, xiii, 98
Energy demand, 143–144
Energy efficiency, 18–39
    fenestration, 24–37
    orientation of structure for, 19–22
    University of Texas Dallas Student Services Building, 212
Energy generators, facades as, 65, 130, 131, 149–153
Energy performance modeling, 8
Energy Standard for Buildings except Low-Rise Residential Buildings, 10–11
Environmental Health Laboratory Building (CDC), 107–109, 229
ETFE (ethylene tetrafluoroethylene), 122–123
Exhaust air-curtain flow in double-skin facades, 146
Expanded polystyrene insulation, 41, 55, 56, 70, 75
External shading elements, 211–217

F

Facades, functions of, xiii, 8
Fans, 144, 146–148
Fenestration, energy-efficient, 24–37
Fins:
    Arizona State University Science & Technology Building, 160, 166
    for energy consumption reduction, 61
    horizontal, 98
    King Abdullah Financial District Parcel 4.01 Building, 193, 194, 197
    King Abdullah Financial District Parcel 4.10 Building, 203, 204, 206
    Kuwait University College of Education, 182–184
    and light shelves, 98
    and orientation constraints, 22
Foam insulation, 44, 55, 56, 220, 223, 225, 226
Framing:
    brick cavity walls, 40
    brick veneer facades, 40, 55
    design strategies, 11–13
    dew-point analysis, 71
    embodied energy of, 65–66
    hygrothermal analysis, 75

INDEX

importance of design, 25
King Abdullah Financial District Parcel 4.01 Building, 193
opaque facades, 18
precast concrete panels, 42
pressure-equalized rainscreens, 47
R-values for brick veneer, 55–57
U-value reduction, 59
Fraunhofer Institute for Building Physics (IBP), 74
Frit/fritted glass:
    back-coated glass, 53
    Center for Urban Waters, 174–176
    components, 52
    daylighting, 103–105, 107
    ETFE membrane, 123, 124
    King Abdullah Financial District Parcel 4.01 Building, 193–195
    King Abdullah Financial District Parcel 4.10 Building, 203, 209
    Kuwait University College of Education, 182
    solar heat gain reduction, 25, 61, 62

G

GFRC, *see* Glass-fiber-reinforced concrete
Glare, 109
Glare reduction, 109–115, 182, 184
Glass, *see* glazing entries, e.g.: Insulated glazing units (IGUs); *specific types of glass, e.g.:* Laminated glass
Glass, surface temperature of, 91–94
Glass-fiber-reinforced concrete (GFRC), 132–135, 182, 183, 185
Glazed facades:
    acoustic performance, 117–118
    defined, 18
    heat transfer analysis, 79–83
    materials, 48–54
    origins, 18
    R-values, 58–59
    thermal bridging, 58
    U-values, 59–60
Glazing:
    aerogel inserts, 124
    Center for Urban Waters, 167
    curtain wall thermal performance, 51
    double-skin facades, 137, 142, 144
    Kuwait University College of Education, 183
    materials for, 92–94, 101
    and thermal comfort, 92, 93
Glazing units, *see* Insulated glazing units

Green Building Council LEED certification, *see* LEED Gold certification; LEED Platinum certification
Gypsum board, 55, 56, 65–66, 71

H

Heat transfer, 66–69, 182
Heat transfer analysis, 79–83
Heat transfer coefficient (U-value):
    ASHRAE recommendations, 12–13
    Bigelow Laboratory for Ocean Sciences, 223, 225
    for curtain walls, 59–60
    defined, 11
    for glazed facades, 59–60
    King Abdullah Financial District Parcel 4.01 Building, 194
    for triple-insulated glazing unites, 129
    vacuum-insulated glazing units, 124
Hector Garcia Middle School (Dallas, Texas), 38–39, 228–229
High-performance sustainable facades, 2
Human body:
    light's effect on, 95, 97
    and thermal comfort, 86, 87, 89
HVAC systems:
    and air quality, 118
    and daylighting strategies, 95, 96
    and intelligent systems, 154
    and interior air pressure, 93
    and self-shading exterior skin, 182
    and solar air heating, 149
    and thermal comfort, 86, 89, 93
Hybrid ventilation, 141, 146
Hygrothermal analysis, 74–79

I

IAQ (indoor air quality), 118
IBP (Fraunhofer Institute for Building Physics), 74
ICBs (insulating concrete blocks), 41
ICFs (insulating concrete forms), 41
IECC (International Energy Conservation Code), 6–8
IESNA (Illuminating Engineering Society of North America), 96, 109
IGUs, *see* Insulated glazing units
IIC (impact insulation class), 116
Illuminance, 96, 110
Illuminating Engineering Society of North America (IESNA), 96, 109

Impact insulation class (IIC), 116
Inclination angle, for PV cell efficiency, 150–152
Indoor air quality (IAQ), 118
Inert gases, 25, 59, 129
Inorganic phase-change materials, 129
Insulated glazing units (IGUs):
    aerogel vs. vacuum insulation, 131
    Bigelow Laboratory for Ocean Sciences, 223, 225
    Center for Urban Waters, 175
    and curtain wall thermal performance, 51–52
    glass property calculation with WINDOW software, 81
    King Abdullah Financial District Parcel 4.01 Building, 194
    King Abdullah Financial District Parcel 4.10 Building, 203, 204
    Kuwait University College of Education, 182
    low-e coatings for, *see* Low-emissivity coatings
    phase-changing materials for, 129–130
    and thermal comfort, 92–93
    U-values for, 59–60
    vacuum-insulated, 124–125, 131
Insulating concrete blocks (ICBs), 41
Insulating concrete forms (ICFs), 41
Insulation. *See also specific types, e.g.:* Batt insulation
    glazed facades, 51–54
    opaque facades, 40–42
    R-values, 12
    U-values, 25
Intelligent facades, 153–154
Interdisciplinary Science & Technology Building, Arizona State University (Tempe, Arizona), 159–167, 231
International Building Code, 116
International Commission on Illumination (CIE), 109
International Energy Conservation Code (IECC), 6–8

K

Kendall Academic Support Center, Miami Dade College (Miami, Florida), 42–46, 229
King Abdullah Financial District Parcel 4.01 Building (Riyadh, Saudi Arabia), 186–199, 233
King Abdullah Financial District Parcel 4.10 Building (Riyadh, Saudi Arabia), 200–209, 233

K

Koppen Climate Classification System, 3–5
Kuwait University College of Education (Shadadiyah, Kuwait), 178–186, 232

L

Laminated glass, 117, 126–128, 130, 131, 182
Landscaping, 168
Latitude, PV cell efficiency and, 150–151
Lawrence Berkeley National Laboratory, 97
LEED Gold certification:
    Arizona State University Science & Technology Building, 167
    Bigelow Laboratory for Ocean Sciences, 226
    Kuwait University College of Education, 186
LEED Platinum certification:
    Center for Urban Waters, 177
    University of Texas Dallas Student Services Building, 216
Life-cycle assessment, 62, 138
Lighting, *see* Daylight; Daylighting
Light shelves:
    Center for Urban Waters, 170, 173, 174
    daylighting strategies, 101–103, 107, 110
    defined, 98
    summer vs. winter performance of, 101
Light-to-solar gain (LSG) ratio, 22, 60, 61
LIM (Lowest Isopleth for Mold), 79
Liquid crystals, 126–128
Louvers:
    Arizona State University Science & Technology Building, 160, 166
    CDC Environmental Health Laboratory Building, 107, 108
    daylighting strategies, 103
    in spandrels, 54
    University of Texas Dallas Student Services Building, 214
Low-emissivity coatings:
    advanced glazing materials vs., 131
    Arizona State University Science & Technology Building, 164
    Center for Urban Waters, 175
    and daylighting strategies, 103
    for double-skin facades, 141–143
    effects on energy consumption, 62
    King Abdullah Financial District Parcel 4.01 Building, 194
    King Abdullah Financial District Parcel 4.10 Building, 203, 204
    Kuwait University College of Education, 182
    light-to-solar-gain ratios for, 60, 61
    and thermal comfort, 92–93
    U-values for, 59–60

for vacuum-insulated glazing units, 124
WINDOW software for evaluation of, 80–81
Lowest Isopleth for Mold (LIM), 79
LSG (light-to-solar gain) ratio, 22, 60, 61

M

Materials, 40–66
    advanced, 122–126
    Bigelow Laboratory for Ocean Sciences, 218–226
    embodied energy of, 62–66
    glazed building facades, 48–54
    opaque building facades, 40–42, 46–49
    properties, 54–66
    smart materials, 126–131
Mean radiant temperature, 86, 87
Mechanical ventilation:
    Case Western Tinkham Veale University Center, 146
    Center for Urban Waters, 168
    double-skin facades, 135–139, 141
    and thermal comfort, 89
Moisture resistance, 66–83
Mold, 67, 68, 74, 79, 118
Monocrystalline silicon PV cells, 150
Mullions:
    Bigelow Laboratory for Ocean Sciences, 223
    curtain walls, 49–53
    King Abdullah Financial District Parcel 4.01 Building, 193
    shading strategies, 62
    thermal bridging, 57

N

National Fenestration Rating Council (NFRC), 59, 80
Natural light, *see* Daylight; Daylighting
Natural ventilation:
    and acoustic performance, 118
    Center for Urban Waters, 167, 168, 171
    and design strategy, 10
    for energy-efficient facades, 18
    Kuwait University College of Education, 182
    and thermal comfort, 88, 89
NFRC (National Fenestration Rating Council), 59, 80
Noise, 115–118

O

OITC (Outdoor-Indoor Transmission Class), 116–118

Opaque facades:
    acoustic performance improvement, 117
    Bigelow Laboratory for Ocean Sciences, 220
    defined, 18
    hygrothermal analysis for, 74–79
    materials, 40–49
    R-values for, 54–55
    steady state heat and moisture transfer analysis, 69–73
    Vincent Triggs Elementary School, 24
Organic phase-change materials, 129
Orientation:
    Arizona State University Science & Technology Building, 159–167
    Bigelow Laboratory for Ocean Sciences, 220
    Center for Urban Waters, 167–177
    and daylighting, 97
    for energy efficiency, 19–22
    Hector Garcia Middle School, 38–39
    King Abdullah Financial District Parcel 4.01 Building, 188–189, 194
    King Abdullah Financial District Parcel 4.10 Building, 201
    Kuwait University College of Education, 179
    for PV cell efficiency, 150
    Vincent Triggs Elementary School, 23
Outdoor-Indoor Transmission Class (OITC), 116–118

P

Panels, *see specific type of panels, e.g.:* Precast concrete panels
Passive design:
    for air circulation in hot and arid climates, 141
    Arizona State University Science & Technology Building, 159, 160, 167
    Bigelow Laboratory for Ocean Sciences, 220
    Center for Urban Waters, 168, 171
    King Abdullah Financial District Parcel 4.01 Building, 186, 194, 199
    Vincent Triggs Elementary School, 22
Passive solar energy/solar heating:
    Bigelow Laboratory for Ocean Sciences, 218, 220
    Center for Urban Waters, 170, 171
    defined, 149
    facade design strategies, 10
    light-to-solar gain ratio, 22
    and orientation, 19, 22
    solar air heating curtain walls, 149
    solar dynamic buffer zone curtain walls, 149

PER (pressure-equalized rainscreen), 47, 48
Permeance, 68
Phase-change materials (PCMs), 129–130
Photocatalysts, 128, 129
Photovoltaic (PV) glass, 130, 131
Photovoltaic (PV) panels, 64, 149–152
PMV (Predicted Mean Vote), 87, 91
Pollutants, airborne, 118, 122, 128, 129
Polycrystalline silicon PV cells, 150
PPD (Predicted Percentage of Dissatisfied), 87–88
Precast concrete panels, 41–47
    embodied energy, 63, 65, 66
    Kendall Academic Support Center, Miami Dade College, 42–46
    for opaque facades, 18, 24
Predicted Mean Vote (PMV), 87, 91
Predicted Percentage of Dissatisfied (PPD), 87–88
Pressure-equalized rainscreen (PER), 47, 48
Princess Nora Bint Abdulrahman University for Women Academic Colleges (Riyadh, Saudi Arabia), 132–135, 230
Punched windows, 24, 38, 168, 220
PV (photovoltaic) glass, 130, 131
PV (photovoltaic) panels, 64, 149–152
Radiance (lighting simulation software), 97, 98, 109
Radiant temperature, 86, 87
Rainscreen facades, 46–49, 168, 174–176, 203, 205, 207

R

Relative humidity (RH):
    defined, 67, 86
    dew-point analysis, 69–71
    in heat transfer analysis, 81
    in hygrothermal analysis, 74, 76, 77
    and isopleths for mold, 79
    and thermal comfort, 8, 9, 86–87
    and weather patterns, 8
Retrofit projects, vacuum-insulated glazing units for, 125
R-value, *see* Thermal resistance

S

Salts, 129, 220
SDBZ (solar dynamic buffer zone) curtain walls, 149
Self-cleaning glass, 128–129
Self-healing materials, 131

Shading:
    Arizona State University Science & Technology Building, 160, 166
    Bigelow Laboratory for Ocean Sciences, 221
    Center for Urban Waters, 168, 174, 175
    double-skin facades, 137, 141–142
    ETFE and, 123
    external shading elements, 211–217
    King Abdullah Financial District Parcel 4.01 Building, 189, 193
    King Abdullah Financial District Parcel 4.10 Building, 203, 204
    Kuwait University College of Education, 181–185
    and solar heat gain, 61–62
    and thermal comfort, 94
    University of Texas Dallas Student Services Building, 212–214, 216
Shadow boxes, 53, 203, 204
Shaft box double-skin facades, 136, 138
SHGC, *see* Solar heat gain coefficient
Silica aerogel, 52, 124
Silicon PV cells, 150
Single glazing, 51, 117, 137
Single-skin facades, 135, 141, 143, 144, 148
Smart materials, 126–131
Solar cells, 64, 130, 131, 149–152
Solar dynamic buffer zone (SDBZ) curtain walls, 149
Solar energy/solar heating, *see* Passive solar energy/solar heating
Solar heat gain:
    Bigelow Laboratory for Ocean Sciences, 218
    Center for Urban Waters, 168, 170
    King Abdullah Financial District Parcel 4.10 Building, 202
    Kuwait University College of Education, 182
    orientation and, 19
    shading devices and, 61–62
    University of Texas Dallas Student Services Building, 212
Solar heat gain coefficient (SHGC):
    ASHRAE recommendations, 13–14
    defined, 11
    for glazed facades, 58
    for triple-insulated glazing units, 129
    variability in electrochromic glass, 126
Solar orientation, *see* Orientation
Solid cell photovoltaics, 149
Sound transmission class (STC) rating system, 116–118
Spandrels:
    Bigelow Laboratory for Ocean Sciences, 225
    Center for Urban Waters, 175

    in curtain walls, 52
    embodied energy in, 66
    King Abdullah Financial District Parcel 4.10 Building, 203
    Kuwait University College of Education, 183
    and photovoltaic devices, 130, 149
SPD (suspended particle device) glass, 126–128, 131
Spray-foam insulation, 55, 56, 220, 223, 225, 226
Static air-buffer flow pattern in double-skin facades, 146
STC (sound transmission class) rating system, 116–118
Steady state heat and moisture transfer analysis, 69–73
Steel, embodied energy of, 64–66
Steel framing:
    brick cavity wall, 40
    brick veneer facades, 40, 55
    design strategies using, 11–13
    dew-point analysis, 71
    embodied energy, 65–66
    hygrothermal analysis, 75
    King Abdullah Financial District Parcel 4.01 Building, 193
    opaque facades, 18
    precast concrete panels, 42
    pressure-equalized rainscreens, 47
    R-value calculation problems, 57
    R-value for brick veneer with, 55–57
Stick curtain wall systems, 49, 51, 205
Sunshades, *see* Shading
Suspended particle device (SPD) glass, 126–128, 131

T

Tectonic sun exposure control, 178–209
    King Abdullah Financial District Parcel 4.01 Building, 186–199
    King Abdullah Financial District Parcel 4.10 Building, 200–209
    Kuwait University College of Education, 178–186
Terra cotta, 47, 214, 216, 217
THERM (software), 80–82
Thermal behavior, 66–83
    heat transfer, 66–69
    heat transfer analysis, 79–83
    hygrothermal analysis, 74–79
    steady state heat and moisture transfer analysis, 69–73
Thermal breaks, 50

Thermal bridging, 57–59
Thermal comfort, 86–94
    defined, 86
    facade design for, 91–94
    facade properties affecting, 8–9
    methods of measurement, 87–91
Thermal Comfort Model, 89–91
Thermal comfort zone, 159, 167, 186, 211
Thermal conductivity:
    aerogels, 124
    aluminum mullions, 50
    and material selection, 54
    terra cotta, 216
    vacuum-insulated panels, 126
Thermal gradient, 70–73, 80–83
Thermal performance, *see specific metrics, e.g.:* Heat transfer coefficient
Thermal resistance (R-value):
    aerogels, 124
    ASHRAE minimum recommendations, 11–12
    brick veneer facades, 55–56
    defined, 11
    facades at Center for Urban Waters, 175
    glazed facades, 58–59
    opaque building envelopes, 54–55
    thermal bridging and, 57
    vacuum-insulated glazing units, 124
Thin film photovoltaics, 149
Thin-shell precast concrete panels, 44–45
Ties (brick), 57, 58, 70
Tinkham Veale University Center (Case Western Reserve University, Cleveland, Ohio), 145–148, 230–231
Tinted glass, 51
Titanium dioxide, 128, 129
Transient-analysis method, 73–79
Triple-insulated glazing units (IGUs):
    acoustic performance, 118
    phase-changing materials for, 129–130
    and thermal comfort, 92, 93
    thermal performance, 51–52
    U-values, 82

U

Ultraviolet radiation, 95, 122, 128, 129
Unified Glare Rating (UGR), 109, 114–115
U.S. Green Building Council LEED certification, *see* LEED Gold certification; LEED Platinum certification
Unitized curtain wall systems, 49
University of California at Berkeley–Center for the Built Environment (CBE), 89–91
University of Texas Dallas Student Services Building, 211–217, 234
U-value, *see* Heat transfer coefficient

V

Vacuum-insulated glazing units, 124–125, 131
Vacuum-insulated panels (VIPs), 126
Vapor, 67
    dew-point analysis, 69–73
    diffusion, 67
    hygrothermal analysis, 74–79
    non-rainscreen facade systems, 46
    thermal comfort and, 86–87
Vapor barriers, 46, 68–73, 75, 77
Vapor infiltration, 67
Vapor pressure, 70–73
VCP (Visual Comfort Probability), 109, 110, 114–115
Ventilated air cavities, 47, 135, 141–148
Ventilation:
    acoustic performance, 118
    Center for Urban Waters, 167, 168, 171
    control systems for, 153, 154
    courtyards as source of, 23
    and design strategy, 10
    double-skin facades, 135–148
    energy-efficient facades, 18
    Kuwait University College of Education, 182
    as portion of commercial building energy use, 2
    thermal comfort, 88, 89
Vincent Triggs Elementary School (Las Vegas, Nevada), 22–24, 228
VIPs (vacuum-insulated panels), 126
Visual comfort, 8–9, 95, 96
Visual Comfort Probability (VCP), 109, 110, 114–115
Visual transmittance (Tv), 60, 61, 129, 194

W

Wall assemblies. *See also* Curtain walls
    Bigelow Laboratory for Ocean Sciences, 218–226
    dew-point analysis, 71
    hygrothermal analysis, 77

Princess Nora Bint Abdulrahman University for Women Academic Colleges, 132–135
R-values, 55–56
U-values, 59–60
Water vapor, *see* Vapor
Wind, 47, 80, 160
Windows:
    acoustic qualities, 117–118
    Arizona State University Science & Technology Building, 160
    ASHRAE thermal comfort measurement, 88
    Bigelow Laboratory for Ocean Sciences, 220, 223
    box window double-skin facades, 136–138
    Center for Urban Waters, 168, 170, 173–175
    daylighting, 95–103
    double-skin facades, 135, 136, 141
    energy consumption management, 141
    glare, 110–115
    King Abdullah Financial District Parcel 4.10 Building, 203
    Kuwait University College of Education, 182
    thermal comfort, 91–94
WINDOW (heat-transfer analysis software), 80–81
Window-to-wall ratio (WWR), 25–37
    Bigelow Laboratory for Ocean Sciences, 220
    Center for Urban Waters, 175
    daylighting and, 97
    Hector Garcia Middle School, 38, 39
    King Abdullah Financial District Parcel 4.01 Building, 193–194
    King Abdullah Financial District Parcel 4.10 Building, 202, 209
    thermal comfort and, 91–92, 94
Wire ties (brick), 57, 58, 70
Wood, 64–66, 79
Wood-framed walls, 12, 13
WUFI® (Wärme und Feuchte instationär) software, 74, 79
WWR, *see* Window-to-wall ratio

Z

Z-girts, 57–59
Zone method, for R-value calculation, 57